LIVING DIVINITY

by

Shakuntala Balu

LIVING DIVINITY

Shakuntala Balu

SAWBRIDGE ENTERPRISES
LONDON

ISBN 0-907555-00-4

1st Edition 1981
2nd Edition 1984

Published by Sawbridge Enterprises Ltd.
37 Sydney Street, London SW3.

Printed by Fretwells Ltd. of Hull.

Acknowledgements

First, I would like to acknowledge my gratitude to Swami for his generous permission, inspiration and guidance in writing this book. It has been a very great spiritual experience for me. I humbly dedicate this book to Swami.

My special thanks go to Sri Vemu Mukunda for his invaluable assistance in introducing overseas devotees who have had Sai experiences.

Photographic credits go to Sri. T. L. Ramaswami, Shri Dhiraj Chawda, Mr. Mistry, Signor Dante Bighi and to the students of the Sri Satya Sai College at Whitefield: Shri Bhimeshwar Sharma for the cover photograph, to Shri U. Pithawala and to Sri Bhuvan Swami.

Special thanks are due to my husband for encouraging me to take up this work. He felt it was my duty to write it for the sake of those who do not yet know the Essential Sai.

My sincere thanks to all the many Sai devotees who were kind enough to relate their own thrilling Sai experiences and who have allowed their names to be recorded in this book.

My thanks also go to Mr. Homer Youngs for the wonderful photographs of Puttaparthi taken by satellite.

Shakuntala Balu

Note:

In this book, Sri Sathya Sai Baba is referred to variously as Sri Baba, Sai Baba, Bhagwan, Bhagwan Baba, Baba, Swami, Sathya, Satyam and Bhagavan.

Note from the Publisher

The manuscript of 'Living Divinity' was completed by the Author in September 1978. It was not however prepared for the present publishers.

The Publishers therefore beg the indulgence of readers, especially Sai devotees, in adding the lapsed time wherever needed in the text and the Introduction.

It was felt that to correct every reference to time and calendar years would inevitably detract from the clarity and feeling the Author has put into her work.

August 1981.

GURU DIVINE

Why Sai Baba?
They ask.
My answer is silence
And reverence
For Sai Baba
My Guru,
Who bade me seek
Within me
Latent divinity
Patent in Him.
I chanted My Guru's name
And beheld the Lord's feet.
I began thinking of
My Guru as God,
But now know
God is my Guru!

. . . Shakuntala Balu

CONTENTS

CONTENTS—*continued*

INTRODUCTION

The Sai Charisma.

Whitefield is just 16 miles from Bangalore where I have lived now for nearly twelve years. But, it was only two years ago that I got a chance to meet Sri Sathya Sai Baba. I realized then what I had missed all along!

Sri Sathya Sai Baba has incredible charisma and the Sai world, which spins around this 52-year-old phenomenon of the 20th century, is a wonderful world indeed. I saw people worship Sri Sathya Sai Baba as a living god and derive immense joy and fulfillment *(ananda)* from their worship. It is a fabulous feast for the eyes of devotees to behold him in his physical form *(darshan)*; it is ecstasy to talk to him *(sambhashana)*; it is bliss when they hear him discoursing; a precious boon granted to touch his feet; and pure rapture to chant his soul-stirring songs of devotion *(bhajans)*, a rapture that transports them to heights of unsullied happiness.

At first, it seemed strange to me that people should organise chanting sessions *(bhajans)* and ritualistic prayers *(puja)* for a living being and that they should worship him in a traditional temple *(mandir)* at Puttaparthi. But, during the past two years, I have had several opportunities of studying the countless happenings around Sri Sathya Sai Baba and have had many glimpses of his fascinating multi-faceted personality. His spiritual stature is immeasurable, but he is short. His form is frail, but the huge halo of dark hair rests naturally on his head. His orange *dhoti* and robe, much like a maxi dress, lend a mod touch to his personality, a personality both grand and simple. Innocence and goodness are writ large on his face, the pristine beauty of which has never been caught on camera. Actually, photgraphs project him as a huge person without bringing out his handsomeness or his childlike innocence. He moves quickly and with agility but gives the impression of one gently floating on earth.

It is difficult to understand the little movements of his hands: he moves his fingers intriguingly in the air as if writing in space, sometimes turning the palm of his right hand upwards, he moves it round and round in small circles, his red lips (red with chewing betel nut leaves) moving inaudibly. At *bhajan* sessions, one often sees him close his eyes and put his right hand forefinger in the centre of his brow.

It is pleasing to see him give a gift of blessing *(prasad)* to people. He turns his right hand, palm down, making quick circular movements and out pours sacred ash *(vibhuti)* like spray from his fingers. His right palm can also bring out many other forms of blessed gifts, like rings, pendants, lockets, chains, etc. When he moves among the rows and rows of devotees sitting in quiet lines, he sometimes touches a packet of holy ash or a photograph in an outstretched hand, thus sanctifying them. Some offer flowers or a letter which he takes, at times passing his hand gently over the letters. (I have been told that once his hand touches a letter, he knows its contents!)

What does all this add up to? Why does Sri Sathya Sai Baba do all these things? I have been told that his hand movements and writings in the air are messages, telegrams as it were, to help or save people in distress; that when his forefinger is pressed to his brow he is on one of his short transcorporeal journeys. The way his devotees speak of Sri Sathya Sai Baba leaves no doubt that he is the presiding divinity in their hearts and lives. And, indeed, the discipline, fellowship and love between them are all very much in evidence.

Sri Sathya Sai Baba is a star attraction to people of all ages and from all walks of life. Politicians and peasants, scientists and statesmen, artists and generals, leaders and pleaders, scholars and singers, priests, poets and philosophers, engineers, economists and elementary school teachers, householders and housewives, professional women and ladies of leisure, lawyers and lecturers, doctors and wheeler-dealers – all come to Sri Sathya Sai Baba's centres at Puttaparthi and Whitefield in the hope of seeing him and, if lucky, talk to him. What is this magnetic charisma? What is there about him that draws people from all over the world? Is it the miracles? Is it because they have seen him in their dreams or in some other inexplicable vision? Is it due to the materialisations of holy ash and other substances on their photographs of him? Or, could it be plain curiosity?

I have talked to many people, believers and non-believers. I have poured over books, articles and essays written about Sri Sathya Sai Baba. And more than that, I have had many opportunities to hear Sri Sathya Sai Baba on various topics and have also personally talked to him. He is a mine of information on different subjects and an ocean of knowledge on *Vedanta* and religion, despite the fact that he has had little or no formal education.

Everyone who has had the privilege of an interview with Sri Sathya Sai Baba has felt his tremendous spiritual vibrations and has instinctively acknowledged that they were in the presence of a great and superior power. It is not surprising therefore that Sri Sathya Sai Baba instills instant respect and makes chit chat and loose talk impossible in his presence. Whatever subject he speaks of, he always returns to love *(prema)* as a means of realising the divinity latent in every human being.

In this book, I have tried to record faithfully, as objectively as possible, all that I have seen, heard and learnt of Sri Sathya Sai Baba. There have been occasions when I have had direct experience of his omnipresence, omniscience, omnipotence and omnifelicity. Much has happened to me spiritually in a short period: Sri Sathya Sai Baba is a wondrous physician of the soul. Though I first went to him as a casual observer, I am now convinced that he is both fully human and fully divine. It is with that conviction that I now humbly offer this small endeavour as a petal at the graceful lotus feet of the Living Divinity, Sri Sathya Sai Baba.

PART I

In the World of Sai . . .

"To understand the idea of a mountain, can it be enough for you to be shown a stone and told that it is a million times bigger? No. You would have to see a real mountain to know its nature, even if from a distance."

. . . Sri Sathya Sai Baba

1

FIRST MEETING

Meeting Sri Sathya Sai Baba for the first time was an unforgettable experience. I felt shattered and went through an inner upheaval which lasted several days. I realised that he had awakened in me a deep spiritual urge which until then had lain dormant.

The *Bhagavad-Gita*, studied word by word during my collegiate years, became newly significant. Then, it had been just a text, a mystic conversation between Lord *Krishna* and *Arjuna* – something my elders told me to read. Reciting stanzas from the *Gita* had once been a way to win approval, now, after meeting Sri Sathya Sai Baba, each stanza has a special meaning.

The meeting thrilled me, a joy such as I had never experienced before. In a worldly sense, I had already won some recognition as an artist and writer and had experienced the satisfaction of being known, noticed and publicly honoured. But, I had often wondered: so what? and what next? Now, a little voice had entered my heart and it fluttered like a leaf in the wind. "What is this life for?"

To return to that first meeting: it was an experience that I had been looking forward to with trepidation. Very tense, I prepared a few questions to put to Sri Sathya Sai Baba with the intention of writing an exceptionally lucid feature on a personality held by many to be controversial.

My husband cautiously repeated, "It all depends on Baba. If you are lucky, he may give you time; or else, he may just see us for a few minutes. Be prepared." I laughed and replied, "You already talk like a devotee."

"Don't make fun of me. I may not be a devotee, but when I met him to arrange this interview, I could feel that he was superhuman," he said.

I was silent for a while, unable to understand how he could have been so completely bowled over by Sri Sathya Sai Baba.

But then I replied confidently, "Why do you say that Baba will give us time if we're lucky? He will certainly do so since he has already agreed to meet us." It also pleased me to think that we had succeeded in getting the interview with Sri Sathya Sai Baba for everyone had said that it would not be at all easy. But, again my husband cautioned me.

"Do not ask Baba anything if you have doubts about him."

I assured him of my sincerity but stressed that I was doing this interview as a journalist, not as a devotee. I would certainly hope to have some answers to my questions.

I knew I would be respectful towards my subject. However, I had heard that with Sri Sathya Sai Baba outward respect alone would never get by: one's words had to be in tune with one's thoughts. I had been told that he read minds and so knew every thought one ever had.

As we set out for the interview, I suddenly felt unsure of myself and wondered if, after all, I might feel tongue-tied in his presence, the painstaking preparation notwithstanding. Another friend who had dropped in had said, "Baba is a person of great love, but maintains a distance, even with the closest of his devotees. Nobody can take liberties with him."

"My God," I thought as we parked the car and walked through the gates of Brindavan, "what have I let myself in for?"

Directly we walked into the grounds there were rules to obey. "Men on one side, women on the other," said a volunteer. "One may not go into the inner compound to meet Baba. When he comes out, he will see or talk to those he wants to talk to. No one should stand up or approach Baba as he walks or disturb all the other seated people waiting to see him."

We went near the entrance to Sri Sathya Sai Baba's residence and said to another volunteer that we had a definite appointment. Nevertheless he stopped us going in. The man in charge explained that he could not let us go further unless Sri Sathya Sai Baba himself called us in or sent word to that effect. So, we sat down on either side of the cemented path and waited. I jotted down some questions and even wrote a page of preamble to my article. Devotees gathered in the round shaded pavilion behind us appeared to be getting restless and some were heard to ask the volunteers whether Sri Sathya Sai Baba was coming out to see them at all, since in any case it was not one of the days scheduled for a public audience.

We had arrived at Whitefield at four o'clock that afternoon. Time went by, the air cooled and the shadows lengthened. Many people came out through the inner gate; others went in and yet others went in and out of a small side entrance to the house. We told several people we saw going in that we were here by appointment for an interview. They all listened to us but no one did anything. The man in charge again told us, "Baba has to ask for people to be brought in. We may not tell him." But, small mercy, everyone added, "If he has asked you to come, he will surely see you. Please wait."

Hours later there was still no sign that Sri Sathya Sai Baba would see us. The devotees crowded around the grounds slowly dispersed. It was now six o'clock and soon it would be night. The volunteer guarding the inner gate told us that Sri Sathya Sai Baba had briefly emerged from the house to stand on the steps, but had gone in again. Suddenly, it rained and this decided the issue for the crowd of devotees and they went home.

Slowly, my confidence about the interview ebbed away like the sea of devotees going home. According to believers, we had no right to complain if we did not meet Sri Sathya Sai Baba. After all, they said, did not hundreds of people leave without even a murmur? They would all return again the next day with the renewed hope of glimpsing Sri Sathya Sai Baba. Many of them had come from faraway places in India and abroad. If they had all come and gone without complaint, what right had I to expect preferential treatment? How was I better than them?

My ego would not accept this line of thought. "I am not a devotee. I only came because I was promised an interview."

Seconds ticked by. It was past half past six now. Every single person from the assembled crowd had left and so had the volunteers. There seemed to be much activity inside the house. We were told that Sri Sathya Baba was addressing a meeting.

A stout gentleman emerged from the darkness and brusquely said, "Please go away. Time is up."

My husband replied, "How can we go away without letting Baba know that we're here? He has asked us to come."

The man looked us over and said decisively, "The time for interviews is over. He will not see anyone now. And he will be busy after the meeting has ended."

But my husband was persistent. "Baba himself asked us to come today."

Came the quick retort, "He may have told you, but he has not told me!"

Then he joined his hands in front of him and said, "Please leave now. If you wish to try again, come tomorrow."

By now, I had become very annoyed. I felt undeservedly insulted. My husband asked me, "Shall we go or wait?"

A dozen people had joined us by this time. A few had been allowed in, the others stopped. We could hear intermittent clapping coming from the house. It seemed as if even the house was crowded, and indeed, we could see that many people were seated on the steps and in the portico.

An agitated man, well dressed and carrying a briefcase, arrived at the gates and sent urgent word. Our stout friend reappeared on the scene and scoldingly stated, "You are very late." The new arrival explained, "I have come straight from the airport. The 'plane only just landed." The stout gentleman went back to the house promising to obtain instructions regarding him.

Now, my disappointment was turning into anger. I had taken the appointment for granted and the ensuing frustration was almost unbearable. I was seething. My husband came to me. "Why are you so upset?" he wanted to know, "let us go away and come back another day."

My fury broke upon him like water through a dam. "Come again? Never! If Baba does not see us today, I will never come here again." My husband was aghast at my words. And then it happened. I looked up and caught a glimpse of the orange robe in the portico. Sri Sathya Sai Baba had come to distribute the blessed gift *(prasadam)* of food. The sight of that elusive figure, like a flame in the darkness, rekindled all my hopes.

Soon, a volunteer came and said, "Baba has asked you all to wait and to take the *prasadam*." A metal bucket full of that particular *prasadam* was brought to the gate. While a senior devotee was wondering out loud whether he should distribute it or not, a young boy came running to announce that Sri Sathya Sai Baba himself was coming to distribute the *prasadam*. "Everyone," he gasped, "please wait."

A thrill of anticipation ran through my body. At last, Sri Sathya Sai Baba was coming. This was our chance to tell him that we had been waiting. We might not get another. But, I knew at the same time that I would not be able to say a word. For it was my husband who had met him twice. He had never even seen me.

Sri Sathya Sai Baba walked towards us. He was short, slender and frail; the orange robe and the bushy crown of hair were striking. He distributed the *prasadam* quickly and gracefully and it was lovely to watch him. Seeing my husband, he asked, "When did you arrive?" and my husband replied instantly, "Swami, I have been waiting here since four o'clock. You told us to come then." There was more than a hint of grievance in his voice. Sri Sathya Sai Baba's hands continued giving portions of *prasadam*, but his face turned towards us full of compassion: "*Aiyo . . . Paapam!* (oh dear, misery). Nobody ever told me. I was in a meeting."

But, my husband was in no mood to let the injury pass. "Baba," he intoned, "I requested so many people so many times to tell you. I told them that Baba has asked us to come. But, no one took any notice at all."

"What to do? I havn't any time now," said a troubled Sri Sathya Sai Baba. His glance rested on me for a moment and passed on to the gentleman with the briefcase who then came close and whispered something in his ear. Sri Sathya Sai Baba reassured him, "I will look after everything. Do not worry." And in the same breath he told my husband, "Go in and wait. I will see you in a few minutes."

The devotees reacted with alacrity. "Go in, please. Baba wants you inside," they whispered urgently. Some ladies insructed me to take the *prasadam* from Sri Sathya Sai Baba before going into the house. Accordingly, I sat down and Sri Sathya Sai Baba gave me the *prasadam*, then he handed over the bucket to an attendant. Briskly, he walked back to the house and summoned us in.

Sri Sathya Sai Baba told my husband, in a sweet and gentle way, that he was very sorry that we had had to wait so long. He was so kind and thoughtful that I was visibly moved. I felt wretchedly small at having elicited an apology from him. I had even said that I would never return without knowing the essential Sri Sathya Sai Baba.

"I don't have time now. Can you come tomorrow so that we can talk?" asked Sri Sathya Sai Baba with such genuine concern and affection that I was flooded with emotion. We then bowed at his feet and he blessed us both.

"Why were you so annoyed? Once I make an appointment, I do not disappoint. You have been fretting since seven o'clock . . . but, your heart is good. There is even a lot of *Vedanta* in it," Sri Sathya Sai Baba said to me and continued, "I know you want to bring your children to be blessed. Bring them, by all means." Then he spoke a little about me saying things like, "You sit late into the night writing, writing. You are now working on a book." Then he asked me in *Telugu, "Bangaru, prasadam kaavalna* (do you want *prasadam)*?" I nodded and he materialised some holy ash *(vibhuti)* for me. Sri Sathya Sai Baba's love was like an avalanche cascading down into our hearts, sweeping away the weeds of our minds. It was as though he felt our grievance was justifiable and pampered us soothingly. Indeed, it was tonic and worked wonders – that special charm that is his and only his.

My husband said, "Baba, we would like to interview you. My wife has prepared many questions."

"I know," he said, "but what shall I do? There isn't any time now. Can you come tomorrow morning at half past nine? I can then talk to you properly." Then he made circles in the air with his hand and materialised some holy ash *(vibhuti)* for my husband. He went to a window sill and brought back two pieces of paper to wrap and keep the holy ash *(vibhuti)* he had given us.

"Don't worry," he said to me, "we will do the interview tomorrow," to which my husband was quick to reply, "Baba, your people will not let us come inside and we will not be able to meet you."

"No, no. I will tell them," he said. Once again we asked to be allowed to bring our children. As we bowed, he patted my head and blessed me with the words, "Be happy!" and touched my husband's cheek in an affectionate gesture. He came outside with us, called his volunteers and told them, "They are coming back tomorrow before ten o'clock. Bring them straight in." He smiled at us and once again said, "Come directly inside. There will not be any problem." Then he bade us an affectionate farewell and went back inside.

However much I tried to control myself, I felt shaken to the core. I felt chastised and yet so happy and so light. My husband said my eyes were starry with tears of joy and I felt everyone around was watching us. Sri Sathya Sai Baba's attentiveness towards us in turn drew attention to us. We heard someone murmur, "How lucky that Baba called them in at this hour."

Now there was a carefree spring to our steps and our hearts drummed joyfully as we left Brindavan and went to our car.

Unlike his usual self, my husband stepped hard on the accelerator in his jubilation.

"Don't you think this grand climax was worth all the waiting?" he asked.

I could not reply. I could not speak for quite some time. Sri Sathya Sai Baba had had a very deep effect on me.

After a while, I asked, "Do you think Baba came out just to see us? Or did he do so for the sake of the gentleman who had the message sent in to him?"

"I think Baba came out because of you and your bald statement that you wouldn't come again unless he saw you today," was my husband's opinion.

"I was annoyed because it was he who gave us the appointment and . . ." I started to explain away my wrath.

"It must have been your anger that went straight to Baba," said my husband, adding, "My God, how he literally overwhelmed us with love!"

"Yes, I think you are right. It was only after seven o'clock that I'd been fretting."

Sri Sathya Sai Baba had offered no lame excuses. Quite the contrary, his kindness and concern for us, his humility and gentleness showed that he cared and wanted to do things to soothe and reassure people. I felt full of energy and a bit other-worldly – certainly not my old self. I knew that this was the most sublime meeting I had ever had anywhere and the most impressive one, for it had had such an impact.

Does Sri Sathya Sai Baba leave such a magnetic impression on most people? I wondered.

"Had we come away without meeting Baba, how disappointed and angry we would have been. But now we're so full of joy," said my husband.

Sri Sathya Sai Baba had forged a strong link in the fifteen minutes he spent with us. And it was a remarkable, even though traumatic, event in our lives. At home, the boys were thrilled to learn that they too would be able to see Sri Sathya Sai Baba the next morning.

"It is my task to transform people's hearts."

. . . Sri Sathya Sai Baba

2

THE INTERVIEW

The next morning, we reached Whitefield at half past nine and got a lovely welcome. Even as we were parking the car near the gates, some children told us that Sri Sathya Sai Baba had already come out into the grounds and was inspecting the building of a college hostel. We hurried to catch a glimpse of him and spotted the orange-robed figure in the middle of a heap of rubble and other building materials. Something about him that morning reminded me of a picture of Christ on a hill I had seen many years ago in my primary school book. The straight long robe made me think of missionaries and the shock of black hair, seen from an angle with the sunlight streaming down, looked like the halo usually depicted around Christ's head.

I told a lady volunteer that I had an appointment with Sri Sathya Sai Baba and did not want to sit in the line of ladies waiting to glimpse him in the grounds. She immediately asked if we were the people who had come last night and, on hearing that we were, told us to go into the house to wait as, she said, "Baba will come there." We were relieved to be able to get into the house so easily. Then, at the portico, a volunteer asked us if we were the Balus. When we said yes, he invited us to come in and sit down and explained to us the reason for our royal treatment, "Baba told us this morning that when you arrived we were to bring you straight inside."

We sat down together in the entrance hall and someone immediately reminded me that I should be seated on the other side. Men and women are separated when they go to see Sri Sathya Sai Baba, although he may summon them to him together. I moved to the ladies' side and, remembering something else I had been told, wrapped the end of my *sari* so as to cover my back and arms.

How my attitude had changed in the past twelve hours! This morning I sat waiting for Sri Sathya Sai Baba without any hesitation or doubt or apprehension. The carpeted hall where we sat waiting was a narrow rectangular, like an enclosed verandah. A variety of pleasing photographs of Sri Sathya Sai Baba hung on the walls. His chair and footstool were near the door. A student devotee dashed in and placed white handkerchiefs on both arms of the chair. This, I later learnt, was for him to wipe his hands after giving holy ash *(vibhuti)* or to wipe his mouth (which he often did because of his habit of chewing betel nut leaves.) This rather human trait puzzled me and I wondered why he indulged in it. Just then, the call arrived and all thoughts of human frailty came to a halt.

Sri Sathya Sai Baba was courteous and often used the word please. "Please come in," he said, "and please sit down." He sat on his chair and allowed us to bow at his feet. He materialised enough holy ash *(vibhuti)* to give to all of us. As he distributed it, he asked our sons their names and where they studied. They were still stunned with having witnessed the much-debated materialisation of holy ash performed so naturally and effortlessly that they had not even realised it was being created. There were no flourishes. He simply made a few circular movements with his right hand and lo! there was the holy ash *(vibhuti)* in his palm.

My husband had brought along a tape recorder and I had dutifully carried my notebook, with all my questions and thoughts carefully noted down. When my husband tried to switch on the tape recorder, Sri Sathya Sai Baba said "No! don't record on that. Record it in your heart, then it will always be with you." So we all sat around and listened to him, occasionally interrupting him with a doubt or a question.

He floored the children by giving each one an exact description of himself: character, characteristics and behaviour. He spoke so kindly, his words laced with love, that the boys felt ashamed of their faults. And there was such humour in his description of the boys' pranks that they could not help but laugh with him.

His way of addressing them as *"bangaru"* (golden) touched their hearts and they absorbed his advice to "always speak sweetly." "Sweet words *(madhura swara)* are always right," he said, "remember that you can't always oblige a person, but you can always speak to them obligingly." This is just one example of how Sri Sathya Sai Baba wins over young hearts with sweet sayings.

I said that I would like to write about his message to youth. He was happy and said that he has always had a special corner in his heart for the young.

"Not that I don't love others, but young people are always something special for me," he said.

Sri Sathya Sai Baba spoke in a soft gentle voice but often so fast that it was difficult to keep up with him mentally. I tried to absorb everything he said, but soon realised that it was in vain: some of the things he spoke of were so profound and, as I started to concentrate on them, I found that he had already moved on to another thought and so my mind had to race to catch up with the new thought. I realised that I had to be all attention, a hundred per cent alert, to take in all he said in such flowing swiftness. My knowledge of *Sanskrit* was useful that morning. Sri Sathya Sai Baba explained the highest philosophy very simply and in a manner that others reserve for talking about the weather.

Besides high philosophy and the idea that God is immanent in all of us, he spoke of the behaviour of students; their lives and living habits and how to spiritualise their daily activities. It was interesting to note the way in which he returned, time and time again, to the theme of divinity in man. Though he covered a wide range of subjects, like a good teacher he repeated some ideas to drive home his main message. Once, he said, "You breathe all the time. Listen to your breath: it says '*sohum*.' Have you heard it? Try listening to someone who is asleep." Sri Sathya Sai Baba's sense of humour and his childlike glee in innocent fun were on display as he turned to the children and asked, "Have you watched men when they snore? grrr, grrr, with their mouths open? Well then, when man is asleep the sound is '*Om*.' So, in your sleeping state you are with *Om*, the divinity. In your waking state too you should realise the God in you."

He then asked the boys which was greater, 9 or 1? They answered 9. Sri Sathya Sai Baba said, "No. One is greater. Nine is made up of 1 + 1 + 1 + 1 + 1 + 1 + 1 + 1 + 1. Therefore, it is one that is important. That 'one' is the individual man." He emphasised this point by saying that zeroes which followed one had value. Without the one, the zeroes were worthless. The boys were fascinated by these mathematics which said that it is the divinity in every 'one' that gives value to life.

He spoke of the evils and temptations that abound in society. But a determined person can overcome these and achieve anything at all through will power. "The young of today do not realise the strength within them and so they slowly slide into bad behaviour. Idle gossip, frequent trips to the cinema, reading bad books – these have all become the pattern of their existence. Because they have not been made to understand how useless such pursuits are," he said.

Gently he admonished my eldest son for his laziness. "Going to your room, lying on the bed and reading worthless books – that is not the way to behave, *Bangaru*. I know what you have been doing. Why do you want to read all that useless stuff? A student should study only his textbooks. Remember the maxim, start early, go slowly and reach safely, and so accordingly, be slow, sure and steady. Why do you cram everything into your head in the last two months and fill your head with mere information without understanding its significance? These days students arrive at examination centres, there they empty their heads of whatever they have managed to fill them with and return completely empty-headed. Is learning only in order to pass examinations?" he asked. "That is why I think the present system of education is wrong. They say a student has passed his examination if he can obtain 35%. Does this not mean that his ignorance is allowed to be as much as 65%? Once these kind of graduates go to work, they forget even the paltry 35% they have learnt and the nation pays a heavy price for the resulting inefficiency. A real pass grade should be 100% as in the *Gurukula* system of old where the *gurus* erased all doubts and ensured that their students had learnt all they had to learn. That keen interest in becoming proficient and in gaining knowledge should again be inculcated in students."

Sri Sathya Sai Baba spoke at length about the working of the Sai colleges and hostels. "The key principle there is discipline and good habits. The students wake up at four o'clock, have a cold watei bath and say their prayers. Then they have breakfast before going on to their study periods. After the study is over, they have games and, before dinner, they sing devotional songs *(bhajans)*."

"Most of the students not only live in the hostel, they also run it, taking turns at different duties. They cook, shop, serve, clean and budget for their own hostel. This helps to make them responsible and self-reliant. They are also encouraged to handle small electrical repairs and to do other minor maintenance work."

"The spiritual content in the educational syllabus at the Satya Sai College will help them when they leave to go to work. Wherever they go and whatever they do, they will not only be honest and hard-working, but will also spread the gospel of love by example. Much is accomplished by setting an example. Even at school, one learns instantly from the gymnastics teacher how to perform a certain movement if he demonstrates it by doing it himself. Compare this with a history lesson where the teacher can teach only through words."

"My boys have been topping the lists in study achievement. They have won many ranks in universities. Even in the All-India accountancy examinations, several have come through with flying colours. It is similar in the Sai Women's colleges. The accent is on training in good home management and childcare. Prayers, meditation, games and rural welfare work – all form part of their curriculum. The girls help village women to learn about hygiene and nutrition. They also help them during sickness, childbirth, etc."

"After all, a man is so many things. Isn't it wonderful? At eight he's a boy, at forty a man and a grandfather at sixty. So, does that make him one or three? What do you say?" he laughingly asked my youngest son, Sanjay.

Sanjay has always been good at drawing. "He is *Ravi* (artist)," said Sri

Sathya Sai Baba, "he constantly wants to draw and has inherited the talents of both his parents. But, he should be a *Kavi* (poet). He must learn a few things first. *Kavi* is better than *Ravi* for he can write much and reach many more people," advised Sri Sathya Sai Baba.

To Vivek, my second son, he said, "Playing is not everything. Why do you not eat properly and why are you so weak? You play all the time. You throw off your school satchel and run off to your friends waiting round the corner. You should not be like that. Life itself is a game and first of all you must prepare yourself to face it. For, nothing is more important than the game of life."

I ventured to ask, "How shall we keep them on the right track? There are so many temptations along the way these days."

"Temptations? Oh . . . " He turned to my eldest son, Ashok. "If I were to tell you you had a cobra in your hands, wouldn't you instantly fling it away? Would you slowly, inch by inch, let it drop from your hands? When you realise that you have developed bad habits as poisonous as a cobra, no doubt you would hurl them from you in the same way. Don't think you can correct your ways little by little, for that is not practical. Make an unshakable resolution and hold to it."

Sri Sathya Sai Baba then spoke of the need to have a pure mind. He said that the boys might also like to remember another saying: less luggage, more comfort, make travelling a pleasure. He explained, "By luggage, I mean the weight of desire and by travel, I mean the journey that is life." Thoughts and ideas, blending with humour, poured down on us like a cascade of clear cool water from Sri Sathya Sai Baba. He spoke with such sweetness and affability that his simple and direct words made his message stimulating to all of us, whatever our ages and temperaments.

My husband presented Sri Sathya Sai Baba with a print of one of his collage paintings of *'Ganesha Shakti.'* He looked at it with interest. "Yes," he said, "I know you are a part-time painter." My husband then voiced all our thoughts, "May we invite Baba to our home some day to see our paintings?"

"Of course, I would like that. I shall certainly come. I am going now to Puttaparthi. When I return, I will come," he said. We rejoiced at the prospect of Sri Sathya Sai Baba visiting our house, honouring us with his presence and blessing our home.

Sri Sathya Sai Baba then spoke on the role of parents. "It is their duty to discipline their children and bring them up, from an early age, according to the codes of right conduct. Do you know how a snake gourd is straightened by tying stones? At first, a small stone is tied to it with a string, then as it lengthens, bigger stones are used. Similarly, disciplines change according to the age of the child. A young plant can be made straight even if it has begun to bend. But, can you straighten a fully grown plant?"

As he spoke, Sri Sathya Sai Baba's hands mimed the planting of a sapling, the tying of a stone, the straightening of a plant. Both his gestures and his voice were beautifully eloquent.

I marvelled at the way he captured young hearts, meeting them more than half way with little sayings and quizzes that delighted their growing minds and held their attention. He also had a few maxims for daily living.

"There are four F's that youngsters should remember: Follow the Master, Face the Devil, Fight to the end, Finish the game."

He explained things so simply that what he said was easy to remember. "God is mirrored in your heart. If you can't see Him, it is because your heart is covered with the dust of desire and indiscipline. Remove the dust through discipline, duty and devotion and you will see the divinity within you."

"However big a man, if he forgets God, he is not big. A hero is a zero if he isn't God-minded." He warned us, "Do not attach undue importance to money or material possessions. Remember that money comes and goes, but morality comes and grows."

My children sat absorbed in attention throughout the interview, drinking in every word, such were Sri Sathya Sai Baba's appeal and magnetism. He brought serious philosophy to life and made it relevant to our lives. His smile and the way he patted their cheeks and talked to them made it such a loving occasion for them that they were reluctant to end it.

At one point, Sri Sathya Sai Baba's handkerchief fell on the floor and my son picked it up and gave it back to him. Pointing to it, he said, "This is cloth. If you remove the threads that make it up there won't be any cloth left. Cloth is full of thread and it's thread that is woven to form cloth. The thread is made of cotton, but when you take it apart, you don't see the cotton, you only see the thread. Similarly, your desires are within you like threads. Remove them one by one and destroy them. Then there won't remain the cloth of illusion *(maya)* to worry you. And you can be happy. It is only disgruntled people who find fault with the world. It is those who have no peace in their hearts who cause disturbances in the world. They are restless, so they in turn engender restlessness in others and then think it a rotten world. I want young people to remember this well and always. For, after all, the journey through life is longer for the young than for the old. So, if life is a train travelling fast, the elderly get off after only a stop or two, but the young can travel on to the last station."

Sri Sathya Sai Baba also dealt with the subject of knowledge. "You should know what to do; have the right knowledge, the right judgement and the right action. If you want to see the whole world coloured green, you should know enough not to attempt painting everything green, but simply to wear green tinted glasses."

I requested him to say a few words about his work relating to medicine *(vaidya)*. "Have you seen the nearby hospital? Try to see it. Everything there is free. The doctors there give their services free. They are good, kind people. Those who come to the hospital are usually villagers to whom proper medical assistance is not available. And too, in general hospitals, they are often badly treated or not treated at all! When people are in pain, they crave kindness, a sweet soothing word and love *(prema)* – these medicines as well should always be freely available in our hospitals." He strongly emphasised that people in the medical profession should possess the quality of mercy and be messengers of love. The Sathya Sai Hospital at Whitefield is new, clean and well equipped. It is run by qualified doctors to care for the sick and is a centre of concerned love *(prema)* to ensure the right climate for medical treatment.

By now, we felt that we had taken a great deal of Sri Sathya Sai Baba's time, but he never gave any sign of impatience. He asked, "Are you happy? I think I have answered all the questions you intended asking me. Is there anything else? Ask me." I was surprised that he had, indeed, answered all the questions I had jotted down in my notebook. My husband had one last query, "Baba, what of the controversies at present going round? Would you like to say something to set the record straight?"

Sri Sathya Sai Baba laughed. "*Bangaru*, there isn't anything in them to be troubled about. They are transient, like passing clouds," he said, his hands describing the gathering and dispersing of clouds.

Suddenly, he made a few circular movements with his right hand and before we could utter a single sound, there was a shining silver ring in the hollow of his palm. He drew my husband's hand to him and slipped the ring onto his finger, saying, "Wear it, it's the right size." We were quite overwhelmed by this unexpected kindness.

As we bowed and took leave of Sri Sathya Sai Baba, we marvelled at how welcome and wanted he made us feel, as though we had been very near and dear to him. My youngest son, Sanjay, requested his autograph and he gave it to him with a warm smile. He did not hurry away, like any other important person might have done, but came with us to the door and again graciously asked if we had any more questions for him. He himself closed the door after us.

The interview was over. Outside, we saw that there were still a few people left waiting to catch a glimpse. I sensed that it was of us they talked among themselves. They were devotees and knew what it meant to have so much time with Sri Sathya Sai Baba. They looked at us and their expressions said, "You have truly been blessed by Baba!" We reached the car still basking in the light that Sri Sathya Sai Baba's attention had turned on us.

The children were thrilled with the materialisation of their father's ring. They crowded round him to stare at the perfectly etched face of Sri Sathya Sai Baba on the ring, a beautiful and perfectly finished ornament.

Our hearts were full and we felt dazed. The boys repeated the sayings and jokes and wondered how he could read their minds so accurately. "There's no doubt that he is superhuman," was their unanimous verdict. They had already and indisputably become Sai fans. They were all happy to have found someone to whom they could always look up. They made instant resolutions to be guided by Sri Sathya Sai Baba and to win his approval. It really was a red letter day in all our lives. Sri Sathya Sai Baba had roused the Good that was in them and thus the God in them. For the rest of the day they talked of no one and nothing else. The two older boys wanted to read about his life and to learn all about him. They were so happy and so excited, their faces suffused with the remembered joy of the unforgettable interview.

As for me, I felt as if an electric current had passed through me, leaving me with an inexplicable joy. The thought of Sri Sathya Sai Baba kept returning as though he had cast a spell on me. But I brushed aside the thought since it seemed unfair to attribute such motives to him. After all, it had been I who had gone in search of him to interview him. It was I who wanted to know him. He most certainly was not in need of more devotees. There are tens of thousands, even millions, of them all around the world, many of them multimillionaires who would do anything he wanted them to. I had also heard that among his followers were celebrities of all kinds and many of the world's most talented and creative people and that they, too, heard his word as law. I wondered if Sri Sathya Sai Baba had the same effect on everyone he met as he had on me. Does he inspire people to such an extent that they think only of him? As he is considered the Incarnation of God, does this mean that one's thoughts can so easily be switched over to the Divine?

Though I tried, I could not forget the moments spent with Sri Sathya Sai Baba. I heard later that soon after the interview, he left for Puttaparthi, the village of his birth. I had never even heard of it. Where was it? I realised that I knew precious little about Sri Sathya Sai Baba. I did not know where he was born, or how he had become so revered a spiritual figure, nor how he had built up such an efficient organisation around him. All I had ever known about him were the miracles he performed and the numerous controversies they generated, keeping him in the news. So I bought all the nine volumes of his speeches and a few other books on him and set out to educate myself.

"In Baba's life, up to sixteen years, leelas . . . from sixteen to thirty-five years, miracles . . . from thirty-five to sixty years, teachings and miracles. After sixty, Baba will be beyond the public, but will continue his work till he leaves this body in his ninety-sixth year."

. . . Sri Sathya Sai Baba

3

HIS STORY AND HIS GLORY

Miracles and illusions *(maya)* have surrounded Sri Sathya Sai Baba since birth. His advent was heralded by mysterious omens in and around the village of Puttaparthi in Andhra Pradesh. The *tambura* (a stringed instrument) and the *madaala* (a drum) in the family home would sometimes play sweetly on their own in the middle of the night. His father, Pedda Venkappa Raju, consulted a learned *pandit* about this phenomenon and he told him that such music presaged an immensely auspicious event. His pregnant mother, Srimati Easwaramma, prayed to Lord *Sathyanarayana* and performed rites after which she felt the start of birth pangs. The day that Sathyanarayana was born, according to the *Hindu* calendar, was a most auspicious day in the month of *Kartika* and the year of *Akshaya*. And his star was *Ardhra*.

The date, according to the prevalent solar system, was the 23rd of November 1926. Soon after he was born, Sathya performed a miracle. A cobra under the sheets gently rocked the baby and the baby smiled serenely as the air filled with the sweet scent of jasmine blossom. Astrologers tell us that the events that surrounded his birth correspond to the events that precede the advent of an incarnation of God *(Avatara)*, as explained in the *Viparita Raja Yoga* (Extraordinary Royal Characteristics), a study within the art and science of astrology.

Little Sathya charmed everyone with his smiles. When asked to sit down to a meal, he would often reply that an old man had already fed him. No one knew which old man or even if one had come by. But, there was never any doubt that Sathya's stomach was full because his hands and mouth would smell of the most delicious food. From a very early age, he would insist that his schoolmates sing devotional songs *(bhajans)*, perform rites *(puja)* and celebrate holy festivals. As a result, even then he was accepted as a leader and called *"Guru"*.

Sathya loved to put *vibhuti* and *kumkum* on his forehead. He was born into a family of meat eaters, but remained vegetarian from childhood. He found support in this from his grandfather, Sri Ratnakaram Kondama Raju, who was the only other vegetarian in the family, and made his wife, Lakshmamma, cook separately for himself and his young grandson. Later, when his grandmother died, Sathya took on the task of cooking for his grandfather and himself in a separate room. Sri Ratnakaram Kondama Raju was very devout and built a temple to *Satyabhama* waiting for her Lord *(Krishna)*. The grandfather encouraged his favourite grandchild to participate in village dramas and to sing.

Sathya had an elder brother, Seshama Raju, and two older sisters, Venkamma and Parvatamma. Sathya was always a good and lovable boy. He attended school at Puttaparthi and the neighbouring village of Bukkapatnam where he delighted his friends with his miracles. Often, he would produce sweets and other gifts from empty bags. And, apparently from nowhere, he would produce *"prasad"* for the *bhajan* singers. When asked to explain, he would say that an angel brought them to him at his command. He gave these gifts only to good children and so they all tried to earn them by being good.

When he was ten, he formed a *pandari bhajan* group in the village. It was a great success. Sathya composed songs about *Krishna's* life. He and his group enacted the stories in song and dance. He danced well and played difficult parts with effortless ease. He imitated the then popular stage artiste, Rishyendramani. He also composed *bhajans* in honour of Shirdi Sai Baba who no one from the village had heard of. He also wrote a play with a moral called 'Do You Act as You Speak?' and that, too, was very successful.

During this stage, Sathya was sent to Kamalpur to continue his schooling. There too he was a popular boy and much loved at school. He gave a hint of his powers once when a schoolmaster punished him without reason and made him stand on a bench. When the bell rang for the end of class, the schoolmaster found that he could not get out of his chair. When he stood up, the chair came with him, firmly stuck to his posterior. Mahbub Khan, another teacher, who knew that Sathya was no ordinary child, came to the rescue by asking the punished boy to sit down. And, as soon as Sathya was seated, the chair detached itself from the unfortunate teacher and he divested himself of it.

Sri Sathya Sai Baba tells of another instance of his pranks. He had two close companions who were not too good at studying. When the examination results were given, they were astounded to have received first class marks. Sathya, with his special powers, had written all the correct answers for them and in their respective handwriting.

Sathya knew that his parents could not really afford to educate him. So he used to earn the money to buy his school books composing little ditties advertising various products on sale at the shop of Kote Subbanna. These little compositions were then sung by children in the streets to popularise the goods on sale.

Sathya had only the minimum amount of clothes. During an address in later years, Sri Sathya Sai Baba described how he used thorns like safety pins on buttonless shirts. He never used his powers to obtain anything for himself.

Later, Sathya went to live with his brother at Uravakonda and attended high school there. He was already well known at the new school as people had heard about the strange and unusual gifts he could materialise. Many asked for his help in finding stolen or lost items. He had an uncanny ability for locating stolen articles. "But I never used to give them the full names. Only the first and last letters of the names of persons possessing the lost articles and they had to do the rest." His miraculous powers were fully appreciated when he found a teacher's lost pen and a Muslim gentleman's lost horse. His fame began to spread and the Muslim community started to heed this wonder boy.

On the 8th of March 1940, Sathya suddenly became stiff and unconscious. No one knew the reason, but some said it was because he had been stung by a big black scorpion. Possibly, this was the first known instance of his transcorporeal journeys (leaving the gross body to travel in the subtle body). Later, people knew what this unconscious state meant, but at that time, no one knew. His brother called in doctors and they tried to chase away the evil spirit that they feared might have taken possession of him. A few days later, Sathya revived. But his behaviour was extraordinary. He was silent most of the time, he recited poetry or *Sanskrit* verses or expounded the highest forms of philosophy. His brother, Seshama, was worried and thought he should send a messenger to fetch his parents. But, Sathya said, "You need not send for them. They are already on their way and will be here in half an hour." And he was right.

But, Sathya's strange behaviour and frequent trances continued. The family called in an exorcist who departed in great haste having perceived in Sathya the God he worshipped. On another day, Sathya said unexpectedly to his sister, "Here, bring the sacred flame here . . . the gods are passing across the sky."

The family were seriously concerned and feared that he might be a victim of black magic. So they gave him over into the charge of a sort of witch doctor who put him through, what amounted to, pure physical torture.

First, he removed all the hair from the young man's head, made cuts all over his scalp with a knife till they spurted blood; then he squeezed lime juice into them. Sathya sat calmly through all this, showing no emotion at all. The witch doctor was insensed. He then squeezed acid, garlic juice and red chillies into the wounds. The boy sat serenely through even this ordeal. Other "treatments" were the pouring of 108 buckets of cold water on Sathya's head each morning and severe thrashings with a stick to drive away the evil spirit. His ultimate treatment was to rub a fiery eye-salve called *kalikam* into Sathya's eyes. The result was alarming: Sathya's face swelled and tears poured from his red eyes, his face was unrecognisably bloated and distorted and his body shook with pain. His parents thought they were on the point of losing a son, but Sathya called them near and explained where to get a certain herbal medicine. An application of the herbal remedy instantly dismissed all the symptoms and his parents took him away from the terrible sorcerer.

On the 23rd of May 1940, Sathya called all his family to him and, with a wave of his hand, produced sugar candy, flowers and sweetened milk-rice for them. His father, Venkappa Raju, was angered by this ostentatious behaviour and took a stick to his son, shouting, "Now tell me, are you a god or a ghost or a prankster?"

The historic statement made in answer thus began the era of the spiritual world of Sri Sathya Sai Baba. "I am Sai Baba," he said and further declared, "I belong to the *Apasthambha Sutra* and the *Gotra* of *Bharadwaja*."

A gentleman known to be a follower of Shirdi Sai Baba was brought from Penukonda. He said that he thought Sathya must be mentally deranged. Sathya replied, "You do not recognise the very Sai you worship," and materialised handfuls of sacred ash *(vibhuti)*. All the others bowed to him and he bade them worship him every Thursday and keep their minds and houses clean. Accordingly, the worship began.

One Thursday, Sathya was challenged and asked to prove that he was Sai Baba. He asked for jasmine flowers which he threw on the floor. Where they fell, the jasmine flowers formed, in *Telugu* letters, the two words Sai Baba. But, Sathya's father did not want him to give up school and took him back to it.

At school, Sathya was regarded as a prodigy and was soon acclaimed a prophet. He materialised pictures of Shirdi Sai Baba, sacred ash, dates (something else that Shirdi Sai Baba had often given) and pieces of orange material which, he said, were from Shirdi Sai Baba's *kafni* gown. Sathya's *leelas* (divine playfulness) became increasingly evident.

One day, he and his followers went to see the ruins at Hampi. There, in the temple dedicated to Lord *Virupaksha*, the divine patron of the Vijayanagar dynasty, Sathya's image was seen on the *Shiva lingam*, though he himself was not even in the temple. This vision made people worship him with *bhajans* and *namasankirtans*. Instant cures of two cripples were taken as further proof of his powers.

On the 20th of October 1940, Sathya was walking to school with Sri Anjaneyalu who was devoted to him. He seemed to have a special halo round his head and face. Suddenly he changed his mind about going to school and returned home. He put his school books away and announced, "I am no longer your Sathya. I am Sai." His sister-in-law saw the luminosity about him. She was awe struck. He turned to her and said, "I am leaving. I do not belong to you. My devotees are calling to me. I have work to do . . . I cannot stay any longer." To his brother he said, "Do not try to 'cure' me anymore. I am Sai. I do not consider myself your relative."

He left his brother's home then, at the age of fourteen, and never returned to it. He went and sat on a rock in Sri Anjaneyalu's garden. People gathered to see him and he taught them a prayer on that eventful day. He sang,

"Manasé Bhajaré Guru charanam, Dustara bhava saagara Tharanam" (with all your mind worship at the feet of your *guru* and cross the endless ocean of life and death).

Sri Anjaneyalu performed a rite to worship his feet *(paada puja)* and was his first declared devotee.

Soon, the singing of devotional songs *(bhajans)* and the giving of blessed gifts *(prasad)* became a daily pattern and Sri Sathya Sai Baba was acclaimed *Guru*.

One day, a photographer came to take a picture. He took photographs despite the fact that there was a stone obstructing his view of the young *Guru*. But when the film was developed, the stone had changed into the form of Shirdi Sai Baba.

His family persuaded Sathya to return to Puttaparthi and they promised not to stand in his way anymore. But, his parental home was too small to receive the growing number of devotees and visitors, so Sathya went to stay in the house of Karnam Subbama, a *Brahmin* lady, whose home had always been a second home to him. Subbama looked after him like a mother and welcomed devotees with open arms. A new stage in the life of Sri Sathya Sai Baba was beginning. He was no more the boy, Sathya. He was more and more being accepted as an *avatara* (Incarnation of God) or God Himself, and many came to worship him. Several fortunate devotees had unusual spiritual experiences and all were enchanted by the ceaseless flow of miracles.

Sri Sathya Sai Baba composed many songs and *bhajans* and taught them to his devotees. He taught them about Shirdi Sai Baba, about his temple at Shirdi and the way worship was practised there. He spoke in great detail about the *udhi* (sacred ash), the blessed gifts *(prasad)* and the margosa tree at Shirdi. Venkamma, one of Sri Sathya Sai Baba's sisters, asked for a photograph of Shirdi Sai Baba and received it mysteriously on a day that her brother was not in town. She had been sleeping when his voice woke her and she found a rustling piece of paper which turned out to be the photograph.

Sri Sathya Sai Baba used to produce every kind of fruit imaginable from a certain tamarind tree that stood near the River Chitravati. It became known as the wish-fulfilling tree, *Kalpataru*. The banks of the Chitravati were often the setting for Sri Sathya Sai Baba's early discourses and the sands in the dry riverbed frequently manifested his creations.

As a young man, Sri Sathya Sai Baba did not like to be tied to a schedule and, often, he used to wander off on his own to escape from the heavy atmosphere of adulation. Everyone adored him for he was like a young *Krishna* returned to earth. They loved him, his pranks, his songs, his *leelas* and his miracles. They wanted nothing better than to gaze constantly upon his face and his form.

People thronged to see him and Sri Sathya Sai Baba insisted on feeding them. Like Christ before him, he kept up an unending supply of food – he would either wave his hands over the pots full of cooked food or break coconuts and sprinkle their water over them.

Old devotees recall how they sang *bhajans* regularly every evening, sometimes when Sri Sathya Sai Baba was himself away, wandering somewhere near or far. But always when it was time for the *aarati*, he would return, often breathless, to receive the *araadhana* as promised. Frequently, he would be with other young boys by the banks of the River Chitravati when, suddenly, he would announce, "They are about to perform the *aarati*. I must go." Then he would run to wherever the *bhajans* were being sung.

During those days, the young Sri Sathya Sai Baba had to contend with much jealousy and opposition from some of the local people. Once, they set fire to his shed and he brought down heavy rain to put out the flames. On another occasion, the would-be arsonists failed to set fire to his shed because not one of their matchsticks would light. At last, Sri Sathya Sai Baba went up to them and offered a "Sai matchstick" with which to burn his shed, but they fled. Srimati Nagamani Purnaiya, one of the early devotees, has written a compact book entitled, *'Leelas of Bhagwan Sathya Sai Baba'*. Equally, Sri N. Kasturi, a Sai historian, has recorded the many miraculous episodes in that remote village, the amazing Sai happenings that drew pilgrims in their hundreds. The trek was arduous in those days, but that did not present any obstacle to those who had already been captivated by him. They wanted to be near him whenever they could.

Those were the days when Sri Sathya Sai Baba was full of laughter and youthful pranks and delighted in giving divine visions to his devotees. He would show the cosmic form *(Vishvaswarupa)* to a few, appear as *Shiva* to someone and as *Vishnu* to someone else. He also appeared as *Rama, Krishna, Lakshmi, Durga,* and *Ganesha*. In short, he appeared as the *Ishta Devata* (chosen deity) of the particular devotee and thrilled him or her.

Most of those who have been with Sri Sathya Sai Baba since the early days happily confess that, "after one look at him, or one *namaskar*, we knew in our hearts that he was God, the Universal Lord, the Divine

Incarnation." They never doubted or questioned his divinity and were instantly drawn to him. This power to draw people to himself, the charisma and the charm, are characteristic of *avataras*. The name *Krishna* is derived from the word *akarshana* (attraction, that which attracts). *"Ramayathi ithi Ramaha*," means that which pleases is *Rama*. Both these qualities also belong to Sri Sathya Sai Baba, say the devotees of their *Sai Krishna*, their *Sai Rama*.

Srimati Purnaiya has recorded a very interesting incident of those early years. The young Sathya was bitten by a cobra while trying to save a girl from it. He turned to a nearby devotee and said, "The snake has bitten me. Take my *shakti* (power)," before becoming unconscious. The devotee used this power to produce sacred ash *(vibhuti)* which he quickly applied to Sri Sathya Sai Baba and it revived him instantly.

Dr. M. B. Sunder Rao relates similar transferences of power during later years. Once, for a few days, his legs were paralysed due to wanton poisoning. The devotees around him could bear it no longer, so Sri Sathya Sai Baba consented to make himself well again. He sprinkled some water on one leg and it immediately returned to normal. Dr. Sunder Rao asked him how he had done it. Sri Sathya Sai Baba replied, "You can also do it if I give you my *shakti*," and told him to try. So the good doctor sprinkled water on the other leg and, straight away, that leg too came back to life.

There is another instance of Sri Sathya Sai Baba having eaten poison. This time, the poison was in some *vadas* (similar to fried doughnuts) and he brought it out later without it having harmed his system. Devotees speak of other occasions when he has remained unaffected by poison – whether from snake bites or doctored food.

Instances of Sri Sathya Sai Baba healing wounds and illnesses abound, as do stories of surgical operations miraculously performed by him. And there are thousands of stories about his creation of trinkets like rings, chains, pendants, lockets, photographs and coins, and also idols of gods. On several occasions, he has brought out large images of gods from sand banks, seashores, and hilltops.

Miracles were a legion then and, for a chosen few, his personality was irresistible. They were the lucky ones, who cared nothing for the hardships of the journey or for the relative unimportance of the little village of Puttaparthi. They perceived the divinity in young Sathya, enjoyed the privilege of his close companionship and basked in his love and spiritual radiance. He lived with them, ate with them and moved with them. It is only now that he has private living quarters and has to have fixed hours for meeting devotees

Sri Sathya Sai Baba often delighted his devotees by creating delicious snacks. If it was not sugar candy, it was dates or some other succulent fruit or sweet. On other special occasions, he would materialise a pot containing a sweet liquid with an other-worldly taste. He called it *amruta* (nectar) and shared it out between fortunate devotees.

As Sri Sathya Sai Baba's fame spread, people flocked to Puttaparthi in their thousands, although the journey was difficult and lodgings inadequate.

In 1944, some devotees built a small temple for Sri Sathya Sai Baba. It is referred to today as the Old Temple *(mandir)*. Sri Sathya Sai Baba insisted that a photograph of Shirdi Sai Baba be kept next to his in the temple. Festivals like *Dassera* were celebrated with gusto. A palanquin full of floral decorations was used by the devotees to carry their young God in procession. Men and women used to take turns carrying it.

It was on those palanquin processions that they saw some of the most wonderful miracles. All of a sudden, the lines in Sri Sathya Sai Baba's forehead would fill with sacred ash *(vibhuti)*, then change into red dots of *kumkum* (cochinella powder) or yellow dots of turmeric, and his face would glow with an extraordinary lustre. At times, he would pick a few flowers from his garland and scatter them about and, as they fell, they would turn into medallions, each carrying a portrait of one of a myriad deities. Such spectacular manifestations quite naturally drew an ever increasing number of peope to celebrate festive days in Puttaparthi. The Old Temple became too small to hold the surging masses and, in 1950, Prashanti Nilayam (the abode of supra peace) was built. It was officially inaugurated on Sri Sathya Sai Baba's 25th birthday. Since then, the three main festivals of *Dassera*, Sri Sathyas Sai Baba's birthday and *Mahashivaratri* have been celebrated at this new Nilayam.

A new dimension was given to Sathya Sai activities in 1957. Upto then, Sri Sathya Sai Baba had spent time with and given al fresco lectures only to devotees and to close followers. But, in 1957, he presided over the All-India Divine Life Conference at Venkatagiri in Andhra Pradesh. He delivered a brilliant keynote address to the Conference and, as a result, Swami Sadananda, Swami Sachidananda and other scholars invited him to visit Swami Sivananda's *ashrama* at Rishikesh. Swami Sivananda was delighted with the visit. Sri Sathya Sai Baba's speeches were greatly appreciated by him and they had long discussions on many aspects of *Vedanta*. As Swami Sivananda was unwell at the time, Sri Sathya Sai Baba materialised sacred ash *(vibhuti)* for him which worked wonders and improved his condition generally.

Sri Sathya Sai Baba went to various parts of India and everywhere he performed miracles. At Badrinath and Somnath, he brought out hidden *lingams* and performed consecrational rites over them with fresh flowers and with gold and silver flowers, all instantly created by him. In Varanasi, he adorned the golden crest of the famous Kashivishwanath Temple with remarkable jewels shaped as *bilva* leaves, the crescent moon, and bearing *vibhuti* markings as on a devout forehead – all produced by a wave of his hand. In Srisailam, he created medallions of Lord *Mallikarjuna* and his consort, *Brahmarambha*.

When devotees in Tamil Nadu expressed a wish to build and dedicate a temple to him, he said that it should be for Shirdi Sai Baba. And, in Madras, as he stood on a cloth, his feet produced on it the imprints of Shirdi Sai Baba's feet! In the tiny village of Kothnagatta, near Sravanabelgola in Karnataka, he manifested an image of himself next to one of Shirdi Sai Baba in the *Shiva lingam* of the village temple. This was mainly to please two little boys, but it also gave the villagers a Sai *lingam* to worship.

There appears to be no end to Sri Sathya Sai Baba's miracles. At Kanya Kumari (the tip of the Indian peninsula), he gave devotees the rare experience of seeing a pearl necklace materialising on the waves of the sea. In Assam, in Eastern India, he materialised an ancient copper plate with an archaic inscription to be installed in a temple. Similarly, he brought out a sacred plaque to plant under the Tree of Meditation in Puttaparthi. At the festival of *Krishna's* birthday *(Krishna Jayanti)*, he turned jasmine flowers into gems, each one bearing a miniscule image of Lord *Krishna*.

In 1958, Sri Sathya Sai Baba started his now famous magazine, *Sanathana Sarathi* (eternal charioteer). In 1961, the first volume of his biography, entitled *Satyam Shivam Sundaram*, by N. Kasturi was released. In 1965, Sri Sathya Sai Baba started the Prashanti Vidwan Mahasabha to encourage *Vedic* scholars and other *pandits*. By 1966, Prashanti Nilayam had grown to such an extent that it was constituted a township on its own. Many buildings had been built to house devotees and a special canteen building was erected to provide regular meals. Festivals were celebrated on a grander scale and there were more facilities available for those who attended them.

In 1968, the second volume of the biography, *Satyam Shivam Sundaram*, was released and the Bombay centre, Dharmakshetra, was inaugurated. Dharmakshetra includes a lotus-shaped residence for Sri Sathya Sai Baba. During the same year was held the first World Conference of the Sri Sathya Sai Baba organisations at the newly inaugurated Bombay centre. Thereafter, Sri Sathya Sai Baba held these meetings annually. It was also the year he made his first, and as yet only, trip abroad to East Africa. The Women's College at Anantapur in Andhra Pradesh was opened during 1968 and, in 1969, the Boys' College at Brindavan in Whitefield near Bangalore. The third volume of *Satyam Shivam Sundaram* came out in 1972. It was also the first year of the now annual Summer Course on Indian Culture and Spirituality.

Sri Sathya Sai Baba started writing a series of books entitled, *Prema Vahini, Sandeha Nivarini, Geetha Vahini, Bhagavatha Vahini, Rama Katha Rasa Vahini*, and *Bharatiya Paramartha Vahini*. All these books are, as a rule, first serialised in the magazine, *Sanathana Sarathi*, and then issued in book form. There are also nine volumes called *Sathya Sai Speaks*.

At present there are more than 12,000 Sathya Sai *Samithis* all over the world and the number of devotees exceeds 20 millions. *Seva* (service) activities are organised through *Seva Samithis, Mahila Vibhags* (women's divisions) and *Bala Vikas* (children's centres). Keen students of spirituality *(adhyatma)* have study circles and there are quite a number of these in India and abroad. The *Sathya Sai Seva Dal* is an important unit of volunteer workers (men and women) in every state of India.

There are hundreds of *Bhajan Mandalis* around the world. They constitute a vital link in the Sathya Sai programme, for Sri Sathya Sai Baba has repeatedly stated that *namasmaran* (constant repitition of the Lord's name) is the only short cut to God in this age *(Kali Yuga)*. He always stresses the importance of singing the glory of the Lord with purity and devotion in the heart. The *Bhajan Mandalis* help in congregational singing and confer happiness on their communities in general.

There is always ceaseless activity around Sri Sathya Sai Baba. Projects of various kinds, different sorts of educational programmes and cultural events are constantly being planned and arranged under his guidance. More and more people are becoming involved in these programmes. It is a way in which devotees are encouraged to make their own distinctive contributions in their own special fields. Their talents are exploited for the good of society as a whole. And those around Sri Sathya Sai Baba quite naturally take to *sadhana* (spiritual endeavour) and *seva* (service).

The fiftieth birthday of Sri Sathya Sai Baba was a great and unique occasion for his devotees. More than a quarter of a million devotees assembled in the little village of Puttaparthi. There was hardly any standing room, so Sri Sathya Sai Baba took to a helicopter to grant *darshan* to all! There was a flag hoisting ceremony near the recently built *Sarvamatha Aikya Stambha* (Pillar of Concord) denoting the unity of all religions. The pillar not only commemorates the fiftieth birthday, but also reminds people that the religion of Sai is based on the essential one-ness of all religons.

Since his fiftieth birthday, Sri Sathya Sai Baba has intensified his teaching mission. This was predetermined by him even as a young boy. In a letter written years ago to his elder brother, he outlined all his future activities. At the time he was a village boy without any financial means, but he wrote to his brother that, in years to come, he would have millions of devotees and temples dedicated to him; how educational institutions and other activities would be organised. After forty years, one sees the truth of these prophecies. This particular letter is displayed at the *Pragyam Pradarshan*, a museum of spirituality within the Boys' College grounds at Brindavan.

The Sathya Sai educational institutions consist of colleges and schools *(vidya viharas)*. There are plans to start several more of these institutions in regular phases. Meanwhile, the Sai system of education has attracted the attention of policy makers at government level. The government of his home state, Andhra Pradesh, is the first government to acknowledge, accept and introduce the Sai model of spiritual education at primary level. Sri Sathya Sai Baba courses in orientation have been organised for primary school teachers under his direct supervision and guidance. Sri Sathya Sai Baba continually demonstrates a dynamic leadership, working in the midst of people for their spiritual evolution, turning their aims Godward.

"When leaving the Shirdi body, I made a sankalpa to be born again for dharma samsthapana."

... Sri Sathya Sai Baba

4

SATHYA SAI AND SHIRDI SAI

No records are available of Shirdi Sai Baba's life before the age of sixteen. Sri Sathya Sai Baba says that Shirdi Sai Baba was born in the village of Patri, the third child of a boatman called Ganga Bhavadia. His mother's name was Devagiriamma. She had had a divine experience in which Lord *Shiva* blessed her and told her that he would be born to her as her third child. After the birth of Shirdi Sai Baba, Devagiriamma was compelled to abandon the child in a forest and to follow her husband into the wilderness where he was determined to realise God.

The child was kept alive by honey trickling into his mouth from a beehive on a branch of the tree under which his mother had left him. A childless couple, the Patils, journeying through the forest, found him there, took him home and brought him up as their own son.

Mr. Patil died while the boy was still young and Mrs. Patil found it difficult to look after the boy on her own. He had been to a *Hindu* temple and had recited the *Koran* there; and he had installed a stone *lingam* to be worshipped in a mosque. Both parties were angered and complained of his behaviour.

On one occasion, he played a game of marbles with the *sahukar's* son. Suddenly, he dashed away to a house where he knew a *shaligram* was worshipped and brought it back as his marble. When the offended elders came to reclaim it, he swallowed it. "It was because of this that I brought out *Shivalingams* at *Shivaratri*," joked Sri Sathya Sai Baba. He has said, "In this body, I will not become old or infirm as in my old body." As he chewed *pan*, he remarked, "Then it was *hookah*, now it is *pan*."

Shirdi Sai Baba was in Shirdi by the time he was sixteen. There, he performed many miracles, curing the sick, assisting the helpless and protecting the village from epidemics of one kind and another. At first, he was respected as a saint. Later, he was revered as a divine personage.

In Puttaparthi as elsewhere, all celebrations and events are also woven around Shirdi Sai Baba. Every Sathya Sai devotee knows about Shirdi Sai. Though unknown to foreigners during his lifetime, the Shirdi Incarnation is today well known to all Sri Sathya Sai Baba's foreign devotees. When Sri Sathya Sai Baba materialises medallions and rings, he often has only the Shirdi Sai image on them, at other times, the images of both Sai Babas are on them. At Puttaparthi, the main altar in the temple has a life-size photograph of Shirdi Sai Baba beside that of Sri Sathya Sai Baba. And at every Sai festival, Sri Sathya Sai Baba performs *vibhuti abhishekam* (sacred ash cascading from an empty vessel) to a silver idol of Shirdi Sai Baba. When devotees have wanted to build temples to Sri Sathya Sai Baba, he has always insisted that they install only Shirdi Sai images or the imprints of his feet in their temples. Hundreds of thousands of Sai devotees have learnt of Shirdi Sai Baba through Sri Sathya Sai Baba.

Sri Sathya Sai Baba has said that there will be one more *Sai Avatara* called Prema Sai. The third Sai will be born in Gunaparthi, a village in the Mandya district of Karnataka. Thus, Sri Sathya Sai Baba refers not only to his past, but also to the future form he will assume as Prema Sai.

Some devotees of Shirdi Sai Baba have recognised Sri Sathya Sai Baba as Shirdi Sai Baba. People like Shri M. S. Dixit, a Shirdi Sai devotee, at first thought Sri Sathya Sai Baba looked rather melodramatic, with his bushy hair and flamboyant mannerisms, and compared these to the rather simple old man who was Shirdi Sai Baba. But, Sri Sathya Sai Baba gave him many proofs – recognising his uncle's photograph and relating to Shri Dixit his experiences with Shirdi Sai Baba – that Shri Dixit could not doubt for long that Sri Sathya Sai Baba was indeed his beloved Shirdi Sai Baba come again.

Those who do not believe in his Shirdi *Avatara* nevertheless realize that he does not need to boost his public image by identifying himself with Shirdi Sai Baba. And yet he does because, as he says, "It is the truth. When I know that I am the *Avatara* of Shirdi Sai Baba, why should I not say it? Why should I suppress it? There is no way for all of you to know the truth or to prove it. Only I know it to be the truth." That is why Sri Sathya Sai Baba remains unconcerned by those who disbelieve, for he knows absolutely that he was Shirdi Sai Baba and he has come back to the world with a purpose: the uplift of humanity.

"When among men, I am a man; among women, I am a woman; among children, a child. Alone, I am God."

. . . Sri Sathya Sai Baba

5

BABA IS MY BROTHER

Venkamma is Sri Sathya Sai Baba's elder sister. She is deeply devoted to him as well as being attached to him in family feeling. Her devotion is the result of her realisation of him as divine, but the attachment of a sister to a younger brother who she looked after and coddled still exists.

Asked about Sri Sathya Sai Baba's infancy, Venkamma said, "Sathyam was an attractive baby, chubby, with big eyes and fairer in complexion than all of us."

"Our family was very big, with nearly forty members, aunts, uncles and cousins; and the village was poor. We could hardly get milk for the child. Milk was always scarce in Puttaparthi then. So, it wasn't everyday that baby Sathyam got milk. Sometimes, it would be goat milk, or buffalo milk. But he was not a greedy child and never any trouble," she said thinking back to the Puttaparthi of old with all its snakes and snake pits. "After the advent of Sathyam, conditions improved and the place overflowed with milk, curds and butter." There was a smile on her face as she continued, "There is nothing surprising in this since Sathyam is also thought to be Lord *Krishna*, the divine cowherd."

The early devotees of Sri Sathya Sai Baba invariably say that, in those days, one could have lived on just the dairy products of Puttaparthi.

"Young Sathyam was different as a young boy, exceptional in his goodness, but also because of his obsession that he was God," recalled Venkamma. "All the village children loved him as he could 'produce' gifts for them from empty bags. Today we know what Sathyam is, but then we worried about his strange ways. Wouldn't you feel anxious if a youngster maintained he was divine or if he claimed to have been fed by some invisible intruder? Naturally we, his family, feared it might be a kind of madness. The elders wanted to do their best to cure him, or drive away any evil spirit that might have taken possession of him, and make him normal, more like other children," she said.

Venkamma loved to read and could read up to the 5th class standard. "I've always read and kept in touch. Even today, I cannot sleep without reading late into the night." This was her way of explaining why she knew so many myths and legends. She has a soft sweet voice and the ability to learn songs very quickly and remember them forever.

One evening, she treated us to many songs, *bhajans,* and folk songs taught her by Sathyam when young. "After Sathyam announced he was Sai Baba, his main wish was for us to learn *bhajans* and, indeed, most of the time we sang them. Because I was fond of singing, I always loved learning new songs from him," said Venkamma whose repertoire of songs is vast.

Her first Sai experience came soon after Sathyam's announcement that he was Sai Baba. She was curious about this Sai Baba and someone gave her a small photograph of Shirdi Sai Baba. She liked it very much and began worshipping it everyday. One day, Sathyam saw it and said, "It's such a small photograph. Would you like a bigger one?" "Who could say no to such an offer?" said Venkamma. After that, for about a week, she kept asking him, morning, noon and night for the promised photograph.

One day, while Sathyam was visiting a neighbouring village, she was sleeping when she heard his voice calling, *"Ammaji, Ammaji."* Then she heard the rustling of paper and there it was, right in front of her eyes, a nice big photograph of Shirdi Sai Baba. But, Sathyam was not there. Then how could she have heard his voice? How had the picture arrived? She couldn't explain it, but was convinced that it was all Sathyam's doing.

Sathyam has always fascinated her and, when she was young, she loved to go with him to other towns and cities as a member of his entourage. Sathyam has always treated her as he does his other devotees. He severed all his family ties when he announced that he was Sai Baba and expresses equal love towards all.

Venkamma has seen a myriad *leelas* and miracles. And now she observes the great living miracle that is Puttaparthi. The people have changed. She senses the change since the establishment of Prashanti Nilayam and the building of the Easwaramba School. And too, the Muslims of the area are now happy. Sri Sathya Sai Baba has had a big mosque built for them. There are several Muslims there, some of them craftsmen, but they had nowhere to worship. Now they do and they are content.

Sri Sathya Sai Baba once visited the mosque during the month of

Ramzan and told the adepts that Mohammed the Prophet had received the divine revelation of the *Koran* in the month of *Ramzan*. He materialised seven silver lockets bearing the word Allah inscribed in Arabic, and gave them to the religious head of the mosque to distribute among the Mosque Committee members.

"Isn't the mosque in Puttaparthi something wonderful?" Venkamma asked, her voice full of admiration for her brother's efforts, the brother who she now calls Swami.

"There is only one free will, and that is God's will."

. . . Sri Sathya Sai Baba

6

HOROSCOPE OF SRI SATHYA SAI BABA

Sathyanarayana, who later came to be known as Sri Sathya Sai Baba, was born on the 23rd day of November 1926, in the village of Puttaparthi (14° 12′ N and 77° 46′ E) in Andhra Pradesh, India. The time of birth was early morning, just before sunrise and, according to the Indian calendar, the year was *Akshaya*, the month *Kartika* and the day was *Somavara* (Monday). The Indian calendar calculates a day as starting from sunrise, unlike the Occidental system which marks a new day from midnight. So, the day, according to the Indian calendar, was between Monday the 22nd and Tuesday the 23rd of November. While the Occidental calendar marks it as Tuesday 23rd, which has now generally been accepted as the birthday of Sri Sathya Sai Baba, named Sathyanarayana, with the birth star *Ardhra*.

Sri Sathya Sai Baba's horoscope shows all the aspects of a *mahapurusha* (great being) and there is a conjunction of *chatur-graha* (four stars) in the *lagna*. They are the rising Sun in the star *Anuradha*, second *paada*; the moon in *Ardhra,* fourth *paada*; Venus; and Mercury. The *lagna* has touches of *Tula* (Virgo), but the predominant aspects are those of *Vricchika* (Scorpio) which is accepted as Sri Sathya Sai Baba's *lagna*. The time is the *Brahma muhurtam* and the day between Monday *(Kartika Somavara)* and Tuesday *(Krishna Chaturdashi)*. The star *Ardhra* is sacred, because it is the star of *Shiva*.

The study of planetary combinations and readings of horoscopes are confined to aspects that are patent rather than to deep spiritual dimensions. Even so, astrologers have pointed out that the most important aspects of Sri Sathya Sai Baba's horoscope is the characteristic of the *Vipareeta Raja Yoga*. The Sun is also in the ascendant, representing Self. The Sun in that position signifies everything relating to *dharma*, God, rituals, worship, etc. Also, there is the symbolic merging of the Sun and Mars which connotes a spirit of determination and self-confidence. That is why, when confronted by hurdles, Sri Sathya Sai Baba assures devotees, "My *sankalpa* (will) will prevail and nobody can stop my work." The combinations have made the 'Self' emerge as an incarnation of 'God'. Saturn on the ninth *bhava* and its association with the ninth lord assures great fame and endearing. The planetary conjunctions also ensure appeal to the masses and the longlasting nature of the fame inspite of criticism and opposition.

Sri Sathya Sai Baba's short stature and preference for red robes are considered to go with the nature of Mars, the *lagna* lord of his horoscope. Special attention or meticulous care to personal appearance and dress, luxuriant curly hair – are all attributed to the Sun, Venus and Saturn combination in the *Tanu bhava*. The other characteristic aspects of *Kuja* (Mars) are seen in Sri Sathya Sai Baba's slender waist and curly, shining hair. His *somya* (pleasing nature) is a typical characteristic of Scorpio.

Astrologers also predict that after 1980, *Ketu dasaa* will commence for Sri Sathya Sai Baba, when people may witness miracles that surpass all previous phenomena. In 1982, there may be a revelation as significant as the one when he revealed himself as Sai Baba of Shirdi in May 1940. After 1985, there will be crucial events, which will show his great powers and miracles. Sri Sathya Sai Baba's uniqueness as a phenomenal person on earth is vouchsafed in astrology.

"Love is God. God is Love."

... Sri Sathya Sai Baba

7

THE TESTIMONY OF AN AURA EXPERT

Professor Frank Baranowski, an American, specialises in research on auras and works at the University of Arizona. He is an expert in bio-magnetic field radiation photography. He has photographed and interpreted the auras of countless men and women with the ultra-sensitive Kyrillan camera.

He has examined the auras of very many holy men and *yogis* in India and elsewhere. The Kyrillan camera is so sensitive that it registers the aura extending from and beyond man, which is not usually visible to the naked eye. This camera, named after its inventor, was first produced in Russia in 1939, but kept secret. In 1969, an American called Kendell Johnson invented it once again and today the Kyrillan camera is used in over forty countries. It is more like an X-ray camera, without a lens, and faithfully records the fields and colours of an aura.

Professor Baranowski explains that some people possess the ability to see auras with their own eyes and he trains such people to use this gift correctly. He is in touch with experts in the psychic sciences and with hypnotists in regard to several studies conducted by him on the subject of reincarnation. He has Kyrillan photographs showing the energy rays and colours emanating from people. It is through these and similar studies that phenomena like faith healing are presently being interpreted.

Professor Baranowski read several books about Sri Sathya Si Baba, among them Samuel Sandweiss's 'Sai Baba, the Holy Man and the Psychiatrist.' He wondered whether such a person really existed and whether all that was written about him was factual. As one writing a book on reincarnation, on the basis of case studies and other findings, he was interested in Sri Sathya Sai Baba's claim of being a reincarnation of Shirdi Sai Baba. He wasted no time in writing to Sri Sathya Sai Baba to request him to write a forward to his book. Having no personal experience of Sri Sathya Sai Baba, he offered him a percentage of the royalties! There was no reply to the letter.

Professor Baranowski says that in the course of clinically examining 16,000 people, he found that almost 90% could recall, under hypnosis, experiences going back 300 years. During hypnosis, they regressed to different names and spoke other languages, such as 17th century French. To Professor Baranowski, all this seemed to have much bearing on the question of *karma* and reincarnation.

During Christmas 1977, Professor Baranowski was a guest at a home where they sang *bhajans*. Unused to this form of celebration, he withdrew to an upstairs room on his own. He was resting there quietly in a dark room when he was startled by a candle on a table suddenly bursting into flame. The bright flame illuminated a nearby picture of Sri Sathya Sai Baba.

He could not understand who could have lighted the candle. He was alone in the room. There had not been any sound and no one had come in. How could a flame appear all of a sudden on the wick of the candle? He stared at the picture and it did many things to him. It seemed to penetrate into him and to beckon him. To a man of science, the occurrence was totally inexplicable.

The thought of Sri Sathya Sai Baba remained in him long after the candle experience. He decided to go to India and visit Whitefield. The first time he went there, he saw Sri Sathya Sai Baba appear on the balcony. He was left breathless by the aura and the colours emanating from him. Large thick bands of white and pink flowed out from him – white, the colour of energy, and pink, the colour of love. And what amazed him were the bands of gold and silver. He had never seen these bands before although he knew, in theory, that they existed. For the first time, he was seeing a person with a golden aura, brilliant gold, moving and shining like sunrays on water. It was breathtaking.

He observed Sri Sathya Sai Baba in the Brindavan grounds for almost a week. "So much energy flowed out and so much love. The pink encompassed the people, went in and came out. His aura spread, extended to and enveloped the area in one mass or cloud of pink. It was all energy in the form of love that flowed from him. So much of his energy is used up by people. It simply flows out of him to the people and they all absorb it," said Professor Baranowski with emphasis.

Everyone has an aura. At times, the aura is of a prominent colour. But such a shade of pink, deep broad bands of pink, is something totally extraordinary. A person can only have this kind of aura when he or she loves absolutely – extends and expresses love, speaks and lives love.

Sri Sathya Sai Baba also has very large bands of blue aura beyond the white. This is at least twice as much as any ordinary person's. These are then surrounded by pink. These are all considered good colours and excellent combinations. Professor Baranowski explains that there are five different shades of auras *(tejas* in *Sanskrit)* denoting aesthetic, spiritual, intellectual, physical and moral aspects. These can all be scientifically explained. But the aura around Sri Sathya Sai Baba is beyond explanation.

Professor Baranowski explained to me that Sri Sathya Sai Baba's aura is at its fullest when *bhajans* are sung. Then the pink surrounds the people singing in the hall and extends beyond them.

"I cannot find a scientific explanation for this unique phenomenon,"said Professor Baranowski, "the love that he generates envelops you. His love goes into you. So many of you draw on his energy . . . His energy seems to be boundless, like his love. Otherwise no ordinary human being could survive so much activity after so many have drawn away so much from him."

Professor Baranowski saw him talk to a small girl in a line of people waiting to see him. The girl was an invalid in a wheelchair. "Sai Baba's aura became immense as he touched her with kindness and his love *(prema)* flowed out and into the girl."

When he looked into Sri Sathya Sai Baba's eyes, the Professor had an unforgettable experience. For, as he says, "Sai Baba's eyes glow inside, too, with a diamond like brilliance. I have seen many brown eyes, but none that can glow like that inside, but they do! He is love. He is exactly what he claims he is: an incarnation of love."

Sri Sathya Sai Baba created a gold ring set with nine gems for Professor Baranowski when he least expected it. He was stunned. "The event took place inches before my eyes which have been scientifically trained. It is something unbelievable how, using energy, he can make a gift of gold."

"I was not raised with *Hindu* beliefs. I am a Catholic raised in the Christian faith. And I belong to the scientific community. In my country, it is difficult to accept anyone as God. For it is not scientific. When I say that I have looked into the face of divinity whose eyes show light, I am placing my scientific reputation at stake and my colleagues may think I have lost my mind. But, I do not mind. For, in my estimation and experimentation, Sai Baba is, aura-wise, exactly what he says he is and what he asks you all to be. He is love, pure and simple. He is love walking on two feet. Such an unselfish love is nothing other than divinity."

"Seers of Ancient India prophesied that change in the world will be brought about by Sri Sathya Sai Baba around 1980. This was predicted 5600 year ago in the Upanishads. They say that the Sai Avatara will have three incarnations."

8

THE PROPHECY OF THE *SHUKA NAADI*

Naadi is the collective name given to palm leaf manuscripts written by ancient sages describing the characteristics, family history as well as the life story of certain significant individuals. The sages *(rishis)* who wrote these *naadis* had such remarkable foresight that they accurately foretold the entire future of mankind. *Sanskrit* scholars in different parts of India have in their safekeeping several *naadi granthas* (volumes) of ancient palmyrah leaves written by the great *rishis Bhrugu, Vasishta, Agastya* and other venerable saints.

A well known professor of astrology *(jyotisha acharya)* of Bangalore, Sri Ganjur Narayana Shastry, recently traced a *Shuka Naadi Grantha* (a volume of palm leaf manuscripts by Sage *Shuka*) on Sri Sathya Sai Baba, entitled *Saicharitamrita Grantham*. It consists of hundreds of palm leaf manuscripts written in *Sanskrit* and is thought to have been set down over five thousand years ago. It describes, accurately and at great length, Sri Sathya Sai Baba's family tree and many facts about him. It gives interesting details of all that he will accomplish in this present life and also the great miracles to come.

Among many other things, the palm leaves of Sage *Shuka* say: Born in *Akshaya* year, in the month of *Kartika*, on Tuesday *Krishna Chaturdasi*, in *Ardhra* Star (fourth *paada*), like anima, etc., this person of divine aspects was previously *Shirdivasi* (resident in Shirdi). He is a great *sankalpa siddha* (a master of the will) and one of great powers, but without any attraction to worldly wealth or glory. All *rishis* declare that he will have the power of *ichhamarana prapti* (the ability to die at will) and that he is one in the *Nirvikalpa Samadhi* state, living only for *dharma paripalana* (the nurturing of righteousness) and *dharma upadesha* (the preaching of righteousness). His mission will be of *prajopakara* (relieving the distressed) and, for this, he will distribute and spread all appropriately *(sadviniyogam)*. He will be born to propagate righteousness *(dharma prachara)* and the place where he will live will become a holy land *(punya bhoomi)*.

He will be able to assume different forms and be seen in several places simultaneously and to remove difficulties and obstacles and to avert danger. He will establish an *ashrama* near a place where there are *bahu-chakra-vahana* (vehicles with many wheels) and will also re-establish educational institutions of spiritual strength. He will show his omniscience in many ways to devotees who, if they surrender to him in full faith, will be given the opportunity of shedding their sins and of finding peace and goodness *(shanti* and *punya)*.

His glory will spread far and wide and many people will come to him. But all shall not receive his grace due to past actions. The *Shuka Naadi* says that this great person will be a *Brahmachari* (celibate) and will help others in establishing righteousness *(dharma)*. His attitude towards men and women will show equality (equal concern). He will be as a mother among women. He will be an Incarnation of Love *(Premaswarupa)*, Joy *(Ananda-swarupa)* and Wisdom *(Jnanaswarupa)*, but only those who are enlightened will be able to experience him as joy *(ananda)*.

He can be experienced, but not expressed; as a dumb mute can eat but not speak. Total equanimity will be his. He sees the world as a blade of grass *(thruna)*. He will not be concerned with public opinion and will do only what is right.

He will be a representative of Shirdi Sai Baba and will be born as a result of the prayers addressed to Shirdi Sai Baba. He will give *Samadhi Darshan* to Shirdi Sai devotees; and similarly, after he has flown from this body, Sathya Sai devotees will have *Samadhi Darshan* at Whitefield which will be venerated as sacred soil.

His life will be for the good of mankind *(loka kalyanam)* in the way described by *Krishna* in the *Bhagavad-Gita* – *"yada yada hi dharmasya glanir bhavati Bharata, abhyuttaanam adharmasya tadatmaanam srujamiham."*

The *naadi* astrologer says that *adharma* (unrighteousness) has grown to three-fourths proportion. When it increases by one more fourth, that is, when all is unrighteousness, Sri Sathya Sai Baba's full powers will come into play and be known in the world. In other words, evil has to rise to its uttermost before his divine quality can be fully realised.

As things stand at present, Sri Sathya Sai Baba displays only one tenth of his real self. After a while, his efforts to save the world will increase tenfold – particularly at the time of *pralaya kaala* (the end of one cycle of the world). He will show that he alone can control the fury of nature. He will also plant a tree in Brindavan, Bangalore, and that place will become a *siddhi kshetra* (a field of energy) and the tree a *kalpa vruksha* (a wish-fulfilling tree).

The *Shuka Naadi* states that good will accrue to anyone who only sees Sri Sathya Sai Baba. *Sainatha's* (Lord Sai's) birth is for *loka upakaar* (succour of mankind) only and so everything pertaining to him is for the good of the world. Though he is fully aware of his own powers, he will reveal them only when he has to and always at the appropriate time.

His grace will make people overcome their problems, surmount difficulties and guide them towards progress. In a short time, his greatness will spread further and there will be universal worship of Sathya Sai. He will show himself in many places simultaneously, though he will actually be in one place, and there will be many divine acts and manifestations.

He will erect a flag staff of righteousness *(dharma dhwaja)* at a significant time and thereafter righteousness will visibly increase. What he does may appear simple to us, but the effects of his actions will be immense and far-reaching.

He is tolerant and compassionate of nature and treats everyone equally. He does not hurt feelings or express anger when errors of ignorance are committed. Often, he speaks in jest, but he speaks Truth. When he publicises any aspect of himself or his activities, which is not always, he does so at particular times and it is only and always for the growth of righteousness: instilling good ideas of life and creating an atmosphere of goodwill.

Sage *Shuka* refers to this as spreading the gospel of righteousness *(dharma)* so that people may be enlightened. It is known from time immemorial that God incarnates again and again for the re-establishment of righteousness *(dharma)*: Sri Sathya Sai Baba will prove in the course of time the truth of the saying, *dharmo rakshati rakshata* (*dharma* is protected by the protector/protection).

Sri Sathya Sai Baba will have *jnana vidya* – knowledge of wisdom, rather than merely mundane knowledge. His early schooling was in Uravakonda, a village that once had a *Lingayat Mattham* (an *ashrama* of the sect of *lingam* worshippers). He was born to devotees of his Shirdi days upon whom he could not, as Shirdi Sai Baba, bestow full grace. Even now, though there is the relationship through birth, he is towards his family as he is towards all.

Sainatha (Lord Sai) will teach people that this world is illusory. His divine powers will be known in all the world. Even though in India, he already blesses people in other parts of the world with his vision and presence. Many worship his photographs. They keep a separate room for him in their homes for they believe that he is always with them and lives with them.

If people recognise the truth of Sri Sathya Sai Baba, salvation will not be long to follow. Trust in God becomes easy and one can rise from worldly existence to true reality. The importance of bodily life will lose value as one realises that the body will soon be dust or ashes. The Sai Path demonstrates that self-inquiry *(atmachintana)* and adoration of God *(Daiva prarthana)* are essential on the way to ultimate liberation.

By listening to Sri Sathya Sai Baba, people will be guided onto the right path; their minds will be cleansed and all doubts will vanish. All inessential mind activity will die for He is the Divine in fleshly form, born to elevate mankind.

Sage *Shuka* also refers to another aspect of Sri Sathya Sai Baba. He says that this *Avatara* will have healing powers and the power to cure himself by the sprinkling of water. This power is beyond nature's laws and not found anywhere in the world. Sri Sathya Sai Baba will use his healing powers not only for the people of this world, but also for the beings of other worlds, and on a higher plane of existence *(devatas)*. At times, there will be inexplicable situations when he takes on the illnesses and sufferings of these other-worldly beings to save them from the curses and the ill will of others. In such cases, he will cure himself when the danger has been averted.

He also has the power to lengthen life and there have already been a few cases of people being given a longer lease on life. But, there are many whose sins are so great that they still bear their fruits and may not receive even Sri Sathya Sai Baba's grace. When the *Kali Yuga* influence grows even more intense, then people will see his true might and will acknowledge that he is the Supreme Power. Then mankind will bow to him as to a great emperor and he will be revered as the greatest living being *(Mahapurusha)* in the world.

Sainatha (Lord Sai) does everything according to a plan he has; for he is born with a purpose, a mission to fulfill. He is all-knowing *(sarvajna)*. This is God's natural state and not a state achieved through education. He does not forget anything. There is nothing that he does not know. And these are qualities that are always his.

He has great purificatory powers. Merely the sight of him, or the slightest of word exchanged with him, can purify one. Everyone needs such purification for, if we are born into this world, it can only be as a result of some faults in a past life. But, by exposure to such a divine personage and by his influence, they are automatically diminished, even nullified.

The *Shuka Naadi* emphasises that *Sainatha* (Lord Sai) is *Mahavishnu Swarupa*, a form of Great *Vishnu* Himself. Seeing him is the same as looking upon Lord *Vishnu*. Sage *Shuka* gives Sri Sathya Sai Baba a lineage other than the one generally known. He says that it was *Kabir Das* who returned to earth as Shirdi Sai Baba, who in turn is now Sri Sathya Sai Baba who will also return to earth in another form. But, this is nothing new: so far, he has had a hundred and one lives and always for the good of the people and the world. As Shirdi Sai Baba he willed another birth to relieve the distressed of the earth and so is now reborn as Sri Sathya Sai Baba. In this life, he is fully divine, full God. This is a life of total sanctity, fully endowed with *Brahmajnana*.

Those who, without understanding and without even the will to understand, criticise him commit a sin. But, very soon, more and more people will come to accept his divinity, for they will have seen his divine powers. After the Spring of 1979, the tide will turn and *dharma* will slowly reassert itself, atheism will begin to decrease. India will come into better days, too, and once again, the influence of the present *Mahapurusha* or *Mahashakti* will be decisive. Sri Sathya Sai Baba will perform ever greater miracles, more wondrous than any he has performed upto now. One of the examples of his miracles mentioned in the *Shuka Naadi* is when he will keep an aeroplane airborne for a long time after it runs out of fuel, through his will alone.

The *Shuka Naadi* also mentions that Sri Sathya Sai Baba will always retain a youthful look, age notwithstanding. He will teach great truths, even smile at the human weaknesses of his listeners. Very soon now the days of his great glory as *Mahapurusha*, the Incarnation of Lord *Vishnu*, will be upon us.

The erudite astrologer, Sri Acharya Shastry, says that there are many more details in the ancient manuscript of Sage *Shuka*, but it is not possible to include many more in this book. But, Sri Acharya Shastry plans to write down the *Shuka Naadi* in book form retaining all the original material. It will, of course, also retain its original name, *Sai Charitamrita Grantham*.

Sri Acharya Shastry says that he was not a Sai devotee before discovering Sage *Shuka's* prophetic manuscript. But having been through it with a toothcomb, he realises that what we have in out midst is God Incarnate. So, he took himself off to see Sri Sathya Sai Baba. With the first glimpse, he knew himself to be in the presence of a *Mahashakti* (great power). Sri Acharya Shastry feels that he must make a transcript of Sage *Shuka's Sai Charitamrita Grantham* available to the public. He feels certain that learning about Sri Sathya Sai Baba, his birth and his mission can only be of immense benefit to lectors.

I wanted to know from Sri Acharya Shastry if he had become a Sai devotee. He said that he bows to Sri Sathya Sai Baba as a great power, but has not analysed his feelings beyond that. However, he related a lovely Sai experience. He made up his mind to translate Sage *Shuka's* prophecy and started doing so. Sri Sathya Sai Baba appeared in his dreams, hand raised in benediction, and confirmed Sathya Sai's omnipresence. Sri Achraya Shastry thinks that the *Shuka Naadi* is a *chaitanya grantha* (a book of soul power) written by ancient seers to form a bridge spanning time and space.

"Swami creates objects in just the same way that this material universe was created. It is his swabhava (nature) to create. His sankalpa (resolution) can bring forth objects in a moment."

. . . Sri Sathya Sai Baba.

9

MYSTIC MANIFESTATIONS

The actions and activities of Sri Sathya Sai Baba are not confined to his physical form. He has often made himself felt in his cosmic form. Devotees are full of stories of these glorious incidents. Substances such as sacred ash *(vibhuti)*, cochinella powder *(kumkum)* and nectar *(amruta)* appear first on photographs of Sri Sathya Sai Baba, and later, on pictures of other gods. There are two rare instances of perfumed oil steadily oozing from a picture of *Guruvayur Krishna* and of butter forming in his hand in another picture of him and *Yashoda*.

The advent of Sri Sathya Sai Baba was announced by just such wonders to people who had had no direct physical contact with him. At the time, no one had heard of such events taking place for the good of mankind. They associated these mysterious manifestations with black magic of some sort, all the while hoping that the unexplained appearance of auspicious substances *(kumkum, vibhuti* or *amruta)* could not augur the advent of evil.

Since the day young Sathyanarayana revealed that he was Sai Baba, he has materialised and handed out *vibhuti*, forging an unmistakable link between himself and it. So, whenever *vibhuti* forms on Sai photographs, devotees quite naturally take it as acknowledgement of the their devotion.

Sri Sathya Sai Baba has bestowed this grace not only on people already on the path of devotion *(bhakti marg)*, but also on others less advanced along the way to goad latent devotion and turn them Godward. And, indeed, *vibhuti* materialisations on photographs have proved a very effective method of arousing dormant *bhakti*. Not only do the recipients benefit, but so do their friends, relatives and all others who come in contact with the phenomenon. They then join the *bhajan* sessions or perform *puja* for themselves to earn God's grace and, sometimes, receive acknowledgement of their efforts.

Speaking to Professor N. Kasturi about unusual *vibhuti* manifestations and the appearance of photo letters was an illuminating experience. He first learnt of the *vibhuti* manifestations twenty-five or more years ago when a Sai devotee wrote to him asking what the appearance of *vibhuti* on a photograph of Sri Sathya Sai Baba meant. "Did it mean," he inquired in anguish, "that his lost son was dead and that these were his ashes?" Sri Sathya Sai Baba directed Professor Kasturi to reply to the distressed gentleman that the *vibhuti* was a symbol of his grace and his reassurance that all would be well. That was the first confirmation from Sri Sathya Sai Baba of his many manifestations.

In thousands of homes, encrustations of *vibhuti, kumkum* and turmeric appear on photographs and pictures. In some homes there are showers of *vibhuti*. It is said that, during the time Sri Sathya Sai Baba visited Saurashtra, hundreds of homes there experienced such manifestations. Professor Kasturi owns photographs of unique formation patterns of the *vibhuti*: one was in the form of the letter *Om*; in the drawing room of a Bengali lady the *vibhuti* appears in a round, forms the shape of a *Shiva lingam*, increasing in size as the *vibhuti* showers down on it like an *abhisheka*; another unusual case is the formation of *vibhuti* on a blank wall in the house of a devotee, a completely bare wall. There are the regular forms of manifestation as well, but many unusual cases have also been reported.

Halagappa lives near Srirangapatnam. He has a tiny Sai locket which oozes *amruta* constantly. It falls in trickles and slowly fills pot after pot. It is now twelve years since the *amruta* started trickling out of the locket. If one holds the locket in one's hand, one can feel it oozing and gradually one's palm is filled with *amruta*. Halagappa lets visitors take it away in bottles.

There are many homes where liquid *amruta* appears, first in droplets and then in slow steady rivulets, out of Sri Sathya Sai Baba's photographs.

There is one manifestation that even Professor Kasturi calls an odd miracle. A priest and devout Sai devotee of many years' standing owns a small porcelain figure of a cow and calf. On one occasion, milk flowed from the cow's udder for a long while and many people witnessed this amazing occurrence. The priest even made clarified butter *(ghee)* with the wonder milk and carried it back to Sri Sathya Sai Baba at Prashanti Nilayam.

SRI SATHYA SAI BABA'S PHOTO-LETTERS

A phenomenon beyond comparison are the letters that fall from photographs of Sri Sathya Sai Baba. The lucky people who receive these letters and notes all have shrines in their houses where Sai photographs seem to behave like mystic postmen. Sri Sathya Sai Baba writes these letters in *Hindi*, English, *Tamil* or *Kannada* to convey Sai news and give guidance on purely private matters.

Professor Kasturi told me about two people who regularly receive photo-letters from Sri Sathya Sai Baba: Mr. Iyer of Trivandrum and Mr. Bhat who lives on an estate in Karnataka. The one received letters written in chaste *Tamil*, the other in eloquent *Kannada*.

Professor Kasturi heard of these letters and went to see them for himself at the estate of Mr. Bhat. On that very day, Mr. Bhat had received a photo-letter saying, "Bhattray (Mr. Bhat), why do you doubt my words when I say that I will come to your house one day, just as Kasturi comes today?" Imagine the surprise of Professor Kasturi on reading this! He had not told Sri Sathya Sai Baba of the trip as it was a decision taken on the spur of the moment.

Professor Kasturi remembers another photo-letter to Mr. Bhat. There had been talk of a helicopter for Sri Sathya Sai Baba, an offering from an American devotee. It had been discussed at Brindavan at the time of Professor Kasturi's departure. When he reached Mr. Bhat's house, he was stunned to find that Mr. Bhat had already received a photo-letter about the helicopter. "Bhattray, I am thinking of buying a helicopter – Baba," said the latest phantasmagoric communication. That put paid to Professor Kasturi's conscientious discretion about the latest happenings at Brindavan.

Mr. Bhat once received a photo-letter in which he was asked not to scold his children for tearing paper out of their notebooks since it was he, the author of the photo-letters, who was responsible; the children were quite exemplary in caring for their school books. And indeed, it was true that sometimes the photo-letters had arrived on a scrap of paper hastily torn out of a school notebook.

Mr. Bhat had quite a collection of these letters and notes. One day, when he went to look at his collection of carefully preserved Sai letters, he was startled. The bundle had vanished and in its place was a solitary new letter. The letter was also from Sri Sathya Sai Baba and it said that all his letters had been taken away because they had resulted in the arrival of many curious V.I.P. visitors. It went on to say that Mr. Bhat should not lament the loss since he would continue to receive more letters from Sri Sathya Sai Baba.

Mr. Iyer of Trivandrum in Kerala was once told in a photo-letter not to become angry and to control his emotions. The photo-letters he received from Sri Sathya Sai Baba often discussed daily happenings or commented on his family situation.

Sri Sathya Sai Baba sent letters to Mr. Iyer not only through the photograph in the *puja* room in his house, but continued the marvellous correspondence even when Mr. Iyer went to Prashanti Nilayam to see him. And so there existed for a while an ethereal correspondence between Sri Sathya Sai Baba in his earthly abode and Mr. Iyer in the East Block fifty yards away. Once, Mrs. Iyer made some *halva* for Sri Sathya Sai Baba, but the crowd was so great (it being *Dassera)* that she could not approach him to offer it. So they brought the *halva* back to their rooms and left again to attend the *bhajan* session. When they returned, they found that a portion of the *halva* had been neatly scooped out. And, on an oily scrap of paper lying next to it, they found scribbled, "Look! I have taken some of the sweet you so lovingly prepared for me. That should satisfy you – Baba." The Iyers' joy knew no bounds that day. They could not have been more pleased had they offered it to him in person.

On another day at Prashanti Nilayam, another surprise awaited Mr. Iyer. On that day, Mr. Iyer had been deeply moved by the *bhajans* and the ensuing discourse. His thoughts turned towards obtaining Sri Sathya Sai Baba's permission to leave his home and come to stay at Prashanti Nilayam. Both his sons had settled well into their own lives and he had no more worldly duties to perform. Mulling it over, he went to the canteen. When he opened his wallet to pay, he discovered a letter. Very surprised he read, "It is better that you return home. You still get angry and have no control over your anger or other emotions. You cannot live in Puttaparthi until you gain control over them. – Baba." Mr. Iyer was dazed and poured over the letter over and over again. Imagine! The thought of one single person among the thousands there being caught by Sri Sathya Sai Baba and, even more, an instantaneous reply being delivered into his wallet. He had had the wallet on him all the time and never knew, while he sat transfixed, thinking his thoughts, that the answer was in his pocket. There are no words to describe the divine play of Sri Sathya Sai Baba.

NAGA SAI

Bharat, son of Sri S. Devanathan of Bhopal, was a student who came to Sri Sathya Sai Baba's Summer Course. He is a medical student. He related to me some of the happenings in the home of a Sai devotee in Palghat, Kerala that he and his parents had visited.

The devotee is Sri T. S. Nair and in his home at Kuppam, in Palghat, astounding things happen. *Vibhuti* pours from several photographs and it has different scents and tastes. Small idols of *Krishna, Lakshmi* and *Ganesha* appear in his shrine and they, in turn, materialise *vibhuti* and *amruta*. It is said that this *amruta* has a distinct flavour of its own.

When Sri Nair was mentally and emotionally upset, Sri Sathya Sai Baba blessed him with a divine vision. He also materialised for him a picture of Sathya Sai as *Anandaswarupa* (Incarnation of Joy). In this picture, Sri

Sathya Sai Baba appears ecstatic, his robe exposing *ghunghurus* (dancing anklets with bells) on his ankles, and he is carrying a *vina* (ancient stringed musical instrument) in one hand and wooden cymbals in the other. Everything in the photograph was joy evoking – the dance, the music, the rhythm and Divine Sai, the embodiment of purest bliss. It is customary in that part of India to worship such an image with lotus petals.

Bharat's parents performed the rite with lotus petals for the picture and were blessed with the appearance of *vibhuti* after the ritual had ended. This *vibhuti* was rough in texture, sour to the taste, and had a medicinal flavour. They were told that the arrival of the *vibhuti* denoted the acknowledgement of their worship by Sri Sathya Sai Baba. They heard that others had received different kinds of acknowledgement, *kumkum* and sweets, when they had worshipped the blissful photograph of Sri Sathya Sai Baba with his hand raised in blessing *(abhaya hasta)*. They said that a packet of these photographs had materialised on a plate on New Year's Day and that they gave them out to visitors.

They stayed the next day for the *bhajans*. They had been told that every Thursday was *Naga Sai* day for the Nairs. They explained that on Thursdays, after *bhajans*, a small snake appeared in the worship room and they performed *aarati* to it. Bharat's family, curious, stayed on to see this.

On the day, after about forty-five minutes of singing *bhajans*, the snake appeared. It was bright yellow, almost golden. Bharat could not see the tail as it curved away and shone brightly. It had appeared from behind the idols and pictures, swiftly sliding into the area where the *aarati* was kept ready. As soon as it appeared, Sri Nair performed the *aarati* and worshipped it in ritual fashion. The little serpent acknowledged the *aarati* and the worship, accepted the offerings and then disappeared.

It is said that *Naga Sai* looks different to different people. Bharat saw it as yellow, his father thought it was dark brown, almost black. They were surprised to learn that this extraordinary occurrence had been a regular event for many years.

Professor Kasturi went to Palghat. On that Thursday, they sang *bhajans* for nearly an hour and it was darkening when the little snake appeared from behind the images. Professor Kasturi describes the occasion: "It was a lovely little snake, a small sweet thing that came sliding out, shining like the Brindavan Express at night with its dazzling lights, winding its way across the floor. The little thing shone so brightly. The people remarked that it was wearing *vajra kavacha* (diamond sheath) that day. *Naga Sai* had blessed them with this special aspect. Sri Nair performed the *aarati* very near the snake and it accepted it with dignity. He offered it a little milk and some fruit on a plate and *Naga Sai* tasted the offering. Then it slid away and disappeared."

Professor Kasturi found the experience unforgettable. Some time later, he heard that a burrow had formed of its own in the Nair worship room. The snake now appears from it and disappears into it.

THE *VIBHUTI* MANIFESTATION AND HOW GANGES WATER FLOWED FROM IT

Several people say that they have proof of Sri Sathya Sai Baba accepting the offerings they make to him in their homes.

Srimati Gayatri Sundar Rao's family were followers of Shirdi Sai Baba and are now devotees of the present Sai Baba. They have regular *bhajan* meetings at their house. She described to me a series of astonishing events that occurred during 1978 in her mother's house.

One day, after *bhajans* as was the custom, the vessel of offerings was taken to the *puja* room and left there behind closed doors for a little while. When they went in, they were surprised to see that a portion had been taken from the platter of offerings. It had been neatly scooped out. Who could have taken it from a locked room in which there was God alone? They were puzzled. But, bewildered though they were, they continued their daily worship and *bhajan* singing.

One day, out of the blue, they found that all the pictures and photographs in the worship room had been signed by Sri Sathya Sai Baba. Suddenly, the letter *Om* appeared in *vibhuti* form on a table. They watched and waited in amazement as each day unfolded to some new marvel. One day, Sri Sathya Sai Baba's footprints appeared outlined in *vibhuti*, another day the *vibhuti* wrote *SAIRAM*. Then the *vibhuti* formed the profile of Sri Sathya Sai Baba as they watched. But, what happened next was completely astounding. Sri Sathya Sai Baba's face in a photograph was suddenly crowned by a dome of hair which slowly parted down the centre and from the parting flowed water, just as the sacred Ganges is shown flowing out of Lord *Shiva's* hair. The water trickled down and they collected it in pots knowing it to be holier than any water that flowed on earth. It was a sign of great grace and made them supremely happy.

Shivaratri that year was made even more memorable in the Sundar Rao home. They have a small silver figure of Shirdi Sai Baba in the *puja* room. On *Shivaratri*, *vibhuti* showered over the figure as when Sri Sathya Sai Baba performs the *vibhuti abhishekam* over the image of Shirdi Sai Baba. He does this at Puttaparthi every *Shivaratri* Day. The little figure was almost completely covered in ashes when the *vibhuti* shower stopped as mysteriously as it had begun. Several people came running to see the shower before it stopped. The Sundar Raos freely gave away the *vibhuti*. Later, they regretted not having taken a photograph of the silver figure smothered in divine *vibhuti* before they started giving it away; now, alas, there was barely any left on the idol. As they expressed their regret, a fresh shower of *vibhuti* fell on the Shirdi Sai Baba figure and stopped, as before, with the figure covered in ashes. They could hardly believe the evidence of their eyes. An instant response to a small wish.

Another instance of grace was related to me by one of the many *Seva Dal* volunteers at Whitefield. He sells incense sticks called *Sai Bahar*. He said that on the 4th of August 1972, Sri Sathya Sai Baba's footprints appeared in *vibhuti* in his worship room. He has preserved them by covering them with glass panels and taping the frame to the floor.

Vidyullata, the great grand-daughter of Sri Seshagiri Rao, a staunch Sai devotee, also had an interesting *vibhuti* experience. She was at boarding school at the time and was in the habit of religiously applying *vibhuti* to her forehead every day after prayers. She made certain that, wherever she was, she was never out of *vibhuti*.

One night when she opened the little box in which she kept the *vibhuti*, she was dismayed to find it empty. Obviously, she had fogotten to write in time to her mother to replenish her dwindling stock. She was very depressed at the thought that she could have neglected something so important. And she did not like to think of her mother's reaction. That night, Vidyullata prayed to Sri Sathya Sai Baba not to leave her without *vibhuti* too long and resolved to write to her mother for some more as soon as she was up the next morning. But, even so, she spent a sleepless night.

She woke very late the next morning and had to hurry through her morning routine to get to class on time. She rushed through her bath and prayers, hurriedly applied *vibhuti* to her forehead and dashed off. She was in the middle of a lesson when she was struck with wonder. Her *vibhuti* box had been full that morning. How could that be? She remembered her distress of the night before, but distinctly recalled that this morning, when she had hastily dipped her finger in the box, it had come out covered in *vibhuti* which she put on her forehead. It was there. The *vibhuti* box was full.

Vidyullata was dazed. Silently, she sent thanks to Sri Sathya Sai Baba. Later, she wrote him a letter of thanks in which she also expressed her worries about her school work. As she signed the letter, it occurred to her that he might not know her. There were thousands of people who wrote to him everyday. So, after her signature, she carefully wrote whose daughter, grand-daughter and great-grand-daughter she was, so that Sri Sathya Sai Baba might recognize her.

Months later, Vidyullata went to Brindavan. Sri Sathya Sai Baba came up to her and said, "*Bangaru*, Swami reads every letter he gets." Then he mentioned how worried she had been about running out of *vibhuti*. She was thrilled by Sri Sathya Sai Baba's attention to her.

There are so many more similar instances of Sri Sathya Sai Baba's interest in others. Devotees are very moved when they remember them, these tender episodes that are for them tokens of their Lord's love and grace.

Prabha Sridharan told me about something that happened to her mother, Srimati Yogambal. When she had learnt her first Sai *bhajan*, she played it on the *vina*. As she played, *kumkum* appeared in little sprinkles on the *vina* and, by the time she finished playing the *bhajan*, there were small mounds of it all over the *vina*.

There are several homes where suddenly the scent of *vibhuti* comes wafting on the air. One day, Srimati Shakuntala Lall had just finished reading the first volume of *Satyam Shivam Sundaram* and she set it down reflectively. She felt there was a certain fragrance in the air. Her father smelled it, too, and thought that it was like *vibhuti*. For a while it pervaded the whole house. Srimati Lall, very excited, went to a cupboard and took from it a carefully wrapped packet of *vibhuti* that Sri Sathya Sai Baba had given her. She sniffed it and found that it had the same fragrance that was wafting through the house.

This incident served to strengthen her belief in Sri Sathya Sai Baba's divinity. How else, she thought, could he arrange to have her house, a thousand miles to the north, in Delhi, smelling of *vibhuti?*

Sri Vemu Mukunda, who lives in London, says, "Often I feel Baba's presence in the unexpected scent of Chanel No. 5!" Other people in Sri Mukunda's house, even those outside it, have sometimes had whiffs of the same sophisticated scent. To some devotees, it is the scent of fresh jasmine that heralds Sri Sathya Sai Baba's presence. Some *Seva Dal* volunteers say that when they smell burning camphor in the air, they know that he is there.

Sri Sathya Sai Baba also comes to people in their dreams and in visions no matter where in the world they happen to be. He often appears in dreams to guide and to comfort and to resolve problems. He gives devotees a glimpse of his *avataric* quality through visions of himself in whichever divine form the devotee has faith. And it is known that Sri Sathya Sai Baba has been physically present in two or more places at the same time.

*"Mine is no mesmerism, no miracle or magic . . . .
My body, like all bodies, is a temporary abode.
My power is eternal and all-pervasive."*

. . . Sri Sathya Sai Baba

10

SRI SATHYA SAI BABA AND THE SATELLITE

"It is not science. It is a miracle by Baba," say Lila and Homer Youngs of La Jolla, California. It happened in 1972 when Lila went to India to see Sri Sathya Sai Baba in a group of devotees led by Indra Devi. Homer had remained at home in the U.S.A. Lila had the great good luck of meeting Sri Sathya Sai Baba in group and private interviews.

When she returned home, her husband told her that he had a surprise for her. He had asked EROS (Earth Resources Orbiting Sensor), an American satellite orbiting the globe, to take a photograph of Puttaparthi while Lila was there. He had learnt that the satellite organisation would willingly photograph any part of the world if provided with its exact longitude and latitude.

Homer could not find a map of India showing Puttaparthi. He had to do a lot of research to find the latitude and longitude of Puttaparthi, but in the end he located it for EROS. And they took photographs for him, from 200 miles above the earth, of the Puttaparthi area.

Lila returned exuberant, full of stories of Sri Sathya Sai Baba. Homer brought out the EROS photographs with a flourish, proudly announcing that they were taken by satellite. Lila studied them, expecting to see the *ashrama*, the *mandir*, the apartment blocks, and saw nothing but a barren landscape, pitted and scarred like a moonscape. She asked Homer how much they had cost him and he replied sixty dollars. She was furious. "You spent sixty dollars on these stupid photographs when you know that we need every single cent for our own needs! Anyway, what is Baba going to do with these pits and holes? If he is God, he knows what the earth looks like and if he isn't God, these photographs won't help him." Silently, Homer gathered the photographs and put them away in his office.

The years flew by. The Youngs' finances improved, but they were still not rich. Lila, impetuous as ever, asked Sri Sathya Sai Baba about their financial situation the next time she saw him. He laughed and said, "You have not too much, not too little, just enough money. Is that not so?" Lila gasped, for this was exactly their situation which, earlier when they had had less, she had asked for in prayer. Gradually, she had begun to feel Sri Sathya Sai Baba's presence everywhere, even in her thoughts. She wondered whether the finances would improve. Sri Sathya Sai Baba assured her, "Everything will be all right . . . these things take time." It surprised Lila to think that even divinity needs time and cannot make all things happen in the twinkling of an eye.

Lila still could not forgive Homer for wasting sixty dollars on the useless satellite photographs. They still sat in Homer's office.

A few years later, guests on their way to Tecate, Baja California, for the wedding of Indra Devi's daughter, stopped at the Youngs' home. The Youngs' ran a Sai Book Centre and they also had a fair selection of Sai photographs. The guests poured over the photographs, commenting, appreciating and acclaiming the beauty of some of them as is the way of eager devotees.

Suddenly, Homer said, "I want to show you the satellite photographs," and dashed off to get them while Lila protested in vain. The guests looked at them, at first politely silent. "What else can you expect when people are shown a lot of holes and pits like on the moon?" thought the embarrassed Lila.

One of the guests who had been turning a photograph this way and that suddenly shouted, "There is Sai Baba!" Everyone looked. There he was, his profile clearly visible with his halo of hair and even the mole on the left cheek. Homer peered incredulously. Where had this picture been hiding? It had not been there before, surely. Perhaps, he had not looked at them from every side. That must be it. How else was it possible that all four now bore the profile so plainly?

Homer examined the clearest of the four photographs. He found that the ups and downs of the terrain formed the facial features, the riverbeds and vegetation emphasised the contours to produce the image of Sri Sathya Sai Baba. Homer calculated that, to get such a photograph, one would have to have photographed an area of 20 miles by 40 miles. Was it feasible, he wondered.

Everyone was thrilled and agreed that it could only be another Sai miracle. No other explanation was possible. Since that day, the photographs have pride of place in Lila's house and have delighted the eyes of devotees who have seen them.

Homer, however, wanted to check further to see if the profile was a reality or a miracle. He contacted the satellite organisation and asked for more copies of the photographs. Normally, it is easy to obtain any number of copies through the computer system. But, in this instance, Homer was told that these particular pictures were not available anymore and were officially classified lost. This effectively meant that the only photographs were the four that Homer had and that no more copies were available from any source. This added to their belief that the satellite photographs were a *leela* of Sri Sathya Sai Baba. A *leela* to keep Lila happy!

Lila has now been to India thrice and, each time, she was lucky enough to have interviews with Sri Sathya Sai Baba. He has materialised for her a silver locket, crystal prayer beads *(japmala)* and a silver ring with a full image of Shirdi Sai Baba. Lila is convinced that all the people she brings with her to Sri Sathya Si Baba derive great benefit from seeing him.

Homer has been to India once only, in 1978. How did he feel after he had seen him? "Oh, it was wonderful. I clearly saw a person with light. Oh, I'm not usually gifted to see auras, but I'm sure I saw a luminous aura around him. Also, he is beautiful and so powerful! It was marvellous to look at him."

When did Homer first hear of Sri Sathya Sai Baba?

"I heard of him about the same time as Lila. As a man of science, I could appreciate Sai Baba all the more since matter in this world has dimensions which can only be described in terms of electrical charge, length, mass and time. But man or life cannot be measured in this way. Life certainly has many more dimensions, and we have known that Sai Baba possesses supra or super powers that go beyond known dimensions. He is certainly a supra-being, call him God, *Avatara,* or by any name you like. He has connections with the very source of all energy, power and vitality of life."

When I asked Homer if this was his first visit to India and Sri Sathya Sai Baba, he replied laughingly, "Yes, this time round!" to emphasise his firm belief in the theory of reincarnation. I asked him if, apart from the public audience, he had had a chance to meet or talk to him. "Yes," he said, "there was a big group interview for American ladies. But, I was the only man allowed with them and I heard him talk."

Homer is full of praise for the ineffable peace and effulgence radiated by Sri Sathya Sai Baba's personality and the wisdom of his mellifluous discourses.

Note on Homer Youngs and American satellite programmes.

Homer Youngs is a scientist and inventor and has contributed a great deal to American technology. He now owns a private company in San Diego, California, refining gold and silver. Earlier, he was connected with several aerospace firms working for the U.S. Department of Defence. The Department of Defence (DOD) has four divisions: Army, Navy, Air Force and Marines. The space programmes of the USA are civilian rather than military and, generally, are independent in terms of location, facilities and personnel. The EROS system is civilian and is not connected with any military establishment.

The American method is for independent companies to take out contracts with the DOD, or other governmental agencies, to do particular jobs that would otherwise be difficult for the departments involved to carry out. A private company can be more flexible in their operations and organisations than a governmental body.

Homer Youngs has worked for many such private companies in a technical capacity and, through them, has worked for all the branches of the DOD as well as several other U.S. Government agencies.

Note on satellite photographs.

The photographs were taken at a very high altitude with a wide angle lens. The markings along the edge give exact data. They do not, in fact, show "pits and holes," but do give that impression. Clouds show up as white patches and have darker shadows below them – these look like pits. The distance from which they are taken, their scale, does not allow one to see any man made structures. All one can see are geographic features: the courses of rivers, vegetation patterns and shadows denoting hills, valleys and mountains.

The photographs are black and white. There are four in the set, all taken at the same time. One was taken with green light, another with red light and two with different degrees of infra-red light. They cover an area of approximately 200 square miles.

One kind of human endeavour is visible. Around the villages, there is an increase in the growth of vegetation and this shows up as slightly darker. One can therefore locate Puttaparthi by this and by the pattern of river-beds. Sri Sathya Sai Baba's face is looking towards his *ashrama*.

"The Lord is the Sun and when His rays fall upon your heart unobstructed by the clouds of egoism, the lotus bud of the heart blossoms and the petals unfold."

. . . Sri Sathya Sai Baba

11

A COSMIC PORTRAIT

Signor Dante Bighi is a photographer from Italy. He learnt of Sri Sathya Sai Baba from friends. The first time he went to Puttaparthi was for a week in November, for Sri Sathya Sai Baba's birthday. He was accompanied by an Indian friend.

The day he arrived at Puttaparthi, Sri Sathya Sai Baba was celebrating a mass wedding for a hundred and fifty couples who could not afford grand weddings. Sr. Bighi watched the colourful ceremony and said that he thought Sri Sathya Sai Baba looked like an officiating priest. And, as he moved about, supervising details and participating in the rituals, Sr. Bighi took photographs.

That evening, when Sri Sathya Sai Baba came near him, Sr. Bighi experienced "powerful spiritual vibrations." He felt a strange new peace and knew himself in the presence of a superior power. Sri Sathya Sai Baba materialised *vibhuti* for him. He accepted it gratefully and expressed a birthday greeting. Sri Sathya Sai Baba smiled and said, "What is a birthday? The soul has no birthday. It is only the body."

A few months later, Sr. Bighi again journeyed to India. His only aim was to meet and photograph Sri Sathya Sai Baba. His first meeting had given him so much joy. He arrived in Bangalore, this time with an Italian friend, Sr. Craxi, a businessman and an ardent Sai devotee.

Sr. Bighi had the great good fortune to have several interviews with Sri Sathya Sai Baba and many opportunities of photographing him. He specialises in outdoor photography using natural light and likes to have unusual and exotic effects.

"I want to take a divine picture of Swami," Sr. Bighi told us over and over again.

"Divine picture? How will you take a divine picture? You can only photograph Swami as he is. Don't tell me you will photograph a Cross on him with your lens and get a Divine Jesus photograph of Sai Baba," said my husband.

But, Sr. Dante Bighi brushed aside this pleasantry and said, "No, Mr. Balu, I will get my divine picture of Sri Sathya Sai Baba and you will see it. I want to photograph the Sun and Swami. Oh, it will be fantastic. Swami has such a fantastic personality. Everything about him is captivating to me as a photographer. He is the ideal subject for any photographer, even as he is, but the sunlight streaming down on him, on his crown of hair . . . ah, that will be truly fantastic." Sr. Bighi was imagining how wonderful the photographs would be if only he could take some shots of Sri Sathya Sai Baba in the Sun and against the light.

Sr. Bighi often repeated, "Sun and Swami . . . that will be marvellous, a divine picture."

His determination made us pray that Sri Sathya Sai Baba would grant him his wish and pose for him in the Sun.

Sri Sathya Sai Baba smilingly obliged. Sr. Bighi knelt and crawled to get his shots. He rolled from side to side, made various uncomfortable movements on the ground and carried on, clicking away happily. Sri Sathya Sai Baba, seeing this performance, asked "Is there film in the camera?" Everyone heard and laughed except for Sr. Bighi who had forgotten everything except "the Sun and Swami."

Sri Sathya Sai Baba granted two interviews to Sr. Bighi and went over his whole life and career with him. He materialised *vibhuti* and a locket for him. Sr. Bighi then asked for his robe and Sri Sathya Sai Baba said, "Yes." Sr. Craxi and Sr. Bighi were invited to attend an exclusive celebration at the Cowan Hostel on *Yugadi* (New Year's) Day. Sri Sathya Sai Baba, on that occasion, materialised the fabulous *Kosala* ring, a precious stone dating from the age of *Sri Rama*.

Before Sr. Bighi left, Sri Sathya Sai Baba gave him one of his robes. Sr. Bighi was overjoyed by the gesture. Once back in Milano, he made a special glass case in which to exhibit the robe. He calls it his portrait of Sri Sathya Sai Baba. He has written a poem, describing Sri Sathya Sai Baba and what he means to him. The poem also explains the meaning and different aspects of the "portrait" in the glass case.

Sr. Bighi says that many who visit his studio find the "portrait" too powerful. Some have even said, "Take it away, it is too strong, too much for me." Sr. Bighi is certain that some of Sri Sathya Sai Baba's own extraordinary vibrations radiate from this "portrait."

"How can it be a portrait? It is only Swami's robe," I protested, "you havn't even used some of your photographs to make up the head and limbs."

"Oh. This is a divine portrait. It is Swami's cosmic form in that robe. Photographs of his head and limbs would make it a human portrait. But, I explain everything about Swami in the stanzas of the poem. Is it not better to describe his extraordinary hand through feeling rather than portray it in photographic form?" asked Sr. Bighi. It is his conviction that this "portrait" shows the Formless One, the Omnipresent One. Reactions of those who have visited the studio and seen the robe corroborate Sr. Bighi's view.

Recently, Sr. Bighi sent us a few transparencies of Sri Sathya Sai Baba. Looking at one, my husband exclaimed, "This is unbelievable. Look, Bighi has got the Cross on Swami's heart." I looked and was surprised and pleased. In another one, Sr. Bighi had Lord *Shiva's* crescent moon in his hair and a luminous circle in the middle of his forehead where the third eye is thought to be.

Sr. Bighi would like to photograph Sri Sathya Sai Baba again and again. Asked why, he sighs, "I cannot explain. It is something I feel deep within me and I cannot express it in words. There is no personality like him on earth."

"Why do you waste your time and energy trying to explain Me? If I had come as Narayana with four arms, they would have put Me in a circus, charging money for people to see Me. If I had come as only a man like every other man, who would listen to Me? So, I had to come in this human form, but with more than human powers and wisdom."

. . . Sri Sathya Sai Baba

12

ON *AVATARAS*

The simple definition of *avatara* is God come down to earth in human form. The concept of *avataras* is not new to the West. The term was used for Jesus Christ who is called the Incarnation of God. In other words, *avatara* corresponds to incarnation.

When and why does an *avatara* arrive in the world? The *Bhagavad-Gita* gives this answer: "when righteousness is weak and faints and unrighteousness exults in pride, then My Spirit arises on Earth. For the salvation of those who are good, for the destruction of evil in men, for the fulfillment of the kingdom of righteousness, I come to this world in all the ages that pass." (4:7-8). An *avatara* is sometimes called *Bhagavan* which means one who spreads light. The literal translation of *Bhagavan* or *Bhagavanta* is one who is able to shed light, to illumine.

It is difficult to explain and even more difficult to fully comprehend an *avatara* who is the complete fusion of the divine and the human. *Avataras* may have only a few divine attributes or they may be fully divine. It is the latter that we call integral or full *avataras*. *Sri Krishna* was a full *avatara* and descended to earth to grant peace, joy and fulfillment to humanity.

In his book *Bhagavatha Vahini*, Sri Sathya Sai Baba writes about creation and the concept of *avataras*. The *Bhagavatham* says: "God is not bound by time and space. He is Lord of the living and the un-living. At the end of every cycle of time, the process of involution is completed in the deluge; then evolution starts again. As *Brahma*, He creates Being anew. As *Vishnu*, He enlightens all with a spark of His own glory and puts each one on the path to fulfillment. It is He again who as *Shiva* concludes the process by the destruction of all. Thus, you may see, there is no limit to His might, no end to His potency. There are no boundaries to His achievement. He incarnates in countless ways. He comes as an incarnation of a *kala* (fragment) of His, or an *amsha* (part) of His; He comes as an inner inspiration for a definite purpose; He comes to close an epoch or to inaugurate a new age *(Yugavatara)*."

The *Bhagavatham* is the narrative of these incarnations. The story of the *Yugavatara* is well worth studying, its purpose being that of restoring righteousness in the world and morality in men.

The *Bhagavatham* also speaks of the origin of *Brahma*, the Creator. Creation precedes the beginning of time. First, a lotus arose from the navel of the Primal Person, here called *Narayana*. Then, from the lotus, the Lord manifested Himself as *Brahma*. *Brahma* felt the urge to look upon all directions and has four heads.

The one divine principle works through the three forms, *Brahma, Vishnu* and *Shiva*, to complete the circle of *srishti* (becoming/existence). The three are fundamentally the same; none is higher or lower; all three are equally and completely divine. When creating, the Divine is *Brahma*; when protecting or nurturing, It is *Vishnu;* and in dissolving, It is *Shiva*. But, when the Divine comes down to earth, assuming a particular form for a particular purpose, then that is what we call *avatara*.

Manu and *Prajapati* are divine persons who *Brahma* entrusted with the mission of peopling the earth (everything can happen only in accordance with the Divine Will). *Brahma* deputed *Manu* to create living beings on earth. *Devi*, the feminine principle, eluded him and took the earth away to the nether regions. *Brahma* then sought the help of *Vishnu. Vishnu* took the form of a boar and brought the earth back and placed it among the waters. Later, *Vishnu* assumed the form of *Prithvi* (the earth) to level the ground. This is how an early incarnation, *Varaha* (the Boar), occurred to serve a divine purpose.

It is the Lord's will and His will alone that is always at work and worked out in the grand scheme of things.

The Lord originated the *Vedas* for the preservation of man through the practice of morality and spiritual exercises. The *Vedas* contain names that liberate and rules to be guided by. When the *asuras* (demoniac beings) stole the *Vedas* and hid them under the waters, *Vishnu* incarnated in fish form, *Matsya*, to bring them back.

Doubt may raise its ugly head when reading the story of creation and the early history of man on earth. The processes of the Divine Will are mysterious and beyond the grasp of normal mental faculties. God never performs a deed without a purpose. Everything everywhere is because it is His will.

For creation to occur there must be the urge to create. So, *Brahma* created two in body and activity: the feminine and masculine aspects, one which attracts and the other that is drawn to creation. The progenitors were *Manu* and *Shatarupa* (*shata* = 100, *rupa* = aspect, form). *Brahma* bade them mate, beget and people the earth. And that was how the earth was filled with people.

The *Bhagavatham* speaks of Emperor *Parikshit* who, because of a curse, had only seven days to live, Sage *Suka* tells him not to waste a single moment, but to use them all in listening to the story of *Madhava*, the Lord of the Universe, and to drink in the stories of the incarnations as the nectar of salvation.

In it, *Brahma* explains His own nature to celestial *Narada*: "Creation is My task. I will and creation happens. I lay down rules and codes which, when neglected, lead to suffering. I provide on earth divine personalities and sages to set examples. I limit the unlimited increase of beings and, for this, I assume the form of *Rudra (Shiva)*. I am the inner core of every being, but they are unaware of this. They believe the outer world to be real and fall into grief and pain. But, if men concentrate all attention on Me alone, then I bless them and reveal to them the truth that they are Me and I am them. Thousands have thus been blessed and have acquired the experience that Truth is *Dharma*. I am the cause of all causes. I am eternal. I am *Satchitananda* (reality/existence - awareness - bliss). Creation, the universe, is but the projection of My will and has no basis in reality. The clouds of delusion *(maya)* cannot take away the inner consciousness of those who rejoice in the glory and majesty of God. Even when there is delusion, through *tapas* (austerity) it can be made to disappear."

Sage *Suka* also explains to *Parikshit* the many other incarnations of the Lord, such as *Kurma* (tortoise), *Narasimha* (man-lion), *Vamana* (dwarf) that served the divine purpose.

Rama and *Krishna* are two *Avataras* that have shown mankind through example the high standards of conduct within their reach. *Rama* had the quality of *somya* (gentleness, softness, mildness). *Krishna* is considered the most blissful *Avatara*. *Krishna's leelas* were all as significant as they were amazing. They were not in any way tinged with an urge to brandish his divine powers. No one can correctly comprehend or interpret his *leelas*. *Krishna* alone can interpret his own play.

There is something we can say with confidence about *avataras*. God manifest on earth as an *avatara* never concerns Himself with personal glory. All that an *avatara* does is done for the good of the world. The underlying current of all *avataric* activities is total renunciation.

Krishna's every movement, his walk, his speech, his smile and his laughter, his gestures, his songs and music and dance - all were brimming with charm and artistry. He was everyone's dearest kinsman and their closest companion. The *gopas* and *gopikas* (cowherds) among whom *Krishna* lived tasted the nectar of ecstasy every time they saw him and even when they thought of him. The power and mystery of the *Krishna Avatara* were such that merely to see him was joy, to hear him bliss, and to touch him was enough to attain fulfillment.

SRI KRISHNA AND SATHYA SAI

Krishna is one with *aakarsh* (the power to attract), one who ploughs your heart to produce fruits of peace. For *Krishna* is also a derivative of the *Sanskrit* word *krishi* meaning to plough or cultivate.

Many miracles performed by *Sri Krishna* have also been performed in abundant measure by Sri Sathya Sai Baba. For example: giving illuminating visions; seeing events occurring in faraway places; multiplying food and other material things; appearing simultaneously in several places; healing the sick, the crippled, the deformed with a touch; and, on rare occasions, bringing the dead back to life.

Sri Sathya Sai Baba, it is said, has the same height and build as *Sri Krishna*. This is how he defines the purpose of the *Sai Avatara:* "the *Avataras* of the past appeared to vanquish powerful demons or wage war against the forces of evil to restore the balance of righteousness. The *Sai Avatara* has come fully aware that it is man's intellect *(buddhi)* that needs to be corrected."

It is not physical prowess that is needed to overcome evil in the nuclear age, in an era when a single bomb can destroy thousands of people and wipe out whole nations. But, if the mind of man can be altered, if the people in power and those they rule over can be made to realise the futility of violence, then the nuclear holocaust can be averted; and the evil and the unrighteous among us can be brought back to reason and to goodness.

Sri Sathya Sai Baba believes in the complete eschewal of destructiveness and violence. This is perhaps why the *Sai Avatara* does not use His powers to destroy or cause gloom even among the gravest sinners. There is no doubt that there are people who have reservations about accepting Sri Sathya Sai Baba as an *Avatara*; but, there is no one who can say that, in all the fifty-two years he has been with us, he has ever hurt or caused injury to anyone. Quite the contrary, he has poured out love and beneficence to all.

Sri Sathya Sai Baba knows, better than all, that the spiritual uplift of mankind is a long drawn out process. It cannot be achieved in a single life span. That is why the *Sai Avatara* is to incarnate thrice: Shirdi Sai in the past, the present Sai now, and Prema Sai in the future. It follows that not all mankind is influenced in one fell swoop. The change is gradual in most cases, spread over a space of several lifetimes. For man has to work off, at varying rates, his accumulated *karma* (past action).

Sri Sathya Sai Baba stresses that religion and spirituality are not meant just for the other or next life. Spirituality is a way of living and loving God. Man's everyday actions delineate his future, just as his past shapes his present. Man cannot leave the cycle of birth, death and rebirth until he realises God and thereby attains liberation *(moksha)*.

Sri Sathya Sai Baba knows the past, present and future of every human being. He often says of this knowledge: "It is not a gift I have acquired and use on you when you stand before me and I reel off your past!" He knows the exact spiritual level of each individual and guides him or her onward accordingly. That is why, as he frequently says, he materialises gifts for people. It shows them his love and makes them happy, and it also demonstrates that he wants nothing from them. And often he confers other boons, easing worry, and puts minds at rest. "I give you what you want so that you will want what I want to give you," is the way he puts it. If a person responds to his spiritual call the journey becomes easy. For, as he says, "If you take one step towards me, I will take three towards you." So, all come to Sri Sathya Sai Baba, the desirous *(arthi)*, the avaricious *(artharthi)*, the intellectual *(jignaasu)* and the fulfilled *(jnani)* – all come seeking to Sri Sathya Sai Baba, the divine physician of the soul.

Says Sri Sathya Sai Baba, "I call you to me and even bestow worldly boons on you so that you may turn Godward and follow the path of *Sathya* (truth), *Dharma* (righteousness), *Shanti* (peace) and *Prema* (love). My activities and my actions will never change. I shall not stop nor reverse a step I have taken. Not even the greatest scientist can understand me through his laboratory knowledge. I am always blissful. That is why I can impart joy to you and lighten your burden. I never exult when I am extolled nor do I cringe when I am reviled . . . "

Sri Sathya Sai Baba's life and *leelas*, his nature and his personality resemble those of *Sri Krishna* according to several scholarly devotees. Not only does he often speak of *Krishna*, his life and his message, but he has also materialised ornaments and gems of the *Dwapara* and *Treta Yugas* (periods of time relevant to the *Krishna Avatara)*.

On the 30th of May 1978, in a discourse to students at the Summer Course, Sri Sathya Sai Baba resolved the much debated subject of *Sri Krishna's* end. He stated very simply, "*Sri Krishna* attained *nirvana* at midnight between the 17th and 18th February in the year 3102 B.C."

What often baffles and astounds his audience is the way in which he talks of the *Avataras* – with such easy and intimate knowledge that one is left feeling that he is talking about events that he himself took part in. Upto the moment Sri Sathya Sai Baba spoke, no one had given a date to *Krishna's* end with such accuracy. And too, never before has the Christian (Gregorian) calendar been used to date an event of *Hindu* significance. Legends and stories of *Sri Krishna* have often skirted the kingdom of fantasy and so Sri Sathya Sai Baba's unequivocal statement has finally given the stamp of authenticity to *Sri Krishna's* life on earth. People sometimes wonder if *Sri Rama* and *Sri Krishna* really lived and others have questioned the validity of the *avataric* theory, preferring to believe in the *Aadi Deva* (Original God) alone. In this context, an exact date in *Sri Krishna's* life has helped to dispel doubts of his existence. *Sri Krishna* is not, after all, a figment of the imagination of wishful religious teachers or the superstitious.

The advent of the triple *Sai Avatara* was prophesied five thousand years ago in the *Upanishads*. The three *Avataras*, Shirdi Sai, Sathya Sai, and Prema Sai, are also mentioned in many ancient palm leaf manuscripts *(naadis)*. A conversation in the *Mahabharata (Aranya Kanda)* describes the coming of an *avatara* in orange robes during the *Kali Yuga* (the present cycle of time). A devotee of Sri Aurobindo remembers his Master saying, on the 24th of November 1926, that an *avatara* had arrived to help in the ascent of man. Later, it became known that Sri Sathya Sai Baba was born the day before. Dr. V. K. Gokak refers to him as a colossus among men with all the powers of an *avatara*: omnipresence, omnipotence and omniscience, and to these he adds his special characteristic of omnifelicity.

Sri Sathya Sai Baba once said that Shirdi Sai Baba was born in Patri, a village in Maharashtra; he himself in Puttaparthi, Andra Pradesh; and that Prema Sai will be born in a village called Gunaparthi in Karnataka. He has also said that as no other person could know him to be a reincarnation of Shirdi Sai Baba, he had himself declared it. When asked why his *avatarahood* should be doubted by some, he replied casually, "Every *avatara* faces this during his lifetime. *Sri Rama* was not recognised as an *avatara* at all. Though the sages knew his divinity, they did not spread that knowledge, to help *Sri Rama* fulfill the purpose of the destruction of evil. So, Sage *Vishwamitra* taught his divine pupil in the same way as he taught other royal pupils. *Sri Rama*, too, always behaved as an ordinary human being, even allowing his wife to be kidnapped. Had he willed it, he could easily have vanquished *Ravana*. But, he wanted to accomplish his mission as a human being. *Sri Krishna*, too, was the target of similar doubts and accusations. If he had wanted it, his Uncle *Kamsa* and others would have been vanquished in no time. But, *Sri Krishna* waited and accomplished his task in stages, undergoing many trials and tribulations, in the way of mortals."

Sri Sathya Sai Baba often says that the belief or non-belief of others cannot deter him. His efforts will not be deflected; he knows what he wants to do and knows how to do it.

Once, in Ootacamund, a hill resort in Tamil Nadu, he materialised a map. Even scientists would not have disputed the fact that the map was a creation rather than a transference for it was a map of the future. On it were indicated all the Sai Institutions that would be established before he sheds his present form.

Sri Sathya Sai Baba routinely materialises *vibhuti* and scores of other items, but his materialisations on special occasions have been breathtaking. Twice, during 1977-78, he performed such miracles for his devotees and in particular for the students of the College at Whitefield – both these manifestations were linked to the *Rama* and *Krishna Avataras*. Such links through his materialisations are not new. A few years ago, Sri

Sathya Sai Baba created a most unusual Crucifix for Dr. John Hislop: it is made from the wood of the very Cross on which Christ was crucified.

On the occasion of *Krishna's* birthday, *Janmashtami*, the 6th of September in 1978, Sri Sathya Sai Baba spoke to the students of the College at Whitefield. In his discourse, he explained that *Sri Krishna*, the full incarnation of love, is the present *Sai Avatara*. He said that *Sri Krishna's* grandfather had given him the *Kaustubha* gem which he then always wore. He asked the boys if they had any idea what the *Kaustubha* was. They could only reply with puzzled looks. So he moved his hand, palm down, in the familiar circular movement and they saw a flash as he turned his palm up and something glittering in it. He had materialised the original *Kaustubha* jewel for the boys to see. What they saw was a big emerald, bluish-green and rectangular, surrounded by diamonds, hanging on a golden chain. They stared in wonder and rejoiced that they should have witnessed such an extraordinary event. Sri Sathya Sai Baba strolled around showing the *Kaustubha* to everyone. He even asked a devotee who was a jeweller to value it. The jeweller could only say that it was priceless and that never had he seen anything like it.

On the same occasion, Sri Sathya Sai Baba further gladdened the boys by showing them how *Sri Krishna* used to wear his headgear. He said that he did not wear a crown, only a longish piece of cloth wrapped turban fashion. He added that the peacock feather was not a permanent feature of the headgear as depicted by artists, but that, peacocks being plentiful in those days, *Sri Krishna* had playfully stuck one in his turban. These were unforgettable moments for all those who were there that day – to see Sri Sathya Sai Baba demonstrate the way *Sri Krishna* wore his turban and to be shown an ornament worn by him more than five thousand years ago!

Sri Sathya Sai Baba's book, *Rama Katha Rasa Vahini,* was officially released on *Yugadi* Day (New Year's Day; in 1978, the 8th of April) and there was a special inaugural for it during the week celebrating the birth of *Sri Rama*. The day is called *Ramanavami*. That evening, Sri Sathya Sai Baba treated the students of the same college to another glorious event. At the student hostel, he regaled them and other devotees with the story of how King *Kosala* rewarded *Sumantra*, a minister of King *Dasaratha*, with the *Kosala* ring for finding his lost daughter, *Kausalya*. She later married King *Dasaratha* and was, indeed, *Sri Rama's* mother. As he neared the end of the tale, his hand began to make circles in the air and the lucky audience again saw a flash like lightning. And there it was, in the palm of his hand, a sturdy gold ring bearing a large stone.

"This," he said, "is the *Kosala* stone. See how it shines, like fire. Look at the light inside. See the three colours of the stone, honey, yellow and white." He pointed out every significant detail, then he moved down the assembly lines showing the jewel he had materialised from an age long, long past. The ring was huge, suggesting the size of people in the age of *Sri Rama*.

"Life with desire is Man;
life without desire is God."

. . . Sri Sathya Sai Baba

13

CHRIST AND SAI

During the Summer Course held in 1978, I met two young girls from far away: Laura Ross from Mexico and Theresa Hartmann from Ojai, California.

Theresa said that Sri Sathya Sai Baba was quite definitely a Christ-like figure. Laura said that she had always felt sorrow and regret for the way Christ was treated during his brief sojourn on earth. She often spent hours thinking how she would try to make it up to him if only he would return. She heard about Sri Sathya Sai Baba and what she heard she found riveting. So she went along to the shrine dedicated to him at Indra Devi's house in Tecate, Baja California, Mexico. She went there several times and, soon, she began to see Sri Sathya Sai Baba in the image of Jesus Christ.

Theresa first learnt about Sri Sathya Sai Baba from people who had visited Puttaparthi. She read books on him and listened to the miraculous experiences of Sai devotees. Her curiosity was aroused. She saved money and journeyed to India. When she saw Sri Sathya Sai Baba something told her he was superhuman. She watched him do many things and the conviction grew. His kindness, compassion and self-giving love made her feel that he was none other than Jesus Christ walking the earth again.

Many Christian Sai devotees from other lands like to visit India at Christmas. They consider the experience of Christmas more rewarding when celebrated with Sri Sathya Sai Baba. They decorate his residence and the College auditorium with colourful trees. They sing Christmas carols and look forward to the discourse he gives in the student hostel before the Christmas dinner. They feel themselves twice blessed to be able to hear Sri Sathya Sai Baba on the many facets of Christ's life on earth. Many confess to a deepened understanding of the essence of Christianity since hearing him speak of Jesus Christ. They quote him when they say, "Christ's birthday is when He is born in each person's heart. That is the only day anyone can really celebrate Christmas."

A Sai Christian expressed the feelings of many who attended the Christmas celebrations of 1977. "Christians are not new to the incarnation theory and so can understand the Incarnation, or *avatarahood,* of Baba. After all, Jesus of Nazareth, though human, was considered God come down to earth. Many of us feel, because of our experiences, that Sai Baba is none other than Christ."

A Malaysian lady related her own experience. She had gone to a Sai *bhajan* session out of curiosity alone and sat staring at a photograph of Sri Sathya Sai Baba. At first, she did not find it captivating, but soon, she saw a most extraordinary thing happening to it. The photograph seemed to part down the middle creating a vista of space. Into that space rose the figure of Christ who stood for a while blessing her. Then the two halves of the photograph came back together and showed Sri Sathya Sai Baba in the same pose as she had seen Christ. She rubbed her eyes hard, but realised that she had not imagined any of it. The vision was real and indicated to her the identity of Sri Sathya Sai Baba.

The lady became a more devout Christian after that experience. She has photographs of Sri Sathya Sai Baba now and feels that whether you worship him or Jesus Christ it is all the same, the advantage of Sai worship being that he is available in human form, too.

Dr. Benito Reyes, of the World University at Ojai, and his wife have had experiences of seeing Sri Sathya Sai Baba as Christ. They have a pure and devotional attitude towards him and he has responded in full measure to their spiritual work.

There are many people in many countries who take time off to come to see Sri Sathya Sai Baba and, often, they stay in Whitefield or Puttaparthi. They have to adapt to alien surroundings and put up with the lack of creature comforts. Though Sri Sathya Sai Baba's lifestyle is admittedly the ideal, what most of them find especially significant is the spiritual experience of meeting divinity in human form. They are attracted to his way as the only religion he represents is the one that springs straight from the heart. They find in him a deep unfathomable source of love and a repository of inexhaustible compassion. They invariably see his gentle and loving figure as Jesus Christ. They understand his mission to be that of bringing the vision of the Divine to the planet Earth.

In 1972, on Christmas Day, Sri Sathya Sai Baba elucidated the meaning of something Christ had said. 'He who has sent me will come again' – he explained that the He referred to is himself. Sri Sathya Sai Baba also said that Christ had said, "'His name would be Truth.' Sathya means truth. 'He wears a robe of red, a blood-red robe (at that point he looked down at his own robe), He will be short, with a crown (his hair).' Christ did not say that He would come again. He said, 'He who has sent me will come again.' And so, that He, this Baba is here."

It is not only the sick, the troubled and the needy who come to Sri Sathya Sai Baba. The rich and the successful also come to him. For, having attained all there is to attain in the material world, they still feel an emptiness of the heart. Some, already spiritually inclined, are attracted to him as a great teacher whose life is his message: one who gives freely and who does nothing for selfish reasons. His charisma and his suprahuman powers draw millions of people, even from the most distant corners of the world.

Sri Sathya Sai Baba always advises people to adhere to their own religion. He preaches universal truth: the brotherhood of man under the fatherhood of God. He emphasises that the purpose of life is the realisation of the divine within oneself and thus the release from the futile cycle of birth and death.

Everyone is born with a divine spark which chooses a particular field of activity while on earth. There is no work that is superior or inferior, nobody higher or lower. All have the same divine element, the same divine energy. It is the way one uses this energy that matters. It is the way one chooses to add plus and take away minus points to this energy that decides the form of the life to come. That is what is known as *karma* (action) and it follows the soul like a scent, good, bad or indifferent, according to the actions performed by the body during a lifetime. Death is just a transition, a change of bodies, like changing into new clothes.

The difference between him and others, Sri Sathya Sai Baba points out, is that he has incarnated himself of his own will, and not as a result of past *karma*. That is also why he is an embodiment of all the aspects of God.

Ancient palm leaf manuscripts say that, so far, Sri Sathya Sai Baba has reincarnated a hundred and one times. While, according to popular belief, there are ten incarnations of Lord *Narayana*; and according to the *Bhagavatham*, there are twenty-two, some fully divine and some partially divine. The concept of *avataras*, or incarnation in the case of Jesus Christ, is slowly gaining acceptance in the world outside India.

Before the advent of the *Avataras*, the ancient seers *(rishis)* of India described God as bliss-form. "Later, the Lord began to come down to earth in human form and move about among men, so that He could be listened to, communed with, loved, revered and obeyed. He had to speak the language of man and behave as a man, one of a species. Otherwise, he would either be negated and neglected or feared and avoided." *Avataras* became necessary as man moved farther away from the purpose of human life, the realisation of God. He began to attach greater importance to material things and forgot his goal, his natural path. So God had to descend to human level as an *avatara (Sanskrit: avatarishyati iti*, one who descends) to work for the uplift of man to divinity, from the human to the super-human level. In other words, God descends to man so that man may ascend to God. An *avatara*, then, is the descent of God for the ascent of man.

Sri Sathya Sai Baba, while explaining the universality of all religions to teachers attending an orientation course in 1978, drew a parallel between *Vedantic* thought and Christian concepts.

Jesus Christ at first said that He was the messenger of God, then He said He was the Son of God and, finally, He declared, 'I and My Father are one.' In *Vedanta,* there is the principle of duality *(Dwaita)* in which God and the worshipper are two separate entities, as in God and His messenger. Then there is qualified non-dualism *(Visishtadwaita)*, such as the father and son relationship in Christianity. And there is the monism *(Advaita)* principle, where there is only One and man has to realise his fundamental divinity, expressed by Christ as, 'I and My Father are one.' Sri Sathya Sai Baba used the example of *jyoti upasana* (meditation on light) to explain this. 'I am in the light' is the first step of this meditation: the I and the light are separate entities. The next step is 'the light is in me'; now the relationship between the I and the light is closer as the light is no longer external. The final step is to realise that 'I am the light.'

The three steps of this meditation correspond to both *Vedantic* thought and Christ's statements about God and Himself. 'I am the messenger of God' is the *Vedantic Dwaita;* 'I am the Son of God' is *Visishtadwaita;* and 'I and My Father are One' is *Advaita*.

Sri Sathya Sai Baba also said that there is a stage beyond the above three which is known as *turyavastha,* and that is akin to the Holy Ghost in Christianity. In similar ways, Sri Sathya Sai Baba often stresses the basic unity of all the religions of the world.

The Sathya Sai emblem bears the symbols of five major religions: Hinduism, Zoroastrianism, Buddhism, Christianity and Islam. At Puttaparthi, where there is a pillar dedicated to the unity of all religions, there is a short legend under each of the five religious representations. Under the Cross of Christianity it reads, "Cut the I feeling clean across and let your ego die on the Cross to endow on you eternity."

He often points out how important it is to conquer the ego in order to reach God. He has a formula, too. Man – Ego = God (Man minus ego equals God). And it is this that is emphatically expressed in his words beneath the Cross. Cut the I feeling clean across, if you do, the I becomes a Cross.

When Sri Sathya Sai Baba materialised the Crucifix for Dr. Hislop, with wood from the Original Cross, he pointed to a hole in it and said that it was from that point that the Cross had been hung from a tree. Dr. Hislop was intrigued. It has always been depicted as standing dug into the ground. He had the materialised Crucifix tested for time and the test proved that the wood dated from the period of Christ's Crucifixion. And it appears that new evidence is beginning to emerge that the Cross could have been suspended from a tree.

Sri Sathya Sai Baba has been throwing light on Jesus Christ continuously; the same facts are then corroborated from various sources by unrelated research. Addressing the Christmas gathering in 1977, he said that Jesus had spent five of the missing years of his youth in Kashmir. It was here, in this sacred land, that he realised the truth of 'I and My Father are One.' Given this perspective, it may well follow that Father Hera's theory that "the three wise men who followed the star to Bethlehem were Indian saints" will prove to be factual.

During His lifetime, Jesus showed how a messenger of God and a Son of God can ultimately become God the Father Himself. While in the spiritual land of India, He realised the eternal truth and then returned to His earthly homeland to preach the new gospel. With just a dozen disciples, in a few years He established the foundations of Christianity which, in the centuries to come, would spread around the world.

Like the *Avataras* of India, Jesus tried at every stage to set an example and be a model for man's humanity to man to increase. Every Indian *avatara* has done the same and, in this way, they destroyed the forces of evil, establishing in their place the great truth that good must in the end triumph over evil.

The *Sai Avatara* has the same goal: of drawing the mind towards God, of making men abandon evil ways and attaining God through love. One of Sri Sathya Sai Baba's favourite little sayings is: "Start the day with love, fill the day with love, end the day with love. This is the way to God."

Many Christian Sai devotees believe that Sri Sathya Sai Baba is fully divine and fully human, that this perfect God-Man lives on earth and moves among men solely for the good of mankind. They have seen him perform many more miracles than are known about Christ, leading a life of total selflessness, showing patience, tolerance and kindness even to those who criticise him, leading the ideal human life, even as Jesus Christ did.

Like Christ, Sri Sathya Sai Baba uses his unfailing magnetism to make people accept the simple truth that GOD IS LOVE. His miracles, his gifts and his life all serve the one aim – that of making people into true children of God, enthroning qualities of peace, love, truth and righteousness.

Many see Jesus in action when they see Sri Sathya Sai Baba pouring love on all those who go to him, an unqualified and boundless love. They feel that he is God Incarnate for he can establish and maintain a personal relationship with each one of his millions of devotees. He has taken the initiative to be reborn on earth so that, like a loving parent, he can guide his erring children onto the right path.

Sri Sathya Sai Baba has explained the real meaning of his name, making it up thus: SA+AI+BABA, one who is both mother and father (SA is a prefix denoting goodness, AI is mother, BABA is father). That is why he declares that he represents both the *Shiva* and *Shakti* aspects of creation, embodying both the male and the female qualities of God as worshipped by *Hindus*.

"Worship Me in any form you like, whichever pleases you, for I am in everything," he often assures people and sometimes adds, "There is only one God, He is omnipresent; there is only one caste, the caste of humanity; there is only one language, the language of the heart; there is only one religion, the religion of love."

"Art is outside, heart is inside. Art should come from the heart."

. . . Sri Sathya Sai Baba

14

DIVINE PAINTING

Srimati Vijayam Rajagopala Iyengar is a pious lady in her late sixties. She took up painting and the fine arts after her sixtieth year, when all her seven children had grown up and she had time to indulge her own wishes.

"I have memories of having done only a few drawings in my childhood days. I got married when I was ten and never even touched a paint brush. Very late in life, I had a sudden urge to paint Lord *Venkateswara* of Tirupathi who I worship, so I set about collecting canvas and paints. Then I started painting the Lord against a backdrop of the Seven Hills. The painting emerged of itself, I should say, for I forgot myself as I painted. I was not conscious of anything at all except the thought of the Lord."

One afternoon, as she was painting, her daughter walked in and asked, "Where could that smell of camphor incense be coming from at this time of the afternoon?" They looked round and found to their astonishment that it came from the painting. At the time, Srimati Iyengar was painting the act of offering burning incense to the Lord and the fragrance emanated from that very spot on the canvas. They were full of wonder. Soon, they came to realise that whenever Srimati Iyengar painted flowers, the room was filled with the fragrance of whichever flower she was painting. Each flower would spread its own scent round the room from the canvas. When once she painted *tulsi* leaves, the whole house was filled with its fragrance.

Srimati Iyengar went on to paint other divine figures whenever and wherever she was inspired. Each painting gave her new mystical experiences that surpass everyday comprehension. One day, as she painted a fire in front of a god, she felt its heat. And always, wherever she painted, that place would smell like the sanctum sanctorum of a temple, with a mixture of strong joss sticks and burning camphor.

Srimati Iyengar has had many such experiences by now. When she was painting the Goddess *Raja Rajeshwari*, a spray of fragrant yellow water appeared on the Goddess's head and flowed down the canvas as if someone were performing *abhishekam*. When she painted Lord *Krishna*, a flute played sweet notes in the room where there was none but herself with her paints and her brushes.

Many of these events are so astounding that Srimati Iyengar prefers not to talk about them, lest they be disbelieved or worse, ridiculed. Once, in a dream, *Sri Rama's* youngest brothers, *Shatrughna* and *Bharata*, asked her, "Why have you not given us the sacred thread that you have given our elder brothers in your *Ramayana* painting?" Startled, she woke up and went to the unfinished painting to find that she had indeed not given *Shatrughna* and *Bharata* the sacred thread. Another day, she wanted to draw in detail the jewels of Lord *Venkateswara*. Quite unexpectedly, someone from the temple came to her and took her and her husband into the temple for a private visit. And she was able then to take all the time in the world to study the jewellery and later faithfully translate what she had seen onto canvas. Srimati Iyengar has experienced great joy and satisfaction while painting the images of gods and goddesses.

Shanta, Srimati Iyengar's youngest daughter, is a nuclear physicist and a Sai devotee. She asked her mother to paint her a picture of Sri Sathya Sai Baba. The mother had never seen him and so could promise only to try. But, Shanta said, "You can't just paint Baba, you have to have his permission."

That night, Sri Sathya Sai Baba appeared in Srimati Iyengar's dreams. In the dream, he gave her a slip of paper which had written on it *'Om Sri Sai Ram'*. She understood that this was the permission she sought. She took a postcard her daughter had given her as a model and started painting.

Since the day she started the painting, Sri Sathya Sai Baba appeared regularly in her dreams. She did two paintings in as many months and, during that period, he appeared in her dreams almost every night to guide and inspire her.

This experience convinced Srimati Iyengar that Sri Sathya Sai Baba was just like all her other gods, a god who came to her as she painted and gave her many spiritual and divine experiences. Therefore, she thought, he too must be divine. Or else, how could he come and talk to her in the same way as her own Lord *Venkateswara*?

Srimati Iyengar has also done portraits of ordinary people living today as well as several mythological and literary figures, i.e. *Shakuntala*. But these people have never come to her in dreams or visions nor given her any mystical moments. Sri Sathya Sai Baba is the only actual contemporary person who came to her in dreams and visions, the only one to give her spiritual experiences. That, more than anything else, proved to her that he was a living god.

Sri Sathya Sai Baba helped her in many ways to paint his portraits: he posed for her in her dreams and gave her glimpses of his personality. She could not have painted him properly otherwise, as she had never seen him. He also showed her many other things. Once she had accepted his divinity in her mind and started to paint him with her customary devotion, she thought of the painting as her offering to him. Thereafter, wonderful things started to happen in her dreams. Those two months became the most glorious, an experience of and for a lifetime.

"What were those wonderful dreams about?" I asked.

"Oh, so many things . . . I've told my daughter about some of them in detail and she has written them down. One day, he walked ahead asking me to follow. It was a bright moonlit night and I could see the tall trees we walked past till we arrived at some caves. He took me inside a cave in which the light was very dim, but I could see that there were a lot of paintings and sculptures. He showed me all of them, explaining some of them in detail. He told me I should paint those gods and that I should experience spiritual joy in painting such sacred subjects."

In another dream, he offered her *vibhuti* and *kumkum*. In another, he brought out a golden pot and gave her nectar from it. In many of the dreams he appeared singing *bhajans*. In yet another dream, she saw him sitting at a desk and writing.

"He appeared so many times that after a few times I began to think of him as someone close to me, like a member of the family. When he talked to me, he always addressed me as *ammah* (mother). Once, he appeared as a small boy selling vegetables. He came and bent near me and that was when I saw how his hair was," said Srimati Iyengar.

She asked him why he had such a profusion of curly hair. He answered her by asking her to look at his hair closely. As she watched she felt her gaze penetrating deep layers and unravel hidden meanings. Then suddenly, she saw an extraordinary thing. Each strand formed the *Sanskrit* letter *'Om'* so that his whole head was crowned with thousands of *Oms*. It was a deeply thrilling sight.

Srimati Iyengar began to feel that truly she was in the presence of divinity and eagerly looked forward to her dreams.

One night, Sri Sathya Sai Baba showed himself in all the forms of the *Dasavatara* (the Ten Incarnations). She found it difficult to believe her great good fortune when, again, he appeared in a dream as *Sri Rama* chasing the deer *Mareecha*. In another dream, he came as *Sri Krishna* on the hood of the Lord of the serpents, *Kalinga*. She watched, fascinated, as the entire

Kalinga episode unfolded in the dream with Sri Sathya Sai Baba as *Sri Krishna*. He came one night and sat cross-legged. He said that he was going to speak on *Gitopadesha* (the message of the *Bhagavad-Gita*) and spent hours explaining the chapter on the *Vishwaswarupa* (cosmic aspect) and the significance of this huge form of God.

In many of her dreams Srimati Iyengar worshipped him and offered him food and drink. She had these experiences at night. During the day, when she had finished her housework, she would paint. When she finished the two portraits of Sri Sathya Sai Baba, he stopped visiting her dreams.

Srimati Iyengar never made any effort to see Sri Sathya Sai Baba in reality. Then one day, her daughter said that it would be wonderful if she could get him to sign one of her paintings. She took a painting to Brindavan, but she had mixed feelings. The dreams had given her a feeling of such closeness and she felt great affection for him. But, would he recognise her and talk to her now out of the dreams? She was anxious. Some of her relations had envied her dream experiences as they, though they had seen Sri Sathya Sai Baba, had never dreamt of him. They had seen him, spoken to him and even had interviews with him. Her elder sister-in-law, a Sai devotee for many years, had even received crystal prayer beads *(japmala)* from him which gave off a sweet fragrance. But even she had never once dreamt of him.

So, one day, Srimati Iyengar rushed into the Brindavan compound just as Sri Sathya Sai Baba had ended his round and was preparing to return into the house. She was late. She ran across the area and stood near him watching him closely. He looked at her once; then, he looked at her again for a long moment. Then it was over. There had been no word, no sign of recognition. Why? Says Srimati Iyengar, "Of course he looked at me twice. His look conveyed a thousand things to me. I am pleased, thrilled . . . I am ecstatic to have seen a living representation of God. That is enough. Oh, how wonderful to have his *darshan*, to see him in person at such close range. His features are perfect, the eyes and the nose especially. But, he is darker than I expected, dark blue, like all my other gods."

"The Lord is Kavi (poet), like Valmiki. Both create, one with loka (world), the other with shloka (stanza)."

. . . Sri Sathya Sai Baba

15

TWO *PUNDITS*

Two *pundits* of *Sanskrit* from Shimoga in Karnataka were honoured with shawls at the valedictory ceremony of the 1978 Summer Course. They came back to Bangalore with us in our car, and we had the opportunity of talking to them about Sri Sathya Sai Baba. They were both very pleased to be able to talk about him.

One of them said, "This is the first time I've been able to recite the *Vedas* in Baba's presence."

I asked them if they thought of him as an *avatara*. One of the *pundits* quoted from the *Bhagavad-Gita* (10:41): *"yad vibhuti muth satvam shrimath urjitha mayva va; tat tat yeva avaguchatvam mama tejomsha sambhavam."* (Whatever there is in this world of unusual and extraordinary power, know that it is but an Incarnation of Me, the Divine). The *pundit* went on to say that all these years Sri Sathya Sai Baba has been manifesting so many and such varied superhuman powers "which clearly show that he has *daivamsham* (the element of God)."

The second scholar said that the greatest quality of Sri Sathya Sai Baba, that which designates divinity, is the absence of *swaartham* (egoism) in all that he does. "Nothing he does is for himself and everything he does is for the good of mankind."

The first *pundit* then spoke of Sri Sathya Sai Baba's beautiful discourses.

He dwelt upon the pure sound that wells up with such resonance from his navel *(naabhi)* referred to as *naabhi dhvani* (the umbilical sound) and this, he said, is characteristic of a pure *brahmachari* (celibate) and an *achaara sheela* (one who follows all the sacred disciplines). His voice is not just loud and clear, it has the majesty of sanctity and the sweetness of purity. The contents of his discourses bear the stamp of authenticity and truth due to his purity and pristine power.

The second *pundit* then told us of the first time he went to Brindavan. On that occasion, he sat himself down in a chair in the third row. Sri Sathya Sai Baba, at one stage, came and sat at the end of the same row. The *pundit* looked at him and wondered, of all things, about his hair. He puzzled over whether or not it was a wig. But soon, his attention was drawn back to the stage where a new orator had arrived. But, his speech was heavy and tedious and the *pundit's* attention again wandered. He glanced down the line of chairs, but Sri Sathya Sai Baba had moved away. He had walked back to the end of the hall where the College students were. The speech was by now so boring that the good *pundit* nodded off. Soon, he woke with a start for there was something bristling against his fingers. He was more than a little taken aback to see that Sri Sathya Sai Baba was sitting in the chair directly in front of him and quite deliberately brushing the *pundit's* hand with his hair, as if to say, "now you may feel my hair and decide for yourself whether it is real or fake."

"This in response to a small fleeting doubt that flitted across my inattentive mind. What powers of telepathy, but more than that, what magnificent tolerance and patience in clearing a real doubt," said the *pundit*. He is convinced that Sri Sathya Sai Baba is no ordinary mortal.

He then told us of another incident. He had been to Brindavan several times and had never talked to or bowed down to offer a *namaskara* to Sri Sathya Sai Baba. One day he prayed fervently to be given a chance to offer *namaskara* or to talk to him and, instinctively, his mind lighted on a *Kannada* song which said, 'O *Govinda*, give me a chance to seek your lotus feet.' When Sri Sathya Sai Baba emerged in public, as if the song had been sung on a private hotline, he walked directly to the *pundit* and stood near him, gently holding his robe so that his feet were available for the *namaskara* so ardently prayed for.

"Is he not God?" asked the *pundit*. "He possesses all the *avataric* qualities listed in our scriptures and his life is spent bringing goodness to the people for the sake of *dharma*."

Both *pundits* were firm in their conviction that Sri Sathya Sai Baba is divine.

AT BRINDAVAN

(A) The *Bhajan* Bridge

(B) A Hostel is Opened

"Bhajans must invite all to share in their ecstasy, joy and peace."

. . . Sri Sathya Sai Baba

16

(A) THE *BHAJAN* BRIDGE

I first heard Sri Sathya Sai Baba giving a public discourse in December 1976, a month after the interview he had granted us. It was a talk addressed to an assembly gathered at Whitefield for Medical Services Day. It was given in continuous *Telugu*, without any translation, and its impact has left a profound impression on me.

Before he spoke, Sri Sathya Sai Baba sang a verse in *Telugu*, in his sweet musical voice, setting the theme of his talk. His music has a haunting quality and reaches the innermost chords of one's heart.

"Was this due to the spiritual timbre of his music?" I wondered, "A music that cannot be explained but only experienced?" Months later, talking to a Hawaiian devotee, I felt I had been right about the rare quality of his voice and music. The Sai devotee from Hawaii said, "Hearing Baba's voice in song and speech through a long-playing record played in my room made me realise that this was no ordinary voice, but the voice of God."

The crowd, over three thousand, sat waiting in pin drop silence in the gaily decorated grounds of Brindavan. There was no special dais and Sri Sathya Sai Baba spoke from his usual place under the *bhajan* canopy. His voice rang clear, then he ended the song and began his address with the word *'Divyaswarupalara'* (forms of the Divine). What a marvellously different form of address! Indeed, he never stops telling people that "the divine is in you" in private conversations, just as he reminds them in public.

The talk was a simple but enlightening one on health, laced here and there with ethical messages and light touches of humour. Small episodes, incidents and stories were used to illustrate or clarify points and to drive home important ideas. The audience was variously addressed as *'divya-swarupas'* (forms of the Divine), *'premaswarupas'* (manifestations of love) and *'pavitratmaswarupas'* (forms of the pure *atma*). These terms of address helped to build a high level of communion between him and the audience. Certainly, it made me feel I belonged to and was part of the occasion, not only an observer. His expressions, with graceful gestures and the endearing and instructive tone, reminded me of a good teacher giving an interesting talk to children of all ages. The points Sri Sathya Sai Baba made were simple to grasp, but lofty in concept.

"Health is very important and can be protected only by discipline. Worry is one of the contemporary problems that affect the health of people. They worry and get ulcers. What is this worry? Can anyone tell me the size and shape of worry? What can people gain by worrying except poor health? Things never improve or even change just because one worries . . . "

"People often overeat. This causes wind in the stomach and leads to chest pains. Doctors immediately suspect heart trouble and then the patient works himself up to that condition to justify the diagnosis. Frequently, physicians start fears in the minds of their patients due mainly to their very wide knowledge of the variety and scope of diseases." Sri Sathya Sai Baba described an instance of death from cholera in a village. He explained how fear of cholera had claimed more lives than the disease itself. "Worry and fear," he said, "are more serious diseases than the disease itself."

"Another obstacle to good health is people's greed for food. If they see food, they want to gorge themselves. Somebody's birthday becomes an excuse to eat; if there's a wedding, then that becomes the reason to over-indulge; profit in business, too, is a signal to eat to excess. Thus, people eat and eat and eat. Even a committee meeting to discuss health first says, 'come to tea!' So, control of the tongue and palate is made more difficult."

He stressed the need for doctors to use the more vital therapy of kindness, honesty, sincerity and integrity. He brought his address to a close with *bhajans* sung in his wondrous voice. He led and the audience followed, singing each line after him with great devotion. The *bhajans* were *'prema mudhita manasé kaho, Rāma Rāma Rāma'* and *'Subrahmanyam'*. (See page 337 for full texts).

The second *bhajan* produced waves of a wholsesome feeling deep within me. If I had already been captivated by the song at the beginning and the cascading flow of thoughts in his discourse, the sweet lilt of his voice, then the *bhajan* singing at the end was an enthralling experience that words cannot describe. Words like "wonderful" and "exciting" and "brilliant" cannot describe the totality of a spiritual experience.

It was a whole education to me to see the effectiveness of congregational prayer. Led by the lead singer, Sri Sathya Sai Baba, the singing with one voice of the devotees seemed to gain a special devotional significance that electrified the atmosphere with sacred reverberations and mystical vibrations. I felt it was perfectly possible for devotional music to reach directly to the divine and establish a connection with God. There were moments, particularly during the loud singing of the strongly rhythmic '*Subrahmanyam*,' when I completely forgot myself and my surroundings, so lost was I in bliss.

The bond that a *bhajan* builds between a Master and his disciples is indeed a strong spiritual bridge.

"The end of wisdom is freedom. The end of culture is perfection. The end of knowledge is love. The end of education is character."

. . . Sri Sathya Sai Baba

16

(B) A HOSTEL IS OPENED

I had never before seen Brindavan look so festive as on the afternoon of the 28th April 1977. It was full of animation too and filling steadily with more and more people. A new student hostel was to be opened by the then Acting-President of India, Shriman B. D. Jatti.

The huge compound was decked with rows and rows of colourful bunting. *Toranas* (festoons) of fresh mango leaves and flowers hung above every gateway and door, banana plants adorned them and floral *rangolis* (mosaics) added their brightness to the ground, like a carpet from the portico of the house to the main gate. It was as if ardent devotees and volunteers of the *Seva Dal* had vied with each other to give Brindavan a look of divine festivity.

College students in immaculate white acted as ushers guiding and seating the steady stream of devotees. There were a few chairs on the sides, but most people sat on the ground facing a rostrum on which there were a few more chairs.

Bhajans began an hour before the inauguration. Then, at the appointed hour, a procession started from Sri Sathya Sai Baba's house and proceeded to the hostel. There was a military band, followed by Sai Geetha (Sri Sathya Sai Baba's elephant) in all her finery, and many *pundits* chanting *Vedic* stanzas and carrying the *purna kumbha*. Then came Sri Sathya Sai

Baba, majestic as a king, gentle as a saint, smiling often and raising his hand in blessing. He walked in measured steps accompanied by Shriman B. D. Jatti.

Shriman Jatti lit the lamp at the new hostel building and Shrimati Jatti cut the ribbon to inaugurate the magnificent new building in the presence of Sri Sathya Sai Baba, the students, hundreds of visitors and Mrs. Elsie Cowan, widow of Walter Cowan in whose honour the hostel is named. Then, Sri Sathya Sai Baba led the chief guests to the rostrum past the lovely statue of *Saraswati*, goddess of learning, playing her *vina* in a fountain below the entrance of the Cowan Hostel.

The formal speeches began on a solemn note. Colonel Jogarao, a Sai devotee, welcomed the guests; next, the then Chief Justice of Karnataka, Sri Govinda Bhat, spoke. Then the President spoke inspiringly, quoting from Saint *Basaveswara*. Mrs. Cowan was visibly moved by the occasion, a celebration paying tribute to her late husband's memory. She said that intelligence and love bring wisdom and that she would always remember what Sri Sathya Sai Baba had once said to her: "What is good for your soul is alone really good for you."

Several students who had gained high university ranks were then congratulated. It was an inspiring and joyous occasion.

The story of Walter Cowan has been told in many books. But it would not be out of place to mention it here once again.

On Christmas Day 1971, Walter Cowan was brought back to life by Sri Sathya Sai Baba. This happened in a Madras hospital a few hours after doctors had certified him dead. His ears had been plugged with cotton wool and his body had been lying covered with a white sheet.

Mr. Cowan has left a record of his experience of death and how Sri Sathya Sai Baba brought him back into the world of the living. Sri Sathya Sai Baba said that he had given him an extra lease on life because his work on earth was not finished. Mr. Cowan was restored to good health as well and was totally free of the diseases, aches and pains he had suffered from before death. He lived a happy and healthy nineteen months doing useful work after his astounding resuscitation. When finally he did die, Sri Sathya Sai Baba sent Mrs. Cowan a telegram saying, "Walter arrived here in good shape," here meaning the blissful world beyond death. It reassured Mrs. Cowan that he had answered her husband's prayers to lead him from death to immortality *(mrutyor ma amrutam gamaya)*.

The story of Mr. Cowan's resurrection has raised many eyebrows in India and elsewhere. It has also shocked many people into awareness of Sri Sathya Sai Baba's superhuman powers. People who disbelieved Sai miracles were forced to take note.

It is said that the Cowans first met Sri Sathya Sai Baba in rather unusual circumstances. The couple had gone on a 'flight,' leaving their material bodies behind and then, somehow, they had difficulty in returning to their bodies. At that point, someone as yet unknown to them came to their rescue. Later, they found out that the person who had rushed to their succour was none other than Sri Sathya Sai Baba. It was after that that they journeyed to India and met Sri Sathya Sai Baba in his physical form. But their occult contact with him continued. Walter Cowan's dramatic resurrection made them want to do their very best for Sri Sathya Sai Baba's mission on earth. The Cowan Hostel is one small offering made to that sacred mission.

In his speech at the inauguration, Sri Sathya Sai Baba underlined the importance of the students' role as future citizens of their country. He sang a beautiful song on the greatness of India, the *Bharat* which had shown the way of spiritual enlightenment for centuries. A college education was meant to mould the character and personality of youth. That is why the students of the Satya Sai College are required to follow the disciplines of prayer, study and obedience. They must become living examples of duty, devotion and discipline in daily living.

Sri Sathya Sai Baba told an anecdote to illustrate how the mindless and superficial aping of Western culture had led to Indians forgetting and even losing the glory of their past. Einstein, the renowned scientist, once met an Indian gentleman called Gupta. Einstein was shocked to learn that Gupta knew nothing about the *Bhagavad-Gita*. He showed the errant Indian shelves overflowing with books on Indian scripture and philosophy and asked how, having been born in a country replete with *Vedic* and *Vedantic* riches, he could not even have wanted to learn *Sanskrit?* Sri Sathya Sai Baba said that this was also the case with most students today. They make no effort to learn the great truths contained in the sacred literature of *Bharat* (India).

Education should not encourage people to chase after comfort and luxury. Students must realise that *bhoga* (enjoyment) leads to *roga* (disease). They must learn from a very early age the art of *tyaga* (sacrifice). Every Indian should know that it is only through sacrifice that one may achieve *amrutatva* (eternal bliss). Education should instill in young minds the abhorrence of sin and the love of God. Man's real strength consists in the moral values practised by him and not in book learning. "*Ravana* was an adept of the sixty-four subjets of knowledge, but *adharma* (unrighteousness) led to his downfall," concluded Sri Sathya Sai Baba.

"Light a lamp in each house; the whole street will be lighted."

. . . Sri Sathya Sai Baba

17

OUR DIVINE VISITOR

On the 15th of May 1977, a wet Sunday afternoon, we went to Bangalore Airport with a friend going to Bombay on the airbus. Then we – my husband, my second son, Vivek, and I – went on to Brindavan. We waited in the compound to see Sri Sathya Sai Baba, but it was raining heavily and he did not appear. At about six o'clock, people were told to disperse. But my husband went into the house, while Vivek and I waited in the car. We waited a long time before my husband came back to the car and urgently said, "Come on! Swami wants you inside." The rain had drenched my satin *sari* but, by then, it had almost dried so, quickly adjusting its clinging folds, I hurried across the compound and into the house.

Sri Sathya Sai Baba called us into a small side room. Sri Gangadhar Shetty and Sri Sunder Rao were with him. He asked, "Shall we think of coming to your house on Tuesday the 17th?" It was such a shattering question that we nearly fainted with joy. "Yes, Swami," we said. Our joy must have shown on our faces because he pinched my son's cheek and smilingly asked, "Happy?" Then he said, "I will come to your house around five o'clock," and turning to Sri Gangadhar Shetty, he continued, "after that, I will come to your house at seven o'clock." Sri Gangadhar Shetty too was overjoyed.

Then I exclaimed, "Swami, you must have some food at our house."

"Oh, whatever there is in the house at the time, I will have a little," then he added thoughtfully, "Your house . . . there will be a lot of people."

"We won't invite many people, Swami," I faltered and said.

He smiled.

We then did *namaskara* and he said to my husband, "Balu, come at about four or half past four on Tuesday to take me."

I consulted Dr. Sunder Rao about the way in which Sri Sathya Sai Baba should be received and about his preferred foods. He replied, "Swami hardly eats anything. He sometimes takes a bite or two of little things like *bhajji* or *vadai*, but he never has sweets." He also suggested we do some *rangolis* (floor mosaics made with coloured powders and flowers) on the doorstep and the floor as at Brindavan. "Please do not forget to greet Swami with a garland and to perform *aarati* when he leaves."

I consulted my parents as well. It was all excitement and planning after that. The entire Monday was spent cleaning the house, rearranging the furniture to make more room for visitors, making festoons and other traditional decorations, planning the menu and all sorts of other preparations. The whole house buzzed with activity.

Tuesday dawned bright and clear. Everything fell into place beautifully. The house looked festive and the main hall bright with its red carpet. The delicate scent of jasmine garlands and roses mingled with the delicious aroma from the kitchen where the cook, with my mother's help, was busy giving the finishing touches to the food. Visitors started arriving even before my husband left to fetch Sri Sathya Sai Baba from Brindavan.

He arrived at half past five. It was marvellous to receive him and to present to him all those who were there. After he was garlanded, several people did *paada namaskara* (touching of feet with hands and/or head). There was a slight commotion as he sat down as some uninvited people suddenly rushed in. People had also swarmed into the compound. The hall was suddenly too full and I had to have the main and side doors shut.

Sri Sathya Sai Baba looked around and said, "If anyone has questions, they can ask."

Mr. S. said, "I hope this will not become a regular press conference."

Sri Sathya Sai Baba replied, "Yes, yes. *Adhyatmic* subjects and doubts about them, not a press conference!" Mrs. S. had the first question: "We women are always entangled in *samsara* (worldly life). How may we strive to attain *moksha* (release)?"

Sri Sathya Sai Baba: "What is *moksha, Bangaru?* You must try to understand that first. No one has to be absorbed in *dhyana* (deep meditation) all the time, or contort the body in all sorts of ways calling it *yoga*, or renounce life and retire to the forest to attain *moksha. Moksha* is not something outside you. It is not a faraway place you have to reach. *Moksha* is in you, within you. You can find *moksha* or God in your everyday activities."

"As you chop vegetables, cut out your desires. As you roll out *chapattis*, flatten out your ego. As the dough grows larger and larger, make your heart and mind expand with generosity. Perform each daily chore in the name of God, without attachment or desires. Perform your duties with love, affection and devotion to attain *moksha* and reach God."

"It is not necessary to regularly worship for hours, or fast, or go to temples or on pilgrimages. Never get angry or irritated with your home and family commitments. Never do your work with hatred or dejection. Do everything cheerfully, be happy at the thought that it is God-given work for you. Don't become fed up with chores; rather, do all as an offering to God. And that will be your prayer."

"If you can find the time to attend *bhajan* sessions or do *namasmaran* (name worship), then do it. But if your home duties don't allow these, then be happy to perform your duties with love and kindness and perform them to the best of your ability, with sincerity and love. Then that will become service to God, or worship. That is the way to *moksha*."

Question: "Is it right to believe in fate or destiny? Does fate control the lives of human beings?"

Sri Sathya Sai Baba: "Fate is the result of your own actions. Everything you did in the past has a result, just as everything you do now will have a result, and that in turn will have effects on your body and your life. Every thought, every word and every deed of yours always come back to you. So, it is not fate that controls you, but you who control fate."

Question: "It is said that *Brahma, Vishnu* or *Maheshvara* (usual name given to *Shiva* in the Trinity) cannot change our fate. How can I change mine?"

Sri Sathya Sai Baba: "True, they cannot change it. But you can . . . through your actions. For, what you do now shapes your future, your next birth."

Question: "It is said in the *Bhagavad-Gita, 'ananyas chintayan-tomaam yejana pariyupaasathay, Tayshaam nityaabhi yuktaanaam, yogakshemam vahaamyaham'*. (In short, if you surrender to God completely, He looks after everything). Is this so? Will God really take care of the worldly needs of devotees?"

Sri Sathya Sai Baba: "If you give God 10,000 *paise*, He will give you a note of Rs 100! As you sow, so will you reap. Whatever your actions, these will be reflected in your life, to the same degree and relation. It's no use at all blaming fate afterwards. Good actions, good words and good deeds alone bring goodness."

Question: "If you say there is no fate, how do you explain death by accident, even at a young age?"

Sri Sathya Sai Baba: "There is no death for the soul. Death is for the body alone. The soul continues to live. It takes on another body in which your actions of today reap the consequences. Take the example of silver. Whether the silver is made into a dish, a plate or a spoon, the silver remains, it does not disappear. Death and birth go on according to the actions performed. They can be controlled and directed by your *sankalpa* (resolve)."

Question: "What is *mukti*?"

Sri Sathya Sai Baba: "Merging with God."

Question: "It is said that if I think of God in the last instant before death that I can merge with Him. Is that true? I can do whatever I like, good or bad, throughout my life; only think of God as I die."

Sri Sathya Sai Baba: "It is easy to say. But, it is very difficult to think of God at the last moment of life unless you have made it a habit through life and the name of God has become a part of your nature."

"Do you know the story of the temple priest's son? An old priest used to ask his son to learn and to master all the prayers and intricate rites of worship. The son kept putting off taking lessons from his father, saying that they were all elementary and that he would be able to perform them quite effortlessly whenever required. The old priest tried hard to teach them to his son, but the young man continued to think that his old father was making a great fuss over something very simple."

"Then, unexpectedly, the old priest died. And it fell to his son to perform all the temple rites. He hadn't expected to take over these duties quite so soon and he hadn't even learnt all the *mantras*. He managed, mumbling inaudibly, to give the right impression. But, when it came to the final rite of offering *aarati,* he found he could not wave the camphor with the right hand and ring the bell with the left. He was surprised at his own lack of coordination. He remembered how well his father used to do it and realised then the need for constant practice if he wanted to do it properly. This little story illustrates how one must practise calling the name of God whenever there is an opportunity so that the thought of God, at any time, becomes easy and natural."

Question: "As Shirdi Baba, did you not attain *mukti*? Did you not merge with God? Why have you come back?"

Sri Sathya Sai Baba: "As I was leaving that body, I willed my return for *dharma samsthapana* (the establishment of righteousness) and so I am here."

Question: "May we see some of your miracles?"

Sri Sathya Sai Baba smiled. He pulled up his right sleeve and materialised *vibhuti* in his usual way. He gave it to Mr. S. nearby. And, as he did so, someone asked him about it.

Question: "How did you get this *vibhuti*?"

Sri Sathya Sai Baba smiled gently and said, "Yes, where did it come from?"

Again he pulled up his sleeve and looked to left and right as if looking for an answer to his own question. Then again he moved his hand in those familiar circles and out popped a ring. Everyone expressed amazement at this spontaneous action performed with such ease. Sri Sathya Sai Baba said that he performed these miracles more for the gladness of those who wanted to see them than for any other reason. He passed the ring on to be examined by all who were curious. Suddenly, a journalist asked, "May I keep this ring?" And Sri Sathya Sai Baba said, "All right, keep it. Do you still have doubts about this?"

Question: "Can you create *vibhuti* with both hands?"

Sri Sathya Sai Baba: "If I can do it with one hand, it can surely be easily done with two."

Question: "I have read about you for many years and heard so much about you. But, I'd never made any attempt to see you until today, when Balu called me. Could you explain why?"

Sri Sathya Sai Baba: "There is a right time for everything. Nothing can happen before the time is ripe for it."

Then I ventured to ask a question: "Are not good or bad qualities innate?"

Sri Sathya Sai Baba: "No, *Bangaru*. Man is not born like that, with specific qualities. *Satva, rajas* and *tamas* are all in him. Each characteristic comes to the fore at different times and in different circumstances. Take your own case. You have been so happy since yesterday looking forward to Swami's visit *(satva)*. Today perhaps, you may have been annoyed with someone for not doing a job properly *(rajas)*. Tonight, you will forget all this in sleep *(tamas)*. So, the three *gunas* take turns making their appearance in human beings. One should always try to control the *rajas* and *tamas* qualities and to cultivate the *satvic* aspect fully."

"People should take life in their stride. You should not fret for the past. That is like crying over milk that has boiled over and spilled on the ground. What is the point in wailing over spilt milk? This is how some people worry about their children when they fail their examinations. Once they have failed, what can you do? What is the use of being upset about it? Instead, you must think of the next step. After all, passing an examination is not everything in life. Let me tell you that I have never felt pain or sorrow for anything."

Someone then wanted to know if it is true that some who go to him as devotees go hoping to solve personal problems.

Gently but firmly, Sri Sathya Sai Baba answered the question with one of his own. "Is it right to discuss other people's personal problems in public?"

Then two people had private interviews with him. After that, we took him upstairs to see our paintings. He autographed a portrait in oil of himself done by my husband, and joked about another one, of me, also by my husband, and said, "Balu has many portraits in his heart, not only these." His hands swept around the studio in a wide gesture. We had some photographs taken: of Sri Sathya Sai Baba with the family as well as one of him next to his own portrait. He spoke to my parents and gave them blessings for greater spiritual development.

Meanwhile, crowds had gathered outside and in the garden. One could hear the noise inside the house.

Next, Sri Sathya Sai Baba blessed our *puja* room. He said to me, "I have had no time to talk to you on *Vedanta* at all." Then we took him to the dining room where he took a little bit of all that we had prepared so that we could distribute it as *prasadam*. He ate a piece of *vadai* and said, "It's good." He did not even taste the sweet but, at our insistence, took a spoonful of fruit salad. After the snacks, we offered him his favourite *pan supari* (betel leaf and nut), spiced with cardamom and clove.

I could not help saying to him, "This is like a dream."

He smiled and said, "I shall come here many more times, *Bangaru*."

It was soon time for Sri Sathya Sai Baba to leave, to visit the home of Sri Gangadhar Shetty. The *aarati* was performed outside the house so that the hundreds of people gathered could also see him and participate in it. Then he left, with affectionate words for all, his hand raised in blessing.

"Good and bad are not in a human being. They are in the way the mind is used. Joy and peace do not exist in external objects; they are inside you, within your Self."

. . . Sri Sathya Sai Baba

18

AT *RAJ BHAVAN*, BANGALORE

The Governor of Karnataka and Srimati Chandra Govinda Narain welcomed Sri Sathya Sai Baba with garlands. Devotees sang a few *bhajans* and then Mr. Justice K. asked Sri Sathya Sai Baba, "When on earth there are such great souls as you, why is there still so much sin?"

Sri Sathya Sai Baba not only answered the question, but also gave a discourse on various subjects such as *papa* (evil deeds), *punya* (good deeds), *atma* and *anatma*, dreams and reality, action and inaction and the purpose of life.

"Sin exists along with good deeds. For there is nothing wholly good or wholly evil. Pleasure is but an interval between pains. When you perform a virtuous deed, it may have some vice in it as well. And further, what is good now may not be good at another time. Let us consider even very ordinary things. Take the case of the foot and the face. Normally, one tends to value the face more than the foot. But, can you take your face anywhere without your feet going there with you? Take another instance. You invite a blind man to dinner. But you cannot dine with only him as he will be accompanied by someone with sight."

"Even the same action can be both *papa* and *punya*. Here is an example. Two shopkeepers have a fight and one of them is slightly wounded by a knife. The police are called in and one of them is charged with assault. But when a surgeon takes a knife and cuts into the body to perform an operation, the police are never called, even should the patient die. Why? Though the action in both cases has been performed with a knife, and indeed, the surgeon may even have made the larger wound, no one finds fault with him because the surgeon has the right to cut with his knife."

"Good and bad are like that, like the body and its shadow, like light and darkness. Unless there is darkness, you would not recognise the value of light. If there is no evil, goodness cannot be known."

"Man must be involved in action. And action invariably produces re-action. Suppose you have a matchbox in your pocket. The matchbox itself is harmless. The matchsticks alone cannot burn your pocket. There is fire in the matchsticks, but it is latent. The fire is contained in the matchstick and can only emerge when the action of rubbing it against the surface of the matchbox has been performed, the friction causing the hidden fire to leap out. Action is the key factor. Similarly, there is divinity hidden in humanity and only right action can make it manifest."

"You are asked where the sky (*akasha* = space) is. You need not point upwards, for wherever there is sound, there is sky (space). The quality of sound characterises the sky and it is omnipresent. It is all around you, in the clap of your hands, in the tap of your foot, in the music your mouth makes, anywhere and everywhere. It is essential to know, to feel and to recognise this omnipresence."

"Everything that happens has a meaning and a purpose. Take the wonder of creation *(srishti)*. Have you studied how marvellously balanced this creation is? Some parents have sons only, others only daughters, yet others have both sons and daughters. But you will find that there is ultimately a perfect balance if you take the trouble to compute the final ratio of men to women. It is *sama* (equal). This will become clear if you study the statistics after world wars. A lot of men were killed during the wars and after that the male birth rate was at its maximum to compensate the loss."

Sri Sathya Sai Baba's hands moved in eloquent gestures as he explained the beauty of balance in creation.

"The principle behind creation *(srishti)* is balance. But there must be vision *(drishti)* to see it. Without sight, how can you see creation, the colours, the objects, the people . . .?"

"In the same way, how can you know about *atma* and *anatma* unless you realise the omnipresence of the *Brahma Tatva*? How can you know that the divine principle is in everything? For that, your heart must become the sky, your intellect the moon, and your mind become as bright as the sun and thoughts merely passing clouds. Clouds hide the sun and the moon and they bring darkness and brightness, light and shadow. We see things differently, in different forms, but the underlying divine concept is the same. *Papa* and *punya* are really only the reaction, re-sound and reflection of your own actions."

"Take a simple instance. When you bang down your fist on a table, you not only hit the table, but the table also hits your hand, and with equal force. That is why your hand feels pain. That is the reaction of your action. In life, good and bad are mixed. You should know how to discard the bad and absorb only the good. If I would like to have a sweet orange, I must first peel its bitter rind. In other words, sweetness coexists with bitterness. Good is often veiled by bad. You must realise that all this world is *maya* (illusion)."

He than told us of King *Janaka* reclining on a soft bed in his palace. His wife sat near him and servants fanned him with feathers. The king drifted into sleep and into a dream. In it, he was alone and poor. He was hungry and begged for food. He found it all painful and wretched. Then, startled, he awoke and found that he was still in his luxurious bed in the sumptuous palace, his queen by his side and his servants in attendance.

Soon, he was awash in doubt. What was real? That he was a king in a palace, or a beggar as in the dream? Which of the two was the dream and which reality?

King *Janaka* then decided to ask the great sage *Viswamitra* who realised then that the King had reached the threshold of wisdom. He had reached the time of dawning, when darkness is in flight and light is just over the horizon. *Jnana* (wisdom) was to dawn on the King and so Sage *Viswamitra* knew he must help. He explained to King *Janaka*, "You were there in the dream when it appeared real and you are here now, in this palace, and that too seems real. Surely then, you must realise that both the dream and your present state are irreal. Only your presence in both predicaments is real. The stages of *jagriti* (wakefulness), *svapna* (dream) and *sushupti* (dreamless sleep) cannot be and are not as real as the real you."

"Take another example. A forty-year-old woman has a son half her age. She dies. The boy, in great grief, wonders, "Mother, why have you left me?" And yet the body which the boy identified as his mother is before him. Even so, he feels bereaved. If the woman's body is the boy's true mother, then why does he consign it to the flames? Surely, even though subconsciously, he realises that it is not the body which was his mother. His real mother is the soul that has discarded the body. The *atma* (Self) is his mother."

"Realisation comes through *sadhana* (spiritual endeavour). *Sadhana* does not consist only of *japa, bhajan, tapa* and *dhyana*. Principally, it is in the exercise of performing well the action of your duty and your given tasks. You must understand the significance of this in your life. Take for instance the eye, any eye. It can look at light only upto a degree; more than that and it will be blinded. The eardrum can withstand only a certain volume of sound; more and it would burst. Anything in excess is bad. People should bear this in mind while going about their business. They should realise that life itself is a limited liability company! You cannot invest £100 and expect a profit of £100,000."

"Man has two eyes. He can only visualise two things: the past and the present. He does not have a third eye with which to see into the future. The word 'eye' has three letters, and that number symbolises many things. *Triguna*, the three *gunas;* the three petals of *bhakti* (devotion), *jnana* (knowledge) and *karma* (action)."

"To realise the divine, there are the paths of *jnana* and of *bhakti*, but the most practical way is that of *karma*: performing your duties honestly and well and taking right action at the right time is that way. Nothing should deflect you from following the path of righteous action. There may be many dangers and obstacles on the way, but you must have the courage of conviction in the right action. Take as example the sugar cane. If you want sugar, you must first extract the juice from the sugar cane, then mix additives and process it. But, if you keep the sugar cane in its original form, what would happen? In a few days the juice dries up and so does the sugar cane. You will not have used the sugar cane at the time it was there to be used. Just so, the divine in you is there as sugar is in the cane. It needs to be 'processed' and realised by conscious effort and right action. Then we need not worry about good and bad. And *papa* and *punya* will take care of themselves."

"God's power is like electricity and our bodies are like light bulbs. The light within can only be seen when the switch of faith is turned on."

. . . Sri Sathya Sai Baba

19

TO PUTTAPARTHI

We found the drive in our Fiat from Bangalore to Puttaparthi exceedingly pleasant. Our happiness was caused by just the thought of meeting Sri Sathya Sai Baba in his own abode of Prashanti Nilayam. We had read so much about the difficulties in travelling to Puttaparthi: bad roads, atrocious roads, even no roads. So, we were pleasantly surprised to reach our destination so smoothly. Except for a few short stretches, the road was fine and we saw hundreds of assorted vehicles on the way.

We left Bangalore after breakfast and reached Prashanti Nilayam before midday. My first impression of it was the similarity to Tirumalai-Tirupathi (a famous place of pilgrimage in Southern India): the shops, the *gopuram*, the blocks of flats and the general appearance of the area. But, the main Prashanti Temple was utterly different. The beautiful and fairly large structure, ornamented by tasteful carvings and domes painted in pastel shades, spoke of high art and ethereal calm. I could not take in the details as we drove past it to the parking area.

We soon got down to the job of settling into a flat. The flats at Prashanti Nilayam are simple and practical. Resting a while in ours, we experienced the remarkably soothing peace of the place. Indeed, the meaning of Prashanti Nilayam translated literally is 'abode of supra-peace.' We were told to be ready by half past four in the afternoon for *darshan* of Sri Sathya

Sai Baba at the *Mandir* (Temple). After an hour's rest, we went to the canteen for some coffee and snacks. It is a well organised canteen with a coupon system for meals, snacks, coffee and tea. The prices are very reasonable and everything is served completely hygienically by volunteers from the *ashrama*.

That afternoon, we waited as bidden for Sri Sathya Sai Baba's *darshan*. But he made only a lightning appearance as he had a *Seva Samithi* meeting to attend. We had a good night's rest and heard the next morning that it had poured during the night. Soon we learnt from Mr. K. Rao that Sri Sathya Sai Baba would grant us an interview after nine o'clock. So, we readied ourselves and hastened down to the main *Mandir*.

That morning, I had had a look at the prayer hall. In it, there are two large portraits of Shirdi Sai Baba and Sri Sathya Sai Baba and also a beautiful silver image of Shirdi Sai Baba mounted on a snake-shaped pedestal. Another smaller portrait of Sri Sathya Sai Baba is regularly worshipped here. A special chair is kept in the prayer hall for Sri Sathya Sai Baba's use during the morning and evening *bhajan* sessions.

The daily routine at Prashanti Nilayam is interesting. The dawn is heralded by the chanting of *Om* twenty-one times, followed by *suprabhatam* on Sri Sathya Sai Baba. All this happens in the main *bhajan* hall and, unless one is near the hall, one can hear neither the *Omkar* being intoned nor the *suprabhatam*.

On that particular morning, I watched the *ashtotara archana* in the *bhajan* hall. (The *ashtotara archana* is the worship of Sri Sathya Sai Baba with flowers performed 108 times while chanting his 108 names). This was followed by *bhajans*. While I was listening to them, a lady from the *ashrama* asked me to go to the verandah of the main building in readiness for the interview. There were others there, too, including two foreigners: a girl in a canvas chair and a middle-aged lady.

Sri Sathya Sai Baba emerged at half past nine and asked us to go into the interview room. The room is small and intimate. We sat down and he materialised *vibhuti* and gave a little of it to each of us. He spent nearly an hour with us all and, later, also granted a short private interview to our family. With one sweep of the hand, he materialised three identical lockets for my sons and said, "Be like the *Trimurti*." He asked Sanjay, my youngest son, to describe the lockets.

"Shirdi Baba and Sathya Sai Baba," replied Sanjay.

He materialised a locket bearing his image for the young Spanish girl in the canvas chair. She had acute arthritis. The older lady was there to translate and the girl's father was also there. There was an Indian gentleman from Singapore who had come to seek Sri Sathya Sai Baba's blessings to build a temple in Northern India. To him, Sri Sathya Sai Baba said, "There are already so many temples. What is important is to look after the old temples rather than build new ones." The gentleman explained that he had taken a vow to build a temple to *Shiva* and that he had already bought the land and paid for the plans. He wanted Sri Sathya Sai Baba's blessing now and, if possible, his physical presence at the consecration. Then Sri Sathya Sai Baba "created" a lovely silver medallion with *Shiva's* face and an *Omkar* embossed on it.

He gave equal attention to each one there. His love, thoughtfulness and grace were overwhelming. To me he said, "So . . . you felt troubled this morning, thinking Swami may not see you. Even as the *ashtotara puja* was going on, all you could think was will Swami see you or will he not see you," he smiled then and said, "Do you really think that Swami would have done that, *Bangaru*?" Then he looked at Sanjay and said, "He has a lot of *bhakti* (devotion) in him. He was born at a good time."

My husband said, "He was born on the day of *Ganesha Chaturthi.*"

"Vinayaka Chaturthi," said Sri Sathya Sai Baba, "but at the time of his birth, the *Chaturthi* was past, it was already *Panchami.*" Then he looked at me and laughed, "See, even she does not remember. Swami remembers and she does not . . . mmm . . . She wanted a daughter because she could have dressed her up prettily in gowns and jewels. But what can one do? The boy arrived. But, she did not grumble. She accepted the boy and felt no regrets at all." I was astounded by Sri Sathya Sai Baba's omniscience.

"How do you find Puttaparthi?" he asked us.

"Very peaceful."

"*Prashanti*, you can feel it, can't you?" he said.

After that, he said, "Swami gives these gifts of love. If you want to give joy to your children, what do you do? You give them presents, like sports shirts and other things. Then you try to persuade them to do things for their own good . . . Swami too gives presents only for that reason, not because he wants to attract or charm people. Swami has so many devotees and each one is near and dear to him."

Then he talked to my sons, playfully pinching and patting them. It was obvious that he was in a relaxed mood and the three boys were at ease with him. Sri Sathya Sai Baba has a way about him that makes children take to him. They simply adore him. They love him so much that they think of him as someone very very close to their hearts, as one of them. So much so that they feel they can more easily share their closest secrets with him than with their parents.

I saw Sri Sathya Sai Baba bending his head down and my second son whispering into his ear. He was all seriousness, all attention. Another sign of his infinite love and loving-kindness. No one and nothing is too trivial for his consideration. He listened patiently to my son's whispers, briefly and softly responding so that none of us heard what he said. It was all so Top Secret and, to this day, I do not know what transpired so earnestly between them.

Sri Sathya Sai Baba then turned to my eldest son. He told him to pay more attention to his studies and less to his friends. He said to him, "You must study well and become an officer like your father so that Swami can find you a wife and celebrate your wedding!" It tickled the other two boys to hear Sri Sathya Sai Baba discussing the marriage of their brother who had only just enrolled at college.

Sri Sathya Sai Baba looked at them and gently admonished them: "See here, boys. You are not to tease your brother about this. Swami can talk about such future things, but you may not make fun of or tease an elder brother. He is older than both of you and you must show him respect."

Then, with great difficulty, the two boys controlled their laughter for they knew perfectly well they had to obey Sri Sathya Sai Baba. And he, seeing their efforts, patted them kindly and the gesture endeared him all the more to them.

Sri Sathya Sai Baba then asked us if we had any questions for him.

My husband asked, "Baba, is it true that the soul resides between the eyebrows, in the middle of the forehead?"

Sri Sathya Sai Baba: "No, no . . . the spot is recommended as a point to concentrate on during meditation. It is only one point, for the soul is everywhere in the body, in each limb. A man lives on even when he loses his hands or feet, the soul does not die with each limb. The soul is like a flash of lightning in the spinal column. It is called *sushumna naadi.* Between the ninth and the twelfth vertebrae, it is very sensitive and moves in curves like flashes of lightning. That is why no one can survive without a spine. The soul is present in every part of the body and is not fixed to any one area. But this spinal area is very sensitive."

Then I asked, "Swami, how can one attain the concentration needed for meditation? And why can't we realise God instantly?"

He replied, "Everything you do requires concentration. Can you drive a car without concentrating? Can you eat, read, write or do anything at all without concentrating your attention on the task in hand? People forget this simple truth and think that concentration is a huge feat to be performed only when it's time to think of God. They begin to think of it as far too difficult for them and completely beyond their abilities, and it is this thought which makes concentration more difficult. If you can concentrate on your daily chores, why should you not on your prayers which should, after all, become a part of your daily routine. *Sadhana* (spiritual endeavour) has to be done to enable you to progress Godward."

"Were the ancient sages *(rishis)* all fools to tell us that it takes many ages to achieve God-realisation? If you could realise God that easily, what would have been the need for saints of olden days to go into forests and perform penance for years? They were surely not leading the hard life of jungle-dwellers for rest and relaxation . . . No, no, continuous, constant and concentrated effort alone can lead one to God-realisation. Don't believe anyone who says that after so many classes, or so many courses, and within such and such a period of time, you can be made to realise the Divine. You may be able to achieve the physical feats of *yoga* within a certain period of time, but real *yoga* is union with God. And that God is everywhere: inside you and outside you. That is why you too are divine. The human body has both its functions and its limitations. It needs food for sustenance, exercise for health. A healthy body, healthy habits, a healthy mind – performing one's duties conscientiously on the path of *dharma*, that in itself is nothing other than meditation."

And on that note, Sri Sathya Sai Baba ended the unforgettable and soul-stirring interview.

After the *bhajans* were sung and the *aarati* performed, we went round the Prashanti Nilayam complex. We saw the enormous Purnachandra Auditorium with a seating capacity of over 30,000. It looks like a huge hangar with a series of roll-up shutters on both sides that are, in fact, doors. The hall is unique for it has pillars only on the sides and no support at all in the vast central area. The result is a lovely large and clear area with no structural obstructions of the view onto the podium. The vast expanse of the hall filled me with wonder, both for its immensity and the originality of its concept. It is also an artistic hall, with mosaics on the pillars, sculptures and paintings depicting all the great religions of the world on either side of the stage. There are quotations and sayings of Sri Sathya Sai Baba elucidating the pictures and photographs. It is an auditorium that brings to mind the thousand-pillared halls of famous temples where cultural events are held in praise of the deity. But here, the presiding deity is also physically present, unlike the famous temples where only idols preside over celebrations.

The high façade above the main entrance to the auditorium has a beautiful and enormous relief of *Nataraja* (*Shiva* as Lord of the Dance), every last detail of which is perfect. Opposite this, in the courtyard as it were, is the 50-foot tall *Aikya Stambha*, or Column of Concord, depicting the symbols of the main religions as on the Sai insignia: Hinduism *(Om)*, Buddhism (the Wheel of Eternity), Zoroastrianism (fire), Islam (the Crescent and Star), and Christianity (the Cross). An appropriate legend is inscribed below each symbol.

Under the *Om* it says: 'Listen to the primeval *pranava AUM* resounding in your heart as well as in the heart of the Universe.'

For the Buddhist wheel, the legend reads: 'Remember the wheel of cause and consequence, of deed and destiny, and the wheel of *Dharma* that rights them all.'

For the Sacred Fire of the Zoroastrians, the inscription says: 'Offer all bitterness in the Sacred Fire and emerge grand, great and godly.'

Under the Crescent and Star of Islam, the message is: 'Be like the Star which never wavers from the Crescent but is fixed in steady faith.'

And under the Cross the legend reads: 'Cut the 'I' feeling clean across and let your ego die on the Cross to endow on you eternity.'

This concrete pillar of concord reminds one of the *Ashokan* stone monuments of over twenty centuries ago. They too had inscriptions on them. In the same way, the *vata vruksha* (the sacred Banyan tree) on a hill behind Prashanti Nilayam is reminiscent of the *Buddha* and the *Bodhi* Tree. Instinctively one senses the significance of such sacred trees which withstand the passage of time and offer shelter to generations of mankind who hope, perhaps, to be inspired to meditate underneath their majestic boughs. Sri Sathya Sai Baba planted the Banyan tree above Prashanti Nilayam on the 29th of June 1959. First, he consecrated the spot by placing a thick copper plate (15 ins × 10 ins) into the soil. He had materialised the plate earlier from the sand in the bed of the River Chitravati, and it has engraved on it a multitude of hieroglyphs and many unusual letters and alphabets. The Sathya Sai Hospital stands close to the sacred Banyan tree.

There is a small *Ganesha* idol in front of the Prashanti Mandir. There is also a large image of the Elephant God installed in a small temple on its own behind the Prashanti Mandir facing the rear gateway. This little structure has become a landmark of Prashanti Nilayam. Just outside this gate, there are several small shops and stalls selling Sathya Sai photographs and mementoes, flowers, incense and an assortment of provisions. The noise, bustle, dirt and crowds outside the gate are in sharp contrast to the calm and cleanliness that pervade the *ashrama*.

We went to the banks of the River Chitravati. They say the river is no longer as it was when Sri Sathya Sai Baba was a young boy. Now, there are only thin streams of water flowing in the broad riverbed and the sandbanks are crowded. We were told that Sri Sathya Sai Baba has given up going to the river.

There were a few village boys by the river and they showed us the *Kalpataru* (wish-fulfilling tree) sitting atop a hillock. This is the tree from which young Sathya used to pick a whole range of fruits. The hillock is known as the site of many Sathya Sai miracles and divine *darshans*.

The Sathya Sai *Gokulam* (cow stabling) is on the outskirts of Puttaparthi village. It houses over a hundred cows and it is administered under the strict and direct supervision of Sri Sathya Sai Baba. A graceful figure of *Krishna* with a cow stands at the entrance. The whole area has fresh green patches of lawn and lovely flowering trees. There are clean and bright sheds for the cows and water buffaloes; indeed, the whole place is spick and span. It also has neatly laid out living quarters for the cowherds who tend the cattle.

Sri Sathya Sai Baba had the Easwaramba School built, and named to commemorate his mother, for the children of neighbouring villages.

The old part of Puttaparthi village is tiny, and marsh-like during the monsoon. I saw a small plot of land on which once had stood the house in which Sri Sathya Sai Baba was born as Satyanarayana Raju. Nearby are the houses of his brother, Seshama Raju, and of his two sisters, Parvatamma and Venkamma. Although members of the family go to Prashanti Nilayam everyday, they still live in their own houses in the village.

The Old *Mandir* (temple) is now called the Pedda Venkappa Raju Kalyana Mantap and stands opposite the village temple. It is in a largish compound of its own and has a medium-sized hall. Behind the temple there is a tiny room with an even tinier bathroom. These two diminutive rooms were Sri Sathya Sai Baba's living quarters for nearly twenty years.

Puttaparthi is such a small and underdeveloped village. And yet, today it prospers: because it is the birthplace of the *Avatara* of the Age. And through him, this unknown, unheard of and unsung hamlet is now a place of holy pilgrimage, a place sacred and sanctified. What could have been called a God-forsaken village is today a God-seeking pilgrimage.

"The Avatara behaves in a human way so mankind may feel kinship, but rises to superhuman heights so that mankind may aspire to those heights."

. . . Sri Sathya Sai Baba

20

FESTIVALS AT PUTTAPARTHI

All through the year, the Sai Festivals draw many thousands of people from all over India and from many parts of the world. The biggest draws are the *Dassera* Festival, the *Shivaratri* Celebration and Sri Sathya Sai Baba's own birthday. *Guru Purnima* and Easwaramba Day also draw a fair crowd.

I attended the *Dassera* Festival at Prashanti Nilayam in October 1977. It began with a ceremonial procession as do most festivities in Puttaparthi and Bangalore. Trumpeters and a band accompanied a gaily caparisoned Sai Geetha (Sri Sathya Sai Baba's elephant). Sri Sathya Sai Baba walked behind the elephant under a bejewelled parasol, his right hand raised in blessing, gracefully acknowledging the greetings of the people lining the route. Priests chanting sacred *mantras* preceded him carrying the *purna kumbha*. (*Purna kumbha* is a ceremonial pot which is full, symbolising the fullness of everything. It is carried at auspicious events and it is also a respectful way of heralding the arrival of a revered personage.) Girls from the Anantapur College formed the band that day and marched through the central avenue to the main courtyard and stood in formation until Sri Sathya Sai Baba arrived and signalled to them to disperse. It was exactly nine o'clock in the morning.

Sri Sathya Sai Baba led the Governor of Karnataka, the Chief Guest, to his seat on the podium and sat next to him. The Governor, in a short speech full of reverence for his host, commended the many Sathya Sai *Seva Samithis* for the service they rendered their communities "under the divine inspiration of *Bhagavan* Baba." Then, Sri Sathya Sai Baba spoke. His speech on that day stressed that divinity always blesses those human efforts which are sincere and selfless. Then began the *Vedapurusha Saptaha Yagna*. This is a *yagna* (sacrificial rite carried out over seven continuous days) in honour of the Lord Himself, for He is *"Vedapurusha"*, the originator of the *Vedas*. Learned *purohits,* dressed in silken *dhotis*, chanted *mantras* as they churned a piece of wood on a block of wood to make it ignite. Lighting a fire in that way, by friction, is taught by the *Shastras* and the *yagna* is performed strictly in accordance with scriptural injunctions.

When, after some effort, a thin wisp of smoke came from the turning and churning wood, the *Brahmins* redoubled their efforts. They were visibly thrilled when a flicker of flame appeared. Then, by more methodical churning, they made the flicker a single tall flame until, at last, with the help of wood shavings, it burst into flames and was a proper fire. Sri Sathya Sai Baba blessed the flames and the fire was then taken to the *homa kunda* (sacred pit) where the *yagna* was performed around it. More wood, pure and costly, was added to the fire to the sound of ancient *mantras* and, slowly, a blazing fire was built up. Several ingredients were put into it, but the main sacrifice was always *ghee* (clarified butter). The *Brahmins* intoned *Vedic* hymns dedicated to *Rudra (Shiva)* known as *Namaka* and *Chamaka*. To one side of the stage, the *Devi Bhagavatham* was being read and worshipped simultaneously until all 18,000 stanzas were read. On the other side, the *Shri Chakra (Meru Chakra)* was being worshipped according to prescribed injunctions and *araadhana* was performed with *Lalitha Sahasranaama*.

The *Brahmins* then chanted the *Chandi*, enumerating the *Shakti* aspects of the Divine. The *pundits* also chanted the *Saptahasathi* which forms part of the *Markandaya Purana*. Then, a *Brahmin* sat at an allotted spot and recited the *Sundarakanda* of the *Ramayana* and another one performed the *Surya namaskar* (bowing to the Sun). The Sun is a visible symbol of the Supreme Power and that is the very aspect that the powerful *Gayatri Mantra* defines as 'that power that illumines the Sun.' Groups of *Brahmins* and *pundits* then performed the various propitiatory rites and, on each of the seven days at noon, the *yagna* ceremony ended with the *aarati* performed at the altar of the *Shri Chakra*. Sri Sathya Sai Baba attended the *aarati* which was performed to the chanting of the beautiful and moving *Mantra Pushpam*. He was then garlanded and offered the *prasadam* (offering) which he accepted. These ceremonies were carried out for seven days and, each evening, Sri Sathya Sai Baba gave a discourse which was then followed by a cultural programme on stage.

Vedapurusha signifies the Supreme Lord *(Purushottama)*, as glorified in the *Purusha Suktha*. The deities thus propitiated include *Lakshmi,*

Saraswati and *Durga*. *Dassera* is the festival dedicated to the primal urge that caused the infinite and beginningless equilibrium to be disturbed by this divine delusion we call Creation. The Universe *(jagata)* is in constant agitation, trying to recapture the equanimity that was lost then. When that equanimity is regained, all ideas of past, present and future, of manifoldness, of gain and loss, of pleasant and unpleasant, disappear. The three characteristics of calm, active and dull (the three *gunas: satva, rajas* and *tamas)* affect consciousness and hence we pay homage to the three aspects of *Mahakali* (Great *Kali* or *Durga*), *Mahalakshmi* (Great *Lakshmi*) and *Mahasaraswati* (Great *Saraswati*). The three goddesses are each worshipped for three days during the *Dassera* Festival for, with their grace, it is possible to recapture that original equanimity.

Dassera celebrates the victory of righteousness over wickedness. The tenth and ultimate day, called *Vijayaa Dasami* (the victorious 10th) is the grand finale, the day of *Purnahuti*, the full offering, the complete sacrifice.

Sri Sathya Sai Baba arrived in procession again and, as the *Purushottama* or *Vedapurusha*, he received the valedictory offering near the central *vedi* (sacrificial pit). Then, his hands started to rotate in the familiar way and materialised a *navratna mala* (a nine-gem necklace). He gave it to the chief officiating priest and told him to put it round his wife's neck. That lady, clad in the traditional nine-yard *sari*, had been present on stage throughout the ten day festival as the *Sahadharmini* (co-performer), performing the rituals prescribed for her as the female half of the officiating *Brahmin*. She was, of course, overjoyed to receive the gift of grace from Sri Sathya Sai Baba.

Sri Sathya Sai Baba moved his right hand again and, this time, the nine gems that appeared were offered to the sacrificial fire. God is sometimes referred to as *Ratna Dataa* (the giver of precious stones) and on that *Vijayaa Dasami*, Sri Sathya Sai Baba justified the title by creating the gems through his own will *(sankalpa)*. He explained that the number nine is auspicious. It is significant in numerology and represents the nine steps on the way to God. (One of Sri Sathya Sai Baba's car registration plates reads 999!)

Other articles wrapped in silk bundles were also offered to the fire. Sri Sathya Sai Baba has often explained about *loka kalyanam* (the good of the people), the good that accrues to the world by similar offerings made at *yagnas*. People should not look upon such sacrifices as a waste of *ghee* (clarified butter) and other materials. He drew an analogy to this kind of sacrifice by describing a farmer who put aside a portion of the harvest to sow back into the soil. To the ignorant it may look as if he is throwing his hard won grain into the dirt, but they could not know about future harvests reaped with those seeds flung onto the earth. Mankind will reap three times as much *ghee* than that offered to the sacrificial fire. The sanctifying effect of the fire is great. Do people ever pause to think of the effect of all the *ghee* they have swallowed? Do they believe that indulgence is not waste?

More *ghee* was poured into the fire after the *Purnahuti* offering. This was done with a grooved bamboo stick so that the flames shot upwards, high above the *vedi*. Then Sri Sathya Sai Baba moved his hands over the fire and a shower of rice grains poured from them into the flames. To see this is to be blessed. Many *yagnas* are performed but it is very rare indeed to witness the offerings being accepted by the *Vedapurusha* Himself. (In Scripture, there is mention of the descent of the Divine to accept *yagna* offerings.) Then the *Brahmins* and *pundits* went to the River Chitravati to perform more rites. Finally, the stage was set for the *vibhuti abhishekam* (shower of sacred ash) performed by Sri Sathya Sai Baba over the silver image of Shirdi Sai Baba while devotees sing *bhajans*.

The image of Shirdi Sai Baba sits on a silver pedestal in the shape of a coiled snake. A painted wooden urn is used for the *abhishekam*. First, Sri Sathya Sai Baba created a small ornament and placed it on the forehead of the Shirdi Sai image.* He then performed *abhishekam* with water, milk, honey and other liquids. Next, he carefully wiped the image dry and rolled up his sleeves. The *bhajan* singers began to sing a *bhajan* called '*Om Shivaya*' and Sri Sathya Sai Baba put his right hand into the empty urn which was held by a *sannyasi*, (Swami Karunyananda, a devotee) upside down over the Shirdi Sai idol.

The moment he put his hand in the pot and shook it, *vibhuti* showered down onto the Shirdi Sai image. He continued to shake the pot by twisting and turning his hand inside it and the *vibhuti* rained down and a cloud of sacred ash formed around the cascade. Slowly, the Shirdi Sai idol was covered in *vibhuti*.

Sri Sathya Sai Baba changed hands. The *vibhuti* cascade stopped when he removed his right hand from the pot, but it started again as he put his left hand into it. The climax was reached with almost a cloudburst of *vibhuti* tumbling down, fast and furious and in huge quantity. Then Sri Sathya Sai Baba removed his hand and the *abhishekam* was over.

This is the usual pattern of *vibhuti abhishekam* at *Dassera*. On one occasion at *Dassera*, there was not only the grey *vibhuti*, but also red *kumkum* and yellow turmeric that poured out of the urn in turns; then, near the end, it was again *vibhuti*. On yet another occasion, precious gems

*On seeing this for the first time, Dr. S. Bhagavantam (a noted physicist who now translates Sri Sathya Sai Baba's *Telugu* speeches) wondered how the small object could remain fixed to the statue. He could not take his mind away from the problem. How did Sri Sathya Sai Baba stick it there? Two metal surfaces cannot adhere together spontaneously – this is very simply impossible scientifically. And yet Sri Sathya Sai Baba had not used an adhesive. How had he managed to keep the ornament on the metal image? Why did it not fall away?

Sri Sathya Sai Baba's answer was simple. "Some wonder how this little jewelled ornament was fixed to the metal surface. Cannot one understand that one who can create the ornament can also make it stick?"

tumbled out of the urn, clanking down onto the silver idol of Shirdi Sai Baba.

The front of Sri Sathya Sai Baba's robe was almost white with *vibhuti* and his hands and arms were covered in it, as if he were wearing dress gloves! He rushed off to change and, within minutes, he was back looking clean and fresh as always, without a trace of *vibhuti*.

The priests had returned from the river by then. One of them carried the *abhishek teerth* (holy water) in a vessel. Sri Sathya Sai Baba walked ahead carrying a sheaf of *kusha* grass blades. He dipped the sheaf into the holy water and, walking among the congregation, sprinkled water on all. It is said that these sanctified drops falling on one is equal to having a purificatory bath.

The dawning of *Vijayaa Dasami* Day was very festive and different. There was a silver *jhula* (swing) occasion. For this Sri Sathya Sai Baba, robed in purest white, reclined on a swing, swaying gently, while P. Susheela (a devotee who is a playback singer) sang *bhajans* and music was played by her own musicians.

What is the significance of these ceremonies and rites? Sri Sathya Sai Baba explained it during the evening *Dassera* discourses. The *vibhuti abhishekam* is performed "to inspire you to renounce desires." He stressed the need for inner *yagna* (sacrifice) in the minds of individuals watching the outer *yagna*. People should not only give up evil thoughts and desires, they should try equally to cultivate a sense of sacrifice and practise detachment. They ought to take the example of Emperor *Bali* (son of *Prahlada*) who renounced all when the Lord, as *Vamana*, came to him asking for the extent of three paces. Though *Bali* had been forewarned by his *guru*, he did not hesitate for a moment in granting *Vamana's* wish. Though he was very short, *Vamana's* first two paces covered the three worlds: *Bhur, Bhuvah* and *Suvaha*. *Bali* was indifferent to the loss of his empire and happily offered his head for *Vamana's* third step.

Sri Sathya Sai Baba also spoke of the importance of cultivating equanimity. It is said that *samatva* (equipoise) is *yoga* (union). He said that *sadhakas* must try to achieve equanimity in every way: physically, socially, occupationally, philosophically and devotionally. Equanimity is the result of *Paranjyoti* (the illumination of consciousness). This is the final flash of the luminous revelation called *Prakanti*, which, in turn, is the culmination of *Prashanti*. This is earned through *sadhana* (spiritual endeavour) and contemplation to drive out the *ashanti* (dissatisfied restlessness) that prevails in the world at large and in the minds of individuals.

One evening, Sri Sathya Sai Baba explained, simply and lucidly, the significance of the four *Mahavakyas* (Great Phrases). We find *Pragyanam Brahma* (Divine Wisdom is *Brahma*) in the *Rig Veda*; in the *Yajur Veda*, we find *Aham Brahmasmi* (I am *Brahma*); the *Sama Veda* declares *Tat Twam Asi* (That Thou Art); and the *Atharva Veda* says *Aham Atmabrahma* (this *Atma* is *Brahma*, or I am *Atmabrahma*).

Pragyanam is eternal wisdom. Sound is the basis of *Brahman* (universe, creation). The *Rig Veda* teaches us that divine wisdom and *Brahman* are one. The *Yajur Veda* says that God is not the actual doer, but is the witness to everything. Ordinarily people think of their bodies as themselves; more knowledgeable people think their souls are their true selves; but truly wise people know that each 'I' is God.

Sri Sathya Sai Baba illustrated these three ideas with the simple phenomenon of the moon reflected in water. The moon seems to tremble on troubled water: this would be dualism. The moon and the water are two different things and the reflection is troubled when the water moves, which is the natural reaction. This is the *Dvaita* concept, or dualism. But, if the water is in a pot, or in a still well, the moon's reflection too will be still. This is *Visishtadvaita* (qualified non-dualism), where both are stationary. While in *Advaita* (non-dualism or monism), you see the moon in its place in the sky. With this illustration, we have the same moon in three different views: one, in the sky; two, stationary in still water, and three, moving in the waters of a river.

Turning to the *Tat Twam Asi* concept in the *Sama Veda* (from which all musical compositions take their origin), he said that *Tat* (That) is permanent and has no form and no name. He gave the instance of a rock being chiselled into an idol by a sculptor. After that the idol is installed in a temple and worshipped as divine. The unused chips chiselled out of the same rock may say "we are also that", since indeed they are of the same rock. But no one acknowledges their divinity. All worship only the idol as God, though both are from the very same substance.

Sri Sathya Sai Baba then pointed out that while the human body is impermanent, man's soul is everlasting. That soul and the omnipresent and universal soul are one and the same. We must therefore realise the truth: "That and this are One."

In another discourse, he spoke of divine grace and the debts man has to discharge. Man has three debts: a debt to God, to the *rishis* and to his parents. God gave him life, the *rishis* wisdom, and his body is the gift of his parents. These debts can be discharged by promoting sacredness and purity and by following the maxim: be good, see good, do good. By earning a good name and leading a good life, one pleases everyone and brings credit to one's family and country. Our ancient traditions and customs all have meanings and there is a purpose in them all. For example, even the simple custom of decorating the floor of the entrance of a house *(rangoli)* is done with rice flour so that birds, ants and other small insects can feed off the decorations on the floor. This decorating held compassion in it, "while today we forget that and think only of its appearance and so we use powdered chalk which is useless to ants and insects." Cultivate open heartedness and share freely with all. Glory and wealth are transient. People should have *Daiva Preeti* (love of God) and *Papa Bheeti* (fear of wrong-doing).

Sri Sathya Sai Baba explained that *karma* (action) alone is responsible for both good and bad. "God is not responsible for man's problems and sorrows. All the pain and the troubles are results of man's deeds. Do not blame God or say, 'Oh God, why do you cause this pain?' For God is only the witness." If you are ignorant on the subject of God, it is better not to talk about it.

A mother may love her child, but when the child has a stomach ache, all she can do is give it medicine. The child must suffer the pain alone until it passes. Beyond the grave, only God accompanies man; family and friends must halt at the graveyard.

Only a few people have been able to know God or have divine experiences. However, no one has been able to prove to others the existence of God. But, everyone senses that there must be a creator of this world, someone must have made it.

Sri Sathya Sai Baba pointed to a little bit of material sticking out of his closed fist. "You are able to see only a bit of cloth. You do not know what the entire cloth is like, its shape or its size, until I open my hand and show it to you. Man's position is similar. He knows precious little about divinity and has no idea at all of the whole. That there <u>is</u> God is truth, a truth more fundamental than the atom."

We must believe in divinity and cannot argue that because we do not see God with our eyes, God does not exist. We do not see stars in the daytime, but that does not mean that they are not there. We do not see them because the sunlight blinds our eyes.

Sri Sathya Sai Baba then defined the word *Bhagavanta* (God). '*Bha*' stands for lustre or light. '*Ga*' means spreading light. So *Bhagavanta* means one who sheds (or spreads) light.

He told the story of Jesus Christ to illustrate how he shone brighter than everyone else. He did only good and tried to spread knowledge with an unwavering mind. In Jerusalem, the grounds of the temple were being used for unholy practices. They used them to barter and bargain in and kept them dirty. Jesus told them not to pollute the holy ground with their unclean activities. Bartering and commerce should not be done there, he said. They also sold pigeons to offer as sacrifices. Jesus told them that God is omnipresent and lives in every being. Why kill poor pigeons on His altar?

The religious leaders thought that Jesus, with these revolutionary new ideas, was trying to change ancient traditions. So they made plans to get Jesus away from the temple. Judas was among his twelve disciples and they won him over with thirty silver coins. When Jesus was alone, with the help of Judas, they caught him and tortured him. Later, Judas repented his betrayal of Jesus Christ. But none of this prevented Christ from performing his mission of spreading light.

SHIVARATRI:

Thousands and thousands have always congregated at Puttaparthi for *Shivaratri* to watch the *Lingodhbhava*. Sri Sathya Sai Baba no longer produces the *lingams*, but people still come in myriads.

Devotees speak of something that happened many years ago in the Old Temple at Puttaparthi. Sri Sathya Sai Baba asked a man to dig in a specific place. From it they took several pedestals such as are used to place *Shiva lingams*. He is then reported to have said: "Yes, the images for these pedestals are here!" pointing to his stomach. At the time, the devotees did not understand what he meant. Later they knew when, on the night of *Shivaratri*, as *bhajans* were being sung, Sri Sathya Sai Baba suddenly showed signs of severe stomach pains. He writhed around, pressed his hand on his chest, retched and, out of his mouth there emerged a streak of light followed by a *sphatika* (crystal) *lingam*. He caught it and held it high for all to see.

The *lingam* is an ellipsoid and is the symbolic representation of *Shiva-Shakti*. Worship of the *lingam* is one of the highest forms of prayer. Most *Shiva* temples have only this form of God in the inner sanctum.

People who have witnessed the *Lingodbhava* have experienced profound joy in it. They know that it is a rare spiritual event and that it is indescribable.

Usha Pillai, a devotee, recalls that she had taken a lady with her who had never witnessed this miracle. The lady was not a devotee of Sri Sathya Sai Baba, but the miracle of the *lingam* produced spiritual stirrings deep inside her. She felt moved beyond measure. Soon, a strange restlessness and a longing for self-expression took hold of her. In a few more hours, she knew what she wanted to do. Her spiritual experience inspired her to compose *bhajans* and *kirtans* – a talent she never knew she possessed. In the course of the next forty days, she created forty beautiful songs, all inspired by the birth of the *lingam*.

Sri Sathya Sai Baba has brought out *lingams* of stone, metal and crystal. Often the translucent *lingams* have an inner light that glows and changes colours. Sometimes, only one *lingam* emerges from him, at other times a pair, and there have been occasions when a whole stream of them are regurgitated, in gold, silver, jade and crystal. No one has been able to fathom why Sri Sathya Sai Baba brought out *lingams* from within his own divine body. He did this for several years on every *Shivaratri*, undergoing physical agony. Nor does anyone know why he does not produce them anymore.

The *lingams* thus produced were always given away by Sri Sathya Sai Baba to devotees, with instructions for their worship.

An Assamese devotee, a devout old lady, is one of the lucky recipients of a *lingam*. She has worshipped it diligently and she says she sees in it "at times, the form of *Shiva*." At other times, she sees in it the form of *Sri Krishna*. She sees many forms and many images in it during worship and derives great *ananda* (bliss) from it. In 1978, on the day of *Shivaratri*, Sri Sathya Sai Baba was driving from Ooty to Bangalore when he ordered the car to stop. Followed by a small group of people, he walked to a secluded spot. A student of the Satya Sai College requested permission to photograph Sri Sathya Sai Baba. The permission was given and Sri Sathya Sai Baba said, "When you click, you will capture my real form." When the polaroid photograph was pulled out, everyone was astonished to see on it the form of Lord *Dattatreya* – the Trinity, the composite divine unity of *Brahma, Vishnu* and *Shiva*.

Sri Sathya Sai Baba told them, "Because I am with you in this human form, I move about among you as one of you. You therefore do not understand Me nor do you realise that I am *Dattatreya* amidst you."

That night, he materialised a medallion showing the entire surface of the moon for a boy who wanted it, and a space type wristwatch for another devotee. Later, at Whitefield near Bangalore, he spoke to a large crowd on the meaning of *Shivaratri* (the night of *Shiva*), which he described as the divine night or the night of consecration, dedication and illumination. He explained that the mind is ultimately linked to the moon *(Chandra)* which is therefore recognised as the presiding deity of the mind. *Shivaratri* is a celebration dedicated to the moon, hence the night-long vigil, *namasmaran*, worship and fasting prescribed for spiritual progress.

In numerology, the first three syllables/sounds of the word *Shivaratri* (i.e. shi, va and ra) signify the numbers 5, 4 and 2. Together they make eleven, representing the five senses of perception, the five senses of action and the mind. Senses and mind cause only sorrow, so one should aim for the soul to illumine one's intelligence.

Sri Sathya Sai Baba explained the significance of the *tandava* (the cosmic dance of *Shiva*) which the *Puranas* say occured on *Shivaratri*. The *tandava* was a divine plan to attract *Prakriti* in the same way that miracles are divine ploys to attract people to the divine presence in order to mend their ways and cleanse their minds, to strengthen their faith and to lead them in the way of *sadhana* and service – so that they may melt in ecstasy into the ever-conscious bliss-form.

The *tandava* was such a fierce dance that fire emanated from *Shiva's* body. *Parvati*, his consort, trying to cool him, placed the Ganges *(Ganga)* and the crescent moon in his hair, smeared cool sandal-paste all over his body and made cold-blooded snakes coil around his limbs. At last, *Parvati*, daughter of Himalaya, sat on his lap. All these ministrations cooled the fire of *Shiva* and then both *Shiva* and *Parvati* danced together to the everlasting enchantment of all.

This story is related to show how to please the Lord and win His grace. People ought to try to understand the underlying meaning of festivals and celebrations, and they should observe the required austerities with devotion. For there are no short cuts on the spiritual journey.

In another discourse the same evening, given at the boys' hostel, Sri

Sathya Sai Baba talked about the four stages of a man's life: *Brahmacharya*[1], *Grahasthashrama*[2], *Vanaprastha*[3], and *Sannyasa*[4]. When life is correctly led in these stages, man can attain the goal of self-realisation through self-confidence, contentment and self-sacrifice.

At the *Brahmacharya* stage, a student should fix his mind on the blossoming of spirituality and guard against the plagues of hate, greed, lust, pride and envy. The mind is like a mirror. Unless the mirror is kept clean and straight, the reflection will distort truth. By conscientiously following the *Brahmacharya* discipline, young people will be able to obtain a clearer picture of *Brahman*.

Sri Sathya Sai Baba then talked about the philosophy of Gautama the *Buddha* who said that all is sorrow *(sarvam dukkham)*. With the awakening of the desire for joy comes its shadow, sorrow. A happy event, even the birth of a child, heralds a crop of cares: the child's health, its studies, its future and so on. The *Buddha* also taught that all is void *(sarvam sunyam)*, an unavoidable fact often faced by the *grahastha* (householder) who finds that nothing in the household has real or lasting substance.

In the *Vanaprastha* stage, one can come to understand another part of the *Buddha's* teaching: *sarvam Shiva swarupam* (all is an aspect of *Shiva*).

The ultimate lesson to learn is *'sarvam kshanikam'* (everything is transient, momentary). The final stage is *Sannyasa* which means total renunciation excepting only one ardent desire, to merge into the Divine. *Sannyasa* is not just the outer donning of the yellow robe.

Service performed in the true spirit of love is the surest way of winning God's grace. Sri Sathya Sai Baba told the students, "Through holy merit you have earned human life. You have the added good fortune of proximity to the *Avatara* of God. Do not let this magnificent opportunity pass you by."

GURU PURNIMA CELEBRATION

At a *Guru Purnima* gathering in Whitefield, devotees had a chance not only to hear their Divine *Guru*, but also to see him in the role of director of a play called *'Bhaja Govindam'* by *Adi Shankaracharya,* performed by the boys of the Brindavan College. The play, a musical, had English dialogue and *Sanskrit shlokas* (stanzas). It taught the highest of philosophies in the gentlest possible way, through music. The performance was such a success that All India Radio broadcast it several times as part of their youth programme.

I went to Puttaparthi for *Guru Purnima* in July 1978. Sri Sathya Sai Baba

1. Youth and celibacy.
2. Householder with family responsibilities.
3. Life in the forest, away from all worldly ties.
4. Total renunciation.

addressed a large gathering in the Purnachandra Auditorium and spoke of the qualities of a *guru* who can guide human beings on the path to divinity. There are three types of *gurus*: the *badha guru*, the *bodha guru* and the super *guru*, or *Avatara*, he said.

"A *guru* is one who has transcended all attributes. He is one who has conquered body-consciousness and *moha* (desires) and he is capable of any *tyaga* (renunciation). One can take *Prakriti* (manifest nature) as the first and foremost *guru*. For trees offer shelter to all without distinction of caste and creed; mountains teach us how to bear both heat and cold; birds can teach us to be content with what food we receive each day. Ultimately, God with His perception is the greatest *Guru* of all," said Sri Sathya Sai Baba.

Then, he explained the importance of *Vyasa*. *Vyasa* was the great sage who gave us the *Puranas* which contain those profound truths that are relevant to our day to day life. They also treat of other-worldly aspects and *moksha* (release or liberation). "The sacred literature of the past is intended to help people to lead a righteous life on earth and to show them the path that leads to life beyond the earthly confines," said Sri Sathya Sai Baba.

"Sometimes there are needless questions about who wrote the *Puranas*. The authorship of the *Puranas* is far less important than their contents which can bring solace and everlasting joy to man. They discuss issues beyond modern science and contain much greater knowledge of astronomy, geography and other fields than is known to contemporary science. Today's scientists do not understand *Sanskrit*, the language of the gods, in which the *Puranas* are written. Man's ultimate goal should be perfection, for his life is governed by his actions alone. His thoughts and deeds today will bring him the life he deserves tomorrow, just as this life is governed by the *karma* of a past life."

"Some can lead their lives without the help of others; but everyone cannot, particularly in the spiritual field. With the right kind of spiritual help, divinity can blossom in every individual. This kind of help cannot come from books alone: it needs the help of a *guru* (a great teacher) with *anubhuti* (experience)."

"Divinity in man is related to the cultivation of his own humanity. Learning from books alone can only sharpen the intellect and encourage argumentativeness. Only *sadhana* enables one to grasp the significance of divinity. Man first worships God in human form because that is the only way in which he can visualise divinity. After that, he can come to recognise the divine essence, *Ishwaram sarvabhutanam* (God is in all beings), the all-pervading presence."

"*Sri Krishna* says in the *Bhagavad-Gita* that a true student should be like *Arjuna* who had a pure heart *(pavitra hridaya)*, courage and conviction, and never doubted that the Lord in the heart *(Hridayasthayi)* would become *Yogeshwara* and turn into the Divine Teacher, *Krishna*. Only with a pure heart can one visualise divinity."

"Man should take to the godly path with an open mind. Doubts about God that disturb the mind are deterrents. Any *sadhana* (spiritual endeavour) that holds doubt, even of the existence of God, will be in vain. The heart can be purified by reading Scripture and with *sadhana* under the direction of the right *guru*. For, as it is said, the *guru* is *Brahma*, the *guru* is *Vishnu*, the *guru* is *Shiva (Maheshvara)* Himself!"

"On *Guru Purnima* Day, one should light the lamp of knowledge and dispel dark ignorance from the heart. The supra-consciousness in the heart is the Lord, or the Divine *Guru* who resides there permanently. When people realise this, then that will be the day of fulfillment. The real *Guru Purnima* Day will dawn when the lotus of the heart opens up fully in response to the inspiration of the *Puranas*, the wisdom engendered by *satsang* and the supremity of the *guru's* teaching," concluded Sri Sathya Sai Baba.

BIRTHDAY CELEBRATION

Sri Sathya Sai Baba's birthday, on the 23rd of November, is one of the most important occasions at Puttaparthi. It is customary to offer special prayers in domestic shrines to different deities and *avataras* on their birthdays. Thus *Krishna Jayanti* is celebrated as *Sri Krishna's* birthday and *Rama Navami* celebrates the birth of *Sri Rama*. In the same way, devotees gather at Puttaparthi on the 23rd of November each year to have *darshan* of their own Living God and to celebrate the day as a true holy day.

While Sri Sathya Sai Baba's parents were alive, they used to mark the day by, among other things, applying oil to his hair. Then this would be followed by elderly lady devotees dipping a flower in the oil and putting it in his hair. Since their death, however, this is no longer done.

One of the highlights of the birthday celebration is the *jhula* (swing). Sri Sathya Sai Baba sits for a while in the evening on a silver swing. He arrives dressed in white and reclines on the swing which is gently rocked by devotees to the strains of melodious music. Usually, this music is provided by well known musicians. In 1977, it was Ravi Shankar with his *sitar* who gave the birthday concert, thus paying a devotee's homage to Sri Sathya Sai Baba. In 1978, it was the turn of M.S. Subbalakshmi, also a devotee, to sing songs of exquisite devotion.

The grandest birthday celebration was in 1975 when Sri Sathya Sai Baba was fifty. Then every inch of Prashanti Nilayam township was packed with people. Those who came from afar stayed in improvised shelters; camps and tents were pitched wherever there was space. The larger tents and *shamianas* (canopies) often housed hundreds. The total number of people gathered there was thought to be over half a million. The result was that it became impossible for many to catch even a glimpse of the orange robe. So a helicopter was brought in and, to the delight of all, Sri Sathya Sai Baba gave *darshan* to all from the overflying helicopter.

On his birthday in 1977, Sri Sathya Sai Baba called upon his devotees in ringing tones to do their utmost for the people left destitute by the cyclone and tidal wave on Andhra Pradesh's East coast. He emphasised that service to humanity in distress is service to God. The response to his call was monumental. Sri Sathya Sai Baba started a snowballing effect by donating Rs. 100,000/– from his Central Trust. Within the next few hours a million was added to this. Many offered help in kind, others came forward to help in person. Under Sri Sathya Sai Baba's direction, a *Seva Dal* Unit started straight away for the areas most affected by the twin natural disasters.

This incident made clear how a spiritual teacher, like Sri Sathya Sai Baba, can motivate and guide people onto the path of service to mankind, spirituality in action, at a time of great need. Indeed, a spiritual leader is not one who doles out "religion" as opium for the masses. Those *Seva Dal* workers who volunteered to help in the worst hit areas worked in a spirit of total dedication, cooking and serving food with love to over twenty thousand people everyday, distributing new *saris, dhotis* and children's clothes made by students of the Satya Sai Women's College in Anantapur.

Addressing an All-India conference of Satya Sai organisations, Sri Sathya Sai Baba said, "Sathya Sai has nothing to do with money. He does not concern himself with your riches, but with your *gunas* (characteristics), your virtues and the quality of your lives. There is no need for money to carry on a *bhajan mandali*, or *satsang*, or a study circle, or even for *Bal Vikas* wherever there are children and *gurus*. And that is not all. *Seva* (service) is the most excellent wealth."

Speaking of the Satya Sai organisation, he said, "The *Sai Samithi* is the thumb; the *Mahila Vibhag* is the forefinger; the *Seva Dal* is the middle finger; the *Bal Vikas* is the ring finger; and the *Bhajan Mandali* is the little finger. They are all limbs of the same hand. They should all co-operate with and help each other."

Sri Sathya Sai Baba pointed to a new direction for *seva* (service). Unlike many others, he underlined the need for *seva* in urban areas. The people who live in cities and towns are rapidly forgetting how to distinguish between human beings and animals. People living in rural areas have preserved, at least to some extent, a few sacred aspects of life such as devotion to God and compassion towards others. They need *seva* only when they are afflicted by droughts, floods, fires and other natural calamities. But in the cities, there is always work to be done in spreading morality, virtue, mercy, charity, brotherhood and love – as they are becoming scarce. So, Sai devotees must set the example of their own lives and exert a healthy influence on their misguided brothers and sisters.

Sri Sathya Sai Baba also said that in *bhajan mandalis*, which were springing up fast in cities, towns and villages, people of all religions could participate since the Sai religion accepts and respects every religion as authentic. It holds that all holy scriptures strive to cleanse the consciousness and to reveal divinity to mankind. "So," he concluded, "encourage everyone to sing their own prayers and share in the joy of congregational *bhajan* singing."

Sri Sathya Sai Baba's guidance is available to the whole vast network of Satya Sai organisations which function under the three wings of the *Seva Samithi*, the *Mahila Vibhag* and the *Seva Dal*. They, in turn, work through and under the Sathya Sai Trusts in every state of India and are controlled by the one Sathya Sai Central Trust. There is also a World Council which co-ordinates the activities of the thousands of Sai organisations in different parts of the world.

"Education without character, science without humanity, commerce without morality are useless and dangerous."

. . . Sri Sathya Sai Baba

21

INFUSING SOUL POWER INTO EDUCATION

The annual Summer Course organised by Sri Sathya Sai Baba has been praised by many people and institutions. What does the Summer Course consist in? What needs does it fulfill?

This course, called the Summer Course on Indian Culture and Spirituality, was started by Sri Sathya Sai Baba to activate youthful dynamism by making students and others more aware of India's great heritage. It is also designed to instill in them the value of virtues such as renunciation, integrity, justice and truthfulness.

Sri Sathya Sai Baba feels that "the current system of education makes no provision for the development of soul power. Our students have forgotten this inner power which is many times more potent than brute force. Soul power nurtures an integrated, harmonious and balanced personality." In his daily evening address during the month of the Summer Course, he relates episodes from the great epics (like the *Ramayana*, the *Mahabharata*, the *Bhagavatam*). These are shown to be guideposts on the right way of everyday life so that the students may realise in which way Scripture has relevance to all times including their own.

Students who attend the Summer Course are chosen through a written entrance examination. About twelve hundred students from all over India and two hundred from other countries attend the Summer Course. They listen everyday to Sri Sathya Sai Baba's evening discourse and to lectures from eminent persons who speak on themes set out in a suitable syllabus by Professor V. K. Gokak. The general subjects that cover the five daily lectures are Indian Culture and Art, World Religions, Great Saints of the World, Systems of Philosophy, Sacred Indian Texts and *Yoga*.

The students sit a written examination at the end of the course and certificates are awarded to those who exceed 50% in given marks. During the course, they stay in the College and follow its daily routine and discipline which are those of a *gurukula*. Boys and girls have separate dormitories, of course, and the same arrangement applies to the observers. Strict rules forbid any social mingling. It has not passed unnoticed that six hundred boys and six hundred girls spend a whole month in close proximity without not so much as exchanging a look. They all go about their own work in an atmosphere of absolute peace. Silence, cleanliness and punctuality are compulsory. Observers and leaders of each separate group have the duty to check on daily routines and discipline.

Students are up at half past four and, after ablutions, participate in the *Omkara suprabhatam* and *nagar sankirtan*. They attend *yoga* classes before bathing and breakfasting. Each morning they hear three lectures and two in the afternoon after lunch. After the tea break, they reassemble for *bhajans* and to hear Sri Sathya Sai Baba's discourse. This last session closes with *bhajans*, this time with Sri Sathya Sai Baba. After they have had their dinner, the students are encouraged to go to bed as their day begins so very early.

It is always heartening to see how well the dining hall is run by the boys of the Satya Sai College and without any help from *Seva Dal* volunteers. These boys, the hosts as it were, cater to more than two thousand people four times everyday in the dining hall which has separate sessions for men and women. The food is vegetarian, clean and simple, but not without a bow to taste and variety. Very systematic planning takes place in the organising, preparing and serving of the food. The boys help in chopping vegetables, making *chapattis*, assisting the cooks whenever required, and in serving the prepared food. The washing up is scrupulous and the dining hall is cleaned methodically after each meal and schedules are adhered to with clock-like precision. Silence reigns supreme during meals. Before they eat, the students chant prayers of thanksgiving to God the Munificent, the giver of the food.

The Summer Course teaches communal living and encourages a spirit of co-operation and friendliness among the various groups of students: the simple living in dormitories with common bathrooms where co-operation becomes vital if discipline and punctuality are to be observed. In every act, they feel the presence of Sri Sathya Sai Baba. They revere him and wish to please him by the righteous conduct that he expects of them. They eagerly look forward to Sundays when their schedule calls on them to do social work. They go to nearby villages where they clean streets while they sing *bhajans*.

Sri Sathya Sai Baba's discourses during the Summer Course cover a wide range of subjects. The most abstruse philosophy is elucidated by him in the simplest way. His inimitable method of narration, his oratory and rhetoric, his marvellous sense of humour, his alliterations and onomatopeia in lucid *Telugu,* help to make his speeches an exquisite treat and a truly heavenly experience.

SAI MODEL OF EDUCATION

1978 saw the application of the Sai model of education at the grassroot level of primary education in the State of Andhra Pradesh in Southern India. For this reason, a ten day orientation course was arranged at Whitefield for the initial six hundred primary school teachers under the personal supervision of Sri Sathya Sai Baba. What was the principal aim of this orientation training?

Sri Sathya Sai Baba explained: "*Bharatiya* (Indian) culture believes in the concept of the happiness of all beings. Real *vidya* (learning) is that which brings liberation from perpetual birth and death. Therefore, along with the knowledge of how to earn a living, people should be taught the real *vidya* of how to build character from an early and impressionable age. True education must din into children the value of *satya* (truth), *dharma* (righteousness), *shanti* (peace) and *prema* (love), reverence of their elders and *gurus*, service to the community and the love of all faiths and all peoples. From a tender age, children must be taught the care of their bodies and encouraged to lead disciplined lives, for the body is the temple of the Divine."

"Primary teachers should themselves be exemplary in what they practise and preach. Otherwise children, and they are shrewd, will not respect teachers or their words. The training course is to help remind the teachers of their sacred role in moulding the character of children and in sowing the seeds of love, discipline and patriotism in their hearts."

Many of the teachers who did the training course felt that it was a spiritual experience. They readily admitted that not only had they absorbed universal values from the discourses of Sri Sathya Sai Baba, but they had also been taught lessons in conduct by observing the students of the Satya Sai College who demonstrated enormous dedication in all they did. They were surprised to note that all their duties were performed as offerings to God.

Several teachers became convinced that spirituality is not only to be delved into at the end of one's life, but that it should be an integral part of life from childhood onwards. They were pleased and gratified to learn that the orientation course was aimed at emphasising the unity of all religions and the universal good as upheld in all the world religions. They acknowledged that the Sathya Sai system of education promotes integration of thought, word and deed and shows life to be a way of living and loving.

"In ancient days, by the power of mantra, an aeroplane could fly."

. . . Sri Sathya Sai Baba

22

THE SACRED THREAD CEREMONY AND THE *SAI GAYATRI*

In many *Hindu* homes, a variety of rites and rituals are celebrated. *Ayusha homam* (first birthday celebration), for instance, when the ritual includes piercing the earlobes of the child; *anna praasana* (the first cereal given to the child); *aksharabhyasa* (initiation into formal learning); *upanayanam* (the bestowal of the sacred thread).

Sri Sathya Sai Baba celebrates such occasions with some of his devotees. Mr. N. Kasturi writes in the second volume of *Satyam Shivam Sundaram* of an incident that occurred during a sacred thread ceremony. Suddenly it was discovered that the boys who were to receive the sacred thread had not had their ears pierced in infancy. Sri Sathya Sai Baba waved his hand and materialised as many gold earring wires as were needed and then pierced their ears himself.

The 17th of May has become a red letter day in my family. That was the day in 1978 that Sri Sathya Sai Baba chose for the *upanayanam* of my two sons, Ashok and Vivek. That morning, fifteen members of my family travelled to Brindavan and gathered in the interview room. Sri Sathya Sai Baba entered the room at the exact moment appointed and showered us with gifts of grace. He materialised *vibhuti* and distributed it among us all. We garlanded him and bowed at his feet.

The ceremony began with Sri Sathya Sai Baba asking my sons if they knew the meaning of *upanayanam*. He then explained to us the significance of the rite. The word *upanayanam* literally means near *(upa)* and sight *(nayanam)*. *Nayanam*, meaning eye, also signifies here the opening of the inner eye, the divine eye of man. Man is born the first time to his mother, and the second time when he receives the sacred thread, since with it he receives the holy *Gayatri Upadesha*. This takes him to his third birth which is said to be when he becomes *vipra* (a wise man). After the third birth, he is set to travel on the road to realisation of *Brahman* (God). Hence, a real *Brahmin* (or *Brahmana*) is one who has realised *Brahman*.

All at once, Sri Sathya Sai Baba's right hand made the familiar circular movements. As Ashok and Vivek looked on breathlessly, two *upaveetams* (sacred threads) appeared from his hand. The threads had arrived fresh and yellow and neatly tied up. Sri Sathya Sai Baba carefully unravelled them and explained the significance of each of the three strands tied together in the knot of *Brahma*.

"The three strands represent the three worlds: *Bhu*, the earth we live on; *Bhuvaha*, the atmosphere; and *Suvaha*, the heavens. They also denote *Trikalam* (the three time stages), past, present and future, and *Trigunam* (the three attributes of man), *satva, rajas* and *tamas*."

The *Gayatri Mantra* starts with *Om*, a word of three separate sounds, A, U and M. He than demonstrated the right way to chant the word *Om* (or *Aum*) with correct low, high and low intonations. He advised the boys to chant the *Gayatri Mantra* everyday saying one could chant it for daily protection. It is wrong to think that women may not chant this *mantra* when the very name *Gayatri* is that of a goddess. Given that it is the name of a female deity, what basis is there for prohibiting it to women? In olden days, *upanayanam* was performed for girls as well. In the *Ramayana*, we find that King *Janaka* performed the sacred thread ceremony for his daughter, *Sita*. The important thing is the initiating of every individual, male or female, to the sacred and shielding power of the *Gayatri Mantra*.

Sri Sathya Sai Baba then went on to explain that in the course of time the sacred thread given to a girl became the *dhorakam*, the thread that is put around her neck when she is married. Before the wedding, she is given it to tie around her wrist. Equally, she wears sacred threads round her neck and wrists after the performance of important *vratas* (fasts) and *pujas* (rites) and the saying of certain prayers.

All this is true for *Om* chanting too. Everyone can and must chant *mantras* that do good not only to themselves but also to others. Both the *Gayatri* and the *Om* are universal *mantras*.

'Gayantam Triyati iti Gayatri': *Gayatri* is that which protects the one who chants it. In other words, the *Gayatri Mantra* acts as a *raksha* (protective talisman) for those who always utter it. Sri Sathya Sai Baba explained its characteristics. It is *Shabda Brahman* (God in the form of sound); it is *charachara mayi* (that which is connected to mobility and immobility); it is *jyotir mayi* (that which is of the light); it is *vang mayi* (that

which is connected with speech); it is *nityananda mayi* (that which is connected with infinite bliss); it is *paratpara mayi* (that which is connected with this and other worlds); it is *maya mayi* (that which is of illusionary nature); and it is *shri mayi* (that which is connected with aspects of prosperity/ fullness).

He taught the boys to repeat after him the sacred sounds of the *Gayatri Mantra:*

Aum Bhūr Bhūvah Suvāhā
Tat Savitūr Varenyam
Bhargo Dévasya dheemahí
Dhiyó yó nāh prachodayaat.

After that, Sri Sathya Sai Baba applied turmeric powder to the sacred threads. He made both my sons and ourselves, the parents, hold the threads in the centre and himself held them as he blessed them. Then he carefully put one around the neck of each boy and blessed them by sprinkling grains of rice on them. He then gave each boy a sacred *mantra* of his own, covering himself and the boys, one after the other, with a towel and whispering into the ear of the recipient alone. This is the personal *mantra* which is kept secret for greater potency. It has to be repeated regularly and daily in a spirit of dedication and devotion. After this, he asked the elders to bless the boys.

Sri Sathya Sai Baba explained the true significance of *mantras*. These days, rituals are followed and meaningless actions accepted as custom because people are too indolent to inquire into their real meaning. The word *mantra* is a composite of *manana* and *trayate* and means that which saves through constant reflection on its meaning. The *Gayatri Mantra* is a prayer addressed to the universal intelligence to kindle the *dhee shakti* (the discriminatory power that enables man to analyse himself and to realise his true nature). Initiation into the *Gayatri Mantra* sets man on the road to exploring the reality of the divinity within him. J.B.S. Haldane wrote that the *Gayatri Mantra* ought to be inscribed on the door of every laboratory in the world. Sri Sathya Sai Baba said, "Westerners have investigated the vibrations produced by this *mantra*. They found that when it is recited correctly, as laid down in the *Vedas*, lustre is evidenced in a circular form; but when said disregarding the pronunciation and right accents, nothing happens and there is only darkness."

He than chanted the *Gayatri Mantra* to demonstrate how it should be recited with all the correct intonations. He started with *AUM* and said that it is very important to observe the correct way of reciting the *pranava mantra (AUM)*. The 'A' sound must begin in the *naabhi* (navel) and rise gradually as it turns into the next sound, 'U', which must originate in the throat. This must be taken to a crescendo to complete the inhalation. Then the 'M' sound is slowly and gradually exhaled. (This breathing in and breathing out process through AUM can be performed in another way as well, known as the *Hamsa Gayatri* method. Here, SO is inhaled and HAM is exhaled; together they form the *mantra* 'SOHAM' in both breaths.) Sri Sathya Sai Baba showed us how the timbre of the voice must be both majestic and even during the rise and fall of each syllable of the *mantra*.

The exact meaning of the *Gayatri Mantra* is as follows: "*AUM*. O Divine Power, you who illumine the great Sun and the three worlds of Earth, Air and Heaven, we implore you for that illumination which will lead us from darkness into light." Sri Sathya Sai Baba explained that, in essence, this means, "O Divine Mother, our hearts are filled with darkness. Please lead us away from this darkness by nurturing the illumination within us."

The *Gayatri Mantra* is in three parts; praise, meditation and prayer. First the Divine is praised, then it is meditated upon with reverence and, lastly, the appeal is made to the Divine to awaken and strengthen the intellect and the discrimination (between good and evil) of man. It is addressed to the Immanent and the Transcendent Divine, and to *Savitir (*that from which all is born). The *Gayatri Mantra* is considered the essence of the teaching of the *Vedas* (*veda* means knowledge). The *Gayatri Mantra* is usually to be said at dawn, midday and at dusk. But, God is beyond temporality and one can say it always and everywhere.

Sri Sathya Sai Baba recommended the boys to recite the *Gayatri Mantra* when they bath, thus making of the bath an *abhishekam* (offering) to God. Instead of humming film tunes in the bath, they ought to chant the *Gayatri Mantra* with purity of mind. Bathing makes the body clean and, while cleaning the body, let the mind and intellect also be cleansed by the *Gayatri Mantra*.

He told the boys never to forget the *Gayatri Mantra* as "it is a treasure you must guard all through your lives so that it guards you in its turn. You should recite it several times a day, at least. It will protect you from harm."

When he had explained the meaning and importance of the *mantra*, Sri Sathya Sai Baba told the boys to ask him questions if they still had any doubts about it. In answer to their question, he explained about changing the sacred thread's position from left to right. He then emphasised that one should follow rituals only when one understands their inner significance and not because a priest tells you to. He then related an anecdote about a priest's son who thought it was necessary to cover any cats in the house with baskets before praying or performing *puja*. The real reason for this was that his father had once done that to prevent a cat from soiling an area that had just been cleaned.

Sri Sathya Sai Baba allowed the boys to do *paada namaskara* (bowing to the feet) and blessed them. He gave *prasad* (blessed food) to all and accepted *pranams* (respectful bows) and garlands. We performed *aarati* to him with a sense of unending joy and with complete contentment.

On our way home, we remembered an occasion in Brindavan in 1977. Gandhikota Subramanya Sastry, a noted scholar, gave a talk in *Telugu*, which Dr. Bhagavantam simultaneously translated, in the presence of Sri Sathya Sai Baba.

After a general talk on spirituality and on *avataras,* Sri Sastry recited for the very first time the *Sai Gayatri* composed by him:

Sayeeshwaraya Vidmahé
Sathya Dévaya Dheemahí
Tannassarva prachodayaat.

Then the erudite *shastri* presented another and alternative verse:

Yo Dévā Sathya Sayeena
Buddhim Dharmādhi Gocharam
Prérayeth Tasya Téjaha
Tadvarenyamupasmahé

The *Gayatri* prayer is thus addressed to Sathya Sai *Deva* and entreats Him "to enter our minds and inspire such thoughts as would make our deeds beneficent." The meaning of the verse is as follows:

"O, Lord Sathya Sai, make my thoughts search in the direction of *Dharma, Satya, Prema* and *Shanti*. I pray for Your effulgence in directing my thoughts and my intelligence in this way."

In addition to this *Gayatri* prayer, which conforms with the traditional *Gayatri Mantra*, the *shastri* explained how the *Sai Gayatri* is a *chatur vimshathi Gayatri* (a *Gayatri* prayer of 24 letters/syllables), 8 syllables for each of the 3 lines. He said that the *mantra* had come into his mind of its own due to divine will. He felt happy to be offering it to *Devata Sayeeshwara* in the way of ancient sages who were called sages because they had "seen" a *mantra*. He was very glad to be associated with the composing of this *Gayatri* prayer. Finally, he asked everyone to recite the Sathya Sai *Gayatri* 108 times a day and thus earn divine grace and blessings.

PART II

Some Sai Experiences . . .

"More than all other forms of prema, man's first endeavour should be to fix his love on the Lord."

. . .Sri Sathya Sai Baba

1

SOME FAITHFUL OLD SAI DEVOTEES

Srimati Sunderamma is one of the old devotees who have known Sri Sathya Sai Baba since he was a boy of sixteen. Her father, Seshagiri Rao, came to Sri Sathya Sai Baba after her and because of her but it was he who was instrumental in starting several *pujas* and *sevas* that are widespread today.

"In Swami's discourses on the *Bhagavatham* during the recent Summer Course (1978), he spoke a great deal about the sacred relationship between *Krishna* and the *gopikas*. As he told these stories, I felt he was relating incidents from his own early life. There is such a striking similarity between the two, so many parallels between *Krishna leelas* and Sai *leelas*." Sunderamma went on reminiscing and recalled many episodes which she felt fortunate to have witnessed.

How did she come to know Sri Sathya Sai Baba? Sunderamma said that one day long ago, her mother-in-law and her daughter, Sucharita, who was six at the time, went to Puttaparthi to see a relative of theirs called Karnam Subbamma. This lady, Karnam Subbamma, figures prominently in Sri Sathya Sai Baba's early life since it was she who, believing him to be someone 'special,' helped to organise *bhajans* for him. While Sucharita was playing, she heard young Sathya Sai Baba (then sixteen years old) say to her grandmother, "This girl's mother is not at all well and her life is in danger. She is pregnant and wants a son as she already has three daughters.

Her mother will indeed give birth to a boy. Her father, too, is unwell and has eczema all over the body."

Sucharita's presence went unnoticed by her elders. Later, she went to the *bhajan* session and marvelled at how a handsome youth was worshipped like a god.

When she came back to Bangalore, Sucharita told her mother (Sunderamma): "Sai Baba, who they all say is God, said your life is in danger." Sunderamma's mother was disturbed because she had not wanted her daughter to know this. And, after hearing what Sri Sathya Sai Baba had said, Sunderamma's mind was in a turmoil of fear. A few days later, she heard that Sri Sathya Sai Baba was in Bangalore (in Chamarajpet) and urged her husband, Mr. Sharma, to take her to him. Her husband did not have much faith in *sadhus* and *sannyasis* and so, although he took her there, he remained outside in the street. He told his wife to see Sri Sathya Sai Baba and to come away as soon as she could.

Sunderamma went in and found that her pregnancy made the other women waiting make way for her and, as a result, she was the first one to go in to see Sri Sathya Sai Baba. He looked at her and said, "Yes, I know her little daughter who has been to Puttaparthi." Then he blessed her. He slipped away without anyone being aware that he was gone, but returned to sing *bhajans*.

Later, Sunderamma's husband told her an astounding story. As he was strolling about in the street, waiting for his wife to leave the house, that boy with the curly mop on his head approached him and said, "Are you not the husband of the lady who has come to see me? You are not at all well. You have eczema, all over." He waved his hand and materialised a banana which he gave him saying, "Eat it with the skin on it. Your disease will vanish and you will be well." Mr. Sharma said that the boy then disappeared as suddenly as he had appeared, leaving him stunned. But he ate the banana as directed and rushed off home to fetch his mother and his daughter to join in singing *bhajans*.

This then was the advent of Sri Sathya Sai Baba into Sunderamma's life in 1942. The family has had the continuing good fortune of close association with Sri Sathya Sai Baba ever since then. Her sister, Sharadamma, explained that there had been danger to Sunderamma's life during her confinement, and that Sri Sathya Sai Baba had saved her. She had a son as predicted by him.

The women were drawn, more each day, to Sri Sathya Sai Baba, but the men were rather sceptical about a boy who appeared to attract so many women devotees.

Sunderamma's father, Seshagiri Rao, objected when she and her widowed sister wanted to go to Puttaparthi. In the end, he had to give in to their persistence and he took them to the station to see them safely away. He returned home, and sat in meditation before a picture of Shirdi Sai Baba. When he opened his eyes he was astounded to see that, in the picture before him, Sri Sathya Sai Baba was installed in the heart of Shirdi Sai Baba. Mr. Seshagiri Rao could not believe his eyes. He kept looking at it and staring at it, but the image in the heart remained, bright and clear. How could this be? he asked himself. Was it possible that this boy was the reincarnation of Shirdi Sai Baba? What else could explain the sudden appearance of Sri Sathya Sai Baba in Shirdi Sai Baba's heart? This wondrous event kindled faith in Seshagiri Rao.

The very next time his daughters went to Puttaparthi, he went with them. And a very short while after that trip, he became one of the staunchest devotees of the young Sai Baba.

Sunderamma recalled how, once in Puttaparthi, her father went into a trance for three days. For days after that he was in such delirious ecstasy that Sri Sathya Sai Baba avoided direct contact with him until he had calmed down.

Something marvellous had happened to Seshagiri Rao. Sri Sathya Sai Baba had granted him a divine vision: he had shown him the third eye of *Shiva* on his, Sri Sathya Sai Baba's own face. This had put him into the trance, and after that experience, he felt as though he never wanted to leave Sri Sathya Sai Baba. He settled in Puttaparthi and formulated regular modes of worship for Sri Sathya Sai Baba. Other members of his family also tried to "be with Swami as often as possible," and for his part, Sri Sathya Sai Baba showered such devotees with his grace for the deep and strong devotion they displayed towards him.

The journey to Puttaparthi in those days was both hard and hazardous. Sunderamma came from a lower middle-class family who possessed no cars, or any other form of transportation. So, each time they journeyed to Puttaparthi, they had to face a fair amount of difficulties. But they were always undeterred and looked forward eagerly to seeing Sri Sathya Sai Baba. Every trip had to be carefully planned in advance, preparing adequate food, supplies and cooking utensils. At that time, there were no shops in Puttaparthi and one had to trek to Bukkapatnam to buy even a box of matches. And there was no way of reaching Puttaparthi directly from Bangalore. One had first to take a train, then a bus upto a point, then continue by bullock cart and, finally, walk across the river bed to reach the Old Temple where Sri Sathya Sai Baba used to live.

Many were the trials and tribulations they faced on those journeys. Sunderamma described one of their journeys. Their party was made up of about thirty people and they started out from Bangalore in three hired bullock carts in good time to reach Puttaparthi for the *Dassera* celebrations. In the middle of the trip they were caught in heavy rains. Nevertheless, they asked the cart drivers to carry on for, in those early days, there were people in the area who did not believe in Sri Sathya Sai Baba who not only refused help to his devotees, but actually hindered them and could turn nasty, particularly with female devotees. So, the group kept going even though it was raining heavily. At one stage, the carts had to go through swirling waters. The cart drivers baulked at the fast flowing current lest the carts capsized and the bullocks carried away in the torrent. It was becoming dark and there were big black clouds looming over them streaming rain. Sunderamma and others desperately prayed to Sri Sathya Sai Baba.

After a while, four tribesmen appeared. These are people known as *Kaadu manushyuru* (forestmen) who live in the wilder regions. They were hefty-looking men and were undoubtedly very strong, for they said they would bodily carry each bullock cart across the torrent. They asked for a lot of money but they did what they said they would. They untethered the bullocks and let them swim across; then they lifted each cart very skilfully and swam across with each one without tipping it over. It was a remarkable feat.

As the pilgrims again set off on their way, they encountered another obstacle. At a place called Kothacharavu they came to a halt: the one-track path was flooded and it was impossible to travel on in the bullock carts. There was no shelter anywhere around and it was late at night. And they were miserable thinking that they ought to have been in Puttaparthi celebrating the *Durga Ashthami* festival of *Dassera*. Instead, here they were, stranded in the rain and the dark and without even the humblest shelter. The children were hungry and crying. It was cold. The few local people they had seen had refused all help. They felt abandoned.

But, a Muslim youth arrived on the scene wearing white pyjamas and *kurta*. Learning of their sorry plight, he offered to help. He guided them to a nearby school, but they found it locked. He left them and returned with the key and took them inside. There they sheltered for the rest of the night and ate the food they had brought with them. He also produced a lamp and then left, saying he would return in the morning to help them get started on their way again. He declined to stay with them as, he said, his clothes were sopping wet and he wanted to go home to get dried and changed.

The boy was back promptly in the morning. The children demanded their milk, but the women were helpless. Once again, the boy was equal to the task. He brought milk from somewhere and then helped to organise a makeshift stove with bricks. So all were able to have their morning milk and coffee before setting off. They wanted to thank the boy, but he had vanished.

At last they reached Puttaparthi. Eager devotees came rushing up to greet them and asked, "Are you Sunderamma and her party? Since yesterday, Swami has been talking of you. He worried all the time and said you were having problems en route. In the evening, he told us to carry on with the festivities, went to his room and went into a trance. Only now has he re-emerged to give *darshan* and join in the *pujas*."

Sunderamma and her group rushed to Sri Sathya Sai Baba who welcomed them with evident warmth but chided them for journeying unmindful of the rain and all the attendant hazards. It came to them then in a flash that he had come to their rescue at every perilous stage and that it was he himself who had been the helpful young Muslim. How was it possible not to love such a god?

Sunderamma continued to reminisce. On another occasion, also during travels through heavy rain when visibility was very poor, the bullocks of the cart she was sitting in had nearly stepped into a huge well overflowing with water – just as they were about to walk into the well, strong invisible hands hauled the cart and bullocks back to safety without upsetting the balance to the smallest degree. The slightest tilt would have sent the cart and everyone in it into the well. "Those strong hands that pulled the cart and bullocks back to safety, whose hands could they have been but Swami's?" she asked.

She recalls how, although every trip was full of hurdles and perils, not once did any harm befall them; nor did they ever suffer any injury or pain. Quite the contrary, each time in Puttaparthi they had so much enjoyment that time seemed to stand still. They had lovely *bhajan* sessions and other occasions when they sang of Sri Sathya Sai Baba. And he took them very often to the Chitravati sands where he materialised delicious sweets such as candy, *laddoos, amruta* and other things. He would make them climb the hillock near the *kalpataru* tree and take from it whichever fruit or sweet they asked for.

It was on one such occasion, as they were slowly going up that hillock, that Sri Sathya Sai Baba suddenly went ahead swiftly and called out to them to look carefully. Then they saw a huge halo around him, a vibrant circle of moving light like a *chakra* (wheel). As he stood there, they gazed at him and felt one with eternity, as if Lord *Vishnu* stood before them with his *chakra*. He called each one of them as if to ensure that they had all seen the divine vision.

In a while, Sri Sathya Sai Baba joined them and behaved as though nothing unusual or extraordinary had happened. All those who had witnessed the vision felt so radiant with the experience that they felt even greater adoration for Sri Sathya Sai Baba than before. "He is God, when He chooses He shows such *leelas*." Such was their faith. Even so, they were happy that he mixed with them so easily and informally. They felt no inhibitions and, as they fully accepted him in their hearts, he was able to do all that he wanted. His *leelas* greatly pleased both him and them.

Slowly and steadily the volume of people going to Puttaparthi increased. There were families who travelled regularly from Madras and Bangalore; Nagamani Purnaiya, Sakamma and others who became devotees made frequent visits. With the steady growth of devotees, Sri Sathya Sai Baba introduced a few restrictions into the informality.

Once, Sri Sathya Sai Baba materialised idols of *Vishnu* and *Lakshmi*, his consort. The idol of *Vishnu* he gave to a lady from Madras who was a devotee of Lord *Venkateswara*. The *Lakshmi* idol he gave to Sunderamma who performed *puja* to it faithfully, carrying it with her wherever she went.

On a trip to Puttaparthi, when she left the train at Penukonda Station, she discovered that her gold chain was broken and that her *mangalya* (sacred symbol of marriage) had fallen off. Discreetly she searched for it everywhere, but in vain. She could not speak of her loss openly as her mother-in-law and other elders would not only have been angry with her, but worse, they would never have forgiven her for losing the sacred *mangalya*. They would have thought its loss a portent of evil to come. Sunderamma too was worried by such thoughts and decided that she would ask Sri Sathya Sai Baba to set things right.

But, in Puttaparthi, she did not have the opportunity to see Sri Sathya Sai Baba privately even for a minute. He was in the middle of organising a wedding ceremony for the idols of *Vishnu* and *Lakshmi* that he had materialised, especially as both the lady from Madras and Sunderamma were there and had brought the two idols. He announced that it would be a good thing to bring together the long separated pair of *Vishnu* and *Lakshmi* and, with this in mind, he was arranging the wedding. He went about making arrangements as if for a real wedding. Soon all the devotees got into the spirit of it. Sri Sathya Sai Baba gathered the village musicians, drummers and other festive people as well as the different materials required for the rituals.

Sunderamma was in no mood to join in the festivities, but was obliged to do so since she was the mother of the bride, as owner of the *Lakshmi* idol. And too, being a talented singer, she was inevitably in demand as the lead singer at *bhajan* time. And so she was asked to start the auspicious songs.

Sunderamma was annoyed, irritated and angry beyond description and her anger was directed mainly at Sri Sathya Sai Baba. "What is so wonderful about this idea of marriage between two idols when I am so worried about my *mangalya*, the symbol of my real marriage?" she asked herself furiously. In her mind she challenged Sri Sathya Sai Baba: "If you are really the God we all think you are, you will do something about my *mangalya*. I cannot go home and face my family without it."

The wedding was a grand affair. The two small idols were resplendent in their wedding costumes. Priests intoned ancient *mantras*. All of a sudden, Sri Sathya Sai Baba materialised a *mangalya* for the *Vishnu* idol to tie around the neck of the *Lakshmi* idol. The devotees were thrilled. When the wedding ceremony was over, he went to Sunderamma and whispered in her ear, "I have done all this only for your sake. Now you may take the *mangalya* from the *Lakshmi* idol and put it on your chain."

Sunderamma was moved to tears of joy when she saw that the *mangalya* was exactly like the one she had lost with even the white gem in the centre. How could she ever thank Sri Sathya Sai Baba for having gone through an entire wedding gamefully for her sake alone? Sunderamma then recalled how each time Sri Sathya Sai Baba played a *leela* she would compose a song about it and sing it. All the members of the *bhajan* group as well as her family joined in the composing and singing of these songs. Her two young daughters, too, helped with the composing and singing and more, on certain occasions at Sai festivals, they would dance to the songs. It was on such a special occasion that a member of the *bhajan* group, Mani Bashyam, composed a *shloka* on *vibhuti* which has remained popular in Sai circles:

Paramam pavitram Bābā vibhuthim
Paramam vichitram leelā vibhuthim
Paramātmā Ishtartha moksha pradhātam
Bābā vibhuthim idam āshrayāmi

Translated this means:

The *vibhuti* of Baba is most sacred
The *vibhuti* of his *leela* is wondrous
To that which loved by the *Paramatma* and which liberates
To that Baba-*vibhuti* I offer salutation

Sunderamma said that Sri Sathya Sai Baba had always showered her family with his grace. She related an incident of this grace.

Once, in Puttaparthi, her son became very ill with a high temperature. As Sunderamma was worrying about him, Sri Sathya Sai Baba walked in to call her and others to *bhajans*. He found the boy languishing in fever. He wanted to take his temperature and put a thermometer into the two-year-old child's mouth. When they took it out of his mouth, she saw that he had bitten into the glass and swallowed the fragments and the mercury. She was hysterical and immediately turned on Sri Sathya Sai Baba, crying, "Why did you have to put the thermometer in the boy's mouth? Now you have killed my child."

Sri Sathya Sai Baba stared hard at her. Then, without a word, he leaned over the child and vigorously massaged his stomach. Then, still silent, he left and went to the *bhajan* hall. After a while, as Sunderamma lifted her son, she found globules of mercury and bits of broken glass under his clothes in the bed. Everyone was astonished. Deliriously happy, Sunderamma sped away to thank Sri Sathya Sai Baba, but she found him in a trance. So they sang *bhajans* and Sunderamma's voice rose high above all the others' in the fullness of her devotional fervour. Her son recovered completely the same night.

Afterwards, Sri Sathya Sai Baba said, "I had to bring your son back to total normalcy or you would not have left me in peace." Sunderamma's kind of old devotee, with absolutely unshakable devotion to their Lord, and yet unafraid of speaking their mind to him, are rare today.

After this, Sunderamma continued the weekly *bhajan* singing with great dedication and without interruption for an entire year. Her father, Seshagiri Rao, thought that they should celebrate the completion of the year of *bhajan*-singing in suitable style. Each member of the family thought up a different way to celebrate the anniversary in befitting manner, but it was Seshagiri Rao's idea that was adopted: *akhanda bhajans* (unbroken *bhajans*) for one whole day and one whole night. The decision having been taken, they got down to planning the performance at their house – which songs to sing, what *prasadam* to distribute, pooling of resources to obtain the ingredients of the *prasadam*. This was particularly tricky as, in those days, there was rationing of rice and the system had to be worked out fairly in cash and in kind.

After making all the preliminary arrangements, father and daughter went to Puttaparthi to announce their intention to Sri Sathya Sai Baba. He was very happy to hear of their plans and responded startlingly, "I have come only for this reason, for the sake of my devotees. Go ahead with the *akhanda bhajans*. I will go there and be with you throughout the singing."

Sunderamma explained that upto that moment they had planned only a very simple celebration. But, if Sri Sathya Sai Baba was himself going to attend, then she felt she ought to make more eleborate arrangements. Then Sri Sathya Sai Baba said he would take charge of all the arrangements. He asked her to book a place in town and to have the *akhanda bhajans* sung there so that all those who wanted to attend could do so more conveniently. He also advisd her to ask other devotees to assist in the event.

Sunderamma was in a quandary at this unexpected turn of events. To cope with an occasion such as it was turning out to be was a gigantic task in those days when even transportation was very difficult. She calculated that about a hundred regular devotees might turn up for the first *akhanda bhajans* and so had *prasadam* prepared for that number. However, hundreds of devotees turned up on the day. They had learned of the event by word of mouth and in dreams and visions of Sri Sathya Sai Baba. Sunderamma became anxious about how she would provide enough *prasadam* to go round.

Puja to Sri Shirdi Sai Baba's and Sri Sathya Sai Baba's images was performed under a gaily bedecked floral canopy. Sri Sathya Sai Baba materialised a silver figurine of Sri Shirdi Sai Baba to keep beside a large bust of Sri Shirdi Sai Baba especially made for the occasion. Then, with circular movements of his hand, he produced 108 golden flowers for the *puja*. After *archana* (offering with *mantras*) of rare flowers, Seshagiri Rao performed *paada puja* (worship of the feet) to Sri Sathya Sai Baba who lighted the *akhanda jyoti* (everlasting flame) at the *bhajan* meeting.

Sunderamma then requested Sri Sathya Sai Baba to come into the kitchen and pronounce *akshaya* (limitless) blessings over the food. He looked at the cooked food and loudly said "*akshaya*" thrice. Then he sprinkled water on the food and left.

Sunderamma remembers with awe how food prepared for a hundred people fed several thousand people easily, even generously. The pot containing the *prasadam* simply never became empty! At last, before leaving the kitchen, Sunderamma entreated Sri Sathya Sai Baba to let the pot be empty and then it was easily emptied. "Such was the nature of

Swami's blessing that it ensured an unending stream of food," said Sunderamma.

The event was truly remarkable. The first *akhanda jyoti*, organised by Seshagiri Rao, has led to the lighting of thousands of other *akhanda jyotis* on *akhanda bhajan* day in *Sai Samithi bhajan* centres throughout the world. Though Seshagiri Rao is no more, Sri Sathya Sai Baba himself recalled his contribution on one such occasion, by referring to him as "the devotee who was the first to light a *jyoti* to Swami."

Sunderamma has never celebrated any family occasion like the naming of a child even without either Sri Sathya Sai Baba's presence or his blessings. He also celebrated with her her *shashti-abdapoorthi* (sixtieth anniversary) at Puttaparthi when, once again, he materialised a *mangalya* for her.

The family has some beautiful letters addressed to them by Sri Sathya Sai Baba. A postcard he wrote to Sunderamma's young daughters is very interesting. He had retained their mother in Puttaparthi to celebrate Professor Kasturi's sixtieth birthday, so he wrote to comfort the girls who were in Mysore at the time. He wrote, "You have your dog in the daytime to play with and to look after. Remember, at night you have your God with you to look after you. Each one of you will always have me beside you. Thus, you will not be three, but six people." The girls cherish and treasure this affectionate epistle.

Sunderamma says that, in retrospect, "Those olden days were golden days, when Swami had more time for us. But even now, Swami finds the time for old devotees and continues to shower his grace on us. It is possible only for Swami to keep all of us devotees contented, for he is divine. It would be humanly impossible to remember all the trivial details of every old devotee's family and to remember the development of the younger generation."

Sharadamma, Sunderamma's sister, lives in Puttaparthi and is a dedicated devotee of Sri Sathya Sai Baba. When asked "how she and her family began worshipping a young boy like Sathya as God," her answer was simple and direct.

"When we saw him we knew he was God. We never had an iota of doubt. Our *bhajans* were all for him and we were immensely happy singing songs to his glory. To us he was *Rama, Krishna, Parameswara* – there was never any hesitation in our minds. Our *bhakti* for him came spontaneously and from the depths of our hearts. We always tried to obtain his *darshan, sparshan* (touch) and *sambhashana* (speech) at every possible opportunity, knowing that it was the greatest good fortune we could ever have."

They recognised the divinity in him and remained steadfast in their faith. This has been the attitude of the first lot of devotees – unwavering devotion. Today there are millions of Sai devotees all over the world, but they sometimes ask themselves, "Is he really divine?" Whereas, the early devotees easily recognised his divinity more than forty years ago when Sri Sathya Sai Baba seemed to be only a young village boy. How much opposition and ridicule they must have faced then can be imagined. But, so true were they in their devotion that they nonetheless worshipped him. Slowly, many others swelled their ranks, having heard of him or having had dreams or mystical visions.

Sharadamma described those early days when Sri Sathya Sai Baba, in a white *dhoti* and *jhubba*, looking much like any other young boy, visited their homes and stayed with them.

He did not allow them to speak of him as someone with extraordinary powers. He always helped with their chores: cooking, fetching water, looking after the children. Often, after a *bhajan* session, he would escort them back to their own villages. He would carry a hurricane lamp to light the way and a stick to ward off the many snakes that infested Puttaparthi in those days. He saw them all safely back to their homes before retiring to the Old *Mandir*. He never ate any specially prepared food, but sat down to eat with all the other children and shared in whatever they were given. And he never sat down to eat before he had made sure that everyone else had been served.

He used to look after Sharadamma's nieces during the holidays when their parents were absent. "How affectionately and how artistically he used to string flowers and deck the girls' tresses, more fondly than their own mother," mused Sharadamma. The children never felt homesick or missed their parents. On the contrary, at the beginning of term, they would cry when they had to leave Sri Sathya Sai Baba to return home.

This is true also today of the students of the College at Brindavan. The boys who live in the College hostel are extremely reluctant to leave on holiday and, indeed, Sri Sathya Sai Baba has to force them to go home to their parents.

Sharadamma's father, Seshagiri Rao, used to perform regular *puja* to Sri Sathya Sai Baba in the temple, ringing the bell and offering camphor *aarati*. Once, during the *aarati*, there was no one else in the temple, so Seshagiri Rao devised a way to ring the bell and perform the *aarati* on his own. He lit the *aarati* and ran back to the bell and so on. It is essential for *dipa aradhana* (worship with flame) to have both things going simultaneously. But, Seshagiri Rao was an old man and this was exhausting for him. As he turned, panting, once more to dash off down the temple to ring the bell, he heard it ringing. Much relieved that someone had come in and was ringing the bell, he turned his full attention to the *aarati*. The bell continued to ring for the ten or so minutes it was required to ring, but Seshagiri Rao was stunned to discover that it was ringing by itself. There was no one there.

That evening, Sri Sathya Sai Baba said to him, "My hands hurt from ringing the bell for you and that too for *puja* of me!"

Old Seshagiri Rao lived at Puttaparthi in total surrender to Sri Sathya Sai Baba in whom he perceived divinity. Sri Sathya Sai Baba often played pranks on him knowing that he would quite naturally accept everything he said and did to him.

Even after her father's death, Sharadamma remained in Puttaparthi. Sri Sathya Sai Baba cured her unbearable headaches and, more significantly, transformed her nature by granting her several divine experiences.

She remembers an occasion when she had arranged *samardhana puja* in her village. It included the feeding of *Brahmins*. While the *puja* was still under way, an old beggar arrived seeking alms. Sharadamma sent him away saying, "Come later, the *puja* is not over yet." The whole occasion went very well. The old beggar never returned for the promised food and Sharadamma soon forgot about him.

A few months later, in Puttaparthi, she asked Sri Sathya Sai Baba to pay her a visit at home. He looked at her severely and said, "You invite me now, but if I come to you, you may chase me away saying the *puja* is not over yet." With a shock Sharadamma realised that it had been Sri Sathya Sai Baba who had come to her that day to test her. She bitterly regretted her action of that day, but recognised that she had been taught a very good lesson: never to turn away a hungry person who comes begging for food.

Sharadamma spoke of another incident. Her sister's son became very ill soon after he was born. The distraught mother mentally prayed to Sri Sathya Sai Baba and took a vow, "Please save my child. If you do I will offer you his hair."

The boy recovered. But some time later, when he was about eighteen months old, his hair became very knotty and dirty-looking despite all his mother's efforts to keep it clean and neat. No one could understand it.

While the family were in Puttaparthi on one of their periodic visits, Sri Sathya Sai Baba saw the child with the awful hair and remarked, "Why do people make a vow if they do not intend to keep it?" Nobody knew what he meant. But that night, the mother suddenly remembered her prayer when her son had been so sick and the vow she had taken about his hair. She was aghast to think that she could so completely put it out of her mind once the crisis had passed. She begged Sri Sathya Sai Baba's forgiveness and sought his permission to celebrate the hair-offering ceremony. This was given and the occasion went off very well with Sri Sathya Sai Baba himself arranging it all. The older devotees frequently speak with nostalgia of such events.

Sharadamma explained that Sri Sathya Sai Baba never allowed any of the devotees to neglect their everyday responsibilities and their duties in order to stay at Puttaparthi. One had to come there only at an appropriate time without the visits interfering with family life, or else he would promptly send them back. And, of course, they were all well aware that he knew all about them, including their innermost thoughts, and that there was nothing they could hide from him. Therefore they led their lives following all the proper codes of conduct, so as never to incur Sri Sathya Sai Baba's displeasure. He would often admonish them: "Your good conduct and purity of heart should last beyond the frontiers of Puttaparthi. The moment you cross them do not don your old garb."

Had Sharadamma or any member of her family or the early devotees made any special contribution?

Sharadamma replied that they had composed many new *bhajans* and that Sri Sathya Sai Baba himself had composed several songs which he sang in sweet melodious tones. He was exacting about *tala* (rhythm) and *raga* (scales) and taught children how to keep time and sing with devotion. He always insisted that *bhajans* be sung with genuine *bhakti* rather than that the singers achieve mastery in performing them. To Sri Sathya Sai Baba, a devotee without a good voice but imbued with deep devotion was preferable to any well known musician who expertly produced melody devoid of devotion.

The Seshagiri Rao family have a collection of letters from Sri Sathya Sai Baba written in those early days. Some of the letters include songs composed by him, in pure *Telugu*, replete with the essence of Sai philosophy, love and devotion.

Sharadamma considers the hernia operation performed on her cousin to be a miracle. "Baba happened to be present when the family discussed the problem." Quickly he took the cousin into a bedroom and closed the door. This in itself was very unusual and puzzling. Time elapsed and it was all silent behind the closed door. After a longer wait, Sri Sathya Sai Baba emerged and asked for water to wash his hands. When the others were allowed into the bedroom, they found their cousin in bed with a bandage around his waist. There were a surgical scalpel and knife in the basin, and blood: clear evidence of an operation having been performed by Sri Sathya Sai Baba. The cousin was peacefully asleep and the worried relatives were told that his problem was solved and that all would be well. Sri Sathya Sai Baba also reassured them that he never felt any pain as he had been anaesthetised by *vibhuti*.

The next day they realised that even the bandage put on his stomach had been extraneous as there were absolutely no signs of a scar or any other sort of wound.

Sharadamma talked about other experiences they have had in Sri Sathya Sai Baba's company, especially when they accompanied him on trips to places like Ootacamund (Ooty). In those days, he used to go into trances fairly frequently. These trances were to help devotees in distress when he left his body for hours, and sometimes days, at a stretch. On such occasions, they used to guard his body zealously and await his return. Sri Sathya Sai Baba would give them some warning that he might be off on one of these trips by hinting that he would not be needing lunch or dinner or some other daily feature.

Once, in Ooty, they were in someone else's house when he went into a trance. The men and women kept watch over his body but, after three days, the situation was a little awkward. His hosts began to wonder whether he was really all right or dead. The devotees started to pray to a photograph of him entreating him to come back. He returned and asked why they had called him back. They answered that it had become rather difficult for them after three days to explain such an occurrence to unfamiliar people. They asked him to show them a way of calling him back in case things became more awkward and in case of emergencies.

That day, Sri Sathya Sai Baba gave Sharadamma a photograph of himself and said, "All right. In those circumstances, perform *aarati* to this photograph and I will come back from wherever I may be." Sharadamma says, "*Aarati* to that photograph always conveyed the message to him and brought him back."

A few years ago at Puttaparthi, Sharadamma had to resort to *aarati* of the photograph when Sri Sathya Sai Baba went into a trance in the presence of a large milling crowd. The crowd grew restless after an hour of seeing Sri Sathya Sai Baba's inert body on the dais. It was only then that others on the dais realised he had gone off on one of his trips. What were they to do about it? They dared not disturb him physically. So, they summoned Sharadamma from the audience and asked her to rush to her flat and perform *aarati* to the special photograph. No sooner had she done this than Sri Sathya Sai Baba, true to his word, woke from his trance and asked, "Why have you called me back when I am in the middle of work?" But, of course, he understood their plight and concluded the day's festivities on schedule.

The real connection between Sri Sathya Sai Baba and the photograph remains a mystery; as much a mystery as the *vibhuti, kumkum,* turmeric and sweet *amruta* that form on his photographs in the homes of some of his devotees. It is such occurrences that signal to the devotees the acceptance of their *puja* and prayers. Many believe that these manifestations proclaim the advent of the Sathya Sai era.

A question often asked, with awe, is how someone living far away can divine a devotee's prayer in another part of the world and manifest his *prasad* there? Reports of *vibhuti* encrustations appearing on photographs have become common place. One also hears of honey or *amruta* continuously seeping from photographs of Sri Sathya Sai Baba. There are also accounts of *vibhuti* footprints mysteriously appearing in *puja* rooms.

Only very devout devotees know the joy *(ananda)* of such an acknowledgement of their prayers from the very deity they worship. This overwhelming joy makes them turn more and more Godward.

A devotee admitted that the joy he feels at the manifestations of *vibhuti* on the photograph of Sri Sathya Sai Baba in his home is unlike any other feeling of joy or satisfaction one can have in a worldly sense. "This joy is something special. It goes deep inside me and makes my entire being experience a sense of radiant happiness and peace. To be able to have such an experience again and again, only true *sadhana* can do it."

"Swami is our well-wisher," says Dr. R. S. Padmanabhan, cousin of Sunderamma and nephew of Seshagiri Rao. He has been a devotee of Sri Sathya Sai Baba since 1942. Dr. Padmanabhan and his wife, Kamala, are a well-known couple actively linked with several Sathya Sai *Seva* activities.

A genial and highly capable dentist, Dr. Padmanabhan, as Rotary Governor, made his mark with the concept of spiritualising service activities in the Rotarian movement.

Mrs. Padmanabhan said that she first saw Sri Sathya Sai Baba when she was a young girl and he was in his teens. She had been with her old aunt who was a devotee. He had been in a trance and they had waited for him to come out of it.

A few hours went by and Kamala became impatient. She kept pestering her aunt with pleas to go home. As she was uttering one of these, Sri Sathya Sai Baba came out of the trance and beckoned her. She went up to him and he told her, "Very soon you will be married to a dentist. He is a very good man." Kamala was at an age when such an idea meant nothing to her.

In what circumstances did Dr. Padmanabhan meet Sri Sathya Sai Baba?

He said he had many relatives in Bangalore in whose houses Sri Sathya Sai Baba stayed when in Bangalore, or he visited them. Initially, he made no attempt to meet him as he had been told that one had to wait patiently to have an interview with him, that he may not even speak to or look at one, etc.

"Eventually one day, I went. There were nearly a thousand people there that day, even so Swami called me, took me inside and spoke to me about everything in my nature, my work, my ideas and even my thoughts at that moment. This was the beginning of my relationship with Swami and I was hardly twenty-two years old."

The Doctor said that Sri Sathya Sai Baba had advised and guided him at every stage in his career. It was he who had asked him to start a clinic at Malleswaram and he had found it very easy to rent suitable premises and to get adequate equipment. "Swami's divine hands opened the clinic and I've had a good practice from the very first day," Dr. Padmanabhan said, a smile of gratitude lighting up his face. Again, it was Sri Sathya Sai Baba who suggested that he went abroad for specialisation in dentistry. "Like a parent, he evinced a keen interest in all that I did," he said. He said that Sri Sathya Sai Baba had made the time to see his new house and clinic during the construction period. And it was he who gave their son the name of Jagdish.

Kamala said that once Sri Sathya Sai Baba produced a *shaligram* (sacred pebble) and asked her to put it on a string. She found that it had no holes in it for a string to pass through and said so. Sri Sathya Sai Baba took it from her, blew on it and gave it back to her. She saw then that it now had a neat little hole all the way through. She asked, "Shall I use an ordinary thread for it?" Sri Sathya Sai Baba looked at her for a while, then he waved his hand and materialised a beautiful chain. Full of joy, Kamala put the stone on the chain and used it for her *puja* deity.

On another occasion, Sri Sathya Sai Baba materialised small gold flowers for the *bhajan puja* and he gave them to Dr. Padmanabhan as he performed the *puja*. Sri Sathya Sai Baba said there should be 108 flowers in all. After the *puja*, Kamala counted them as she was putting them away, but there were only 107. Sri Sathya Sai Baba then re-counted them and, finally, accosted Dr. Padmanabhan in whose pocket the 108th gold flower was found, to his consternation.

The Padmanabhan family used to spend their holidays in Puttaparthi. "In those days there was flowing water in the Chitravati River. There were only a few of us then and Swami used to talk to us all so often and teach us *bhajans*. We were a tightly knit group and, at times, the men would also be called in to help with the cooking and serving of food." The Doctor also recalled that exemplary behaviour and a high level of conversation were musts at Sri Sathya Sai Baba's *ashrama*. If there was any loose talk anywhere in the Puttaparthi area, even at the faraway river bank, Sri Sathya Sai Baba would immediately know about it and say, "In cities you behave in a thoughtless way. When you come here to the *ashrama*, at least for a few days, you should have only sacred thoughts."

Again it was Kamala's turn to remember. "Even today, especially on the College grounds at Brindavan, Swami immediatly knows if anyone speaks of him." Several years ago, a few streaks of grey appeared in Sri Sathya Sai Baba's hair. One of the College boys talked about this to his friends saying, "What kind of an *avatara* is Swami that he cannot even retain his black hair?" That evening, after the discourse, Sri Sathya Sai Baba called out to the student, "Look at my hair. Has it got grey streaks?" Quaking with fear the student said, "Yes!" Sri Sathya Sai Baba then shook his head a few times and said to the same boy, "Look now." To his amazement, the boy now found that there was no longer a single grey strand in the hair. It had all turned jet black and has remained so ever since.

There have been many anecdotes told and retold about Sri Sathya Sai Baba's crinkly hair which has been the same length for many years now. He never cuts or trims it. People who are close to him say that the hair is always fragrant. This, in turn, led to talk in the *ashrama*, voiced initially by one devotee, that he must surely apply scented oil to his hair for it always to be so sweetly fragrant. The next day, directly he had bathed and with his hair still wet, Sri Sathya Sai Baba sent for this devotee. He asked him, "Do you think that my hair is now in its natural state?" The devotee understood that he had been found out, but nevertheless replied truthfully and agreed that Sri Sathya Sai Baba's hair at that moment could not but be totally natural. Sri Sathya Sai Baba asked him to smell his hair and the devotee was astonished: the same fragrance emanated from his hair, washed and wet though it was. Sri Sathya Sai Baba then explained, "This is natural to my hair. There is no scent or oil in it. The fragrance is natural to it, just like the scent you notice in the *vibhuti* I produce."

The Doctor's family always loved their stays in Puttaparthi. The peace, the pristine atmosphere, the encompassing air of spirituality – all these delighted them. They regard themselves as singularly fortunate to have been able to bask so continuously in the warm glow of Sri Sathya Sai Baba's grace. The Doctor said, "We came to know him when his devotees numbered in the hundreds. Now there are millions of them and so we cherish those days when, so often, he would drop in to see us in our homes, sometimes quite unexpectedly." And young Jagdish added, "There were times when I was still very young when Swami would suddenly walk in. I could have been reading or playing and would simply say that my parents were not in and Swami would go away. When they were there, my parents looked after him. Today, whenever I think of those times, I feel so ashamed. Swami was so accessible then and I fear soon we may not even get to see him. I think he knows about this fear I have. That must have been why, before I went abroad, he wrote of his own will in my autograph book, 'I am always with you, Jagdish, don't have any fear'."

The Padmanabhan daughter, Geeta, who runs a *Bal Vikas* class, related a recent Sai miracle. A staunch and close devotee had to undergo an emergency operation, but she would not agree to it until she received Sri Sathya Sai Baba's permission. It was pointed out to her that there was no time to be lost and that there was no way she could make a quick trip to Puttaparthi to ask for permission. Her answer to this was that she would much rather die than do anything at all without first seeking Sri Sathya Sai Baba's permission. At last and as a last resort, a member of her family decided to put through a telephone call to Puttaparthi. Everyone agreed that telephoning could serve no purpose as there was no way of knowing which passing person would pick up the receiver, nor whether anyone would be able to convey the message to Sri Sathya Sai Baba. All the same, to appease the old lady they rang up.

To the surprise of everyone, the voice at the other end belonged to none other than Sri Sathya Sai Baba! In a casual way he said, "I knew you were trying to ring me. Please call her to the telephone. I will speak to her."

The lady went to the telephone and spoke to Sri Sathya Sai Baba who told her that she must have the operation. But, she was persistent and protested, "Baba, I don't even have your *prasadam*." He laughed and told her to hold her hand out near the receiver and, then and there, *vibhuti* poured into her hands from the telephone. "Are you happy now?" Sri Sathya Sai Baba asked his old devotee. She happily agreed to be taken to hospital. Such indeed is the true *bhakti* of devotees and Sri Sathya Sai Baba's response to true devotion.

The Padmanabhans have a large repertoire of Sai miracles. Sri Sathya Sai Baba blessed Jagdish's wedding too, said Kamala and added, "We liked a girl called Aruna and her family. But there were some questions in our minds as she had been brought up in America. We wondered if she would fit into our family. I went to Swami for advice. As soon as I entered the room and even before I could say a word, Swami said, 'I know you want to become a mother-in-law! Don't worry, the match is a good one for Jagdish. She is a good girl and will suit your family. Her family are devotees of Ramakrishna Paramahansa. It does not matter at all who people follow.

All that does matter is that they take to *sanmarg* (the spiritual path).'"

"Later, we went to show Swami some of the things made for the wedding. Even before we opened the bags and boxes, he knew their contents. He teased the bride's parents, 'Look, we are giving Aruna a diamond ring, but the ring you are giving Jagdish is plain gold. We have had new jewellery made for Aruna and all you have brought is an old necklace of your grandmother's!' Aruna's mother was bemused and said that the necklace was an antique and that Aruna liked it very much; Jagdish's ring, she said, was the same as any American ring. Very soon she understood that Swami was only talking in fun, as family elders are wont to do."

During all their many years of dedicated devotion to Sri Sathya Sai Baba, the Padmanabhans have seen and experienced things beyond human reckoning. Their faith in him has deepened over the years and there has never been a single moment when their faith in his divinity has been shaken by anyone or anything. Dr. Padmanabhan illustrates this with an event relating to the sixtieth birthday of a family friend. "Swami stayed there till late at night. The next morning, our friend died. I rushed to Whitefield to tell Swami about it and he said he knew. So, Swami operates on a completely different plane. His reactions to situations, particularly to death, are so utterly different. We have to realise this and accept that he is a phenomenon and beyond our analysis and reasoning powers. Just because he behaves like an ordinary person, and we see only flashes of divinity, should not make us rush to conclusions, for he is superhuman, someone far above us all in all respects."

Dr. Padmanabhan has witnessed a few instant operations performed by Sri Sathya Sai Baba in the early days. For these operations, Sri Sathya Sai Baba produced surgical knives by a mere wave of his hand and performed all the different surgical tasks like anaesthetising, suturing and bandaging by smearing *vibhuti*. "And whatever Swami materialised and did, it was always for the good of those people," he said.

Of all the extraordinary *leelas* of Sri Sathya Sai Baba that Mrs. Padmanabhan knows about, she remembers most of all something that happened before the birth of her daughter, Geeta. She and her husband had gone to Puttaparthi and they were anxious to return to Bangalore the same night. That was during the monsoon and Sri Sathya Sai Baba had asked them not to travel at night but wait till daylight. The Doctor was restless thinking of the considerable amount of work waiting for him in Bangalore and, moreover, it did not look like heavy rain. So they set off. Twenty miles later, the rain came down, lashing past the windows and drumming on the car. Visibility became very poor and turning back was impossible. Dr. Padmanabhan kept the car crawling on – it was already dark and the road was empty – he felt it was better to plough on rather than stand still in the streaming rain and the darkness. He was also afraid of the car engine dying.

The car bumped along very slowly when, suddenly, there was a flash of light. An old man was waving a hurricane lamp. Dr. Padmanabhan stopped. The old man told them that they were heading straight into a torrent with strong currents as a small barrage upstream had burst. The old man had halted the car just in time: a few more yards and it would have been swept away. "You are lucky," said the old man who advised them to stop for the night as the barrage could only be repaired in the morning. Then he went away. Dr. Padmanabhan drove back to his cousin's house for the night and left again for Bangalore the next morning.

A month later, while Sri Sathya Sai Baba was in Bangalore, he castigated Dr. Padmanabhan for not heeding his words and starting out on the journey at night. "If I had not been on the lookout that night, what would have happened to you?" he asked sternly. The Doctor apologised to Sri Sathya Sai Baba and thanked him for his grace.

"Swami always watches over our *bhajans* and, as he once promised us, always makes it a point to look in," says Kamala. They have had proof of Sri Sathya Sai Baba's presence: Sai photographs and jasmine garlands sway with unusual force for a specific period of time; sometimes flowers fall from Sai photographs into their hands or onto their laps when someone makes a special wish or addresses a prayer to him. They always made a point of carrying on singing until they did receive a sign of acknowledgement from Sri Sathya Sai Baba.

They recalled an occasion when the *bhajans* went on for a very long time without a divine acknowledgement. The women continued to sing determined not to stop until they received a sign from Sri Sathya Sai Baba that he had heard their prayers. Their men kept looking at their watches, but the women would not stop singing. It was past ten o'clock at night when the garland around a Sai photograph swung vigorously and broke into ten pieces and fell to the floor. There were ten women singing *bhajans* that evening.

The Padmanabhan family are absolutely certain that Sri Sathya Sai Baba always "peeps in" on their *bhajan* sessions and they have recent proof of this. There were eight separate homes where *bhajans* were usually held in rotation. However, another lady from a ninth home, who always participated, asked one day if the *bhajans* might be held at her house. They yielded to her wish and, the following Thursday, held the *bhajan* session there.

The very next time they went to Whitefield, Sri Sathya Sai Baba asked them, "Where were you on Thursday? You made me roam all the streets of Bangalore."

They were all mystified, but he went on, "Wherever I went only locked doors greeted me; your house, Sunderamma's house, everywhere there were only locks."

From that day on, they never held a *bhajan* session anywhere but in one of the eight family houses.

"Nothing is too small or too big for Baba and no one is less important or more important. No event is more significant or less significant. Baba is all-knowing and a silent witness to all," said Dr. Padmanabhan.

Once, soon after Jagdish returned from higher studies in the U.S.A., they invited Sri Sathya Sai Baba to their house. He took his place on the chair and carelessly asked, "How was the burglary?"

They were amazed and wondered how he had learnt about the burglar who had broken in a fortnight ago while they were all asleep. But the Doctor replied, "Yes, Swami, we had a burglary and we lost all our watches and a purse with money in it." Sri Sathya Sai Baba said, "Why worry about watches? You can always buy them again." Then he twinkled and asked, "How did you all sleep that night?"

Then they began to see what had happened. For that night the burglar had entered through a grille, gone to each room and stolen things. He had taken the watch and the purse from the Doctor's bedside. The Doctor is a very light sleeper and the slightest movement wakes him up. Indeed, the family had remarked on how even he had slept through the prowler in his room. The police inspector who had been to investigate had said, "Thank God all of you slept so soundly, for this was a professional burglar of rare expertise. If any one of you had woken up anything could have happened."

They understood then and bowed in gratitude to Sri Sathya Sai Baba, thankful that he had watched over them and made them all sleep soundly until the burglar had left the grounds.

"The *leelas* of Swami are stupendous. We feel that each day and always he is with us, but also that we have a long way to go. Often, we feel that Swami has done so much for us that we must do something in return. But, alas, he expects nothing in return. So we strive to become better and better in our thoughts, words and deeds, as this alone will please him."

"The spiritual eye is God. Attain Him and the spiritual eye will open."

. . . Sri Sathya Sai Baba

2

HE CALLED HER AFTER THE RIVER

Mr. and Mrs. Parathasarathy are old devotees uniquely blessed by Sri Sathya Sai Baba.

One day, early in 1957, Sita Parathasarathy first heard of Sri Sathya Sai Baba and instantly she wanted to see him. The next day, Mr. Parathasarathy unexpectedly received some money so they both decided to travel to Puttaparthi from Madras where they live. They had a comfortable journey, easily catching the train, bus and cart connections needed to reach their destination. They knew nothing about Puttaparthi nor had they asked anybody anything. They had no idea what it looked like, nor even what Sri Sathya Sai Baba looked like.

They reached the grounds of Prashanti Nilayam and sat in the shade of a tree wondering what to do. In a little while, Sri Sathya Sai Baba came to them saying, "Oh, you have come. I have been waiting for you." Before they could say anything at all he continued, "Was everything all right? I called you at this time so that you might have a comfortable journey and spend some time with me."

Sri Sathya Sai Baba seemed to them a close member of the family and they offered him their respectful salutations.

He then asked Sita, "Do you have a growth in your stomach which hurts a lot?" She said yes and gasped at the thought that Sri Sathya Sai Baba should know about this three-year-old complaint without her telling him about it.

"Don't worry, it will be all right. Now go and rest," he said.

Sita remembers how incredible they found it to be the only two visitors in the *Mandir*. Sri Sathya Sai Baba had called them at a time when there would be no one else, granting them the privilege of exclusive time. "We were so happy and so fortunate to receive such special attention from Swami at that time," said Sita audibly moved.

"I don't think you need rooms. Stay in the *Mandir*," advised Sri Sathya Sai Baba. He asked Mr. Parathasarathy to sleep in the verandah with an *ashramite*, while Sita was to sleep inside the temple.

In the morning Sita found that her stomach felt lighter, the heaviness and pain which were her constant companions had disappeared. Could Sri Sathya Sai Baba, with just a look, cure in a day an ailment she had suffered for three long years? she asked herself. The grateful couple fell at his feet in total surrender

Their stay at Prashanti Nilayam was a peaceful and blissful experience, with Sri Sathya Sai Baba all to themselves. They marvelled at the way he spoke, in detail, of their family and their plans. On their third day with him, he called Sita to him and said, "Unless you eat something today, I will not talk to you. Do you know how much pain you cause me by staying here and starving?" She realised then that Sri Sathya Sai Baba knew that she had subsisted on coffee alone upto then. She was an orthodox *Hindu* and did not eat anything outside her own home. Sri Sathya Sai Baba counselled her to be less rigid when travelling. The love and concern he showed his devotees were revelations to them. He then gave them permission to leave and asked them to return for *Shivaratri* to stay for eight to ten days.

That *Shivaratri* trip was equally memorable. This time, Sita went prepared to cook for themselves. They were lodged in a large room with a small kitchen attached to it. Sri Sathya Sai Baba said to her, "I will have many guests – musicians and artistes will come – and you must look after them." Sita was only too glad to do that and undertook to cook for and feed some of the guests: the violinist Sethuramiah, for instance, who also was so orthodox that he did not normally eat away from home. Sita recalls that Mr. Sethuramiah performed *puja* regularly each morning and that he believed in religious *niyama* (regulation) to achieve communion with God through the divine medium of music.

Parathasarathy, husband and wife, are singers. Gifted with a good voice and with a sound basis in music, Sita cherished the opportunity of listening to the most excellent musicians who came to Puttaparthi that year for *Shivaratri*. "The musicians too were appreciative of the small services I rendered them. They allowed me to see the gifts Baba materialised for them, pendants, rings, etc." Another great bonus was that when she sang the *Sai Namavali*, they accompanied her on their instruments.

Even the incomparable *Shivaratri* celebration could not match the joy, during this stay, of Sri Sathya Sai Baba strolling into her kitchen to lift lids off saucepans and inspect the contents, sniff the aromas and ask about the selection. Sometimes, he would compliment her on the flavour of a dish.

"Oh, will such times ever come back in our lives? Can we ever dream of such closeness to Swami now?" she asks, eyes brimming with tears.

The Parathasarathys have attended three *Shivaratris* at Puttaparthi. They have seen the *lingodbhava – lingams* emerging from Sri Sathya Sai Baba's mouth. "We were truly privileged, for we sat very near and watched it all from close quarters," said Mr. Parathasarathy. He showed me a photograph of Sri Sathya Sai Baba taken on the 28th of February 1957, *Shivaratri's* date that year. This photograph adorns their *puja* room as do several others given to them by Sri Sathya Sai Baba himself. Sita also recalls many psychic visions and signs affirming her belief in Sri Sathya Sai Baba's divinity.

Sita's musical talent was appreciated by Sri Sathya Sai Baba. He gave her several song books and she set the lyrics to *ragas*. Often she would sing before him and it was pure bliss to her to see his face suffuse with happiness. Her own joy was quadrupled whenever Sri Sathya Sai Baba joined in the singing and repeated line after line. Sita used to sing a few lines of songs that Sri Sathya Sai Baba liked which he would then ask her to repeat; and some *bhajans* too, he would ask her to sing again and again.

These lovely experiences with Sri Sathya Sai Baba made her go to Puttaparthi time and time again. She would set off the moment she thought of Sri Sathya Sai Baba and, often, she went alone. She was never afraid or lonely because she always felt that Sri Sathya Sai Baba was with her.

Once, Sita went to Puttaparthi to have *darshan* of Sri Sathya Sai Baba leaving behind her sick child. He called her then and gently admonished her, "You should not come to see me when you have family duties to attend to. Your son is unwell. Since yesterday I have been looking after him as you have come away here. I am with you. There is no need for you to come to me so often. I will be with you when you need me. Remember that and come only when I call you."

Sita perceived the rightness of Sri Sathya Sai Baba's words and, since then, she goes to Whitefield or to Puttaparthi only occasionally. She says that she finds his presence in her house and even in the person of her daughter, Chitra, who is a 'rare' being indeed.

Chitra's parents feel that she is a blessing of God's grace, so "evolved" is she. This spiritual evolution is felt in her talk and glimpsed in her communion with the Divine.

Chitra was born after her parents had been shown Sri Sathya Sai Baba's grace. Sita was determined that he alone should name the child and waited for the blessing. When the child was eight months old, she took her to Puttaparthi. Sri Sathya Sai Baba spoke to her after three days of waiting. He asked, "As you have not given her a name, what have you been calling her these past eight months?" He picked up the baby, materialised a lot of *vibhuti* and applied some of it on her high forehead and rubbed the rest of it all over her little head. He said, "Name her after the river here. Call her Chitra."

When she was seven, Chitra found she could meditate and have mystic visions. But she kept this to herself for almost ten years. No one knew of the spiritual evolution within her. She finished her basic education and then informed her parents that she did not wish to pursue higher studies, "as she had visions of gods who gave her *upadesha* about things that really matter." Chitra says she sees Sri Sathya Sai Baba either as he is now, as *Tirupathi* Lord *Venkateswara* or as his consort. He appears to her in these three forms and has given her many unusual experiences.

Chitra's conversations mark her as a true *sadhaka* who has clearly realised the ultimate reality. She gives convincing expositions on *atma tatva, chakras, Parabrahman*, the divine nature of Sri Sathya Sai Baba, and the divinity inherent in all human beings.

She told us how Sri Sathya Sai Baba once appeared to her while she was in meditation and told her that he would give her a *Shivalingam*. Since then he has appeared to her many times and taught her several aspects of *adhyatma* and *bhakti*.

Once, her mother brought home a small *Shivalingam* made of ordinary wood. Chitra kept it in the *puja* room and regularly performed *ashtotara puja* to it. One day, while she was cleaning the plate on which the *lingam* was kept, she noticed that it looked different. A closer look revealed that it had been transformed into solid black stone. After that, on another day, Sri Sathya Sai Baba appeared to her in a vision and explained, "This *lingam* is sent by me and contains within it five *lingams:* the *atma lingam, aadi lingam, jyoti lingam, jambu lingam* and *vayu lingam*." He asked her to continue to worship it regularly.

Sita described many *leelas* that have occurred through the medium of this *lingam*. One day, the plate in which it stood was full of water indicating that *Ganga abhishekam* had been performed by an unseen hand. (*Ganga abhishekam* is ablutions performed with water from the holy river, the Ganges). On another day, a shower of *vibhuti* fell on the *lingam*. On yet another day, it was first covered in *amruta* and then in curds. And one day, two precious gems glittered from it. Such have been the manifestations of Sri Sathya Sai Baba's grace.

Chitra has had many divine encounters. For a continuous period of nearly eighteen months, fresh *kumkum* marks regularly appeared on her forehead. And when anyone came to her for help, her hands would brim over with *kumkum*.

Her parents believe that Chitra is a child of God. How else can they account for the lucid philosophical discourses she gives at home from time to time? Often they wonder whether it could really be their daughter uttering the words she does.

Sita speaks of times when Chitra would suddenly say that Lord *Srinivasa* had come, and *Padmavati Devi* had come, and then go on to give talks in clear *Tamil* or *Sanskrit* or English.

They remained puzzled until one day, suddenly, Chitra said, "Sai Baba is here!" and started to discourse in fluent *Telugu*. The voice was hers, but the language and the expressions were those of Sri Sathya Sai Baba; Chitra had never been taught even the rudiments of the *Telugu* language.

Had Chitra seen Sri Sathya Sai Baba or spoken to him? Surprisingly, she said she had not. She saw him for the first time in November 1977 during his birthday celebrations at Puttaparthi. He neither came near her nor looked at her but, at night, she had a vision of him taking her around Prashanti Nilayam and the main temple.

When asked if she would like to live in Sri Sathya Sai Baba's *ashrama*, she replied, "Baba is always in my heart. He is not someone outside. He is all over the world, in my house, in you, in everyone. Why limit ourselves to the thought of physical nearness only? We are tiny specks of that immense universal light, the *Bhagavantha* (God) who is none other than Baba. If you do real meditation, even for five minutes, He is bound to come to you," she says with utter and simple conviction.

Chitra then told us about Sri Sathya Sai Baba when he was young. He had gone with his friends to a *Shiva* temple. In the dark sanctum sanctorum of the temple nothing was visible at first. But suddenly a *jyoti* (light) emanating from Sri Sathya Sai Baba illuminated the *lingam* in the dark interior. And those who saw it also saw the light return to him. Chitra asks, "Is not one such instance proof enough of Baba's divinity?"

Her parents are not keen to have Chitra's spiritual evolution made public. They fear that this would soon bring people who would want her to predict their future, and they would give her "gifts" – and attempt to commercialise her spiritual endeavours. They are even hoping that Chitra will marry soon.

Chitra is certain that marriage cannot bind her to *samsara* (worldly existence). She said, "Why should it when I know how not to become bound?" Then she went on to outline her point of view using similes and parables, sometimes using words and expressions typical of Sri Sathya Sai Baba. I asked if she had read his books and she answered, "No. What Baba wants me to know, He tells me!"

Her parents discourage visitors because Chitra takes everyone's problems very seriously saying, "Let me use this chance to pray on their behalf," and then she might undertake fasts for them in addition to the austere ones she already observes. She believes that if she fasts on behalf of people who do not themselves fast that this will do them some good.

Why does she undertake these fasts? Chitra says she is no different from others. "We are all sparks of the same *Paramatma*. We are all God's children. There is no difference whether it is I who fast or someone else. It is all done to mitigate harm. God's divine aspect exists in each one of us. There is no difference: no good or bad. It is He who wills everything."

Mr. and Mrs. Parathasarathy are convinced that their good fortune and

Chitra's soul power are all due to Sri Sathya Sai Baba's grace.

"Women have equal rights and an equal chance to attain the Godhead."

. . . Sri Sathya Sai Baba

3

THE SHIRDI LINK

Seethamma, the sister of Laxmi Bai, Rani of Chincholi, talked about her family's long association with Sri Sathya Sai Baba.

Her nephew, Krishnaswamy, was only a young boy when he insisted on going to Shirdi. At that time, since Shirdi Sai Baba's death, there were a few people who could communicate with him and one such mediator was Abdulla Baba. When Krishnaswamy was taken to Shirdi, Abdulla Baba told him that in a year Sai Baba would grant *darshan* to his whole family. Exactly a year after that, they found themselves quite unexpectedly in Puttaparthi. It was only after being there and meeting Sri Sathya Sai Baba that they thought of the prediction made in Shirdi. Sri Sathya Sai Baba welcomed them to Puttaparthi saying that he had been waiting for them.

Seethamma remembers how difficult that first journey to Puttaparthi had been, in a bullock cart; difficult, slow and hazardous, but they were very happy that they had made it. Seeing Sri Sathya Sai Baba had brought them peace and happiness. They garlanded him and, Seethamma remembers, how in those days he used to keep his head bent and his eyes down when speaking to women. He spoke to them warmly and said, "I have kept the kitchen free for you." That had surprised them. It had indeed been one of their worries; whether they would have a kitchen to themselves. They had heard that lodgings were almost impossible to get, that there were only very few kitchens, and that people had to cook, eat and sleep together, either in the big prayer hall or in the open air. So, they were truly delighted to be given a kitchen. They were content with the arrangement and never gave a second thought to any more comfort. The young Sri Sathya Sai Baba's presence made up for everything.

Sri Sathya Sai Baba granted them interviews and materialised miniature portraits of himself for them. These portraits were the size of an ordinary postage stamp. Then he materialised scrolls of gold foil and *yantras* with *mantras* engraved on them and asked them to wear them always as talismans.

Did they think, at first sight, that he was God?

"No!" said Seethamma, "I cannot say so for it would be untrue. We felt good to have his blessings, but we did not immediately believe he was divine. That feeling grew slowly as the days went by, as we became more and more conscious of his powers and of the nature of his personality."

On one of the trips, Seethamma's sister, the Rani of Chincholi, went with her. Her husband, the late Raja, had been an ardent devotee of Shirdi Sai Baba. When Sri Sathya Sai Baba saw the Rani, he asked her several things about her palace. He said that he had been a visitor to the palace in his previous body, that of Shirdi Sai Baba, and referred to renovations carried out after his visit. He mentioned them in detail. He then asked what had happened to the stone image of *Maruti* (*Hanumana*, the monkey god) he had given to the Raja.

The Rani was completely ignorant of the things he mentioned. When she returned she had a search made in some store rooms which had been kept locked. She checked up on the repairs and renovations too and found that all that Sri Sathya Sai Baba had said was correct in every detail. For instance, he had said that a certain Margosa tree had been uprooted during the renovations and that was confirmed.

One day, the Rani was having one of the store rooms cleaned, when she came across a beautiful brass vessel called a *kamandala* in *Sanskrit.* This is a gourd-shaped vessel used by monks and holymen to store drinking water. The Rani had it cleaned and polished and put on display in her drawing room.

The next day, she found it encircled by a cobra. She burned some camphor in an *aarati* in front of the snake and it slid away quietly. Later, she took the *kamandala* to Puttaparthi to show it to Sri Sathya Sai Baba and ask him about it.

No sooner had the Rani arrived in Puttaparthi than Sri Sathya Sai Baba sent word asking her to come and see him "with his drinking vessel." He pointed to the two *Hindi* letters engraved on the *kamandala: saa* and *baa*. He had seen them during his lifetime as Shirdi Sai Baba. People wondered why he had asked for this vessel and received the answer during the *Dassera* Festival when the *Vedapurusha Saptaha Yagna* was being performed. The officiating priests asked for a vessel of a particular shape and size as prescribed by Scripture. Sri Sathya Sai Baba produced this vessel for them and it met their requirements fully.

Years later, the Rani of Chincholi found in one of the locked store yards a cart referred to by Sri Sathya Sai Baba. It appeared that Shirdi Sai Baba had travelled in the cart. For a long time it was kept on show in the prayer hall at Prashanti Nilayam. Later, it was used to cart mud and earth when the Purnachandra Auditorium was built.

Once, when Sri Sathya Sai Baba was visiting Hyderabad, he visited nearby Chincholi at the request of the Rani. Seethamma and her mother formed part of his entourage and spent several eventful days at the Chincholi palace with Sri Sathya Sai Baba.

Seethamma remembers seeing Sri Sathya Sai Baba create some small idols. And, during his stay there, he brought out a *Krishna* idol from his mouth and gave it to the Rani. Then he let them see another instance of creation from the sand in the bed of the River Godavari: a set of three idols, two of *Rama* and *Lakshmana* in marble, and one of *Sita* in translucent crystal. Sri Sathya Sai Baba gave these to Seethamma's nephew, Krishnaswamy, with whom he and his entourage had been staying. That night, a serene full moon night, he also materialised a milk sweet for distribution as *prasad*. The he asked everyone to see how the crystal effigy of *Sita* glowed in the moonlight.

Sri Sathya Sai Baba showed Seethamma's mother, Namagiri Amma, a great deal of consideration and affection. Namagiri Amma had had many experiences of Shirdi Sai Baba before meeting this Sai Baba. One of the most dramatic of these had happened at a time when there were communal riots in the area. She was a widow staying in a large house with her daughters and she was worried.

One day, Shirdi Sai Baba appeared at her doorstep carrying a *kamandala*. He poured water from its spout and drew a line with water around the *rangoli* design in front of her house. He said to her, "Do not cross this boundary line and no harm will befall you or your family." Then he vanished. His boon proved infallible, for many homes were robbed and many families humiliated, but nothing awful happened to Namagiri Amma or her family.

Once, in Puttaparthi, she had a dream in which Sri Sathya Sai Baba knocked on her door and asked her to come out and look at a certain spot in the direction of West Prashanti. She followed him out and looked in the indicated direction. As she looked there was a blinding flash of light and then, in the light, she saw Shirdi Sai Baba lifting his hand in blessing as he used to do before he disappeared again – a truly divine vision.

"We have all had several experiences with Swami. But these days, it is very difficult to get anywhere near him because of the crowds . . . However, whenever we really want him or need his counsel, he somehow always sends us his message," said Seethamma.

Recently, Seethamma had a problem with her eyes. The doctor thought she ought to have an operation. In a quandary, she went to Whitefield. As she sat waiting in the *darshan* queue, Sri Sathya Sai Baba came up to her, took a slate from a child sitting next to her and wrote *'Om'* on it. As he wrote the word he said, "Don't have the operation, there is no need for it. Swami will look after you."

"See? The way he knows and can talk to us when we most need his advice?" says Seethamma with thankfulness.

"If the Guru is God, then obeying him, walking on the path he has shown – these are as effective as japam of the name."

. . . Sri Sathya Sai Baba

4

THE PICTURE IN THE ATTIC

Sarojamma Krishnaswami has been a devotee of Sri Sathya Sai Baba for almost twenty years.

In her student days, she was a Communist and when her father suddenly died leaving her with the responsibility of supporting the family, what little faith in God she may have had vanished completely. She became fed up of her mother's constant *pujas* and of her other relatives, all reluctant to pitch in and help. She did not want to accept their grudging help, so she moved to a separate house with her mother and brothers. The family lived on her earnings from her job at the Cottage Industries Emporium.

While unpacking in the new house, she saw a picture of the god *Satya-narayana* and it annoyed her. She flung it away in the attic when no one was watching, so angry was she with God.

At the Emporium, a friend called Miss Kulkarni told her about Sri Sathya Sai Baba. She suggested she went to him for blessings to help her with her troubles. Very unwillingly one day, Sarojamma went with Miss Kulkarni to Whitefield and found that Sri Sathya Sai Baba was not there. Despite that, the visit in some way aroused her interest.

On another day, on an impulse, she jumped into a taxi and drove to Whitefield. Sri Sathya Sai Baba was there this time and she waited to see him along with some others. He emerged to give *darshan*, stared at her and went back into the house. Sarojamma told a devotee, "I have come all the way here to see him. Ask Sai Baba to talk to me." She was informed that the message had been conveyed to Sri Sathya Sai Baba.

Sri Sathya Sai Baba came out again, but he never even glanced towards her. She was furious that she had wasted time and money going to Whitefield. She returned home dejected. That night, Sri Sathya Sai Baba appeared in her dreams: she saw a bungalow, a staircase, a room in which Sri Sathya Sai Baba gave her *paada namaskara* and blessings. The dream intrigued her and she went to her friend's house. When she told the Kulkarnis about it, they said her description of the interior of the house fitted the women's entrance, the staircase and the *darshan* room of Sri Sathya Sai Baba's residence in Puttaparthi. Sarojamma could not understand how or why she had had the dream.

Sometime later, Sarojamma was invited by the Kulkarnis to a housewarming at their new house. Sri Sathya Sai Baba was the guest of honour. She took advantage of his presence and barged into a room where he was sitting all alone. He asked her, "Why did you have to dump that picture of *Satyanarayana* in the attic?" She was startled and wondered, "How does this Sai Baba know something that no one else, even at home, knows? This person must certainly have some powers."

Sri Sathya Sai Baba continued, "You need not be so brutally frank. Everything white is not milk. Be wary!" Sarojamma dismissed this as a piece of general advice which all elders love to bestow. Even so, she felt very happy to have been able to do *namaskara* and receive his blessings.

After this initial meeting, Sarojamma was fairly regular in her visits to Puttaparthi. During one of her visits, Sri Sathya Sai Baba gave her a glimpse of his omnipresence. Wherever she looked, whether at rocks or stones, everything looked like Sri Sathya Sai Baba to her. His face looked down on her from everywhere. She saw hundreds of Sri Sathya Sai Babas – here, there, whichever way she turned. She went to the banks of the Chitravati and he was there, too. Her companions made fun of her and taunted her, saying Sri Sathya Sai Baba was definitely in his room, how could she say she saw him outdoors?

The fact was, though, that she saw him everywhere. It was not hallucination. "He is omnipresent and so is everywhere. This experience wrought a change inside me and, slowly, the change was exteriorised." Soon she was completely convinced of Sri Sathya Sai Baba's divinity.

Sarojamma continued going to Puttaparthi and Whitefield. There were times when she found the confusion caused by well-meaning devotees intolerable. Then, with Sri Sathya Sai Baba's permission, she would organise the milling throng into orderly lines. He would wait patiently until everyone had bowed. Though there were no real rules in those days, she used to tell people that if they were disciplined, they would all be able to receive his blessings.

One day in 1961, Sri Sathya Sai Baba summoned her and asked her to join him on a trip to Badrinath. She was unable to believe her ears. She found the long journey with Sri Sathya Sai Baba a magnificent experience. "He looked after us all so well and with such concern. It was thrilling to watch him perform *pujas* redolent with significance at great shrines. His miraculous manifestations were sights fit for the gods. The *Lakshadipam puja* he performed at Haridwar was unforgettable, and the *Netralingam puja* at Badrinath was beyond description." Sarojamma said it was all so marvellous that she felt time should have stopped then.

She described the *puja* at Badrinath. On the 17th of June, Sri Sathya Sai Baba stood in front of the *garbha graha*, the sanctum sanctorum. First he materialised a golden lotus, then he 'brought out' the *Netralingam*. There was a round hollow at the base of the lotus and he placed the *lingam* in it – and it fitted perfectly. The Governor, Sri Ramakrishna Rao, and his wife were with him. He showed everyone the *lingam* and said that it was one of the five *lingams* that *Adi Shankara* had brought down from Mount *Kailasa*. They clearly saw an eye inside it and understood why it was called *netra* (eye) *lingam*. Sri Sathya Sai Baba explained that he had brought out the *lingam* to 'recharge' it so that it could become as powerful as it once was. The *puja* was performed with water from the Ganges at Gangotri trickling through Sri Sathya Sai Baba's divine fingers. Then he materialised 108 golden *bilva* leaves and dew-fresh white *thumbe* flowers. And with all these he performed the *puja*. When it was all over, the *Netralingam* disappeared. Sri Sathya Sai Baba had sent it back to its secret place in the Alaknanda.

"I never wanted the tour to end. Swami looked after us so well! It was absolutely marvellous," said Sarojamma.

She joyfully recalls the first public meeting she helped to arrange in Bangalore with Sri Sathya Sai Baba as the chief guest. Though he had given many informal talks and had held discussions with devotees, he had not, at that time, liked the idea of speaking from a public platform. It had needed a lot of persuading from Sarojamma and her friends to make him consent to address a public meeting.

"That was a red letter day for us," said Sarojamma, "since we welcomed him openly with *purna kumbha* and arranged *bhajans* as a formal part of the meeting to which we also invited a minister of Karnataka State. It was a memorable occasion and, for the first time, we heard Sri Sathya Sai Baba speak formally. And it was a beautiful speech." She remembers, too, how he had teased them saying he was afraid to speak and that they must ensure that no one would attend the public meeting.

"Oh, they were grand, those early days with Swami. He was always in our midst and so accessible. These days, with the increase of devotees, such a thing is impossible," she says.

Sarojamma talked about how Sri Sathya Sai Baba persuaded her to marry. At first, he dropped a few hints, then he gave her affectionate advice to marry and, finally, he insisted that Sarojamma got married. She did her best to explain to him that she wanted to remain free as an unmarried woman, but he persisted. When he saw that she would not accept his view, he refused to speak to her. Sarojamma found this unbearable and so gave in and resolved to please Sri Sathya Sai Baba. He explained to her that she was her mother's only daughter and that it was her duty to please her mother by marrying. And, indeed, her mother's only prayer had always been that she should see her happily married. In later years, Sarojamma found her marriage a safe anchor, considerably steadying her impulsive nature.

However, marriage restricted her visits to Whitefield and Puttaparthi. Sarojamma's husband was transferred to Bijapur where there were no Sai activities. She felt lost without *bhajans*. So she went around Bijapur and discovered that there were many Sai devotees, but they had never come together. It did not take her long to start a Sai Association and organise weekly *bhajans*.

The birth of her only child, Jayashree, was a turning point in Sarojamma's life. Her health was critical. She had kidney failure after childbirth and she came close to death. The doctors in Bangalore wanted her to go to the hospital in Vellore for special treatment. She refused to go and be separated from her baby. Then later, she said she would go if Sri Sathya Sai Baba gave his permission. She was insistent on this point and so the ambulance she was in made a detour to Whitefield before it took her to Vellore. It remained parked inside the Brindavan compound until Sri Sathya Sai Baba emerged to give *darshan*. Sarojamma cried helplessly and he comforted her, "Nothing will happen to you . . . Swami will be with you throughout . . . Go to Vellore for the treatment . . . Don't worry about your baby, I will look after her." Sarojamma went to Vellore Hospital where she went from crisis to crisis and she survived them all to the amazement of the doctors there. Her stay at Vellore extended over several months and when, finally, she was discharged, she went straight to Whitefield.

Sri Sathya Sai Baba granted Sarojamma an interview. He told her he had given her *punar janma* (another life) and that she should not worry. He blessed her with good health in the future and named her daughter Jayashree (goddess of triumph) since she had brought victory to her mother.

Sarojamma wanted to know, "Why have you given me life now? Earlier, you saved my husband in an accident as well."

Sri Sathya Sai Baba replied, "I cannot explain these things. Take it to be the Divine Will."

When Sarojamma was discharged, she was told she had to return to the hospital periodically for regular check-ups and dialysis. But, since Sri Sathya Sai Baba blessed her with good health, she has never felt the need to return for check-ups or dialysis. Her health is absolutely normal.

Sarojamma resolved to dedicate her life to the service of Sri Sathya Sai Baba. He told her that, once her husband retired, he would let her spend time in Brindavan but until then, he said, her duty was at home. So when her husband, Sri Krishanswami, retired, Sri Sathya Sai Baba allowed them to live in Brindavan.

Sarojamma looks after the ladies' section of the *Seva Dal* and her husband helps with electrical engineering work in which he specialised during his working life.

"The Lord looks for sincerity, simplicity and unwavering joy in the contemplation of His name and form. All are beggars at the gates of Heaven. The hero is he who does not beg or cringe or fawn or flatter. He knows that the Lord knows best. If it is His will, He will grant food and raiment; if not, then let His will prevail. That is the way of sharanagati and of prapti."

. . . Sri Sathya Sai Baba

5

ROYAL DEVOTEES

The late Maharaja Jam Saheb of Nawanagar and the Maharani of Nawanagar were beloved of their subjects in Western India for the good that they had done them. After India attained independence, the Maharaja was Rajpramukh of Saurashtra for a few years and was the cornerstone in the authentic reconstruction of the historic *Shiva* temple at Somnath.

They first heard of Sri Sathya Sai Baba from a friend in 1958. At the time, the Maharaja was a sick man. And they had their own *guru*, a great and realised soul, without whose counsel they never took a spiritual step. The friend told them that Sri Sathya Sai Baba had granted him a vision of Lord *Krishna*, something he had longed for. He gave them a book, a copy of volume I of *Satyam Shivam Sundaram*. The Maharani read it but was not very impressed by it. It read to her like publicity, eulogising Sri Sathya Sai Baba for certain extraordinary powers, but she could not connect them with divinity.

Some years went by and the Maharaja's health deteriorated. The Maharani wished to comfort him. A gentleman called Shri Chudasama mentioned to her that a Dr. Gadhia was a Sai devotee and would be able to arrange Sai *bhajans* for her if she thought this would comfort the Jam Saheb. Dr. Gadhia was duly contacted and he arranged a *bhajan* evening which both the Maharaja and the Maharani appreciated very much. Then a second *bhajan* evening was arranged for the following week, on Tuesday evening the 1st of February 1965, after Dr. Gadhia finished his lectures at the Medical School. But this was not to be, for Dr. Gadhia was summoned away to Puttaparthi by an urgent message from Sri Sathya Sai Baba.

Three days later, the Jam Saheb became critically ill: a gall bladder stone gave him intense and constant pain. The doctors could not ease the pain with any kind of medication and reluctantly suggested surgery. He was terribly frail and the Maharani considered it unwise to move him to Bombay where the operation would have to take place. So, she sent for her *Guru Maharaj* but, alas, he was away. The Maharaja went through three more days and nights of agony. The Maharani could only watch and suffer with him. She felt helpless. The Maharaja's suffering was so unbearable that he said, despairingly and repeatedly, that he would rather die than endure the pain. He pleaded with the doctors that, if they could do nothing else, they could give him death.

On the fourth day, *Guru Maharaj* returned to Jamnagar from a trip around some villages. The car the Maharani had sent brought him to the palace. He went first to the Maharani and asked for details about her husband's illness. He asked her for milk and fruit and it became clear to her that he was marking time. It seemed that he had a purpose in mind for the delay and that he was waiting for the right moment to do something significant.

Guru Maharaj unexpectedly put his hand under the cushion on which he was seated and brought out a rolled sheet of paper which he opened. It was a photograph of Sri Sathya Sai Baba. He asked the Maharani to place it beside the Maharaja's bed and said that he must pray to it and offer it flowers. But, she asked *Guru Maharaj* to speak to the Jam Saheb himself and to give him the photograph personally. The Maharaja was very relieved to see *Guru Maharaj* and glad to receive the photograph of Sri Sathya Sai Baba. He put it on his bedside table for worship, meditation and floral offerings as instructed by *Guru Maharaj*.

The next evening, the post brought another surprise. In it was a letter from a Mr. Dixit, written at the personal instruction of Sri Sathya Sai Baba, asking the Maharani not to worry about her husband's illness and to apply everyday on the area of the pain the contents of the enclosed packet of *vibhuti*. The letter told her that he would be well again very soon.

The Maharani marvelled at the series of events. First of all, when *Guru Maharaj* had come to see her, he had had nothing on him and yet he had produced a photograph from under a cushion – and that a photograph of Sri Sathya Sai Baba. Then he told the Maharaja to pray to it. And never before had he even mentioned Sri Sathya Sai Baba. And then, strangest of all, the next day the letter arrived from Mr. Dixit. They had never been in touch with anyone in Puttaparthi. How did this Baba know all this?

When the Maharani told her *guru* about the letter, he was very pleased, as if in fact he had been expecting it. At her request, he came to see the

Maharaja every morning and applied the Sai *vibhuti* to his stomach. Within twenty-four hours of the first *vibhuti* application, there was great improvement. The pain subsided quickly after that and, in a week, the Maharaja was free of all pain.

"My husband was a changed man after that. He lived for exactly a year after this crisis and it was a peaceful period granted to him by Baba. He became completely religious and spiritual during that one year. It was a change that altered him so completely that he was altogether a different man. It was a change I had never been able to bring about, even with all I did to persuade him," said the Rajmata as she is since the Maharaja's death.

As the Maharaja recovered, the Maharani was happy to arrange for Scripture to be read to him. Slowly, he became a calmer and happier person and longed to meet Sri Sathya Sai Baba. So, efforts were made to arrange a meeting when Sri Sathya Sai Baba was to be in Poona and then in Bombay, but in vain.

Meanwhile, war broke out between India and Pakistan and Jamnagar was badly bombed. Radio Pakistan announced that the Jam Saheb's Palace in Jamnagar had been razed to the ground and that there were no survivors of the royal family. But the truth was very different, for another miracle had happened: several unexploded shells were found within the immediate grounds of the palace. Amazingly, not a single bomb or shell had hit the palace despite three consecutive air-raids on it and a shower of shells aimed directly at it.

After the war, the Jam Saheb's eagerness to meet Sri Sathya Sai Baba knew no bounds and he resolved to take a trip to Puttaparthi and there take his chances. His eyesight was bad and he felt weak. Puttaparthi in those days, 1965, barely had any accommodation or any other facilities, but nothing could deter the old Maharaja from making the journey. And so he reached Puttaparthi and waited a long time before he was called to an interview with Sri Sathya Sai Baba. He asked one of his devotees to bring a chair for the Jam Saheb who could not sit on the floor, although he tried hard. An old cane chair was brought from somewhere and the Jam Saheb was made to sit on it while Sri Sathya Sai Baba talked to him, and showered on him so much love that the old and sick Maharaja was happy as he had never been happy before.

Sri Sathya Sai Baba told him, "Our connection has existed for very long. I know you since the work of rebuilding the Somnath temple began. You have been good, a good king to your subjects." The Maharaja asked to have his eyesight restored so he could see the Lord. "I know well your love for *Dwarkadish* and *Somnath* and that you want your eyes back for their *darshan*. But, why do you worry about outer vision? It is inner vision that is important. You will have the *darshan*. That is my responsibility," Sri Sathya Sai Baba reassured the Jam Saheb.

The Jam Saheb invited Sri Sathya Sai Baba to Jamnagar. "I will be with you in your palace at the right time," replied Sri Sathya Sai Baba and sent him home. The Maharaja was so completely transformed after this meeting that he accepted everything without anger or revulsion. He had achieved the ideal equilibrium. Yet before this, even a small change in diet or routine had upset him. But now he was totally composed and he spent his time listening to readings from Scripture.

At two o'clock in the morning of the 3rd of February 1966, the Jam Saheb began to cough and said that he could not sleep. The Maharani tried to put him to bed again, but he simply refused to lie down. Slowly he walked to an armchair and there he sat quite contentedly talking of this and that. After a while, the Maharani felt his pulse and found none. Doctors were summoned immediately and they, too, found no pulse and no sign of life in the Jam Saheb's limbs except directly above the chest where life was tenaciously clinging on. They told the Maharani her husband had suffered a massive and fatal heart attack and that he should be made to lie down. But, he would simply not lie down.

The Maharani and the doctors realised that something strange was happening. The Jam Saheb appeared to be caught up in an extraordinary force which was allowing him to move and speak. He appeared content and it seemed to those with him, that since there was no blood pressure or pulse in his body, that indeed a miracle was taking place and the Jam Saheb's soul was waiting to be taken. He was completely unaware of the heart attack or of any pain.

At half past four, during *Brahma muhurtam* (the sacred hour of the Lord), the Jam Saheb left this earth. His face in death was supremely peaceful.

The Maharani, now the Rajmata, will always remember. "I felt Baba had come as promised to take him away. Truly, it was a beautiful way of reaching his destination. His body and face were in a perfect state of serenity. It was Baba who was with him at that time, who else? It was God who came to him at the right time to give him divine *darshan*," said the Rajmata who remembers that Sri Sathya Sai Baba had told the Maharaja, 'I will come and cure you of all disease and take you for *darshan* of *Somnath* and *Dwarkadish*.' "And so he came to give him *moksha*, to liberate his soul. The people in the room, all of us, we sensed a superhuman presence there."

This event strengthened the Rajmata's feelings for Sri Sathya Sai Baba and, from then on, she was very eager to meet him. Then she heard he was in Bombay and she asked her relatives from Kutch, who knew him, to help her to meet Sri Sathya Sai Baba. The Maharani of Kutch, a Sai devotee, told Sri Sathya Sai Baba of the Rajmata's wish to meet him and he replied that she should come to the Kutch residence the next evening where he would see her.

There, at the Kutch residence in Bombay, was where the Rajmata had her first *darshan* of Sri Sathya Sai Baba. And he asked her to go the next morning to his residence where he would speak to her.

The Rajmata humorously described her trek that morning, the milling crowd that jostled about even outside the gates. "It was good elbow work!" she commented humorously. Inside the compound, they waited in another swarm of pushing and shoving people. When Sri Sathya Sai Baba came he saw the bevy of royal ladies being pushed about and he smiled. "It must have amused Swami to see maharanis struggling and pushing forward in the middle of an unyielding crowd," the Rajmata laughed.

But soon, a devotee-volunteer appeared beside them and asked them to go along to the house to wait there for Sri Sathya Sai Baba. They waited for hours. Once, he came and gave them a passing glance and went away again. The Rajmata's companions tried to persuade her to leave to have lunch, but she said that Sri Sathya Sai Baba had said that he would talk to her that day and so she would wait. It was late afternoon when he finally talked to her. He told her he knew her many woes, about her family and her son.

This was the start of a time in her life full of wonderful and fulfilling experiences. The Rajmata is touchingly happy that she has reached "the lotus feet of the Lord . . . we are all lucky for he is the Lord Himself and none other," she emphasised the last two words.

On the next day, the 28th of March, she went again to see Sri Sathya Sai Baba. He told her that he was going to Jamnagar and asked her to accompany him. But, she left a day earlier to make preparations for his visit.

How was the Rajmata convinced of Sri Sathya Sai Baba's divinity? Did she have any doubts at all at the outset?

"Of course I had doubts, not one, bur several. But, I have learnt to keep an open mind and that helped me to see clearly and to steadily build an absolute faith."

The Rajmata explained the conflict that had existed in her mind: whether it would be right for her to have faith in and follow Sri Sathya Sai Baba, or should she reserve these feelings for her own *guru* in whom she had had faith for many years? She went to Whitefield and to Puttaparthi, but her loyalties were divided and she felt the pressure of the conflict.

Once, in Puttaparthi, while a celebration was in full swing, she was called away by a telephone call. When she returned, she saw that Sri Sathya Sai Baba had already entered and had taken his place on the dais. So, instead of disturbing others to return to her seat, she sat in a corner and watched from the side as Sri Sathya Sai Baba gave his discourse. Suddenly, she was startled. She rubbed her eyes hard and stared at the figure of Sri Sathya Sai Baba, but there was no mistaking what she saw: the face of her own *Guru Maharaj* on Sri Sathya Sai Baba's form: his body and his flame-coloured robe, but the face of her own *guru* of many years. What could this mean? The Rajmata pinched herself to see if she was dreaming, but no, she was wide awake and it was all true. In broad daylight and in an auditorium filled with thousands of people, she was being made to see the relationship between her *guru* and Sri Sathya Sai Baba. As she understood the significance of the apparition, she looked again at the dais and, once more, both the face and the body belonged to Sri Sathya Sai Baba.

This was an important event in the Rajmata's understanding of non-duality *(Advaita)* and led to her surrender to Sri Sathya Sai Baba. The Rajmata said, "It is better to go step by step in your convictions. Once you gain faith, never doubt or waver. There are bound to be tests on the way when you tread the spiritual path. Strange are the ways of the Divine! You must accept that and continue in your faith. You should not let trials and tribulations discourage you or make you give up the opportunity of this unique experience."

The Rajmata spoke of another significant event which also was one that helped her to fully surrender to Sri Sathya Sai Baba. She did not believe that the *vibhuti abhishekam* (shower of holy ash) performed on important days by Sri Sathya Sai Baba from an empty pot was a miracle. She suspected that the pot was crammed full of *vibhuti* beforehand and that Sri Sathya Sai Baba's hand rotating inside loosened it to cascade down dramatically over the silver idol of Shirdi Sai Baba. She was quite certain it was a trick.

One *Dassera*, while the *vibhuti abhishekam* was in progress, she was looking on as Sri Sathya Sai Baba's left hand was churning inside the upturned pot and the *vibhuti* was pouring down. He suddenly stared at her and changed hands. As the right hand took over, tinkling sounds were heard and precious stones and bits of gold and silver began to fall out of the pot together with the ash. The audience was electrified. The amazing shower continued until the Shirdi Sai Baba idol was covered in it. The Rajmata was shaken. She could not believe that so many precious stones and metals could also have somehow been hidden in the pot with the *vibhuti*. In her mind, she asked for forgiveness from Sri Sathya Sai Baba for doubting him. He gave her a look full of meaning that seemed to say, 'What do you say now?' and went away.

After the *vibhuti abhishekam* incident, the Rajmata had no more doubts left about Sri Sathya Sai Baba. She learned to believe that he was divine through and through, that he was divinity in human form come for the sole purpose of *Dharma Samsthapana* (the re-establishment of righteousness) in the world. Though devotion and surrender to Sri Sathya Sai Baba came gradually to her, the Rajmata is today firm and fixed in her faith in him. His words are divine commands to her as she is convinced that obiedience to him is the best of all things we can do since he is omniscient and omnipresent.

"But such is his greatness that when he is with us he makes it a point to be one of us, like one of the family, so that we never feel overwhelmed by his superior powers. It is this compassion and simplicity that make him so touching, so endearing. He has limitless power, and yet he jokes and laughs like a small boy. And he enjoys not only creating things out of thin air, but doing so much work himself, personally planning and supervising projects in his ever-active, ever-agile way that is so marvellous," said the Rajmata.

Has the Rajmata invited him to visit Saurashtra?

"Yes, in 1970, when the Digvijay Dwara at Somnath was built, Swami graciously consented to inaugurate it." (The Digvijay Dwara is the gateway to Somnath Temple and was named in honour of her late husband.) As one of the trustees of the Somnath Temple, the Rajmata was able to arrange the programme. Normally none but the priests are allowed inside the sanctum sanctorum, but they agreed that Sri Sathya Sai Baba could enter it. However, no one else would be allowed into the holy of holies, but would watch Sri Sathya Sai Baba perform the *puja* from just outside. The *puja* would be performed after the new gateway had been inaugurated.

The *lingam* at Somnath is huge, so Sri Sathya Sai Baba had to stand on a stool to perform the *puja*. The Rajmata remembered, "It was a rare sight, the *Shiva-Shakti Avatara* performing *puja* to Himself, just to please the assembled devotees." With the familiar round movements of his hand, Sri Sathya Sai Baba created silver and gold flowers and leaves and showered the *lingam* with them. Then, with a sudden sweep of his hand, he materialised something that glittered with an intense brilliance. It was the *Jyotirlingam*, the *lingam* of light! It was the size of a peahen's egg and translucent: the inner light was visible from every side. Holding the *lingam* in his hand, Sri Sathya Sai Baba proclaimed that from that day this *kshetra* (field/place) had a true *Jyotirlingam* with its original power intact. This meant that the reconstructed temple had regained all its original potency, sanctity and glory.

All those who attended this occasion at Somnath were awed by the incomparable spectacle they had witnessed. And the crowds outside the temple were thrilled when they heard of the phenomenal events. The Rajmata felt deep fulfillment at the thought that her husband had completed the reconstruction of the temple during his life and that Sri Sathya Sai Baba had re-invested the temple with its pristine potency.

Then the Rajmata remembered another wondrous incident. Sri Sathya Sai Baba and a group of his devotees which included the

Rajmata had wanted to go to the temple at Dwarka. When they reached it, they found the crowd there very large and unruly, so they did not go to the temple. On their way back, they stopped at a quiet beach for refreshments. Some members of the group expressed their disappointment at not having been able to have the *darshan* of *Sri Krishna* at Dwarka.

Sri Sathya Sai Baba heard this and laughed and said, "Surely, God is not a prisoner between four walls. He is omnipresent. If you wish you may have His *darshan* here as well."

Then he began to play with the sand. He made a pyramid of sand and flattened the top. With his finger he drew a shape on the flat top. The Rajmata was seated nearest to him and she watched all this very closely. Suddenly, Sri Sathya Sai Baba exclaimed, "It is ready!" and pulled out of the pyramid a gold idol which was an exact replica of the figure he had drawn: Lord *Krishna*, standing with his legs crossed, playing his flute.

"Swami had a glow all over him then. He appeared so radiant and divine that I could not stop looking at him. I felt he was the very *Krishna* he had created in idol form and not a human being at all. There was an indescribable radiance about him. It was glorious just to have been able to look at him then. That experience is unforgettable." The Rajmata remembers, too, that everyone asked him questions about the idol: what it was made of, how much did it weigh. Shri Ratanlal, a devotee from Bombay, managed to take a photograph, in the darkening light, of Sri Sathya Sai Baba holding the idol. Even in the photograph he looks altered. But seeing him then was real bliss, says the Rajmata, who relives those precious moments over and over again in her mind.

The Rajmata has experienced immense peace in the presence of Sri Sathya Sai Baba. "His guidance, his teachings, his words are so right. Swami believes in doing everything correctly and with propriety. Even when I told him in the beginning that I had to get my *guru's* permission to keep the locket he had given me, he readily agreed that it was the proper thing to do. And my *guru*, too, was only too happy about it and said that I had done the right thing in surrendering to Swami. It is said that the *guru* is very important as he leads you to God. In our case, our *guru* was the one who even gave us our first photograph of Swami!"

Once, at Whitefield, Sri Sathya Sai Baba asked the Rajmata what she had done with the locket he had given her. She took it out of her bag and handed it to him. He looked at it and said, "Not this now," and held it in his fist. When he opened his hand again, there was a different pendant in it, a bigger and more beautiful one made of enamel, with a picture of himself seated in the centre. "Wear it," he ordered. The Rajmata was wearing, as she always does, a double *mala* and the pendant could not be threaded onto it. So Sri Sathya Sai Baba waved his hand once more to produce a small pair of goldsmith's pliers. He put a bigger loop on the pendant, attached it to the *mala* and secured it very professionally. "Now, wear it," he told the Rajmata. Ever since then the Rajmata has worn the pendant. She never takes it off, but not even the sheen of the enamel has faded for, as she says, "It is the handiwork of the Divine Goldsmith! What he makes is different. Each gem, each metal . . . different jewellers give different names to the same stone."

Once, when she was very sick, he produced a *Shivalingam* for her and told her to perform *puja* to it and drink the water from it. This she solemnly does everyday.

On another occasion, the Rajmata requested Sri Sathya Sai Baba to give her a task to perform for she wished to have the chance to do *seva* (service). "You have done enough. Now, do only *charan seva*," (*charan seva* = worship of the lotus feet), was the reply as he materialised for her a lovely silver ring with two tiny feet embossed on it. Down the sides of the ring there are symbols of the various religions contained in the larger Sai symbol – the *Om* of Hinduism, the Wheel of Buddhism, the Cross of Christianity, the Fire of Zoroastrianism, and the Crescent of Islam. This is to show that the Sai faith embraces all religions for they all lead to the feet of the One God. The ring is so marvellous that it makes you wonder how it could have been produced in the wink of an eye.

"Swami looks after everything. There is nothing that happens without his knowledge. One need tell him nothing for he knows it all already. Sometimes he would tell me not to worry about my daughter in London for she was unwell, he would say, and that is why she has not written to you."

Under Sri Sathya Sai Baba's guidance, the Rajmata has started an educational trust in Jamnagar. The trust has a school at the moment and is scheduled to have a college in due course. The instruction in both institutions combines spiritual education with the normal curriculum.

"Swami is like a mirror. He reflects you, you see yourself in him. If you have pure love, he is love. If you have pure thoughts, he is sacred. He is the phenomenon for this age. Those of us in his presence should try to earn the consideration and grace he bestows on us," said the Rajmata with feeling.

She is immutable in her belief that Sri Sathya Sai Baba will succeed in bringing *dharma* back to the world. It may be a slow process, nevertheless it will happen for she senses progress even now. Some of the boys he has trained are already in important positions in the world and they must surely influence others. "This is how the actual working will be. After all, we Indians have lost our self-respect and with it our ability to appreciate our heritage and our traditional values. Once we learn to get back this respect and see our country and its culture in proper perspective, things will begin to change. This is where Swami's role is significant," the Rajmata said with unswerving faith.

"Two sentences can summarise all the eighteen Puranas composed by Vyasa. 'Be good to others; avoid doing harm.' Doing good is the medicine, avoiding harm is the regimen that must accompany the cure."

. . . Sri Sathya Sai Baba

6

FROM PUTTAPARTHI TO TANZANIA

In books about Sri Sathya Sai Baba, one can read how he brought back to life two people: Sri Radhakrishnan of Kuppam in Southern India and Mr. Walter Cowan, an American gentleman. They record that Sri Sathya Sai Baba brought Sri Radhakrishnan back from the dead twice: once from drowning in a well and again at Puttaparthi three days after his "death" when his body had already begun to decompose. Walter Cowan was brought back to life in a hospital in Madras where he had been certified dead and covered up preparatory to being taken to the morgue. Mr. Cowan has recorded his experiences from the moment he died to the moment he was brought back to life by Sri Sathya Sai Baba.

A startling instance is that of Dr. D. J. Gadhia who was involved in a fatal road accident in East Africa in May 1974. A lorry with a trailer, travelling very fast from the opposite direction, crashed head on into his car. At the moment of impact, Dr. Gadhia yelled, "Baba! Baba!" as he lost consciousness. He heard the driver say, "The poor Doctor is dead," as he sank into darkness.

Strangely, the Doctor felt his spirit travel to Prashanti Nilayam. After a long time, he was woken up by an imperious command spoken in Sri Sathya Sai Baba's voice, "Get up, or else the bones will break!"

He opened his eyes and saw two hefty Africans near the car. They had removed the glass, pulled out the seats and cut away the wreckage that had trapped the Doctor in his car.

Later, in hospital, Dr. Gadhia found that no one knew who the Africans were. They had been very efficient and had worked briskly and precisely, like experts who knew exactly what had to be done and how. No amateur Samaritan could have extricated Dr. Gadhia from the wrecked car. So bad was the damage that the steering wheel had been pushed all the way into the boot.

Everyone expected the two Africans to turn up sooner or later to claim their customary reward, but nobody ever turned up to claim it. Then Mrs. Gadhia remembered that the Africans had appeared quite suddenly, shouting, *"kishwahili, kishwahili,"* which means make way in Swahili. And one of the Africans had bent down towards her, as she sat stunned in the back of the car, and uttered soothing words. The Gadhias pieced together all the stray bits of information about the frightful accident and decided that it must have been Sri Sathya Sai Baba who sent help to wrench the Doctor from the jaws of death.

Dr. Gadhia had to stay in hospital for a long time as his leg had been severely damaged. So, he could not return to India till 1978. On the 20th of April, Sri Sathya Sai Baba granted him an interview at Whitefield.

Sri Sathya Sai Baba asked him, "Why do you still need the stick to walk? Throw it away!" Dr. Gadhia put it aside and discovered that he could walk perfectly well without it. Sri Sathya Sai Baba then explained, "I had to give you new life since your spine was completely broken in the accident. Do you remember how I came there as a pair of Africans?"

The Gadhias were thrilled to receive this affirmation, for upto then, they could only surmise. Sri Sathya Sai Baba had heard the call for help in Prashanti Nilayam although it was uttered in Arusha, in faraway Tanzania, and he had rushed to the rescue.

"I saved you because you have a lot more work to do," said Sri Sathya Sai Baba. He asked the Gadhias to stay on and attend the 1978 Summer Course on Indian Culture and Spirituality at Brindavan. Dr. Gadhia runs the Om Satya Sai Dispensary in Arusha, Tanzania. He has been a Sai devotee since his student days in 1959, since the day he saw Sri Sathya Sai Baba cure Mr. Madhav Dixit of acute diabetes. (Mr. Dixit had 240 milligrams per c.c. of sugar as compared to the normal 120 milligrams and was living on very strong insulin injections.) Sri Sathya Sai Baba materialised a special chocolate coloured *vibhuti* for him which cured his diabetes completely, so that not only did he go off insulin, but, better still, he could eat sweet things like any normal person. Mr. Dixit lived for eight years after that and Dr. Gadhia says that his cure was "proof positive of the divinity of Baba." Before this, Dr. Gadhia had many doubts about Sri Sathya Sai Baba's divine powers, but each time, something would happen to rid him of his doubt.

Dr. Gadhia spoke of an interesting incident that occurred in 1962. At half past two in the afternoon, during an interview, Sri Sathya Sai Baba asked him to take down the following notes as he spoke: "Your mother is being operated on now in Kampala and doctors say that she has no hope of survival. But, I will give her new life and she will be all right."

Dr. Gadhia had known nothing about any operation on his mother. So, he wrote a letter to find out what was happening. His brother answered and confirmed that she had been rushed to hospital with gangrene of the intestines and, as a last resort, the doctors had performed emergency surgery on her, but without any real hope. His brother then remembered the packet of Sai *vibhuti* and asked the doctors to apply it on her so that she might have Sri Sathya Sai Baba's blessings as she breathed her last. But, miraculously, she had come through the dangerous operation.

"Baba's grace toward our family has been constant." Once again, during an interview at Brindavan, Sri Sathya Sai Baba told Dr. Gadhia, "I went to Kampala yesterday to save your parents from a car accident." Much later, Dr. Gadhia received a communication about the "nasty" accident in which their car was completely smashed though they had miraculously escaped.

"Why such grace?" asked Dr. Gadhia and Sri Sathya Sai Baba told him, "It is the *bhakti* of your parents and mainly your grandmother who was a very pious soul." Then Dr. Gadhia remembered several stories about his grandmother, a kind and noble lady, blessed by a great saint who said that generations would reap the benefits of her piety and prayers. The Doctor then believed that the accumulated good in his family had helped them to become Sai devotees.

After receiving his M.B.B.S. degree, Dr. Gadhia went to see Sri Sathya Sai Baba. Sri Sathya Sai Baba posed for photographs in the interview room. Then something happened with a flash. Sri Sathya Sai Baba made Dr. Gadhia stand in one corner of the room and blessed him and the Doctor felt as though a current passed through him. Sri Sathya Sai Baba said, "From today you will do my work."

Dr. Gadhia felt blessed and very happy. That was 1963 and when he asked for Sri Sathya Sai Baba's blessings before going back to Tanzania, he materialised a locket for his *raksha* (protection) and said, "Keep this with you always and say a prayer to it whenever you are in difficulties and Swami will take care."

The Doctor showed me the locket which looks like a medallion. It is copper with an enamel design in pleasing colours. The main figure on the enamel is *Vishnu* (also *Satyanarayana*) holding a conch and a mace. In *Vishnu's* heart is the face of Shirdi Sai Baba, below that the face of Sri Sathya Sai Baba and further down, the form of Prema Sai seated on a black flower, in the famous stance of Shirdi Sai Baba, with one foot resting on the other knee. It is a unique composition, presenting the past, present and future Sai *Avataras* in minute representation on a medallion. When the medallion was turned upside down, the figure of Prema Sai resembled the face of Sri Sathya Sai Baba, the black flower forming the familiar frizzy crown of hair.

Dr. Gadhia was stunned to have been given the locket. How could this unique locket be "transported?" It is a piece that would have to be specially made by a goldsmith and it would take a long time to make. "Only divine hands such as his can fashion such a locket instantly!" he said to himself. Such an object could not be bought readymade from a shop since it is not likely that anyone could know what Prema Sai, yet to be born, looks like.

On the day that Dr. Gadhia received his locket, he had with him Swami Shraddhananda, a well known and respected *sannyasin* and a disciple of Swami Vajreshwari. He himself had *ashramas* in many parts of India and abroad, and wanted to meet Sri Sathya Sai Baba. As soon as they came, Sri Sathya Sai Baba asked Dr. Gadhia, "Why have you brought Swamiji?"

"Swami Shraddhananda was insistent," he replied.

Sri Sathya Sai Baba moved his hand in the familiar circular way and Swami Shraddhananda pounced on it and caught it and said, "Don't give me those peppermints!" Dr. Gadhia was aghast, but Sri Sathya Sai Baba remained unperturbed. If proof was needed that he is *Prema Swarupa*, then here it was: in this moment of extreme provocation, he was full of love and spoke gently to the aggressive *swami*, "Let me give the peppermints to those who want them. Then I will talk to you."

Then he posed for photographs, gave a short talk on ethics and materialised Dr. Gadhia's unique locket. He gave *prasad* and interviews to all those present. Finally, he took Swami Shraddhananda aside for a private interview. In a few minutes, Shraddhananda emerged from the interview exultant, tears of joy streaming down his face. Later, when he was more composed, Shraddhananda said, "Baba is a great soul. He is divine. For, when he opened his shirt, I saw my *guru*. Yes, Guru Nityananda on his chest!"

Dr. Gadhia said there are many other realised people in the world. This particular *swami* had come to test Sri Sathya Sai Baba and had come away from the encounter completely convinced of his divinity. There are some higher souls, like Swami Muktananda, who have seen him as Lord *Krishna*.

After receiving the divine blessing of Sri Sathya Sai Baba, Dr. Gadhia launched his Om Sai Dispensary in Arusha. On the day of the opening, Sri Sathya Sai Baba sent him a telegram which said, "Blessings. Cultivate and spread *prema*." Dr. Gadhia has made this message his life's mission.

"Baba has been with me and has guided me all these years," says Dr. Gadhia. His wedding was also celebrated by Sri Sathya Sai Baba in Puttaparthi. He and his wife, Nanda, take an active part in composing and singing *bhajans*, as they take part in many other Sai activities.

Dr. Gadhia makes frequent trips to India to see Sri Sathya Sai Baba. He was privileged to accompany him to Saurashtra where Dr. Gadhia used to work at the Medical College in Jamnagar. Dr. Gadhia recalls with love several enlightening experiences during this trip, "which have proved to me beyond the shadow of a doubt that Baba is a divine personage, operating on a very different plane." Even in far-away Africa, Dr. Gadhia says he can feel Sri Sathya Sai Baba's divine grace helping him in so many ways.

"However high a bird may soar, sooner or later it must perch on a tree top to enjoy quietness. So too a day comes when even the most haughty, the most willful, the most unbelieving, even those who assert that there is no joy or peace in the contemplation of the Highest Self, will have to pray 'O God, grant me peace, grant me consolation, strength and joy'."

. . . Sri Sathya Sai Baba

7

THE STORY OF A WORLDLY MAN

Sri S. N. Singh, a successful businessman and ardent Sai devotee, firmly believes that Sri Sathya Sai Baba is divine. "The greatest quality of Baba is his charisma and the faith he instills in people. Though everyone is governed by the laws of *karma*, the grace of Baba can relieve the *karmic* debt to a large extent," he maintains.

Once, Sri Singh tried to see Sri Sathya Sai Baba when he was visiting Bombay. He waited for two hours without seeing him. He was so despondent that he went straight to Shirdi, two hundred miles inland, to the shrine of the first Sai Baba, to complain. The next time he tried to see Sri Sathya Sai Baba, this time in Bangalore, he not only saw him but was granted an interview with him. Sri Sathya Sai Baba materialised a ring for him with, on it, portraits of both Sai Babas. He became so elated that he dashed back to his hotel and knocked back two Martinis; it was most unlike him to need the relief.

Sri Singh has had many thrilling experiences with Sri Sathya Sai Baba and they have strengthened and solidified his faith. The first time he was in Puttaparthi, and as he stood in the grounds after *darshan*, he thought to himself that nothing in the world was more sacred than the sand and earth touched by Sri Sathya Sai Baba's feet. He went on to think that the greatest thing to have would be a strand of Sri Sathya Sai Baba's hair.

A few days later, Sri Singh returned home to Calcutta. Sri Murthy, the son of Sri N. Kasturi, who is also a noted geologist, was in Calcutta at the time and he invited him to dinner. Late that morning, Sri Singh had returned from a Sai *Samithi* meeting with the idea of changing. It was his custom to keep two or three silk handkerchiefs in his pockets. That day, he happened to have two handkerchiefs in one pocket and one in another. As he pulled out one of the two, the sweet smell of *chandan* (sandal wood paste) came from it. He opened it out and discovered round *chandan* marks on it. He wondered where they could have come from . . . He had been wearing a freshly laundered and ironed shirt and the handkerchiefs had also been washed and pressed. Yet somehow, the *chandan* had seeped into one of them and, what was more astonishing, it was still damp and fresh. It baffled him.

When he put his hand in the breast pocket, he found in the folds of that handkerchief dry grains of earth. Sri Singh excitedly called his wife. The grains of sand were carefully emptied onto a clean sheet of paper and, to their further surprise, they found among the sand one strand of curly grey-black hair.

Then in a flash he had the answer: it had to be an act of Sri Sathya Sai Baba's grace. His silent wish for the dust from under his feet and a lock of his hair had been mysteriously fulfilled. He was deeply moved and exhilerated by these tokens of Sri Sathya Sai Baba's grace.

Later, when Sri Murthy, the geologist, examined the granules of earth, he said they were typical of the kind of earth at Puttaparthi. Sri Singh was truly greatly touched by this *leela* which granted him not only his wish for a strand of Sai hair and dust from under Sri Sathya Sai Baba's feet, but as a bonus, the fragrant *prasad* of sandal wood paste.

This miracle deepened his faith in Sri Sathya Sai Baba for, as he says, "Devotion intensifies in degrees and it is good to build faith gradually. The strongest point to be made about Baba is his 'faith charisma', the touching and endearing ways in which he guides people's faith towards divinity."

Recalling the most active days of his business career, Sri Singh said that he had enjoyed a worldly life to the fullest: he ate meat, drank alcohol and smoked heavily. Indeed, he had been a chain smoker. During his first two visits to Puttaparthi, he had not curtailed his smoking. He used to stay at the Rangappa Hotel outside the *ashrama* grounds where there were no rules to break or code of discipline to follow. Suddenly one day, at dawn, just as he was going out to bath, he lit hls habitual ciagarette, but found that he did not really feel like smoking. He threw it away. And, from that moment on, his urge to smoke simply vanished Then, gradually, he stopped wanting alcohol and meat. Six months after the first time he saw Sri Sathya Sai Baba, he was completely vegetarian and had given up smoking and drinking alcohol.

"This is none other than Swami's doing, without even uttering a word. Why else would I have lost interest in these habits of such long standing? Swami never tells anyone to do this or to do that. His will prevails and he removes from us our longing for useless or harmful activities. I don't miss and never have missed my cigarettes since I gave them up. Normally, it would have been a struggle for a chain smoker like me to have stopped smoking, even on doctor's orders, without becoming irritable and tetchy. But, that is Swami. His miracle consists in changing people, in making them renounce the bad in them of their own volition and without regret."

Sri Singh related another instance of Sri Sathya Sai Baba's life-giving and creative power. It happened in 1975 to his eighty-nine-year-old mother. In the first week of May, her kidneys were found to be totally out of order and, as a result, her leg and ankle were very swollen. All the top physicians of Calcutta had attended her, but none of them could help. The swollen leg was nine inches wider than the other one, she could hardly eat and, for the last six weeks, she had existed on two teaspoons of barley water a day. Sri Singh was devoted to his mother who had brought him up single-handedly as his father had died when he was only four years old. During this desolate period, Sri Singh heard that Sri Sathya Sai Baba was to be in Bombay and he wanted very much to go there to see him. Two days before his intended departure, his mother went into a coma. He sent a telegram to Professor Gokak expressing his regrets and his inability to travel to Bombay.

That night, Sri Singh felt that worldly success, wealth and all its accoutrements were singularly useless, for they could give no succour to his sick and dying mother.

At midnight, he left his mother's bedside and, before going to bed, prayed to Sri Sathya Sai Baba: "Swami, take her away if that is your will. But, please, do not make her suffer. Give her perfect health and a good appetite till the very last and give her these for two or three more months. Then, take her to your lotus feet." A tear escaped down his cheek. He cannot remember how he finally fell asleep.

Next morning, the nurse came running to his wife, excitedly saying that her mother-in-law was sitting up in bed and asking for *khichri* (rice and lentil dish). Mrs. Singh went to her mother-in-law and said, "How can you possibly want *khichri*? You've never asked for it first thing in the morning. And for the last six weeks you've been on liquids only!" The old lady smiled and said that Sri Sathya Sai Baba had come to her in the night with a rope in his hand (such as is used for swings) which he swung about playfully and said, "Eat well and get well . . . I will take you when the time comes." Then he had vanished. She said that as soon as she woke up that morning, she felt absolutely well and quite hungry, so she asked the nurse to fetch some *khichri*.

The mother's condition improved so suddenly that the doctors were taken aback. There was no more need to keep her on a liquid diet. She ate well, very nourishing and even rich food. She could also digest all her favourite food, like *makki roti* (cornflour bread). She was very well indeed. Although the doctors continued to be mystified, the family were very relieved and happy.

Though the old lady had not realized the extent of Sri Sathya Sai Baba's omnipresence and omniscience, Sri Singh attributed her remarkable recovery entirely to him. Later, when Sri Singh was in Puttaparthi, Sri Sathya Sai Baba said to him, "I got your two telegrams."

Sri Singh said, "Swami, I sent only one, to Professor Gokak, about not being able to go to Bombay."

"What about the second telegram from your heart?" he asked, touching Sri Singh's chest. Sri Singh was overwhelmed. Yes, it was true, Sri Sathya Sai Baba was referring to that silent and desperate nocturnal prayer he had addressed to him about his mother's suffering, when one tear had squeezed out of his eye. And, with his miraculous power, he had cured his mother. Sri Singh's heart almost burst with gratitude.

After a while, Sri Sathya Sai Baba turned to Sri Singh and asked, "Your daughter, where is she?" Then immediately, "Come to me in half an hour." When Sri Singh returned, he gave him three packets of *vibhuti* and said, "One for the daughter, one for the mother and one for the wife." He also materialised a *rudraksha* bead for his mother with instructions to dip it in water and then drink that water. "I know," he said, "she has pain and swelling in her leg."

Sri Singh gave the *rudraksha* bead to his mother. She followed Sri Sathya Sai Baba's directions and, in ten days, the swelling disappeared and her leg was back to normal. Once again, the doctors were baffled. She lived for more than eleven weeks in perfect health, and she was happy. When the end came, it was peaceful and over in five minutes. Once more, Sri Singh was profoundly moved by Sri Sathya Sai Baba's grace which allowed his mother to reach the Lord's feet without suffering.

And what happened to the other *vibhuti*? One, he sent to his daughter in London and before it had even reached her, she was on the telephone to him. She had been in excruciating pain and it had been diagnosed as a slipped disc. She was bed-ridden when the *vibhuti* arrived. A few hours after she applied the *vibhuti* to the painful area and swallowed what was left, she felt well enough to get out of bed and do some overdue housework. When she had been X-rayed, her doctor had said that the symptoms indicated a slipped disc; now, he thought the diagnosis could have been wrong.

Sri Singh spoke of several instances of Sri Sathya Sai Baba's mind reading. "By reading your mind, he strengthens it. It is not done just for the sake of reading it. You will then try to control your mind and steady your thoughts and try to have only good and pure thoughts," he explained and continued, "For Baba to know your thoughts, you need not be in his presence. You can be anywhere at all and he will always know your thoughts."

In 1975, while the boys of the Satya Sai College at Whitefield were rehearsing the play *'Harishchandra'*, Sri Sathya Sai Baba personally directed them. These sessions took place upstairs in the house which is his residence there. No one else was allowed to enter that part of the house and all interviews were cancelled. Sri Singh and a few others had gone there to see him and, though they waited for some time, Sri Sathya Sai Baba did not come down to see them. Mr. Chatterjee and Justice Dutta of Calcutta, who were with Sri Singh, said they thought they ought to return since Sri Sathya Sai Baba was busy rehearsing the play with the students and they did not believe that he would come downstairs to give interviews.

Sri Singh thought then, "It is all Baba's wish. What could there be about rehearsals to keep him there? If he wanted to see us, he would stop them and call us." After that, he waited a few more minutes but soon, like the others, he decided to leave. He got into his car and drove off. Hardly had he reached the compound gates when three boys came running up to his car, just in the nick of time, to tell him that Sri Sathya Sai Baba wanted to see him upstairs. This was highly unusual as no one was allowed upstairs during rehearsals. It meant that Sri Singh was being accorded a rare privilege because his thoughts about "reahearsals and why should not Baba stop them and call me upstairs" had apparently reached Sri Sathya Sai Baba who must have decided to indulge a devotee.

Sri Singh freely admits that all his money, and the comforts it can buy, never brought him peace of mind. In the past, he had his full share of an active life and it was not without strains. Like most people in high society, he was wont to throw away money on the sating of meaningless personal greed and on games which were no more than a dignified form of gambling. He owned a string of race horses and also bred them, and he enjoyed a good bet. He had spent a great deal of time and money luxuriously wandering the world. Now he says, "Surrender at the lotus feet of Baba has not only helped me to realise the futility of all such endeavours; it has also helped me to gain peace of mind as never before and to follow along Swami's path of *satya, dharma, shanti* and *prema*."

"Consider all your acts as worship. Duty is God. Work is worship."

. . . Sri Sathya Sai Baba

8

19mm BOLTS INTO 16mm BORES

Dr. Gunasingam and his wife, Gnanasodhy, are from Malaysia, but they now live in Jamshedpur, the iron and steel manufacturing city in Eastern India. Sri Sathya Sai Baba often appears in Gnanasodhy's dreams to clear away her doubts as they arise.

Gnanasodhy first went to Whitefield with friends who were Sai devotees. "One look at Baba changed everything for me. I felt I'd seen a bright streak, a ray of light emanating from his head and I knew instantly that he was divine," she said.

Once, she had had no news of a certain intended wedding in the family and she had been terribly worried. She wrote to Sri Sathya Sai Baba about her worries and enclosed a stamped and self-addressed envelope. In four days, the self-addressed letter had come back with her own letter in it. In the same post, she also received a letter from her mother from which she learnt all the details about the wedding that she had been fretting over. "Of course it is Baba's doing to make my mother write and take away my worries. Nothing is too trivial for him. How else can one explain my letter to him being inside the self-addressed envelope and reaching me in the same post as my mother's letter?" declaimed Gnanasodhy.

She says that Sri Sathya Sai Baba has appeared in her dreams many times to warn her of things to come. Thus, she was forewarned of her uncle's death as she had been of her aunts' deaths – each time, she had been prepared. And it helped her to prepare other members of the family for the oncoming sorrow. She is certain that she was able to mentally prepare her uncle for his end and to turn his thoughts towards God. She was happy that he took up the chant *'Sai Ram'* and was relaxed when death came even though, before that, he had been afraid of the idea of death. "It was Swami alone who gave him the right frame of mind to accept the inevitability of his death and to be unafraid of it."

Gnanasodhy once read a description of the *Garuda* mark on Sri Sathya Sai Baba's chest – a symbol of divinity – and wondered about it. She thought, "What is the use of learning about this symbol? I am a woman and so I will never get to see it." That night, Sri Sathya Sai Baba appeared in her dreams clad only in a *dhoti*. An astonished Gnanasodhy stared and stared and he smiled and pointed to the *Garuda* mark just below his breast. She looked in amazement: yes, there it was, the great eagle clearly outlined. Then Sri Sathya Sai Baba asked her, "Now are you happy that you have seen the symbol?" Then he left her dream.

She has had several dreams in which Sri Sathya Sai Baba has appeared in various attires. She has often said, "There is no one like him. He is so mod!" And so, there he was, giving her "mod" visions of himself . . .

"It is true. I have not imagined anything, never! My God, some of the clothes he wore were so trendy, like tights and bell bottoms. If I described all of them, you would think me crazy but, honestly, it's true. Some of the things he wore were unique, so fashionable that any designer would have loved to copy them." Gnanasodhy is an earnest woman who has unshakable faith in Sri Sathya Sai Baba as an *avatara*, and she feels that everything that happens in life is his doing.

Her husband, Dr. P. Gunasingam, was sceptical when he first went to see Sri Sathya Sai Baba which he did through mere curiosity. He was prepared to think the worst and yet he thought, "Give me just one unmistakable sign of your divinity, Baba, and I will surrender to you." When Sri Sathya Sai Baba emerged from his bungalow, Gunasingam was transfixed: he saw a halo around Sri Sathya Sai Baba's head. It was light gold though the day was not sunny. The halo was bright and beautiful and it came straight to Gunasingam. He felt purified by the luminous beam which immediately established the connection between him and Sri Sathya Sai Baba. From that moment, Gunasingam accepted "all happenings as the divine will of Baba."

"Of course, Baba is in everything. He watches over everything we do," said Dr. Gunasingam. He attends to all his medical wards everyday only after addressing a mental prayer to Sri Sathya Sai Baba. He believes steadfastly that a few cases of childbirth which should have been fatal proved not to be so due solely to his prayers to Sri Sathya Sai Baba.

Dr. Gunasingam is active in the *Bal Vikas* organization and has a team of fifteen Sai workers in Jamshedpur who undertake fabrication and machinery work. They put up office buildings, bicycle stands and the like. He spoke of a Sai experience which got his team out of a tight spot and saved him about Rs. 30,000. – (approximately £1360.00). They had accepted a job to construct a bicycle stand and had made 16mm foundation base plates for it. It was to be a fairly large structure with several columns and "we got everything ready to fit. When we arrived at the site on the eve of the deadline date, we found that the engineer had changed the specification to 19mm bolts. We were frantic with worry, for with the change, we couldn't possibly be ready the next day and this could very well result in the cancellation of the order." In effect, it meant making the holes wider, cutting the base plates and drilling the extra 3mm. It was not the thought of the added cost for the gas and drilling that was daunting, but how they were going to drill the holes in time to meet the deadline next morning.

There was no way of organizing the work at night. Dr. Gunasingam prayed to Sri Sathya Sai Baba "for a solution before the workers report for duty in the morning." "Baba," he prayed, "please tell us how to do the fitting with this 3mm difference," and then he added, "Baba, this is your work. Whatever you want, please do." Then he went to sleep.

In the morning, Dr. Gunasingam was anxious to reach the site early to explain the problem to his workers, but he was delayed. When he did reach it, however, he was amazed. He saw that more than half the columns were ready and in place. His workers had seen the bolts and plates and, not seeing any technical difference, had set to work installing them. How had the 19mm bolts slotted into the 16mm bores? As the work went on, Dr. Gunasingam measured and checked and rechecked. The bolts were bigger, but the fit was nonetheless perfect. He looked at the photograph of Sri Sathya Sai Baba hanging at the site and thanked him from the heart.

"This is just one example. There are several others in which, after doing our best, we still faced unsurmountable obstacles. Whenever we've prayed to him, he has always come to our rescue," said Dr. Gunasingam.

A recent such experience was at Telco where the Sai *Seva* (Service) team had been asked to assist in clearing a blocked sewage unit which no one else had been able to do. It was a job given to them as a sort of challenge since they had proved very efficient in handling other problematic jobs. Dr. Gunasingam and his team set to work at the main unit, but without results. The bio-filter inside was stuck and could not be made to budge an inch despite everything they tried. The people who had given Dr. Gunasingam's team the work were beginning to lose confidence in their ability. Again, at that troublesome stage, Dr. Gunasingam prayed to Sri Sathya Sai Baba as both human and mechanical efforts had failed. As always, they had placed a photograph of Sri Sathya Sai Baba at the site. Dr. Gunasingam sat near it and prayed, "*Bhagavan*, please open this for us. Otherwise your Sai Service Unit could get an unsatisfactory reputation." Then he went back to the jammed bio-filter to give it one last push, and it gave away at the merest touch. The Telco people were completely bowled over.

"Real meditation is being absorbed in the thought of God all the time. God only and only God. Think God, breathe God, see God, hear God, eat God, drink God, love God, live God."

. . . Sri Sathya Sai Baba

9

WHO WAS THE LOVELY LADY?

"The advent of Sathya Sai does not always occur only through miracles and *vibhuti* showers. Let me tell you what happened in the milieu of my own home," said Srimati Sita Mahalakshmi. She has come to stay in Whitefield where she has settled down at last after a brilliant career as a lawyer. Her husband, Sri Sambasiva Rao, is a retired High Court judge. She said, "My name, too, was put up for appointment as judge in the High Court, but I did not take it up. Can anyone have greater happiness and peace anywhere other than near *Bhagavan* Baba? One ought not to waste all one's time and live life without the thought of God." And of this last she is convinced.

How did she first come into contact with Sri Sathya Sai Baba?

It was all so unexpected. Her only son, at the age of eleven, suffered a sudden paralytic stroke and became an invalid. She had studied Law in private while married and, at the time, was practising it successfully. She was also a notable social worker and had started several social service institutions in all the places that her husband had been posted in. She had spent nearly fifteen years in selfless service to less fortunate children.

The doctor told her that her son would never walk again. She tried treatment after treatment with the boy confined to bed in Madras.

Learning of his plight, two colleagues at the Bar called on her to offer consolation. "Do not feel bad," they said, "after all, you have only one son. How can it matter since you are quite well off? You can easily afford to give him a good life. Even President Roosevelt was in a wheelchair."

The words gave her a jolt. She was angry that people should think that money could make up for her afflicted son. That day, she sat on the verandah of her house and said to herself, "Oh God, why have You done this to me? Surely, I do not deserve this punishment when all my life I have done nothing but good and especially to children. Why should the legs of my only child be snatched away from him like this?" Feeling bitter and despondent, she prayed for an answer for she believed that that was her due.

All of a sudden, she saw a very beautiful lady seated next to her on the sofa. Sita Mahalakshmi was dazzled by the radiant beauty of the mysterious lady. She sat stunned into silent admiration of the lovely stranger next to her. Her mind was numbed by grief and she did not question the sudden appearance at her side. The lady smiled and spoke to her gently and very affectionately. "Sita Mahalakshmi, don't be worried or sad. Pray to Sai Baba and your son will be all right," she said.

"I have addressed so many prayers to so many gods. I don't want to pray anymore to anyone," replied Sita Mahalakshmi.

"You are young . . . you think you are earning so much and doing so much . . . Believe me, have faith in Sai Baba and pray to him." And saying that, the lovely stranger vanished.

Sita Mahalakshmi puzzled over this incident. How could she have vanished, just like that? Both she and her son, who had watched everything from his bed, were equally astonished by the event, but they did not discuss it just then. At night, before lights out, the boy asked his mother to pray to Sai Baba as the beautiful lady had advised. So, mother and son prayed sincerely to Sai Baba before going to sleep.

It must have been about midnight when Sita Mahalakshmi was awakened by a sound. Her son was excitedly clicking his fingers and calling out to her, "Mummy, lift me up. I want to walk." It was a most peculiar request for the boy knew perfectly well his own paralysed state. The mother tried to calm him and said, "Go back to sleep, this is hardly the time to walk. If you fall, there won't be anyone to pick you up." But the boy would not take no for an answer. He insisted that he wanted to walk. Then she asked him how his legs felt and he replied, "All these days they have been like tyres without air in them, but now they feel as if they've been pumped up. I feel as though there's an electric current going through my legs. Let me walk, Mummy, please," he pleaded again.

Then Sita Mahalakshmi lifted her son out of bed and put him on the floor and he walked. He walked alone to the light switch and turned on the light. He looked for his shoes and socks and found them and put them on. He wanted to go for a walk! Sita Mahalakshmi could not believe her eyes. She felt dazed.

How had this happened so suddenly? His legs had been useless for months. Even all the doctors had pronounced his a hopeless case. In a state of incredulous ecstasy, she gazed lovingly at her son and saw him with amazement, concern, sympathy and wonder till dawn. At four o'clock, the boy was still pleading to be taken for a walk, so she took him to the palm grove park at Mylapore (Madras). "Oh, it was incredible and so wonderful. The doctors could not believe that my son had been redeemed overnight from his former pathetic condition."

After this miraculous cure, Sita Mahalakshmi asked someone in Madras, "Who is Sai Baba?" She was told that there was a Sai Baba temple at Shirdi in Maharashtra where people went on pilgrimage. At the earliest opportunity, she took her family to Shirdi to do homage to the Sai Baba to whom she already owed so very much.

It was dusk when they reached Shirdi, so they settled down for the night in nearby lodgings. In a little while, a young man of about twenty arrived and said, "Sita Mahalakshmi, get up! I will give you *teertham* (holy water)." She was confused and very reluctant to accept anything from a stranger in a strange place. But, the young man went on, "Everyone thinks Sita Mahalakshmi is very healthy, but she has pain all over her body. Get up!" What he said was true and she was on the brink of a nervous breakdown caused by the agonies she had suffered during her son's illness. She could not get up. Her husband and her son pulled her up and made her stretch out her hand and open it. "Oh, it wasn't just *teertham*, it was *amruta* (nectar) that was put into my hand," she said, "after I swallowed it, there was no more trace of the young man."

The family went to the temple of Shirdi Sai Baba and then returned to Madras. A few days afterwards, Sita Mahalakshmi dreamt that a lady came to her and took her by the hand to a place where there were shining golden hills and there stood a young man in great splendour.

Early the next day, Sita Mahalakshmi and her son went to the house of a Mrs. Hanumantha Rao for the first time. As soon as she entered, she felt she was in familiar surroundings. A young Sri Sathya Sai Baba, twenty years old at the time, stood at the top of a flight of stairs. It was the same glorious young man she had seen in the dream standing on top of a shining hill. He looked at her and said, "Yes, you saw me once last night in the dream." He gave her and her son *prasad*.

"Can you believe it? After all those wondrous events and the miraculous cure, I lost touch with Baba for nearly sixteen years. What stupidity on my part. What wasted years," she said. "I was extremely busy being a lawyer, bar councillor, President of the Bar Foundation and making news in the legal world with victories in Court with crucial civil and criminal cases. I was also a busy housewife and mother, watching over my son's studies. I performed *puja* to Shirdi Sai Baba and carried out my domestic and professional duties in exemplary fashion. And the result was that I never made any effort to see Baba till one day, sixteen years later, Mrs. B. Ramakrishna Rao spoke to me in Hyderabad about the Divine *Avatara* on earth in the form of Sri Sathya Sai Baba."

Then one day, Sri Sathya Sai Baba was in town. Sita Mahalakshmi and her son went to the house where he was staying. He recognized her immediately and reminded her about the dream and their first meeting when "Swami gave *vibhuti* to her and jasmine flowers to the boy." Then he turned to her son, now a grown man, patted him on the back and said, "Sixteen years have passed by." Sita Mahalakshmi was filled with remorse for the lost and wasted years and deeply touched that he had remembered and recalled all the details.

After that, she went to Puttaparthi regularly. Sri Sathya Sai Baba was very kind to her and blessed her son many times. She recalled the many occasions when he came to her house and the great good fortune she had to do *paada seva* (worship of the feet) to him. And he granted her mystical visions very many times. He showered her family with grace, effecting many more miraculous cures. Sita Mahalakshmi gave a few instances, but there are too many to set them all out here.

Her youngest sister was found to have abdominal cancer. She underwent major surgery thrice and then she had to have yet another very grave operation. The very best surgeons in Hyderabad gave up all hope of her survival and were even hesitant to perform the fourth operation though they recognized that it was essential.

Sita Mahalakshmi prayed to Sri Sathya Sai Baba, "I am the eldest and she is the youngest in our large family of ten children. Why is her life in peril when I am so many years older and am in good health?" With true humility she prayed again and again for his intercession. She spoke to him in her mind, "Do you know what people will say? The older sister is hale and hearty and the youngest is gone! So, please *Bhagavan*, shorten the span of my life on earth if need be and add those years to hers. Please give her more years on earth." And, after that prayer, she slept.

Sri Sathya Sai Baba came to her in an early morning dream. She said to him, "Give *abhayam* (fearlessness) to my sister who is about to have an operation." In response, he showed her his *abhaya hasta* (a hand raised in a gesture of protection). Then, he appeared in the Shirdi Sai Baba way on the patient's bed. When the patient questioned him, he answered, "I sit to have your sullied body washed and cleansed." With that assurance in mind, Sita Mahalakshmi's sister faced the approaching operation with confidence. To the wonder and amazement of the doctors and nurses, the operation was a success. Her rapid recovery astonished everyone at St. Teresa's Hospital in Hyderabad and they freely admitted that her recovery was due entirely to the miracle performed by Sri Sathya Sai Baba.

Sita Mahalakshmi and her family, which now includes grandchildren, have realized that the whole universe is directed by the *sankalpa* (will/resolve) of Sri Sathya Sai Baba and that he is all in all. They are happy that he has allowed them to live in Puttaparthi and Whitefield which they have done since 1976. "Living in Swami's *ashrama* is like living in heaven on earth," she said.

Sita Mahalakshmi spoke of another, more recent, miraculous cure. A few months ago, her husband became ill. He had blood in his urine. His condition worsened and he became depressed and felt that he was steadily sinking. Doctors advised that he should be hospitalized immediately in preparation for surgery. But, Sita Mahalakshmi did not want him to be removed from Sri Sathya Sai Baba's proximity and prayed hard to him. The next day, Sri Sathya Sai Baba summoned the whole family to an interview. He materialised a ring with *Shiva* and Sai on it and put it on Sambasiva Rao's finger.

"The bleeding stopped that same day and he has remained well ever since that day," said Sita Mahalakshmi. "*Bhagavan* has been immensely merciful to me and my family. He is everything to us. Even though I am old, I am busy from morning to night, doing as much of the housework as I can and personally looking after my husband's needs. For, after all, *Bhagavan* tells us at every stage that the most important work of a woman is *pati seva* (service of the husband) and that it forms the crux of *Hindu stree dharma* (woman's code of conduct)." She and her husband go to have *darshan*, to *nagar sankirtan* and *bhajans* at Brindavan. They attend every discourse and celebration. Their life revolves fully around Sri Sathya Sai Baba.

Does she perform *puja* and meditate?

"Oh, I was not made for regular *pujas* and fixed hours of meditation. *Bhagavan* is always with me, in my heart. How can I restrict thoughts of him to a few hours only or to *puja*?"

"Sorrows and desires are as the clouds that drift across the sky; they cannot mar the blue depths of the sky. Your duty is to strive on from this very moment. Do not vacillate or postpone. Do you postpone to tomorrow the dinner of today? Nourish the spirit as scrupulously as you now feed the body."

. . . Sri Sathya Sai Baba

10

JAYAMMA AT THE LOTUS FEET

Srimati Jayalakshmi Gopinath is head of the Department of English at the Sri Satya Sai College for Women at Anantapur. She is also Warden of the Hostel. She has had the great good fortune of receiving Sri Sathya Sai Baba's grace since her own student days.

When she first met Sri Sathya Sai Baba in 1948, her father, Sri B. S. Keshav Vittal, was on leave before retirement and she was doing her last year as a post-graduate. There was instant rapport between her father and Sri Sathya Sai Baba. Sri Sathya Sai Baba's ways drew the family close to him and they often went to Puttaparthi and Whitefield. Their family *guru* was Raghavendra Swami and she never thought of Sri Sathya Sai Baba as *guru*, but as Lord *Krishna*, who played on the innermost strings of her heart with his infinite loving-kindness, his grace and his tender charm. Her family had discovered the divinity in him and it was this that had drawn them to him. They were very fortunate, for he stayed with them several times at their house in Wilson Gardens, Bangalore.

Jayamma, as Srimati Gopinath is affectionately called, is a good *bhajan* singer. Sri Sathya Sai Baba often asked her to sing *bhajans* in the Old Temple at Puttaparthi. She remembers how, once, she sang a *bhajan* in a spirit of dedicated devotion, extolling the Divine as mother and father. And instantly a big garland around the photograph of Shirdi Sai Baba swayed violently, broke and fell to the floor. Then she sang the *mahima* (glory) of Sri Sathya Sai Baba and another garland, this time one from around a photograph of Sri Sathya Sai Baba, behaved in the same extraordinary way. Finally, as she sang the moving *bhajan 'darshan do'* by *Mira Bai*, the garland around the silver figure of Shirdi Sai Baba rolled away and fell on the ground. That was the most thrilling experience in her life and it remains with her always, green and fresh as though it had happened an hour ago.

Her father moved in circles very close to Sri Sathya Sai Baba – had he had divine visions?

Jayamma said that, indeed, her father had been blessed with many divine experiences and she described one that he often talked about. One day, Sri Sathya Sai Baba was seated in his special chair. Sri Vittal saw something gleaming near his feet. The brilliance alone was a splendid experience. Later, Sri Sathya Sai Baba said to him, "That which you saw was the precious gem of *Adi Sesha*."

Another remarkable experience he had once was, as he was preparing a bath for Sri Sathya Sai Baba. Sri Sathya Sai Baba stood there wearing only a *dhoti* and he saw, between the breast and the navel, a complete human figure. Sri Sathya Sai Baba smiled and casually said to Sri Vittal that what he was looking at was the form of the next *Avatara*.

"My father once saw the *shankha* (conch shell) and *chakra* (wheel) emblems of Lord *Vishnu* on the soles of Baba's feet as they rested on a cushion," said Jayamma. She said that Sri Sathya Sai Baba had removed many ailments from her father so that he could drive a car and be on his own. On another occasion, he had materialised a vial of medicine which had instantly cured him of chronic dizziness.

Jayamma's mother, too, was a very pious person, totally devoted to Sri Sathya Sai Baba. Once, during prayers, everyone present witnessed a phenomenal sight: *vibhuti* pouring down from Jayamma's mother's forehead. She felt truly blessed. "Swami's grace was on her even at the time of her death. For, she died a *sumangali* (happily married woman) on a very auspicious day in a way considered particularly holy for a woman." Sri Sathya Sai Baba commented appreciatively on the manner of her dying and he also praised Sri Vittal saying, "Vittal Rao deserves a gold medal for the way in which he looked after his wife."

Jayamma related a marvellous incident that occurred after she was married, with Sri Sathya Sai Baba's blessing, to Sri Gopinath. It happened in her house at Vedasandhu near Dindigal while Sri Sathya Sai Baba was on tour in Southern India, visiting Rameswaram and other holy places. At the time, a young *Brahmin* boy called Balaji worked for her and the poor boy had been terribly sick. Doctors had diagnosed his illness as a strangulated hernia. Poor Balaji was miserable as he had many family obligations and his illness became yet another thing to struggle with. And, sick as he was, he could not do much work. He could not even travel in a bus to go to a town to have the operation he needed. It was at this time that Sri Sathya Sai Baba came to Jayamma's house.

Sri Sathya Sai Baba stayed a day and, before he left, he had interviews with many people. At last, he called Balaji into a room and they were alone in it for about forty-five minutes. When Balaji emerged he had red tear-stained eyes, but his face was happy and glowing. Everyone took it for granted that he had been through a trauma. Then Sri Sathya Sai Baba and his train departed and, in a few hours, Balaji regained sufficient composure to speak of what had happened to him while he was alone with Sri Sathya Sai Baba.

That day, Balaji had a temperature of 104 degrees, but he had not put himself to bed for fear of missing Sri Sathya Sai Baba. As soon as Balaji came into the room, Sri Sathya Sai Baba spoke his name with love and held him tight. And instantly Balaji felt his fevered body cool and all traces of temperature leave him. Then Sri Sathya Sai Baba held his hand kindly, made him sit by his side and tell him all his woes. He materialised a photograph of himself and gave it to Balaji, saying he should perform regular *puja* to it. Then he told him, "Don't have an operation. I will make you all right," and with that he materialised a bottle of medicine. He told Balaji to lie down and, with his own hands, applied the medicine to his stomach. Finally, he blessed him again and opened the door of the room to signal the end of the compassionate interview.

The next day, Balaji was full of energy and well-being and he volunteered to go to Dindigal by bus to do the marketing. He announced to an astonished Jayamma, "Many changes have taken place in my body and I can feel them all. I know I have been completely cured." The doctors too were very taken aback when they examined him for they found that he was one hundred per cent normal. "Thanks to Swami's grace, Balaji is now a married man and lives happily with his family," said Jayamma.

Jayamma has vivid memories of a certain event in Puttaparthi. She was asleep in a room with another devotee when, at midnight, she woke up with a start. Her hair stood on end and she felt a psychic reverberation that gave her gooseflesh; so, she got up and looked around. What she saw was completely incredible: all the hill tops were aglow. They seemed to be edged with a silvery band about four feet wide. She could not watch for very long as the glowing light was tremendously powerful. She returned to her room with the strange feeling of having witnessed a phenomenon. Many months later, it was explained to her that it had been a divine act of Sri Sathya Sai Baba, a kind of spiritualisation of the atmosphere around Puttaparthi. And she was told that had she watched longer, she would have seen more that night. But, to this day, Jayamma does not know what that something more was that she missed.

I asked her if her husband had also been a Sai devotee. And I asked her if she had ever asked Sri Sathya Sai Baba why he had died so early in life.

Jayamma replied that her husband had had great respect for Sri Sathya

Sai Baba, but that he had been a theosophist all his life. But, he had respected his wife's faith in Sri Sathya Sai Baba and had told her that one should have firm faith in whatever one chose and that one should never let it waver. When he was posted in Rajahmundry and Sri Sathya Sai Baba visited them there, he performed *paada puja* (ritual worship of the feet) along with his wife. And they went together to Puttaparthi where Sri Sathya Sai Baba showed them a model of the Anantapur College and said, "You will be there and it will be such a college that you will have my protection." Jayamma's husband said that if her services were needed, she should go, but Sri Sathya Sai Baba said, "Not now."

A few months later, in 1971, her husband had a sudden heart attack. She wrote a letter to Sri Sathya Sai Baba and he replied, "Be courageous." When he became ill again, she prayed again to Sri Sathya Sai Baba and again the message that came back was to have courage.

Relatives wanted Sri Gopinath taken to Bangalore for treatment, so Jayamma made lightning calls to Sri Sathya Sai Baba for his approval, but he told her that her husband should not be moved. So his treatment was continued at Rajahmundry and he rallied for a while. Jayamma felt optimistic. The local Sathya Sai *Samithi* helped her a great deal.

On the morning of the 20th January 1972, Jayamma went to the hospital to see her husband. There was a photograph of Sri Sathya Sai Baba beside his bed and the Sai *Samithi* people used to place three roses on it. That day, as she approached the bed, one of the roses fell. Distressed, she looked at her husband and saw that he did not look at all well. The nurse went to fetch the doctor. Sri Gopinath began to gasp and, at that moment, the second rose fell. He continued to fight for his life through the day and, at half past four that afternoon, the third rose fell as he breathed his last.

Jayamma, numbed with grief, was brought to Bangalore. The whole family was stunned, for none of their members had ever died so young. In a few days, Jayamma yearned to see Sri Sathya Sai Baba for all else appeared meaningless to her. His beneficent presence was the only consolation in her life.

On the fifth day after her husband's death, Jayamma went to see Sri Sathya Sai Baba. He saw her, but neither spoke to her nor went near her. The next time she went to see him was a month later, when all the obsequies and rituals were behind her and she felt a little more resigned to her loss.

Sri Sathya Sai Baba called her to him that day and talked to her for a long time about life and death, one's *karma* and the things that everyone must face. Then Jayamma asked him, "Why did you not speak to me the first time I came after my husband died?" He replied, "You would have wept and I would not have been able to bear that sorrow or to look on your tears." Jayamma was so deeply moved at this that she could not speak.

She felt at peace in Brindavan. The very atmosphere was soothing and made her put her sorrow behind her. She never thought of joining in the hurly burly of everyday life again. So, with Sri Sathya Sai Baba's permission, she stayed on at the *ashrama* for many days. He talked to her everyday and gave her insights into things spiritual and divine. Jayamma remembers how it all gave her the sustenance she needed at the time: it gave her the courage she lacked to go back and face the world.

Friends recommended her name for teaching jobs in colleges and urged her to take up a career. Jayamma had been well-provided for by her dead husband and she did not need the extra income. She hesitated, wondering how best to use the remaining years of her life in a fruitful and fulfilling way. Then, Sri Sathya Sai Baba telephoned her father and settled her future for her. He wanted Jayamma to attend the interviews arranged to find a lecturer for the Sri Sathya Sai College for Women at Anantapur. She went to the interview, was selected for the post and, ever since, has been with the College for Women. "Remember how he had shown me the model of the College long ago and said that he would look after me?"

"I can never repay all the love, affection and undestanding that Baba has given me all through life," said Jayamma. She lost her father a few years ago. She remembers how Sri Sathya Sai Baba looked after this old devotee during his last days. Sri Keshav Vittal was conscious all the time, but never knew a thing about his sickness. He had no body consciousness at all in those last few days. He slept peacefully, the serenityof his repose shining from his face, and it was with the same serene look that he left this world, unaware that he was dying. It was a beautiful end.

Jayamma was glad she joined the Sri Sathya Sai College at Anantapur and to be able to use her time to good purpose. After her surrender to Sri Sathya Sai Baba, she came to realize that all that happens in the world is part of divine *leela*. God had given her loving parents, money, education and a noble husband with whom she had shared a good life full of understanding and happiness. "Now, I am in the service of *Bhagavan* and I want to perform this task as *seva* (service), for I know with total certitude that the only reality is his lotus feet. There is nothing else for me in this world or the next," said Jayamma peacefully.

"I do many things for the nidarshana (illustration, example) of devotees. It is for their benefit, for them to derive joy from the manifestation of grace. This is not for pradarshana (exhibition) to others."

. . . Sri Sathya Sai Baba

11

FRAGRANCE FOR TULASAMMA

She came and sat next to me in the canteen at Puttaparthi on *Guru Purnima* Day. There was such a fragrance about her person that I was intrigued. What was this scent that was so delightful and even evoked an unexpected reverence? I asked her, and she pointed to a silver ring she was wearing. It was apparent that the ring was "made by Sri Sathya Sai Baba;" I had seen similar ones on other people. It showed Sri Sathya Sai Baba with his hand raised in a gesture of blessing. The lady turned the ring on her finger and I was engulfed in a fragrance that drove away the spicy smells of the food. Incredibly, that vibrant fragrance came from the ring!

The lady said her name was Tulasamma. She smiled and explained, "Yes, the perfume is from the ring. Swami gave it to me in 1972 and the fragrance has stayed." A murmur ran through the canteen. I heard snatches of sentences: "yes, it smells like the *amruta* (nectar) at Srirangapatnam" . . . "Halagappa's place . . . "

Here, I must digress briefly to explain the Halagappa story.

Halagappa was a thief who, with the grace of Sri Sathya Sai Baba, became an honest man. While still practising his old trade, he bought a plastic ring with a picture of Sri Sathya Sai Baba on it, and he wore it. After he had worn it for a while, he discovered that his finger was damp. He found that the dampness was caused by a sweet liquid with an exotic fragrance oozing from the ring. Soon, the liquid filled his hand and still the ring went on oozing, so Halagappa put it in a glass container. It went on oozing and filled up first that container and then many other bottles. So Halagappa collected the *amruta*. The whole place was suffused with the sweet scent of the nectar.

This exquisite manifestation of Sri Sathya Sai Baba's grace has continued since then, ten years ago, giving joy to all who go to see it in Srirangapatnam where Halgappa lives. He has given away many bottles full of *amruta* to many people. (See chapter entitled Mystic Manifestations).

Tulasamma began to chat and told me of a marvellous experience she had had. She has a house in Bangalore which she shares with a friend. The grinding stone (small stone mill) in her kitchen needed to be chiselled to make it more effective and she wondered how she was going to get it done. (Editor's note: Grinding-stones are still used in some Indian kitchens to wet-grind whole grain). It was early afternoon and Tulasamma saw a man enter her gate. He saw her and came up to her and asked, "Have you any grinding-stones to be repaired? I am a stone mender." He was a tall young man dressed in white and she thought he looked like a Muslim. Tulasamma was delighted that her little problem of the grinding-stone was going to be solved so quickly and easily. So, she took the man to the kitchen and showed him the grinding-stone. He set about honing the stone and, all the time, he kept looking up at a small photograph of Sri Sathya Sai Baba which hung in the kitchen. Suddenly, Tulasamma became suspicious and afraid: had she been wise to let the man into the house and that, too, at noon when not many people are about? Also, how strange that he did not call out his trade in the street as is customary . . . Was he really a mason? What if he were a thief? So, she stayed with him while he chipped away and kept him talking. She told him that she had immense faith in Sri Sathya Sai Baba, that before him there had been a Sai Baba in Shirdi who had been a Muslim, like him. Then suddenly, she was struck by the thought that she had let a Muslim into her kitchen (Editor's note: this sort of doctrinaire discrimination is still prevalent in some orthodox *Hindu* homes). What would the neighbours say? They would probably insist that she perform special purificatory rites in the kitchen before using it again. After all, she was known to be very pious, performing so many *pujas* and cooking offerings for God.

But soon, Tulasamma reprimanded herself, saying, "What is the point of being a Sai devotee if I let silly notions of a Muslim being different from a *Hindu* invade my mind? Hasn't Baba always said that all people are divine?"

The stone-grinder was a conscientious worker and finished his task quickly. Tulasamma opened her purse to pay him, but found that there were only Rs.2. – in loose change in it; the rest was all in Rs.5. – and Rs.10. – notes. She asked him how much she owed him. He smiled and said, "Give me whatever you wish. I never call out in the street. I just select one or two houses to do my work in." So she gave him the Rs.2. – which he gladly accepted and left.

Her neighbours came in to inquire about the mason as they too wanted to have their grinding-stones repaired. But, he was nowhere to be seen in the street and must have gone away very fast. Tulasamma's neighbours advised her to clean the grinding-stone very thoroughly in case remnants of powdered stone get mixed in with the grain. So, Tulasamma decided to clean it, but found it spotlessly clean. How could that be? She never saw the man wiping it . . . It puzzled her. Soon, she also sensed a strange fragrance in the air and wondered whether it could be coming from Sri Sathya Sai Baba's photograph in the kitchen. She went up to it and sniffed. Yes, it was very fragrant.

The next morning, Tulasamma went to market. When she opened her purse, the fragrance that came from it was overwhelming. Dazed, she pulled out the money and saw that she held in her hand the same two one Rupees in loose change she had given to the stone-grinder. The scent from the coins was exactly the same as that of the ring Sri Sathya Sai Baba had given her.

"Oh, could it have been Baba who came to my house to repair the grinding-stone?" she gasped. "Yes, who else?" she thought to herself, "it could only have been him," what with all the proofs she had been given in his inimitable way.

This story of Tulasamma's in the canteen at Puttaparthi had drawn many people from other tables, so I thought it best to discontinue our conversation just then. A few days later, we met again in Bangalore and she told me of many Sai experiences spanning a large portion of her life.

Members of her family were ardent worshippers of Lord *Krishna*. She was still in college when she first saw Sri Sathya Sai Baba at the house of a friend. "Baba was nineteen at the time, very good looking and fair, with a huge mop of hair parted to one side. He was so handsome that I immediately thought if God could create such a good looking person, how beautiful, indeed, must be the Creator! Oh *Krishna*, I must have your *darshan* someday . . ." On that day, Sri Sathya Sai Baba looked at her before he went away. Later, she heard from a friend what he had said about her. He had said: "that girl has a firm mind and she will see God."

After that first encounter in 1942, Tulasamma continued with her life and career and her adoration of *Krishna* and did not think at all of Sri Sathya Sai Baba. She was a Deputy Inspector of Schools in Mysore. In 1962, she still held this post, when the family she lived with decided to go to Puttaparthi. She thought she would go, too, and so she applied for leave. It was refused because the Minister of Education of Karnataka was to visit Mysore at exactly that time. She was unhappy not to be able to please the people whose home she shared, for they were "so nice to me and had taken me into their lives as though I were one of them."

The night she learnt the disappointing news, she had a strange new experience. She woke up in the darkness and saw a diffused light coming into her room through the window. Then, it broke into rays, then it focused on her bed for a little while, and then it vanished. She looked out of the window, but she saw nothing there to explain the light that had come and gone.

She found the incident baffling, but thought it might have something to do with Sri Sathya Sai Baba and the visit to Puttaparthi. She decided to make one more attempt to obtain leave. So, in the morning, she went to her superior officer's house where she pleaded with him and his wife to give her leave from her duties to go on pilgrimage to Puttaparthi. She pointed out that the entire family was going, that she would be left alone and also that never before had she asked for leave. Result: she was given a whole month off!

When they arrived at Prashanti Nilayam in Puttaparthi, they saw Sri Sathya Sai Baba feeding sugar cane to Sai Geetha, his elephant. He saw Tulasamma and came up to her and asked, "When did you come?" She mumbled incoherently, for she was taken aback to see that the film star like personality she remembered from her first and only meeting was now so different. Here was a stern and serious Sri Sathya Sai Baba dressed like a *sannyasin*, with his hair now a circle of abundance without any parting. This person was so "unlike the boy I knew," that she felt unnerved. However, he proved very kind and loving. He summoned an old lady nicknamed Pedda Pottu* and instructed her to look after Tulasamma and the family who had brought her there.

Tulasamma and her group were called to the interview room the very next day. Sri Sathya Sai Baba said to her, "You have come after so many years!" As she gazed on his form, she felt instinctively that she was in the presence of divinity. He asked her what she wanted and she answered, "Nothing. I have no desires at all."

After that first visit, Tulasamma went to Puttaparthi regularly for festivals and special occasions. In 1969, Sri Sathya Sai Baba materialised a locket with his image on it for her and said, "Never be afraid. I am always with you." During another interview, he told her how commendable it was that, despite so many tempting offers of marriage, she had resolved to remain a *brahmacharini* (a virgin, one who has taken the vow of chastity). He explained that this was because of her past two lives in which she had also taken the vow of chastity and pursued the spiritual path.

*Pedda Pottu, whose own name is Sharada, had originally been with Shirdi Sai Baba. He had assured her that she would be with him again in his next incarnation. When she heard about Sri Sathya Sai Baba, she went straight to him to find out for herself if he really was Shirdi Sai Baba come back. Sri Sathya Sai Baba recognised her instantly and spoke to her in *Hindi* in the voice of Shirdi Sai Baba. He also reminded her that she owed him money! And he reminded her of one or two other things – all this reassured the old lady that he was none other than her Shirdi Sai Baba reborn. And, ever since then, she has been in Puttaparthi.

Tulasamma recalled a few of the times when Sri Sathya Sai Baba had really been with her. Once, she was in an accident involving an auto-rickshaw and fractured her wrist. The moment the rickshaw had crashed into a tree, she had shouted *'Sai Ram'* and fainted. A car and driver had arrived in that desolate spot where they had crashed and had taken Tulasamma and her taxi driver home. She knew her wrist was badly injured, but it was only later that she came to know of the greater peril she had been saved from. The taxi driver confessed that he had deliberately driven into the tree. He had wanted to steal Tulasamma's jewels and, with that in mind, had chosen an especially deserted route. He had intended to jump off the rickshaw just before the impact and, while she was unconscious, take her jewels and run. But, Tulasamma had called out *'Sai Ram'* and that had made him change his mind. He was full of remorse that he should ever have wanted to rob so pious a person, one who instantly appealed to God in her distress. And he had been shaken to find that the car and driver had materialised so soon after the crash, in what he knew very well was an isolated place. Tulasamma said, "That rickshaw driver comes to see me now and then. He has become attached to us and is a completely changed young man."

In 1974, Sri Sathya Sai Baba gave Tulasamma two *panchamukhi* (pentagonal) *rudraksha* beads which he materialised for her. They are beautifully encased in gold and emit the same fragrance as the ring. She showed me a visiting card of Sri Sathya Sai Baba which she had in her bag and it, too, had the same fragrance.

"Baba is always *Krishna* to me . . . I address him only as *Sai Krishna*," Tulasamma told me. *Krishna* is the God in her heart. Tulasamma's lips are forever chanting the name of her lord, *"Krishna, Krishna."*

She spoke about an incident in 1974 as she was going, with the two daughters of a friend, to see Sri Sathya Sai Baba. They were in a bus which met with a nasty accident on a bridge. The bus lurched forward, crashed through the side of the bridge and teetered on the edge without anything to hold it back. Tulasamma, in panic, shouted *"Sai Krishna!"* and closed her eyes in prayer.

When she opened her eyes, the miracle had happened. The bus which ought to have plunged headlong into the ravine below had come to a stand still, held fast by a single brick which had broken away in the collision. But, the bus was still precariously perched on the bridge and the passengers had to alight from it very gingerly, one by one, without shaking it in the slightest way lest it fall into the ravine. A kind gentleman who recognized the Inspectress of Schools offered to take her back to Mysore. But the two young daughters of her friend wanted to press on. They said, "It was Baba himself who saved us this time. We must see him."

Late that night, they again found themselves stuck, this time at the Kalasipalayam bus stand in Bangalore. Quite unexpectedly, an auto-rickshaw drew up and the driver offered to take all three of them home.

Normally, an auto-rickshaw only takes two passengers. With great relief, they squeezed into the rickshaw and the driver took them on their way. They could not stop talking about their miraculous escape earlier that day and, before they knew where they were, they were home. The rickshaw driver had taken them straight home although none of them had remembered to tell him where to go! Tulasamma gratefully offered him extra money for the third passenger, but he declined politely and only took the amount clocked up on the meter.

The next morning, they went to Whitefield. There, Tulasamma heard that the previous day, in the middle of a conversation, Sri Sathya Sai Baba had fallen silent and then he had suddenly raised his hand in a forbidding gesture indicating HALT! She found that this had happened at exactly the time the lumbering bus had come to a precarious halt on top of the ravine, arrested on its headlong dive by the solitary brick.

On *Yugadi* Day 1976 (*Yugadi* is the new year, heralding also the harvest), Tulasamma was engaged in *sahasranama archana* (chanting the 1008 names) of Sri Sathya Sai Baba while her friend and hostess, Nagaratna, read out the *namavali* (list of names). As she chanted the '*Viprapriraya namaha*,' saying "I bow to the One who likes *Brahmins*," a *Brahmin* walked into the room and sat on a nearby sofa and watched the rest of the *puja*. She was astonished and a bit rattled. She thought she ought to interrupt the *puja* to feed the mysterious *Brahmin*, but he spoke, "Don't worry. Finish the *puja*. I have come from very far and I can wait."

Tulasamma finished the *puja* and rose to fetch some food, but again the *Brahmin* spoke as if reading her thoughts, "I don't want food, but will accept a little rice, just a handful." That, strangely, was exactly the quantity of rice she found in a plastic bag on the kitchen table. Tulasamma thought, "Let me put a bit more rice in the bag and give it to him. I can't offer so little to anyone." And again, the *Brahmin's* voice from the sofa startled her, "Don't add more rice," he said, "what you have on the table is enough for me."

She gave him the rice and added a few bananas, betel leaves and betel nut on the plate. Both women prostrated themselves before the *Brahmin* who blessed them and said, "May you have all you want." He ate a banana, took the packet of rice in his hand and left the house. But, as they watched him go, they saw that his hands were empty. How had the packet disappeared so quickly? A strong scent of *vibhuti* assailed their nostrils. As they went back into the house, they found that the special fragrance of *vibhuti* was everywhere in the house. Tulasamma was mystified and wondered, "Who could have come for the *puja*? Who was he?"

She ran out to look for the *Brahmin*, but he had vanished without a trace. But soon, she was to know who it was that had "visited" her house.

Sri Sathya Sai Baba was due to return that morning to Bangalore from New Delhi for the *Yugadi* celebration. Could that have been what the *Brahmin* had meant when he said, "I have come from very far"? They rushed to Whitefield. Sri Sathya Sai Baba emerged to give *darshan* almost immediately. People there told Tulasamma that he had only a little while ago come from Bangalore Airport. He came near her and smiled broadly. He gestured to her as if to ask about food and whether she had had lunch. Tulasamma talked about the visit of the *Brahmin* for months after that, reliving the thrill of it again and again.

I asked Tulasamma about the family she lived with, both in Mysore and in Bangalore. Were they also Sai devotees? "Not at first," she replied, "but I feel Baba started showing his grace in such abundance that they too could not fail to become aware of his divine powers."

At first, they had made fun of Tulasamma and her devotion to Sri Sathya Sai Baba. They criticized him a lot and it had made her think of moving out on her own. But Sri Sathya Sai Baba told her not to do that and said she should stay on because, ultimately, everything would be all right. Though they were all terribly fond of her, they could not resist teasing her about worshipping Sri Sathya Sai Baba as God. It was then that the miracles had begun. Tulasamma had been given a small sandalwood idol of *Krishna* which she kept in the shrine. One day, the daughter of the house happened to be in the same room when, all of a sudden, she heard a sharp noise. A grey ball of *vibhuti* had fallen from the forehead of the *Krishna* idol. It rolled to the foot of the idol and separated into particles. She called everyone to see this amazing manifestation. When Tulasamma got there, she saw a dazed little group around the shrine, each with a *vibhuti* mark on the forehead. Naturally, she was delighted. After this incident, no one from the family ever again made fun of her worshipping Sri Sathya Sai Baba. On the contrary, they helped her to perform her *pujas*.

Tulasamma's mind was now set at rest and she could lose herself in worship. One day, she saw a shower of *vibhuti* form into a heap in the middle of the shrine. She was touched by the unexpected shower of grace. When she tried to take a pinch of the *vibhuti* she felt something solid in it. She searched around in it and discovered a small silver idol of the elephant-headed god, *Ganesha*. That was in 1973 and, since then, many silver idols have appeared, one after another, in her *puja* room. Now, Tulasamma has a collection of idols, all of which came to her in the same way, but in different places and not always with *vibhuti:* one arrived on the silver *puja* plate, another on the shelf, several from her small *vibhuti* container, and some from the blue box in which she carries her *puja* idols.

I saw the miraculous idols, all neatly arranged on a platter in Tulasamma's *puja* room. There was a chair-like pedestal for Sri Sathya Sai Baba and a large framed photograph of his feet. Tulasamma performs *ashtotara puja* to this photograph. There is another photograph of Sri Sathya Sai Baba high on a wall in the *puja* room. Both had *vibhuti* encrustations on them. A photograph in the kitchen had an unusual manifestation on it. It was also, of course, a photograph of Sri Sathya Sai Baba and, this time, the *vibhuti* encrustation had formed in three horizontal lines on his forehead and there was a bright round *kumkum* mark in the centre. The lines were so neat and even that it appeared as if Sri Sathya Sai Baba had stood in front of a mirror and carefully applied the *vibhuti* and *kumkum* to his forehead. But, Tulasamma said that no one had applied the *vibhuti* or the *kumkum*, they had just appeared one day, like one of the miraculous *vibhuti* showers. She pointed to an idol of Shirdi Sai Baba and a large doll in the likeness of *Krishna*, both in a glass case. They, too, were often showered with *vibhuti*. The *vibhuti* encrustation on a photograph of Sri Sathya Sai Baba in which he wears a pearl necklace and a *tilak* (dot on the forehead) made of precious stones, on careful examination, resembled Lord *Krishna's* crown.

The small idol of *Ganesha*, when turned around, became that of *Yoga Narasimha*. Other idols included *Annapurna* (goddess of food), *Lakshmi* (goddess of felicity and prosperity), *Puttaparthi Krishna* (a replica of the statue of *Krishna* in the Old Temple at Puttaparthi), many other idols of *Krishna*, including a minute and glittering *Natya Krishna* (dancing *Krishna)* which had made its appearance at Whitefield in Tulsamma's blue *puja* box in 1978 while she was at the Summer Course.There were also idols of *Uma Maheshwari, Hanumana, Rama, Dattatreya, Saraswati, Chamundeshwari*, Shirdi Sai Baba, *Panduranga* and *Subrahmanyam*. Sri Sathya Sai Baba's elephant, Sai Geetha too, was there, as were a horse, a deer, *Kamadhenu* (the celestial cow), *Nandi* (*Shiva's* bull) and a coin struck to commemorate Sri Sathya Sai Baba's 50th birthday. And there were religious symbols: a Crucifix, the Fire of the Zoroastrians, the Crescent and Star of Islam and a *Shivalingam* for the *Hindu* faith.

One day, Tulasamma heard that a new idol of Shirdi Sai Baba was to be installed in a nearby Sai temple, where devotees could make offerings of precious stones and gold and silver. On that day, she found that *navaratnas* (nine stones corresponding to the nine planetary aspects) had materialised in her *puja* room, so she promptly offered them to the new idol being installed in the Sai temple.

On another day, a devotee of *Santoshi Ma* visited her. Tulasamma had not heard of *Santoshi Ma* and asked her visitor to explain who she was. The visitor replied that she is another aspect of the Goddess *Durga*. That day, a small silver idol of *Santoshi Ma* appeared in the *puja* room.

Tulasamma also has an idol of *Mahishasura Mardini* which is much bigger than the others. She told me a thrilling story about it.

She has always had great respect for Ramakrishna Paramhansa and was reading a book about his experiences of the Goddess *Durga* at the Dakshineshwar Temple in Southern India. She had always wanted to go to Dakshineshwar, but had never been able to. So that night, as she read about Ramakrishna Paramhansa, she silently pleaded to him, "Why do you not give me a chance to see your goddess? It is all very well for you to bask in her glory, but what about people like me?" Her mind was full of thoughts of the goddess as she drifted into sleep. As always, she awoke at three o'clock, during the *Brahma muhurtam*, to meditate. She was deep in meditation when she was distracted by the sound of bells, like the rhythmic footsteps of a lady wearing anklets. Tulasamma got up and went round the house and looked out of windows, but there was not a soul in sight. Where were the tinkling footfalls coming from? She was convinced that there was no one about, so she returned to her meditation in front of all her *puja* idols. Suddenly, a warm glow, a brilliant luminosity, lit up the whole *puja* shelf. It started there and soon reached the ceiling. Slowly, the light became concentrated into one luminous figure – the Goddess *Durga* in all her splendour stood before Tulasamma, robed in a shining red and green *sari*. The resplendent figure stood smiling while Tulasamma gazed at her in awe. And as she stood, the figure of the goddess started to shrink very slowly; it became smaller and smaller until there was only a speck of a glow left on the *puja* shelf. Unable to contain herself any longer, Tulasamma shrieked incoherently and Nagaratna, sleeping in the next room, was awakened and came to her. They found a new glowing object on the *puja* shelf: a shining new silver idol of the Goddess *Durga*. Later, Tulasamma discovered that it was the image of the Goddess of Dakshineshwar, *Mahishasura Mardini*. She was overjoyed to have been blessed with the *darshan* of the goddess in person and then to have been left such a glowing memento of the divine visit . . .

Miracles never cease to occur in Tulasamma's life. That day, she had with her a small and solid *Shiva lingam*, one to which she offered special daily worship. She told me about it. She had been to an *Ishwara* temple in Sulya, near Mangalore, on the auspicious day of *Kartika Somavara*. She had performed *pujas* there and, after that, her companion had recited the *Lalita Sahasranamam* (1000 names of the Goddess *Lalita* who is an embodiment of *Shiva-Shakti*). They had made the customary offering on a platter, but when she had looked at it again, there was a shiny new object on it. It was a small pebble-like stone shaped like a *lingam*. At first, she had not known what to do with it: should she take it, or leave it there? At that point, she remembered something that had happened at home. Someone had taken away an old *lingam* saying that Sri Sathya Sai Baba would give her a new *lingam* with enormous *shakti* (power). So, she concluded this must be the promised *lingam* and took it home. As she performed *puja* to it, lines started to appear on it. Gradually, the lines joined and formed a picture of Sri Sathya Sai Baba sitting on a mound. The figure resembled one in an old photograph that Tulasamma treasured and kept in her *puja* room.

Many have felt the power of this *lingam* when they have put it in the palm of their hand. Some felt a strong current flowing from it, electrifying the entire body. Tulasamma was directed to keep the small *lingam* between her eyebrows during meditation. When she does this, she senses a remarkable current vibrating in her head and making her feel at one with infinity. "My head then hums with that unearthly force and I can feel something superhuman within." She also feels energy radiating and, with constant use, the *lingam* itself receives the intense heat from her brow.

In March 1978, Tulasamma went to Whitefield to have *darshan* of Sri Sathya Sai Baba. Seeing her, he materialised *vibhuti* and gave it to her saying she should keep it carefully. When he moved away, she opened her hand and, to her amazement, saw that she was holding a minute pair of silver *paadukas* (sandals) on which were inscribed the initials SSS (Sri Sathya Sai). Naturally, Tulasamma cherishes this souvenir of the lotus feet of Sri Sathya Sai Baba. They, too, have their own vibrations, different ones for different people. In some people's hands, they produce a vibrant tingling sensation; others feel them move, and yet others have experienced "a strong pull from within."

"It appears strange, but such are the ways of the Divine," said Tulasamma. She continued, "Whenever I go out in the dark, a bright spot of light appears from nowhere to light my way. In the beginning it used to puzzle me and, the first time I saw it, I was even frightened. But now, I accept it saying 'lead, kindly light.' I am retired now and every moment of my life is now entirely for *Krishna*. Any doubt, any worry, any trouble and I cling to my *Krishna* locket. All that happens is *Krishna's* wish, *Krishna's* will. This is the universe of his creation."

Had Tulasamma never thought of marriage, and of a family? Does she regret not being a wife and a mother?

"Oh, never! The idea of marriage never entered my head at any stage. I performed my duties well to earn my livelihood, but I only really liked thinking of God. I am happy with my life and have no regrets. In my work, too, I never had any regrets, for I did my job sincerely and to my complete satisfaction. I never had too many longings, nor was I ambitious, and so I was happy. I have a sister who has children. They all love me. And more, I have this adoptive family and they are all very dear to me. With them, I have two homes: one in Mysore, the other in Bangalore. After I retired, I asked Swami to let me buy a flat in Puttaparthi as, by then, I had the required amount of money. Swami replied that there was no need for me to do that as he is always with me. So, I continue to live with my adoptive family and to go for *darshan* to Whitefield and to Puttaparthi whenever I can. I did some work for Sai *Samithis,* but now, *Sai Krishna* is everything to me."

Tulasamma was very happy when Sri Sathya Sai Baba asked her to attend the Summer Course the first two years it was held, as this gave her the opportunity of being near his physical presence and to hear him discourse everyday. "The first Summer Course was truly marvellous for the participants, since it was held next to the main bungalow where he stays in Whitefield. Swami often used to be with the students, or he would watch them from the balcony. Now and then, he surprised them with impromptu visits and, occasionally, he threw down fruit for them to catch. They revelled in his company and in the joy of those unexpected treats," said Tulasamma, remembering and comparing that first session to the 1978

Summer Course which was more formal, with fixed hours for the visits of Sri Sathya Sai Baba. "This shows that, as the years roll by, we have to learn not to expect Swami's company at all times and for everything, although that is what we want most. I only hope that many more students will continue to have the chance of attending the Summer Course. It is the only way of being in Swami's presence for a few hours everyday, thanks to his daily discourses and the *bhajan* sessions."

Do many people know of her Sai experiences? Particularly those who do not know Sri Sathya Sai Baba?

"When they come to me, they come automatically to know about Swami. In general, people have been extraordinarily kind to me always, whether or not they know anything about me or my devotion to Swami."

Tulasamma said, "An important thing happened once in Mysore. I met a famous musician, Keshavamurthi. A great devotee of *Sri Rama*, he asked me if I chanted the *Omkara* along with *sruti* and *naada* of the *tanpura* (sound and rhythm of the string instrument of that name). I said to him, 'God has given me money enough to buy instruments, but He has not given me a big house to live in. That is His will. Wherever I am, He gives me only small dwellings. But, I am happy in all those places. That is why I do not have a *tanpura*. I would have nowhere to keep such a big instrument, though I know how excellent it would be to have *naadopasana* (spiritual endeavour through sound) with the *Omkara* and meditation.'"

"The musician, on hearing this, replied, 'It is evident that you are a person in the *turya* stage (state of infinite bliss). As such, I want to make an offering. I myself have made a *tanpura* which is small and very handy, and it keeps excellent time. It will meet your needs admirably, particularly when you recite the *Omkara*. The sound of the *tanpura* will be in sacred communion since its musical notes will automatically link your vibrations to the Universal Soul. Please try to chant the *Omkara* to its accompaniment and you will experience what I have described'."

Tulasamma bowed reverently to him as the *guru* of the *Omkara-naada-upasana*. He gave her his special *tanpura* which was indeed small and handy. She has used it ever since that day and, with it, her *Omkara* meditation has brought her divine stirrings.

Recently, Tulasamma went to Pondicherry. Meditating near the *samadhi* (cenotaph) of Sri Aurobindo and the Mother, she felt very happy. As she opened her eyes, a beautiful flower among the floral decorations caught her eye. On an impulse, she took the flower and wrapped it in a handkerchief. Her companions admonished her, "You are not meant to touch or disturb those flowers. Why have you taken it?"

She was made to feel guilty, but she said she could not help taking the flower. Her friends opened the handkerchief to look at the irresistible flower and they found, glowing at the core, a tiny Sathya Sai locket. They could not believe their eyes: it was incredible that Sri Sathya Sai Baba should materialise at the Aurobindo Ashrama. But, they thought, with

Tulasamma around, any miracle was possible . . .

Tulasamma bows in deep veneration and says that all this is *Sai Krishna leela*. "The whole world is filled with love and fragrance of which Swami is the central flower."

"Whoever you are, you are Mine. I will not give you up. Wherever you are, you are near Me; you cannot go beyond My reach."

. . . Sri Sathya Sai Baba

12

HAVE FAITH IN GOD. THAT IS ENOUGH

Padma Srinivasan has been a Sai devotee for well over ten years. In the early days, her mother, who was even then a devotee, used to take young Padma to *bhajan* sessions at Sakamma's house and other houses in the Basavangudi and Chamarajpet areas of Bangalore whenever Sri Sathya Sai Baba was present. But, after she was married, Padma lost that contact with Sri Sathya Sai Baba.

Once, she went on pilgrimage to Benares. Her mind was full of worries and woes about a family problem. Then, Sri Sathya Sai Baba came to her in a dream and told her to stop worrying as all was going to turn out all right. She was pleased to have dreamt of him even though she had not thought of him for many years. She returned from the pilgrimage to find an invitation from the Sri Sharada Sevika Mandali, the women's wing of the Ramakrishna Mission. It was to be an anniversary celebration to be presided over by Sri Sathya Sai Baba. Padma attended the celebratory occasion and it was so crowded that she had to stand in a corner. When it was over, to her utter astonishment, Sri Sathya Sai Baba came straight to her and asked, "Why do you worry so much? What is the use of worrying? Everything will be all right." Then, he materialised some *vibhuti* and gave it to her.

From then on, Padma went to Whitefield whenever she could. She also attended some festivals at Puttaparthi.

Her husband and sons were not keen on her devotion to Sri Sathya Sai Baba, particularly her youngest son who was an atheist. He used sarcasm to deride her worship of a human being as God. But one morning, the young atheist, of his own volition, suddenly said to her, "Let's go to Whitefield." It was already nine o'clock and Padma did not think they could reach Whitefield in time for the ten o'clock *darshan*. But, her son was insistent and she, too, wanted to strike while the iron was hot. So, they took an auto-rickshaw to the main bus stand and got onto a bus going in the direction of Whitefield. It was a quarter to eleven when they got there. But, luck was with them: that day, Sri Sathya Sai Baba emerged to give *darshan* at eleven o'clock! Then Padma worried whether her son would be able to see him from near or not. She was not with him as he was sitting on the other side with the men. Imagine her surprise when Sri Sathya Sai Baba walked straight up to her and said, "So, he has come with you. I will talk to him. Both of you may come inside the house for an interview." Their luck held again as he went to her son and told him as well to go to the house. Even today, Padma cannot understand how Sri Sathya Sai Baba recognizes people when they have not been presented or pointed out to him.

It was a very long interview that he accorded the devoted mother and her unbelieving son. First, he advised Padma on family matters. Then he said he wanted to talk to her son alone. He was with him for more than an hour and materialised a small Shirdi Sai Baba plaque for him. He called Padma in again and told her that her son had a very good heart and that she need not worry about him at all. From that day, her son's outlook on life changed direction.

Padma has been the recipient of Sri Sathya Sai Baba's grace and blessings many times. Once, she was to go to the U.S.A. to attend a women's convention. Before leaving, she went to Whitefield and Sri Sathya Sai Baba told her, "I know about your trip. Swami's blessings are with you." He materialised a most unusual portrait of himself: encased in transparent plastic, it was about 2 ins × 3 ins square. He dropped it into her purse. Padma constantly carries this talisman with her and feels protected.

"You will understand this protection when I tell you what happened in Sri Lanka," said Padma. She had taken a group of fifteen women to that island nation. One day, they had to cross a forest and, arrived in the middle of it, their bus broke down. It was very worrying, especially as Padma knew that they were near a dangerous waterfall and in an area that was known to be infested with bandits. Her party of women, moreover, consisted of young girls and elderly women for whom, naturally, she felt responsible. And some of them wore expensive jewellery and others carried valuables with them. All this was worry enough, but more was to follow. It was past midnight when the bus sputtered back to life, but now the driver and the conductor were behaving most erratically. Padma was very alarmed and swamped in worry. She addressed a mental prayer to Sri Sathya Sai Baba and asked everyone to sing Sai *bhajans*. Singing the name of the Lord, they forgot their fears and they hardly realized, at two o'clock in the morning, that they had reached their destination.

Safely back in Bangalore, Padma went to Whitefield on a *bhajan* day. Just like a solicitous elder, Sri Sathya Sai Baba came to her and asked, "When did you come back? But then, why were you so frightened that night in Sri Lanka? Swami was with you and no harm could have befallen you. Anyway, you women! you should have been more careful in organizing your trip and done it through better known and more reliable guides." Padma bowed down with heartfelt gratitude.

Day by day, Padma's devotion to Sri Sathya Sai Baba grew stronger with the love and compassion he showered on her and her family. She recalled an instance of his *leela*. She was in the *darshan* line and wore a ring with a light bluish-grey stone. Sri Sathya Sai Baba saw it and said, "Did you buy it in Sri Lanka? Give it to me." Padma took off the ring and respectfully gave it to him. He held it up as if to look at it and gave it back to her. Her friends who were with her shrieked with delight, for they now saw in it the clear silhouette of Sri Sathya Sai Baba's bust.

"Of all his acts of grace, what Baba has done for my husband is something for which I shall never be able to thank him enough," said Padma and went on to tell me about it. "Three years ago, my husband had a severe attack of cerebral thrombosis and everyone, including the doctors, had given up all hope of his recovery. He was in a coma and all our sons were at his side. Suddenly, I wanted to get Baba's *prasadam* for my husband and asked my friend, Usha Pillai, to try to get some from Whitefield. She went off to Brindavan and, just as she entered the grounds, she saw that Baba's car was about to leave it. But Baba stopped the car, got out and spoke to her. Instantly, he produced a substantial amount of *vibhuti* and said, 'Tell her not to worry. He will be all right.' Then he got back into the car and drove away."

Usha rushed back to the hospital with the *vibhuti*. Padma was in tears when she heard of the way in which Sri Sathya Sai Baba had given the *vibhuti*. Her son bravely put some into his father's comatose mouth, lifeless though he seemed. That night was a night of crisis.

The next morning, Srinivasan slowly opened his eyes and looked around. It was the first day he was conscious after days of being in a deep coma. He asked for coffee! Everyone was totally amazed at his sudden recovery.

That afternoon, Padma's aunt came to the hospital with an interesting story. She was not a Sai devotee and, surprisingly therefore, she had dreamt of Sri Sathya Sai Baba that night. He went around the hospital ward, looking about for a while, then he stopped near Srinivasan's bed for some time and blessed him before vanishing from the dream. The account thrilled everyone and they took it to be proof positive that the divine grace of Sri Sathya Sai Baba had come to the rescue of a devotee's husband.

(Editor's note: it is said that Sri Sathya Sai Baba enters our dream world when he wills it, i.e. his presence in our dreams is an act of his will).

That same day, Srinivasan too spoke of a dream he had had. In his dream, he saw Sri Sathya Sai Baba climb the stairs of his house, enter his room, look at his collection of books and say, "You are wasting your time, thinking far too much of your English accent and trying to impress others in a superficial way. Make a deeper study and write a small book on *Sanatana Dharma* and distribute it freely to people." Still in the dream, Srinivasan wondered how he would find the money to have it printed and, simultaneously, Sri Sathya Sai Baba answered, "Don't worry. Write it and contact Dr. Gokak."

Srinivasan regained his health very quickly and the doctors were amazed by this miracle. A few days after he left the hospital, Padma took him to Whitefield for the *darshan* of Sri Sathya Sai Baba. He was still too weak to join the *darshan* lines, so he sat in the parked car rehearsing a meticulously composed English sentence expressing his gratitude.

Then, without any warning at all, Sri Sathya Sai Baba came and got into Srinivasan's car. He materialised *vibhuti* and rubbed it on Srinivasan's chest and forehead. He said, "Have faith in God, that is enough. I am not concerned with whether you believe in me or not." Srinivasan's heart was heavy with emotion and he felt incapable of uttering a sound, let alone finding the right words. Such kindness, such love – what had he done to deserve so much, he wondered. Padma, for her part, was dazed at the showering of so much grace on her husband who had no faith in the *avatarhood* of Sri Sathya Sai Baba.

Padma spoke about a recent materialisation of Sri Sathya Sai Baba's. He produced a small thin copper foil easily rolled into a scroll. He tapped it and something became inscribed on it. He gave it to Padma and said she should put it into a *dayathu* (cylindrical container) and wear it as a talisman on her *mangalya* (felicity) chain. When Padma returned home, she found a silver *dayathu* into which the little scroll fitted exactly. Even as she spoke, she had no idea how that *dayathu* appeared in her *puja* room. She does not analyse its appearance, she simply feels grateful for yet another Sai miracle.

"Spirituality begins where physics end."

. . . Sri Sathya Sai Baba

13

TO THE *VINA* VIA NUCLEAR PHYSICS

Vemu Mukunda, a nuclear physicist, was well established in his profession and worked in London. He was also keenly interested in music and had learnt to play the *vina* from Vidwan Chandrasekhariah, the grandson of the *vina* virtuoso and composer, Vina Seshanna. His hobbies included the study of spirits and ghosts as well as bizarre experiments to do with death.

Once, some friends took him to a *bhajan* session arranged in a house in London. At first, he did not participate; then his hostess brought him a *vina* and asked him to play. So, Mukunda played a few songs that came to mind and everyone was pleased as he was, indeed, an exceptionally good musician. Suddenly, he looked again and more closely at the *vina* he had just played and saw that it was the very badly damaged one that a friend had asked him to mend. He tried to play it once more, but not a single tuneful note came from it. Intrigued, he looked up and saw a photograph of Sri Sathya Sai Baba. He was baffled by the broken *vina* he had played so well a short while ago. All there said it was a Sai miracle. The incident made Mukunda curious about Sri Sathya Sai Baba and his seemingly superhuman powers.

Soon, Mukunda began to hear of Sri Sathya Sai Baba wherever he went in Europe from a variety of people. "Why is everyone talking to me only about Sai Baba all of a sudden?" he thought rather sceptically.

It was a very disillusioning period in his life. He had begun to wonder whether there was any meaning in living his life as a nuclear physicist. He came in contact with hippies, drop-outs and others of that ilk; he generally drifted about accepting Sri Sathya Sai Baba as just another happening and without any conviction. Then, slowly, he found that everything else was receding and Sri Sathya Sai Baba was becoming a stronger and stronger presence in his mind. But, doubts and questions about him still persisted.

Mukunda wrote a letter to Sri Sathya Sai Baba asking for guidance: "Should I take to *sannyasa* (renunciation), or should I continue with nuclear physics, or should I take up the *vina* professionally?" He wanted an answer from Sri Sathya Sai Baba, directly or indirectly, for he felt incapable of making the decision himself. He did not know why he wrote the letter, for he had not accepted Sri Sathya Sai Baba even as a real spiritual person, though he was aware that "changes were taking place within" him.

Then, he had to go to Paris for some work. On his return, he went to the house of Mr. and Mrs. Sitaram, both Sai devotees. No sooner had he arrived than Mrs. Sitaram said she had something for him. She went away and came back with a photograph which she gave him: it showed Sri Sathya Sai Baba playing the *vina*.

Mukunda understood that Sri Sathya Sai Baba had sent him the answer to his letter. He could not believe it and became emotional. He went to the Sitaram *puja* room and prostrated himself before a picture of Sri Sathya Sai Baba, tears streaming down his face. "That day, I threw down my body and my mind at his feet and wept unashamedly," said Mukunda. But, he did not discuss it with anyone as it had become "a personal treasure of an experience." But he knew now that it was with music that he was to make his career.

From that moment, life became for Mukunda "full of Swami and *vina*." He sat in front of a photograph of Sri Sathya Sai Baba and learnt new compositions. He felt as though he was present with him, for he found that he could grasp even very complex forms of music that he had not been taught by his *guru*. Many new aspects of music opened out before him and he felt knowledge flowing to him whenever he sat in front of the photograph of Sri Sathya Sai Baba.

His life was filled with concerts all over Europe and he gained fame as a *vina* player. He was happier with life than ever before. At the time, 1973, Mukunda's parents kept writing to him to come to Bangalore as he had not been home for quite some time. Mukunda answered by asking his father to "see Sai Baba and get his permission for me to come to India." His father went to Whitefield, but Sri Sathya Sai Baba did not even see him in the *darshan* lines. But, he came to Mukunda in a dream while he was in France. This was the first dream Mukunda had of Sri Sathya Sai Baba. He came to him and stepped on his left toe, pressed it down and asked, "Why are you not coming to India?" Before Mukunda could explain anything, he said, "Come." Then he undid Mukunda's shirt and massaged his heart. This dream decided Mukunda to go to India.

The booking, the ticket and everything else about the journey fell into place despite a few hurdles such as, for instance, an airline strike. Mukunda reached home and heard that Sri Sathya Sai Baba was at Brindavan and he immediately dashed to Whitefield in an auto-rickshaw. He waited in the *darshan* lines, his heart pounding, his eyes glued to the gate through which Sri Sathya Sai Baba was expected to emerge. "Swami came floating like a red flame," said Mukunda. At this, his emotions overpowered him and he could not even raise his head to look at Sri Sathya Sai Baba. In that stupor-like state, he was unaware of everything around him, until he saw Sri Sathya Sai Baba bending down and taking the letter he held in his hands. The impact of the Sai presence was so strong that all a dazed Mukunda could do was watch him move away and, finally, disappear into the house beyond the gates.

The next day, he went back to Whitefield. This time, Sri Sathya Sai Baba sent for him, and he went to the interview room. He undid Mukunda's shirt and rubbed *vibhuti* on his chest to confirm to him the validity of his dream and to demonstrate to him that it was a conscious appearance. He talked to Mukunda about his personal life, mental confusions, his problems and his *vina* playing. Mukunda's doubts were cleared away to a very large extent.

During that stay in India, Mukunda played the *vina* for Sri Sathya Sai Baba once at Whitefield and once in Hyderabad. Sri Sathya Sai Baba thrilled him by materialising a gold chain for him before a vast gathering in Hyderabad. The gold chain had a *rudraksha* bead attached to it and Sri Sathya Sai Baba himself put it around Mukunda's neck. He stayed in India for six months and had many opportunities to be with Sri Sathya Sai Baba and to clear many more of his doubts.

In the past, Mukunda had never really felt any reverence for temples. If at all he went to them, it would be to appreciate their architectural beauty. Now, his family wanted him to accompany them to Tirupathi and he asked Sri Sathya Sai Baba for permission to go. Sri Sathya Sai Baba said to him, "Go! It is good for you." He went expecting to experience something wonderful spiritually, but came away disappointed. For, he had seen nothing but a heavily decorated idol. He made up his mind never again to go to temples in search of divinity. However, the very next time he was in Whitefield, he saw Sri Sathya Sai Baba going to a nearby village to install an idol in a temple. This confused him and he wondered why Sri Sathya Sai Baba would trouble to do that.

Next, Mukunda went to Mysore to see his brother. One day, he went with his brother's family to the famous Chamundi Temple on the hill above Mysore. Reluctantly and with mixed feelings, he entered the sanctum sanctorum and gazed at the idol of the goddess without any feeling of *bhakti* (devotion), or even reverence. But then, suddenly, the *raga Simha Vahini* started unfolding in his mind and, as it did, the whole sanctum sanctorum filled with light and he could no longer see the idol. "What a most beautiful and blissful experience Swami has given me," he thought.

He returned to Bangalore and went to Whitefield. Sri Sathya Sai Baba smiled at him significantly. "Now, I go to temples and churches and I find my heart always fills with the Sai aspect and the presence of Swami in the holy of holies."

After Sri Sathya Sai Baba's fiftieth birthday celebrations, Mukunda closed the international camp he had looked after in Puttaparthi and took leave of Sri Sathya Sai Baba to return to London. At that time, Sri Sathya Sai Baba had told him he would take care of his affairs and that he should not worry any longer. This puzzled Mukunda because he could not see what had to be taken care of. Also, on a few treasured occasions, Sri Sathya Sai Baba had advised him to look after his money. Mukunda was fairly well off and he found these mentions of money mystifying.

While still in Bangalore, about to set off on the long journey back to London, a message directed Mukunda to go to the house of a Sai devotee who, the message said, had something to tell him. When he went there, the lady of the house, Meera, was performing *puja* and so he sat down quietly in her *puja* room. She stretched out her open hands, palms up, to a picture of Sri Sathya Sai Baba and two coins of 25 *paise* materialised in her hands. She gave them to him saying, "Swami wants you to have them," and asked him to keep them safely. Mukunda was perplexed. He returned home unable to understand why Sri Sathya Sai Baba would give him anything through an intermediary when he had been with him only a few hours ago. He could not get any clarification on this point from Sri Sathya Sai Baba either.

Once in London, however, he understood only too well why Sri Sathya Sai Baba had talked to him so much about his finances and also why he had sent the two coins for protection. His bank in London informed him that there were only a few pounds left in his account. He was shocked, for he had always maintained substantial balances at the bank. Later, he learnt what had happened. He had entrusted a friend with some financial transactions and the task of transferring funds. Mukunda, though shocked, knew that with Sri Sathya Sai Baba's blessings, things would soon sort themselves out, and they did. Someone who had bought his boutique and who at the time had been unable to make the full payment, suddenly telephoned to say that she now wanted to pay him the remaining amount. He had had no idea that this money would ever come back to him, but it helped to tide him over a period of urgent commitment. After that, a series of prestigious concerts made him financially sound again. "All because of Swami who promised to look after me," said Mukunda in all humility and added, "Though I am so far away, Swami is in my heart. I can always feel him so close to me."

"To me, Swami is God. I am convinced more than one hundred per cent about it, though I had so many doubts and questions in the first few years. But now, I have none. He has taught me so much and I have had many experiences. Even the dust from his feet can do wonders! So immense are his powers . . . "

Sri Sathya Sai Baba has wrought many changes within Mukunda who has been able to advance on the spiritual path through music and to find in the *vina* both solace and communion with the Supreme.

"Music must be a felt experience. Do not sing with one eye on the effect it has on the audience and the other on the effect it might have on God. Let your heart throb for God; then the raga and the tala will automatically be pleasing and right."

. . . Sri Sathya Sai Baba

14

JAZZ AND THE BLUE LIGHT

A master of music and melody, Sri Sathya Sai Baba responds spontaneously to great music that emerges from and touches the soul. During the Summer Course of 1978, Maynard Ferguson, the internationally renowned jazz trumpeter, gave a concert performance of *Karnatic* music accompanied by *vina* maestro Vemu Mukunda in the presence of Sri Sathya Sai Baba.

Maynard's efforts to learn Indian classical *ragas* such as *Hamsadhwani* and *Chala Naata* (from Vemu Mukunda) and the combining of these with pure jazz were nothing less than marvellous. While playing the second number in *Chala Naata*, Maynard used his trumpet very effectively to produce the startling notes of a trumpeting elephant. The notes rang out in a fanfare, one after another in rhythmic flow, ascending to an exquisite crescendo and producing a divine symphony of melody that vibrated the innermost chords of the listeners.

Sri Sathya Sai Baba rose as Maynard played the last note and, with a brisk movement of his right hand, materialised a long gold chain strung with colourful gems. It had a small round pendant. He put it around the neck of the astonished Maynard who then beamed with joy for all the world to see. His exhileration was so overwhelming that he forgot the next line of music – something that had never happened to him before in all his long and varied professional life. It took considerable effort to regain his composure and go on with the performance. Later, Maynard told us that "The piece I played then was the best I ever played in my life." What had so astonished him was that Sri Sathya Sai Baba had instinctively recognised the touch of genius on an alien instrument playing an alien music, a trumpet producing jazz sounds.

It was only a week ago that Maynard's wife, Flora, a Sai devotee, had brought him to Bangalore for Sri Sathya Sai Baba's *darshan*. On the first day, he saw them for a few minutes and materialised *vibhuti* for them. He asked Flo, "Actress?" She replied, "Not now. For some time I was in films, but that was long ago." He stood there for a few more moments smiling as she reverentially bowed to perform *namaskara*. Then, he said, "I will see you before you go," and walked away to the *bhajan mantap*.

Flo said that in those few moments, Sri Sathya Sai Baba had mentally asked her, "Why have you come?" And she, too, had responded in thought, "I have brought Maynard." This kind of mental communication had been possible for her even in the U.S.A., Flo told us. She has been a Sai devotee for several years "on account of firm faith in the supernatural powers and divinity of Baba." Flo is convinced that Sri Sathya Sai Baba will help in times of stress and strain if one has unshakable faith in him.

Some years ago, Flo and Maynard spent two years in Rishi Valley and this led to Flo taking a keen interest in *Hindu* philosophy and Indian spiritual thought. She read J. Krishnamurti's books. A few years after that, she came to know of Sri Sathya Sai Baba and obtained a photograph of him. From the time the photograph came into her life, good things started to happen to her. She became fully aware of his numinous quality.

At one time, Flo had had an eye ailment and a problem with her skin which looked like spreading and spoiling her looks. Then, it seemed that it might impair her eyes. She became desperate. She prayed intensely to Sri Sathya Sai Baba, "Please save my eyes. Don't let them be disfigured." No sooner had she uttered the prayerful plea than she experienced a luminous impact. Bright blue rays of light came straight at her and went into her forehead between the eyebrows. It was a most beautiful sensation replete with purest bliss. The vision of the blue light had a tremendous effect on Flo's personality and wrought great inner change. She was engulfed in a state of unalloyed bliss for days on end. She knew it was the work of none other than Sri Sathya Sai Baba.

After the experience of the blue light, Flo meditated more often and there were times when she sensed the invisible presence of Sri Sathya Sai Baba in the room with her. She received tangible evidence of his unseen help, given on so many trying occasions.

"This is the essential difference between J. Krishnamurti and Baba," said Flo in a soft affirmative tone. "I've been very interested in J. Krishnamurti's thoughts and have read his books, and they are great. However, in times of need, you can't call out to him for help. But, call Sai Baba from anywhere, from any place and at any time and he will be there to help. Is that not omnipresence? There is no one like Baba."

When has Sri Sathya Sai Baba helped her in any way?

"Oh, several times . . . in small things and big things. As an example, let me state the case of one of my daughters who used to keep wild company. She used to get into a lot of difficult situations, and so, I prayed to Baba. It was Vemu Mukunda who suggested that I also do *mandala puja* for forty-five days with the *mantra 'Om Sai Ram.'* And, please believe me, this had definite results. Today, my daughter is a reformed girl and has no more problems."

In a private interview, Sri Sathya Sai Baba said to Maynard, "I know about your music . . . but, for the past six months, you have not been very happy about it, is that not so?" It was a surprise to Maynard to find that Sri Sathya Sai Baba knew about the conflict in his mind. For, professionally and financially, he had been riding high on the crest of success, but there had been a certain inner dissatisfaction – the genuine artiste in him was not satisfied with mere commercial success. How had Sri Sathya Sai Baba known this, he asked himself. Sri Sathya Sai Baba then told him that things would soon be better and patted him affectionately. Maynard said that he had never been a spiritual person and Sri Sathya Sai Baba said, "I know."

Then Sri Sathya Sai Baba materialised some sugar candy for Flo and told her to eat it. He asked her to give up wine and to take good care of her eyes. Flo talked to him about her children, for she worried constantly about their well-being. "It is quite a job to look after four grown-up daughters in the U.S.A. of today where there is so much violence," she said. Both Maynard and Flo were aglow when they emerged from the interview room.

In the U.S.A., Flo often sensed Sri Sathya Sai Baba's presence during meditation. However, his physical form was "glorious, wonderful . . . . and he is a person of such love." Maynard, too, felt great exhileration in his presence. They are a well matched couple and have been married thirty years. Now Maynard Ferguson, the committed musician, has plans to make records of Sai *bhajans*.

"If you feel attachment towards wife and children, land and property, bank accounts and balances, and when these decline, you will come to grief. Develop attachment to the Universal and you will grow in love and splendour."

"You are judged by your sadhana (spiritual endeavour), not by the number of temples you have entered, nor the quantity and cost of the offerings you make at shrines."

. . . Sri Sathya Sai Baba

15

SAVED BY A PHOTOGRAPH

Mr. K. R. Vasudevan, Editor of the Dinamani Kadir in Madras, related a recent experience. A taxi driver asked him for a photogaph of Sri Sathya Sai Baba. So Vasudevan got one, had it framed and took it to his office for the taxi driver to collect. But, he never turned up and the photograph remained in the office.

One day, when the Editor was alone, a furious visitor walked into the office. Purple with rage, the man announced in a loud voice that he was there to settle scores with Vasudevan for what he termed an affront to his family dignity. His outrage was caused by something printed in the Dinamani Kadir magazine.

Vasudevan saw that the enraged man intended violence. He explained that the offending article pertained to the distant past and was factually correct. He also admitted the possibility of its having an effect on the good name of the man's family. He said he was sorry about it and quietly added, "You see, if you still feel hurt and want revenge, let me send away the *peon* who is the only other person here. Then, whatever you do, there won't be any witness, there will be no one to testify to your actions except, of course, Baba there." And saying that, he pointed to Sri Sathya Sai Baba's photograph on the wall. As the man stared at the photograph,Vasudevan calmly added, "Now, proceed with whatever you want to do with me! . . . Maybe, you are right about the material we have printed. Anyway, it is too late to remedy the situation. So do what you want."

The man stared alternatively at the Editor and the photograph and then, abruptly, turned on his heels and left.

"Is this not a miracle of Baba's? A miracle performed by just a photograph of him. What a transformation he caused in the attitude of the violent caller. If a photograph can do this, what can we say about the impact of Baba's physical presence?" asked Vasudevan who has been a Sai devotee for many years.

How did Sri Sathya Sai Baba come into his life?

Vasudevan spoke of the days when Sri Sathya Sai Baba was young, "And it was much easier to see him, as there were not such crowds as there are today. But, for a long time, I was not interested. Then one day, in January 1958, I saw a photograph of Baba in a neighbour's house." This was in Kalathoor (a village between Vandalur and Tiropporur in the Chingleput District of Tamil Nadu) where he lived. It was prominently displayed in a house belonging to an elderly lady. She was absent and Vasudevan was keeping an eye on it for her. When she returned, he asked her, "Is this Sai Baba still available?"

"Of course," she replied and chided him for not having met him. Then she counselled him, "Go now to Madras and see him. Tomorrow, he will still be there, but he will go away the next day to Hyderabad."

Vasudevan had by then developed a strong urge to see Sri Sathya Sai Baba, so he did as the old lady directed and rushed off to Madras. There he learnt that Sri Sathya Sai Baba was at the house of a Mr. Venkatamuni, so he went there and then wondered what to do next. There was an old woman standing near the house and she asked him, "Are you new?"

"Yes," said Vasudevan.

"Then why have you come empty handed when you are to see him for the first time?" she asked. Vasudevan was annoyed at the way she spoke to him. Unexpectedly, the woman opened her hand and he saw that she had been holding two very shrivelled looking oranges.

"Brother, you take one and I will give one . . . that is enough. You should have something to offer when you see Baba," she advised.

Vasudevan was almost in tears at the thoughtfulness of the unknown old woman who, though obviously penniless, had such a generous heart. Then, she gave him another valuable tip, "You should stand here and watch for him. Baba will come out of the house down those steps to get into his car. When he comes down the steps, that will be your chance to do *namaskaram*. That will be your only chance, grab it! I can wait for another time. You are new." And, in that magnanimous way, she moved aside and let him take her place.

There was no time to think for, at that very moment, Sri Sathya Sai Baba appeared. He came down the steps and Vasudevan hurried forward to perform *namaskaram*. Sri Sathya Sai Baba blessed him and said, "I am going to Hyderabad, but I shall come back on Republic Day. Come then." Dumbfounded, Vasudevan nodded as Sri Sathya Sai Baba got into the car. And then, as if answering another thought, he lowered the window glass and raised his hand in blessing.

That first meeting left a deep and lasting impression on Vasudevan and, for a long time afterwards, he could do nothing but bask in the blissful warmth of that *darshan*.

On Republic Day, of course, Vasudevan was in Madras and returned to Venkatamuni's house in Mylapore for Sri Sathya Sai Baba's *darshan*. But, as he got there, he saw that the crowd was dispersing, and they said that Sri Sathya Sai Baba had already given *darshan* and was gone. Vasudevan wondered why he was so unpredictable about his schedule. At the same time, the thought made him stay on. It was just as possible that Sri Sathya Sai Baba would change his mind and re-emerge, so he lingered near Venkatamuni's house.

There was no one else in the compound. After a while, a cleaning woman saw him and said, "Oh! have you come for *darshan*? Then go upstairs." Vasudevan did not know why she said it, for he had not expected to be allowed to sit even in the outside verandah, but he did not wait to be told again. He dashed to the upstairs verandah and sat waiting. In a while, a tall young man (Rajah Reddy) came to him and said, "Baba said he will give you *darshan* after half past twelve this afternoon at Venkatagiri House near the Thousand Lights in Madras."

Vasudevan pleaded with him, "Can I not just have a peep? I have come a long way from a village and I have to return there for some work."

But the tall young man replied, "He is in his room, you can't see from here. But, he has definitely said that he will see you after half past twelve at Venkatagiri House and you <u>will</u> have *darshan*."

Vasudevan was full of misgivings as he left. He had an important assignment that morning to see the Collector of Chingleput arranged by the late Mr. Kamaraj, Chief Minister of Tamil Nadu at the time. He had to attend that meeting and, what was more, he was to take some tribal people to it. The meeting looked like being a long drawn out affair and he had no way of knowing when he could return. Putting duty first, Vasudevan went to the Collector's office at the appointed time and was told that a knotty problem of protocol had arisen and the Collector was caught up in it; so, Vasudevan's meeting with him had had to be postponed. Normally, this sort of thing would have upset Vasudevan, but not this time. Very relieved, he rushed to catch the bus back to Madras. It was half past one and he wondered if he had already lost all chances of *darshan*.

Arrived at Venkatagiri House, he saw a car with a crowd around it. "Is he leaving?" wondered Vasudevan. The same tall young man who was now at the gate answered, "Do not worry. Baba is still in the house and you are bound to have his *darshan*."

Within minutes after that, Sri Sathya Sai Baba appeared and asked

Vasudevan, "Are you the person who has come from the faraway village?" Then he took him with him to another room and what happened then still thrills Vasudevan today.

Sri Sathya Sai Baba spoke in an unceasing flow of things that had happened in Vasudevan's life. He described in detail a time when Vasudevan had thought of killing himself. "You had gone to the beach. You didn't plunge into the sea, but you walked for miles and miles on the sea shore in a daze." As he described this wretched phase of Vasudevan's life, there was deep anguish in his voice and a few tears trickled down his cheeks. Sri Sathya Sai Baba's words revealed affection, feeling and a flood of love for Vasudevan. He went on to say, "You will have problems and difficulties for another three years, but if you have *bhakti* as you do now, everything will turn out all right."

Vasudevan was aghast and exclaimed, "More difficulties? . . . Oh God." Then, without anymore thought, he returned to his family in the village.

The first sorrow to arrive was the death, from diphtheria, of his five-year-old son. A few weeks before that, Vasudevan had taken his whole family to Venkatamuni's house to have *darshan* of Sri Sathya Sai Baba. His five-year-old son had clung to Sri Sathya Sai Baba's feet and would not let go. Vasudevan gave his dead son a splendid farewell with *bhajans* and sacred recitations on an auspicious day in January 1962. But, his death left a deep wound and he stopped performing his personal *puja*. Instead, he left the *puja* – *Ganesha yantra puja* and the *puja* for Sri Sathya Sai Baba – to be performed by the caretaker in his village house. And he moved away and settled in Tambaram. He bundled up all his books on religion and philosophy and put them away.

Two years went by. Vasudevan and his family faced immense financial hardship. He had to leave the organization he worked for. At the end of 1966 he still had grave difficulties. On the morning of the 1st of January 1967, he saw an old pamphlet with the Sai message and it reminded him of Sri Sathya Sai Baba. A friend told him that that very evening Sri Sathya Sai Baba was going to be at the Sai Temple in Guindy. He took him there. Sri Sathya Sai Baba came and stood next to Vasudevan for a very brief moment and then he left. But that was enough for Vasudevan. A couple of months later, he got a new job in Nagpur and became a professional journalist.

Vasudevan talked about a photograph of Sri Sathya Sai Baba he had bought after his first *darshan*. He wanted to give it to his father-in-law, a retired police officer, but he was uncertain of his reaction. To his surprise, the old gentleman was instantly captivated by it and went to Puttaparthi several times where he was affectionately welcomed by Sri Sathya Sai Baba. On many of his visits there, Sri Sathya Sai Baba had kept him on and asked his aid in policing arrangements on festive days.

Vasudevan has had unforgettable experiences on *Shivaratri*. He saw Sri Sathya Sai Baba's face glow with a reddish hue, a luminous orange and then an ethereal blue. "At *Shivaratri*, Baba does things beyond our comprehension. One has to experience the divinity in Baba before one can realize his *leelas*, particularly at *Shivaratri*," he says.

Things improved for Vasudevan in Nagpur. He went to an interview for a job at the Tribune (an English language daily newspaper published from Chandigarh in Northern India). He sensed that he was being guided by Sri Sathya Sai Baba who was in Moga, also in the North, at the time. A Sai devotee in the Tribune office told him that Sri Sathya Sai Baba's aeroplane was due to take off in a short while and that they should be able to hear it as it overflew them. Was that a coincidence, or divine grace? Vasudevan was being interviewed when he heard the sound of the aeroplane. He was chosen for the job and all his conditions were agreed: the amount of the salary as well as the fifty days he requested before joining. Just as Sri Sathya Sai Baba had told him, three years later things did become much brighter.

Sri Sathya Sai Baba gave Vasudevan an interview on the 22nd of March 1978 in Bangalore during which he received indications that he, throughout the trying three years, had been the recipient of Sai grace. Sri Sathya Sai Baba knew everything that was happening to him, his family, his son who was studying medicine, and his daughters who were to be married, and every other detail. Vasudevan is very sure, therefore, that his efforts in various directions will receive Sri Sathya Sai Baba's blessings.

"What more can one want?" asks Vasudevan.

"Assume silence when anger invades you, or remember the name of the Lord. Do not remind yourself of things that will further inflame your anger. That will do incalculable harm."

. . . Sri Sathya Sai Baba

16

THE DIVINE PSYCHIATRIST

"I was a very highly strung person on the verge of neurosis, and my first visit to Puttaparthi had a soothing effect on me. I experienced peace and happiness such as I had not known for months. One look at my face and my husband knew the visit had done me a world of good." These are the words of N. S. Shantamma who had suffered great mental agony for, being a working woman, she had had to leave her baby son in the care of others. And the baby was unwell, needing constant personal attention and medical care. It was at such a time that she was transferred to Mysore. She could not afford to give up working, nor could she take her baby with her. The situation was fraught. She left the baby with elders of the family who, naturally enough, had their own ideas about bringing up children, particularly sick ones. But there was no choice: Shantamma left her child behind in Bangalore and went alone to Mysore, her heart full of anguish.

In Mysore, she chanced to go to a *bhajan* session at the house of a friend where she bought a copy of *Satyam Shivam Sundaram* by N. Kasturi. The *bhajans* brought her some solace and, with the book in her hands, she prayed: "Let me be transferred back home as soon as I finish reading this book." The prayer occurred to her because she had heard that reading about holy men could lead to the fulfillment of wishes.

"It took me one year and three weeks to read the book. Something or the other would always keep me from it. And, believe it or not, immediately afterwards I was transferred back to Bangalore!"

Shantamma related something else that had happened to her in Mysore. She had taken a room in the Modern Hindu Hotel and, to secure the door, she had borrowed a sturdy old lock and key, a type no longer easily available. One day, she lost the key. Of a nervous disposition to start with, this new fix made her frantic with worry about how to return the lock and key to her friend. It was not at all easy to obtain in the shops. She searched everywhere desperately, but no luck. When the tension became unbearable, she prayed to Sri Sathya Sai Baba. She walked back to her hotel in a state of utter dejection. As she came to a *tonga* stand opposite the hotel, she saw a metallic glint on the ground. She bent down and scratched the loose earth from it and there it was, the lost key. She could not understand how something so small, lost on a heavily used thoroughfare, could still be there. Nor did she understand why she had looked down just at that moment and seen the glint in the dust. It had not looked particularly like a key and, ordinarily, she would not have investigated, but walked straight on. Then she understood: it was the work of Sri Sathya Sai Baba to whom she had prayed.

In 1969, after her transfer back to Bangalore, Shantamma went to Whitefield for Sri Sathya Sai Baba's *darshan*. She liked going to Brindavan which had always and rather mysteriously attracted her. She was drawn to it even though she did not have total faith in Sri Sathya Sai Baba.

Suddenly and impulsively, she decided to go to Puttaparthi. Her husband did not object, for all he wished was that his wife should be free of worries and tension. Shantamma loved the tranquillity of Puttaparthi, and seeing Sri Sathya Sai Baba helped her to regain a measure of peace. She felt radiant and, for the first time, a strange new serenity reigned in her heart. This made her think that it was a power that Sri Sathya Sai Baba had that had brought about the wonderful change in her. She thought for the first time, "Maybe he is God." And that thought gave her more peace of mind. She kept telling herself, "It is not enough to lead a good life. God's grace is more important."

Then, quite suddenly, after she had had these inner murmurings, she was summoned to an interview with Sri Sathya Sai Baba. Upto that point, she had only ever had his *darshan* and his blessings and she had never even tried to have an interview.

There were quite a few people in the interview room with her. Sri Sathya Sai Baba looked at her and said, *"Shabash!"* (well done), signifying to her that he knew that she had at last desired to meet him. "What news? What do you want?" he asked her in *Kannada*. She replied, "I become frightened without cause. I want your blessings and to perform *paada namaskaram*." She remembers that on that day she was too overcome to perform a proper *paada namaskaram*.

After the interview, Shantamma did indeed feel free from anxiety; she was serene. She continued to go to Whitefield. One day, she asked Sri Sathya Sai Baba to autograph a photograph for her. He signed as usual on the front, then he seemed to reflect for a moment, turned round the photograph and signed it on the back, too. It intrigued her, but he offered no explanation. She kept it safe in her *puja* room. When someone was ill, she would fetch the photograph and keep it under their pillow.

"My temper flare-ups and my anger in general were easily controllable after I received the signed photograph from Baba." She became deeply devoted to the photograph and set great store by it. She would not allow anyone even to touch it without her consent.

One day, her daughter was sick and Shantamma put the photograph under her pillow. While Shantamma was away, lecturing in Mysore, her maid changed the sheets. She took the soiled linen off the bed and soaked it in detergent with the photograph still hidden in its folds. Hours later, Shantamma's mother discovered what had happened, but did not have the courage to tell her of it. So, she put the photograph in a cool place where she hoped it would dry off, and then went out. She knew that Shantamma would be hysterical when she saw the drenched photograph.

The photograph had dried when Shantamma returned and it was not damaged, but the signature on the celluloid had been washed away. Tears welled up in her eyes and, after a while, she composed herself and turned it around. The second signature was still there, immaculate. She was very relieved that Sri Sathya Sai Baba's grace had remained with her through the second signature, and she thanked him in silent prayer for having so thoughtfully signed it twice.

Some years ago, Shantamma had a dream. In it, her husband was gravely ill and there were clear signs of his death. She cried out to *Sai Ram* to save her husband. But, suddenly, the dream ended and she awoke. Though disturbed by the dream, she felt happy that she had sought Sri Sathya Sai Baba's help even in sleep.

A few months after that dream, Shantamma's husband, C. S. Suryanarayana Rao, was admitted to hospital in a very serious condition and on the verge of collapse.

One morning, the priest who came regularly to see her mother, told them of a dream he had had. He did not know that Mr. Rao was very sick. In the dream, Sri Sathya Sai Baba told him that Mr. Rao was gravely ill. Then he asked the priest to instruct Shantamma that life does not reside in the heart, but in the spinal column, in the *muladhara*. "Teach her the *Ganapati stotra* and *mantra* and how to recite them from the *muladhara* base," he counselled. The priest duly arrived to see her and was told that Mr. Rao really was very sick. He explained the significance of his dream to Shantamma. He said that her heart was good, but that some past *karma* was obstructing her worship of God. The dream meant that her husband's life force in the spinal cord had become desiccated and that it had to be revitalized by the *Ganapati stotra* recited while concentrating on the *muladhara*.

"In times of crisis," explained the priest, "the doctor and the priest are of equal importance. One is the physician of the body, the other that of the soul." Putting all her faith in Sri Sathya Sai Baba, Shantamma learnt the *Ganapati stotra* in order to sustain her husband's *muladhara*. And from that very day, his condition began to improve.

At this point, Mr. Rao himself took up the tale. That morning, almost at the same time that the priest was dreaming about Sri Sathya Sai Baba, Mr. Rao saw him in a vision. Sri Sathya Sai Baba appeared, embraced him affectionately and said, "I am glad you have come under my influence." Then, as Mr. Rao was drifting into sleep, he felt an inner sensation, as if his vertebrae were cracking and someone were straightening something inside him. When he woke the next morning, he felt better. The lifeless feeling and abject misery were gone and he felt, for the first time, that he was going to be all right.

Shantamma believes that it was Sri Sathya Sai Baba who came to their help and rescued her husband on his deathbed. He made her remove all the obstacles to his recovery by prayer, to remove her past negative *karma*, and granted her peace. There can be no other plausible explanation for the priest's dream in which he was given detailed instructions.

Mr. Rao said that his reaction to Sri Sathya Sai Baba is ambivalent: he feels drawn to him inspite of himself. He is happy to have his *darshan*, but beyond that he does not try to analyse Sri Sathya Sai Baba or his own response to him. "What right have I, or what intellectual equipment do I possess with which to analyse or research his powers?" he asks. And he is extremely grateful to Sri Sathya Sai Baba for what he has done for his wife. "Baba's *darshan* and influence have certainly had a therapeutic effect on her, for hers was a psychological problem."

Whenever Shantamma returned from seeing Sri Sathya Sai Baba, she returned in a peaceful state and her neurotic outbursts were quelled. "No amount of drugs could have had the effect that Swami has had on her. And any effect the drugs would have had could only have been temporary, whereas Swami has brought about a permanent cure."

"How many people can afford scientific cures in medical institutions? How often does science really cure cases of neurosis? They give drugs and more drugs and put the patient into a dull soporific state, never fully in possession of their mental faculties. On the other hand, Baba's is a gentle, gradual and graceful process, making one cure oneself through the simple formula of faith and *bhakti* (devotion)."

"My wife is a full fledged lecturer and has always worked. Would she have been able to continue working if we had launched into a clinical treatment of her neurosis? Actually, people should try harder to understand and to realize the nature of such valuable succour given by Baba," said Mr. Rao who has immense respect for Sri Sathya Sai Baba and the good work he does for the benefit of the people. He never interfered with his wife's trips to Whitefield and Puttaparthi, even though he never accompanied her. "And I also accepted that Baba was a source of joy, light and hope for her and that he had restored her to normalcy."

Mr. Rao, principal of a college, is full of praise for the way in which the Sathya Sai educational institutions are run. "The discipline and culture shown by Satya Sai students are exemplary. I have sent my son to study at one of them so that he may imbibe the right values and disciplines in life," he said.

Shantamma attends discourses and goes for *darshan* regularly. She has experienced Sri Sathya Sai Baba's presence in her house several times: inexplicable scents, the fragrance of *vibhuti* and, on some occasions, the formation of honey on photographs of Sri Sathya Sai Baba.

Today, Shantamma is a completely happy person, all her fears and obsessions gone forever – all thanks to the immense and immeasurable love and grace of Sri Sathya Sai Baba.

"God is like a magnet: just as a magnet attracts pure metal, God attracts pure hearts. If there is dirt or rust on the metal, how can it attract? If the mind contains anger, lust, enmity, jealousy – how can divinity attract?"

. . . Sri Sathya Sai Baba

17

DIVINE THERAPY

"I owe a lot to Swami who is responsible for making me what I am today – a person with pure thoughts and an unwavering mind," so says Dr. John Leiff, a successful psychiatrist from Boston, Massachussetts.

John was part of the so called free society in America. Even so, he did not really want to get caught up in the bad habits of his environment. He tried hard to keep his thoughts in check, but it was difficult not to yield to temptations. It was at this point in his life that he became interested in *yoga* and Indian philosophy. He read about the *Sufis*, Swami Muktananda and various spiritual masters. He also heard some stories about Sri Sathya Sai Baba. He learnt to meditate and tried practising it. Often, while meditating, Sri Sathya Sai Baba's face would appear and, whenever that happened, he sensed great betterment in himself as a person. He became steadier and more confident. He could effectively control his diet. His little weaknesses dropped away without conscious effort. He came to feel that he had found a good anchor in life. So, he meditated with more enthusiasm and seriousness and for longer periods. This gave him peace and brought about a marked change in him. Everyone remarked that he seemed very different and he, too, felt that he was emerging in a fresh personality.

John was in Vancouver, in Canada, for a U.N.O. conference when he went to a "psychic film festival." He saw a film about Sri Sathya Sai Baba, one of Richard Bock's first films. Then, in Boston, he bought volume I of *Sathya Sai Speaks*. The film and the book left deep impressions and, in a speech at the U.N.O., he referred to the thoughts and ideas of Sri Sathya Sai Baba.

He heard some tapes of Sri Sathya Sai Baba's speeches and *bhajans* and, soon, a new thought took deep root in his mind: "when will I be able to see Swami?" He bought several more books about him in the longing to know more. He also joined a church group which conducted classes in religious music and meditation. They sang easy continuous *bhajans* such as *'Om Sri Ram Jai Ram.'* And with all this, John's desire to meet Sri Sathya Sai Baba grew daily stronger. Then, on a Thursday night, he had his first Sai dream.

In the dream, Sri Sathya Sai Baba sat cross-legged in the church. He turned around and said to John, "I have been sitting here, right here, for two years now. What do you want to go to India for?" The dream vision amazed John. He wondered if Sri Sathya Sai Baba meant that he had been with them ever since they had started the *Sai Ram bhajans* and meditation. "It was so wonderful, this dream . . . it made me intensely happy, and so I went to an Indian friend and told him that I would go to India with him at Christmas."

The dream helped to improve him further. It took away some of the obsessions that troubled him and made him a more balanced individual. "For in America," explained John, "the set up isn't like in India and is in such sharp contrast to Swami's *ashrama* rules. American women dress with a view to enhance their sex appeal and every man has a struggle to have pure thoughts." He went on to explain that after coming under the influence of Sri Sathya Sai Baba, he invariably stayed unruffled and unaffected by mundane attractions. "You must know the power of Swami's *vibhuti*, too! Thanks to it, when I massage patients, I never have body consciousness and this is a great boon to a doctor like me who has to deal with women patients as well. I don't mind being frank about this." For, the women who go to him for treatment are not normal disciplined women; they are neurotic, highly strung, emotional people and it is a constant effort to retain one's own poise at all times with these women who trustingly come to him for a healing touch or a soothing massage.

"Swami appearing in my dreams has given me the assurance that he is watching over me and that I should be on my best behaviour always and do my best professionally for all patients. Also, after I felt the influence of Swami in my life, my code of conduct in private life, too, has become highly disciplined," said John.

In another interesting dream, John saw Sri Sathya Sai Baba walking in a garden and talking to him about moral values and the need for having a clean mind and a pure heart at all times.

John arrived in India in 1977. He saw Sri Sathya Sai Baba at *darshan* time and experienced emotional upheaval at first sight. He said to John, "I will see you tomorrow," and instantly John was elated. But, Sri Sathya Sai

Baba was very busy the next day and did not see him, and his spirits sank low. Instead of the hoped for talk, all that happened was that Sri Sathya Sai Baba went up to John, patted him on the shoulder and said, "Don't be disappointed, be happy."

That year, Christmas was on a Sunday and on that day all the foreign devotees dined with Sri Sathya Sai Baba and heard him discourse on Christ. He came near John and said to him, "Very happy yesterday . . . I will see you tomorrow." And the next day, Sri Sathya Sai Baba came and stood next to him and John was able to perform *paada namaskara* (bowing reverentially to the feet) and the touch of his feet had a strong impact: John felt a blast of something inside. He was elated, shell-shocked and energised by turns. One touch and what an impact, he thought wonderingly.

The next day, John tried again to touch the feet of Sri Sathya Sai Baba as he passed by in the *darshan* lines. The touch this time did not have the same effect and John realised that when a *paada namaskara* is granted it has tremendous significance which it does not have in other circumstances. It is a spiritual communion. Even now, when John thinks of that first *paada namaskara*, a special current courses through his being as he remembers the impact of touching Sri Sathya Sai Baba's feet in total surrender.

This first trip was significant. He ruminated over the words that Sri Sathya Sai Baba had spoken to him and learnt a psychological lesson. Sri Sathya Sai Baba saying, "You were happy yesterday, but not today . . . Disappointed? Happy! . . . " These words brought home to him that Sri Sathya Sai Baba was telling him what a wavering, excitable and changeable nature he had. He had indirectly instructed John that "to be happy one day and miserable the next is not good. Try to be equal-minded." This understanding brought great happiness with it.

John was also summoned to a group interview with other American devotees and Sri Sathya Sai Baba told him, "Don't worry. I am going to watch over your total development." This reassurance, quite naturally, was wonderfully heartening.

John's second visit to India was in 1978 when he took part in the Summer Course. He had the very moving opportunity to hear Sri Sathya Sai Baba give talks and sing *bhajans*. He was deeply content to be in the divine presence for a few hours each day.

"At the Summer Course, Baba taught me that I can't separate *sadhana* (spiritual endeavour) from my profession. I must do my work as worship and pursue the work with cent per cent purity of heart and with sincerity," said John Leiff. He is now a happy, confident and calm person thanks to the guidance of his Divine Therapist.

"The Lord is understood only by His bhakta (devotee); the bhakta is understood only by his Lord. Others cannot understand them. So, do not recount matters relating to the Lord to those who have no bhakti (devotion)."

. . . Sri Sathya Sai Baba

18

DOCTOR OF DREAMS

"I had to wait for twelve long years before Baba noticed me and talked to me, though I went regularly to Whitefield for his *darshan*," said Dr. K. Hanumanthappa. He is a Reader in Commerce at the Post-Graduate Department of Commerce and Management, the University of Bangalore.

"So long!" I said, "And you still carried on going there. Did you never become fed up or upset?"

"It is a long story," he answered and recounted it.

When he was at the University of Karnataka, he and his wife, Sharada Devi, went to see Mr. Naidu at his house in Hubli, another town in Karnataka State. As they reached, Sai *bhajans* were being sung and they were both moved by them. They learnt that Mr. Naidu was an ardent devotee of Sri Sathya Sai Baba and saw his flame coloured robe in the Naidu *puja* room. Mr. Naidu gave them a small photograph of Sri Sathya Sai Baba which they gratefully brought home.

Then one day, Sri Sathya Sai Baba came to the University of Karnataka at the invitation of Dr. Adke, Vice-Chancellor at the time. Dr. Hanumanthappa was out of town and so missed him, but Sharada Devi saw Sri Sathya Sai Baba and heard him speak.

When their son was two years old, Sharada Devi found that she was expecting a second child. Then, all of a sudden, she became seriously ill.

The medical diagnosis was grim: kidney malfunction caused by tuberculosis of the kidneys. Her condition worsened rapidly and the doctors' opinion was that her survival depended on surgery which, however, could not be performed while she was pregnant. Her case became a hotly debated topic among specialists. The consensus of opinion was that, at best, she could be kept alive for a few months with regular injections of streptomycin. And, worst of all, there was no way of saving either the mother or the baby, they all told poor Dr. Hanumanthappa.

Sharada Devi had to bear excruciating pain for about two months, being injected daily with streptomycin. In her state of advanced pregnancy and disease, she found the pricking of the needle absolutely intolerable. Strong dosages of drugs made her head reel all the time and she was unable to move without assistance. At her wit's end, she desperately pleaded, "Please, I do not want anymore injections. Let us leave everything to God and let His will prevail. At least, let me not suffer this agonising pain and the terrible swellings of the injections. It is torture!"

Dr. Hanumanthappa could not help yielding to her heart-rending plea. Then, Sharada Devi placed the photograph of Sri Sathya Sai Baba by her bed and prayed ceaselessly, "If I must go, please take me away without inflicting anymore pain on me." After that, there was a turn in events. To the surprise of the doctors, her health picked up and, when it was time for the child to be born, the childbirth presented no difficulties and the newborn baby was hale and hearty. But, alas, the kidney trouble persisted.

When the baby was twenty-one days old, Sharada Devi took it to a *Satyanarayana* temple and placed it at the feet of Lord *Satyanarayana*. She prayed very hard, "Please do with this child whatever you want, for it is yours." All her emotions, restrained for so long, burst out and she wept there in the temple. She stayed there, sobbing, for a long time with her little child, but when she returned home, she felt strangely at peace.

The very next day, a miracle was found to have occurred. Her kidney disease had vanished. No doctor could explain how the tuberculosis had been eliminated so thoroughly. But there certainly was no trace of it and, with time, Sharada Devi's health became perfectly normal, and she became absolutely fit.

The miracle of the healing, after months of agony, strengthened the Hanumanthappas' faith in Sri Sathya Sai Baba and they worshipped him now with increased fervour. But, despite all this, Sri Sathya Sai Baba never came near them, nor blessed them in person, although they went to both Whitefield and Puttaparthi periodically for his *darshan*.

Later, with the establishment of the University of Bangalore, the Hanumanthappas moved to Bangalore. It was his task to set up the Commerce Department. He found a house in central Bangalore quite easily. He learnt that the landlord was a Sai devotee and that, for no particular reason, had kept the house vacant for some time. He gladly offered it to Dr. Hanumanthappa for a very reasonable rental.

The family had comfortably settled in when Dr. Hanumanthappa had his first unusual dream. It was a long, very long, dream in which Sri Sathya Sai Baba appeared and talked to him about building a house. He explained technicalities of construction and said, "Do you think I do not know about building? See what I am building!" Then Dr. Hanumanthappa was taken to a site where construction was in progress.

The dream made no sense to Dr. Hanumanthappa, but he told his wife about it. What was Sri Sathya Sai Baba trying to tell him? he wondered. He had never thought of building a house in Bangalore and he hardly had the money to pay for even its foundation.

That evening, a gentleman turned up and spoke about some plots of land for sale. He got Dr. Hanumanthappa thinking about owning his own house, since it seemed that he was to be in Bangalore permanently. Dr. Hanumanthappa said that he did not have the money to buy a house, and the gentleman replied, "You have a scooter. You can always sell it and pay an advance on the plot, then you can apply for a loan to the University." But, Dr. Hanumanthappa politely declined as it all seemed so extravagant and out of reach. But, the gentleman kept coming back and, one day, he brought along a mutual friend to help in persuading Dr. Hanumanthappa to at least look at some plots. He agreed, though reluctantly, and was taken to see many plots for sale.

One day, the gentleman took Dr. Hanumanthappa to see a site in Tilaknagar. He was stunned when he saw it. It was the one Sri Sathya Sai Baba had shown him in the dream! Instantly, Dr. Hanumanthappa was interested and the deal was made the same day on reasonable terms. He sold his scooter and paid the deposit. He applied to the University for a loan to build a house and it was approved straight away. A small property he owned in Dharwar fetched an unexpectedly high price. And, to top it all, several relatives came forward with offers of financial help. All these helpers and helpful circumstances seemed to converge spontaneously, making it possible for him to buy the land, have it registered in his name and start building his house.

The construction work progressed quickly. The Hanumanthappas went to Whitefield regularly, but Sri Sathya Sai Baba still never even glanced their way. Sharada Devi did her utmost to attract his attention, but he never came near her. Nevertheless, they continued to go for *darshan*.

The house was finally ready. No one had believed that they would be able to finish building such a good house in such record time. Dr. Hanumanthappa was convinced that it was Sri Sathya Sai Baba who had helped at every stage. He had been able to obtain all the building materials with ease and had not had to pay black market rates for the cement or anything else. The work never faltered at any stage, and there were no delays in getting the electrical and sanitary connections. The task was completed in five months; and a well planned, modern and spacious house was ready to be occupied by the Hanumanthappas.

First, they installed a photograph of Sri Sathya Sai Baba in the *puja* room and then Dr. Hanumanthappa performed the *grahapravesham* (ceremony invoking the gods before occupying a new abode), accompanied by Sai *bhajans*.

It was at about this time that Dr. Hanumanthappa had an opportunity to meet Sri Sathya Sai Baba during a college programme. Sri Sathya Sai Baba blessed him, but he did not give any indication of having known him or helped him in any way. This raised some doubts in Dr. Hanumanthappa's mind; nevertheless, the close contact, albeit impersonal, pleased him and made him go on visiting Whitefield. Often though, he could not help feeling how nice it would have been had Sri Sathya Sai Baba physically been present at the house installation ceremony to bless their new home in person.

Matters went on in the same way and the long scooter rides to Whitefield, without any tangible results, began to wear down the Hanumanthappas. There were times when they felt hurt at the total neglect, even though they had been faithful pilgrims for years. Even more aggravating was the fact that they had frequently seen completely new visitors being taken straight inside the house for interviews with Sri Sathya Sai Baba as soon as they arrived. Why was that? And what were, then, their own shortcomings? They had been to Puttaparthi, but not once had Sri Sathya Sai Baba given them even an encouraging look. Why? Why?

On a very chilly day, the Hanumanthappas had come out to Whitefield again. As he put on a sweater, he said to his wife, "Why do we come here like this, even in such beastly weather? Anyway, take a good look at this place, for this is our last time. I think it is best that we think of Baba in our own *puja* room and stop yearning for his physical presence here."

As they were leaving, and Dr. Hanumanthappa had already started his scooter, a student came running to them. "Are you Mr. Hanumanthappa?" he asked and, receiving an affirmative response, continued, "Swami wants you to come inside."

Thoroughly shaken and choked with emotion, they both hurried back and went into the divine house. Sri Sathya Sai Baba came to Dr. Hanumanthappa and threw his arms around him, clasping him tightly and with infinite affection. They were both speechless with amazement and tears of wonder at this unexpected turn of events. Sri Sathya Sai Baba comforted the couple and bade them compose themselves, for he knew the emotional turmoil within them. He made them feel at home, materialised *vibhuti* for them and promised to give them another interview, this time with their family.

Suddenly, for the Hanumanthappas, the world had become an enchanting place and life shone with a thousand brilliant colours. Life is worth living, after all, they thought, if only to have lived for one such glorious moment. All the waiting and the penances had been worth the moment of fulfillment. There hearts full, their faces suffused with joy, they almost "floated on air" on the journey back home.

They waited, all agog, for Sri Sathya Sai Baba to call them back for the promised interview. Days passed and no call came. But they decided they would be patient.

On the 6th of August 1976, Sharada Devi reminded her husband that it was his birthday on the 8th. Dr. Hanumanthappa replied morosely, "What if it is my birthday? For you, your parents might send a gift. As for me, I have not had a father since childhood. There is only Baba to give me something, if at all. No one else." His wife advised him not to be so dejected, but to thank God for all small mercies.

The next day, as Dr. Hanumanthappa was leaving the lecture hall, a student from the Satya Sai College came walking up to him with a large package and said, "Swami asked me to give this to you, Sir." He was surprised to see that the package contained a fair collection of Sai books. His birthday present had arrived on time from Sri Sathya Sai Baba. He rushed home with the package to multiply the joy of the unexpected gift by sharing it with his family. They were thrilled beyond words. Sri Sathya Sai Baba's love for them and his omnipresence had proved too incredibly beautiful. A thought expressed by Dr. Hanumanthappa in his Jayanagar house had been picked up by Sri Sathya Sai Baba in Whitefield sixteen miles away. How fantastic! Dr. Hanumanthappa thought gratefully, "Look at the way he has responded."

On the 29th of August that year, the Hanumanthappa family had the promised interview with Sri Sathya Sai Baba, and it was a fairly long one. Sri Sathya Sai Baba took Dr. Hanumanthappa upstairs to have lunch with him and had food brought to his wife and family in the ladies' room downstairs. He told Dr. Hanumanthappa that he had spoken of him many times to other devotees that he knew. "Have they never told you?" he asked, and Dr. Hanumanthappa admitted that he had never been told any of this. Sri Sathya Sai Baba astonished him by talking about several things with intimate knowledge. It was during a similar subsequent session that he confirmed some things about Dr. Hanumanthappa's dream, and he talked about the many problems that he had had to face, such as his wife's serious illness.

Dr. Hanumanthappa continued to visit Whitefield daily, eagerly anticipating Sri Sathya Sai Baba's company whenever this seemed possible. He developed great reverence and love for him. Nevertheless, a doubt persisted in his mind: "Is Baba really divine? Is he a living god?"

After the meetings and discussions with Sri Sathya Sai Baba, something strange happened to Dr. Hanumanthappa. Sri Sathya Sai Baba began to appear in his dreams almost every night. At first, he did not attach much importance to these dreams. He thought that due to the recent closer contact, it was his subconscious mind's response to the events. But after a while, he sought confirmation from Sri Sathya Sai Baba in an indirect way.

To his amazement, Sri Sathya Sai Baba confirmed the validity of the dreams in exactly the manner in which he sought it. For instance, he would say to himself, "Baba, if this dream is true, you will bless me with your hand three times as soon as I see you," and Sri Sathya Sai Baba would do precisely that! Once, he asked Sri Sathya Sai Baba why he gave visions to people in the sleeping state, and the answer he received was that it was a conscious deed with a definite purpose.

One night, Dr. Hanumanthappa had a very long and exciting dream. Sri Sathya Sai Baba appeared and took him by the hand. Soon, the dreamer realized that he was flying, travelling through space. It was all a lovely blue everywhere and the journey was ethereal. He wondered where Sri Sathya Sai Baba was taking him in that wonderful world of silent space. Soon, he became aware of the silence being broken by the steady chanting of the *Omkara*. The *Om* sound was continuous, melodious and very clear. Just then, Sri Sathya Sai Baba turned to him and asked, "Do you hear the *Omkara*? Can you tell me where it is coming from?" He tried hard to find its source, but Sri Sathya Sai Baba smiled and said, "Try to lower your hearing and listen to your heart to see if it is coming from there." Dr. Hanumanthappa did as he was told, but could not hear the *Om* sound in his heart and said so.

Sri Sathya Sai Baba looked luminous and yet so small in that lovely expanse of blue space. "Try once more to discover the source of the *Om* sound," he urged. So, Dr. Hanumanthappa tried again and very hard, but still in vain. At last, Sri Sathya Sai Baba said, "Well, listen to my heart." So he put his ear to Sri Sathya Sai Baba's heart and there it was, that soft *Omkara*, so sacred, pure, clear and serene as it emanated from the divine heart and gradually became stronger and louder. Suddenly, Dr. Hanumanthappa realized that he was face to face with the *Omkara Swarupa*, the divine originator of the sacred *Om*, the primeval *pranava*. He prostrated himself before Sri Sathya Sai Baba and the dream ended.

Dr. Hanumanthappa was very happy to have been blessed with a divine demonstration of the birth place of the *Om*. A few days earlier, Sri Sathya Sai Baba had materialised for him a ring bearing the *Om* symbol and now, through the dream, he had granted him the realization of its inner significance.

One day, Sri Sathya Sai Baba patted him on the shoulder and blessed him saying, "Don't worry, everything will become all right." He had been worrying about not having progressed very far with his thesis, but after this blessing, he felt positively inspired. He worked day and night and finished the thesis on Financial Management in the Transport Industry in next to no time. And here, too, he sensed Sri Sathya Sai Baba's grace at every stage; for instance, in the ease with which he was able to obtain the right references and data from distant centres. He took the final draft of the thesis to Puttaparthi for Sri Sathya Sai Baba's blessings. Sri Sathya Sai Baba played hide and seek with him, but at last gave the thesis his blessing from the balcony.

"Strange, indeed, are the ways of Baba," said Dr. Hanumanthappa, "when my thesis was accepted and I was awarded the doctorate, I went to Whitefield to tell Baba who said very casually, 'yes, I knew about that the day you came to Puttaparthi.'" Then, to Dr. Hanumanthappa's astonishment, he quoted the comments the foreign examiner had made about the thesis. Dr. Hanumanthappa later checked these out and found that Sri Sathya Sai Baba had quoted the foreign examiner's assessment absolutely accurately.

Despite all this, a doubt that persistently assailed Dr. Hanumanthappa was the question of Sri Sathya Sai Baba being an *avatara* of God. "He looks so human and mixes so naturally with all of us that it is difficult to be certain," he thought. Then he had a dream in which, as usual, Sri Sathya Sai Baba came and took him on a trip. They walked for a long time on lonely roads and paths until they arrived under a bridge and Dr. Hanumanthappa suddenly found himself alone. Sri Sathya Sai Baba had vanished and he panicked. Why had he brought him here and abandoned him like that? He looked around wondering if he would be able to find his way back alone. Then, a light appeared, an unbelievable luminosity. He tried to understand what the unearthly light was and, slowly, he discerned the divine form of Lord *Sri Rama*, radiating pristine beauty and splendour. Dazed but joyful, he fell at the Lord's feet. As he rose, he saw Sri Sathya Sai Baba in the splendour of the same light. He was thrilled to the core that his doubts had been chased away forever. Sri Sathya Sai Baba said to him, "I have granted you nine boons. This *darshan* is one."

A few days later, he sought corroboration. Sri Sathya Sai Baba explained the different aspects of an *avatara* and the divine plan behind God's incarnations. "There are bound to be doubts. They were present even in regard to *Rama* and *Krishna* who faced great animosity and several hurdles. Do you think that *Rama* could not have prevented *Sita's* abduction, or that he really needed *Hanumana's* help to find her? Not at all! This was done to show *Hanumana's* devotion to the world. All others, too, had their roles to play as instruments of the Divine. In the same way, the *Sai Avatara* has as its purpose the redemption of humanity by making them be good, see good and do good."

After being granted the divine vision of Lord *Sri Rama*, Dr. Hanumanthappa knew that Sri Sathya Sai Baba was no ordinary human being, but a real *Avatara*. And yet, another doubt crept into his mind. Why does Sri Sathya Sai Baba say that he is an *avatara* of Shirdi Sai Baba? How can one *avatara* be continued in that fashion as another *avatara*?

That night again he had a dream in which Sri Sathya Sai Baba appeared. He came and sat on a chair and asked Dr. Hanumanthappa to look in the opposite direction. And there stood Shirdi Sai Baba, smiling benignly. Slowly, Shirdi Sai Baba walked towards Sri Sathya Sai Baba and merged into his form. Then there was only Sri Sathya Sai Baba with the same gentle smile seated on the chair. Dr. Hanumanthappa bowed down to him with deep veneration.

Dr. Hanumanthappa's experiences with Sri Sathya Sai Baba are not confined to dreams; he was often physically with him during the day. One day, Sri Sathya Sai Baba called him in to lunch. The boy who was serving put a lot of a certain vegetable on his plate. He was acutely embarrassed by this vegetable called ash gourd for, on a pilgrimage to holy Benares, he had vowed to give it up. This is not an unusual practice: many pilgrims to Benares give up eating something they are inordinately fond of as a kind of minor renunciation. But, in Dr. Hanumanthappa's case, the facts were a little different. What he really liked very much was meat, but he had not felt like giving up any meat preparations; instead, he renounced the humble ash gourd. He had never told Sri Sathya Sai Baba about it. His dilemma at lunch was to figure out how to leave untouched the heaped up ash gourd, especially as everyone knew that Sri Sathya Sai Baba disapproved of wasted food. As he was agonising over this, Sri Sathya Sai Baba called to the serving boy, "Is that the way to serve food? You should not serve enormous quantities of vegetables like that. This is not a meat dish that you should give such a generous helping to Hanumanthappa. And you should ask people's preferences. It is possible that some people gave up certain vegetables when they went to Benares!"

The incident brought home to Dr. Hanumanthappa the omniscience of Sri Sathya Sai Baba and he realized that there is nothing too trivial for his attention. If that were not so, why would he have tuned in to what he, Hanumanthappa, had done years ago in faraway Benares at a time when they had not even met? Also, after this incident, he found that his taste in food changed radically. He no longer relished meat, chicken, fish, etc. and turned to a simple *satvic* diet of vegetables, completely eschewing all that was not vegetarian. Today, the whole family is vegetarian and Sharada Devi wonders how she ever cooked meat.

"There is a certain stubborn element in my make-up. I have to be personally convinced about things and, fortunately for me, Baba has with kindness and patience answered all my doubts and proved his divinity through visions in several dreams," said Dr. Hanumanthappa. He related a dream in which Sri Sathya Sai Baba took him to a lonely spot where, astonishingly, Sri Sathya Sai Baba's form began to grow till it was so vast that it seemed to encompass the entire universe. The form was gigantic and so beautiful that Dr. Hanumanthappa trembled in awe as he realized that he had been given a vision of the all-powerful and all-pervading *Maha Purushottama.* After just a few seconds, he could no longer look at the great form so, covering his eyes, he prostrated himself before Sri Sathya Sai Baba. As he did, he thought of *Arjuna* who was shown the *Vishwaswarupa* (by *Sri Krishna* in the *Bhagavad-Gita*) and how he, too, had not had the strength to bear its splendour and majesty. Very slowly again, Sri Sathya Sai Baba's form became smaller and smaller until it had resumed its usual size and the dream was over.

I asked, "Why does Swami appear in so many of your dreams? Have you ever sought an explanation for that?"

"No, except that he has told me that he gave me visions to explain or to clarify many of my doubts. I pray that I will be fortunate always and continue to have his grace in this way."

A memorable day in Dr. Hanumanthappa's life was the day, 17th of December 1976, when Sri Sathya Sai Baba came to his house. As Sri Sathya Sai Baba was getting into his car at Whitefield, he asked Dr. Hanumanthappa to direct the driver, but he demurred and said, "Baba, don't you know where my house is?" Sri Sathya Sai Baba smiled and after that gave all the directions himself, where to turn and when, and got the car to stop exactly at the gate of the Hanumanthappa house.

That visit is still fresh in the minds of all the Hanumanthappa family. Sri Sathya Sai Baba spent more than two hours with them, moving about their house freely and easily. He remarked on the peaceful atmosphere of their home, very much in keeping with the name of the house, *"Prashanti."* The Hanumanthappas told Sri Sathya Sai Baba that they had missed him at the *grahapravesham* ceremony. "But, I was with you. I was the first to enter, even before you!" he assured them and added, "Don't you know that I was also here when you were building it?"

Sri Sathya Sai Baba saw their *puja* room where he hummed the *bhajan Jai Jagadisha Haré*. Then he called them all to him and made those familiar little round movements with his right hand. When he opened his hand, it held a pair of dainty little silver feet (symbolic of his own feet). Etched on one was the *gadaa* (mace), on the other the *padma* (lotus). The feet were joined together and the toe-holds were exquisitely shaped in the form of the *Omkara* in *Sanskrit*. Sri Sathya Sai Baba blessed them and said, "Swami will remain permanently in this home. So, have no fear for I am always here."

After that, Dr. Hanumanthappa dreamt that Sri Sathya Sai Baba allowed him to do *paada seva* (worship of the feet). He held the divine silver feet in his hands and did *namaskara* (reverential salutation) to them. He examined them carefully and saw that on the soles there was a *shankha* (conch) on one and a *chakra* (wheel) on the other. And then suddenly, from within the feet, a wonderful kaleidoscopic vision unfolded. Dr. Hanumanthappa saw the whole Universe in a series of scenes: space, planets, movements, revolving colours and yet more colours, moving objects. It was breathtakingly vivid, so vibrant and pulsating with life. He was overwhelmed and speechless, for here was Sri Sathya Sai Baba showing him that he held the Universe in the soles of his feet.

Dr. Hanumanthappa says that he has seen the divine aspects of Sri Sathya Sai Baba not only in dreams, but also in person. Sri Sathya Sai Baba takes an interest in people and watches over them. He gave an instance of this aspect to illustrate it. Once, he was annoyed over something and wrote a letter about it which he wanted to post straight away. But, he could not get stamps and so he was not able to post it that day. The next day he was in Whitefield and Sri Sathya Sai Baba came up to him and asked, "Why do you feel so badly? Don't behave like that. You are mistaken." This was said so softly that only Dr. Hanumanthappa heard it where he stood in the verandah. He understood then that Sri Sathya Sai Baba, with his omniscience, knew the contents of the letter.

"Who can ever watch over people like that, even from afar? But, Swami says that he is never far away, that he is present in everyone as the divine essence in every human being," said Dr. Hanumanthappa.

On their wedding anniversary, the Hanumanthappas went to Sri Sathya Sai Baba for blessings. He asked them to return the next morning. And he made them so terribly happy: he asked a student to take photographs of them with a polaroid camera, then he posed with them all and gave them the photographs. Then he said, "I was to leave for Puttaparthi this morning, but I delayed my departure since you wanted to celebrate your wedding anniversary with me. I will go to Puttaparthi this afternoon." Dr. Hanumanthappa impulsively asked, "Can I come with you, Swami?" Sri Sathya Sai Baba happily consented to take him with him in his car. He did not have a change of clothes or any other necessaries with him, but he decided to do without them in view of the privilege of travelling with Sri Sathya Sai Baba.

The drive was enjoyable and very instructive. Sri Sathya Sai Baba looked after him so well, as though he were a small child. He pointed to hillocks and various other landmarks en route and recounted the legends associated with them. Sri Sathya Sai Baba stopped the car many times to give *darshan* to people along the road. On arrival at Puttaparthi, he went straight upstairs to his private rooms, leaving Dr. Hanumanthappa in the lobby.

Dr. Hanumanthappa waited in the lobby for a long time, not knowing what else to do. In a little while, all the other people who had also been lingering there went away. The adjacent *bhajan* hall was locked and the door leading upstairs to the private rooms was bolted on the inside. He felt lost, lonely and hungry. His thoughts went more or less like this: "where has Baba gone? Perhaps he has forgotten all about me and gone into his private rooms. What shall I do now? Where will I sleep? What about my dinner?" This string of anxious little thoughts was interrupted by the door opening. A student carrying a leather suitcase came through and said, "Sir, please come with me. Baba has sent these things for you. We have also prepared a room for you." Dr. Hanumanthappa was very taken aback and very grateful. He was taken to a room where everything was ready for him. He opened the suitcase and was amazed at the amount of things it held: two sheets with the Sathya Sai crest (clearly the ones used by Sri Sathya Sai Baba himself), a *dhoti*, a fresh towel, a new white shirt, soap, a shaving kit, toothpaste, brush and comb – in fact, everything that he would have brought himself. The student then said, "Sir, Baba said that it is all for you. You are to take everything home with you." Dr. Hanumanthappa was overwhelmed at the concern Sri Sathya Sai Baba had shown and the care with which he had gone about arranging every little detail for the happiness and comfort of a devotee.

That night, Dr. Hanumanthappa and a lecturer at the Satya Sai College saw a new book called *Vision of the Divine*. The photographs in it were impressive and Dr. Hanumanthappa expressed a wish to buy a copy if it were available. The lecturer promised to find out and, before leaving him, said that Dr. Hanumanthappa would be having breakfast with Sri Sathya Sai Baba in the morning.

At dawn, Dr. Hanumanthappa was all agog with the idea of seeing Sri Sathya Sai Baba in his sanctum sanctorum. Sri Sathya Sai Baba welcomed him in and asked if he had slept well. The divine living quarters were a great surprise to him. The entrance was quite bare and led to a small and simple room in which there was only a very ordinary wooden bed. Sri Sathya Sai Baba smiled and said, "Take a good look. Is it really as luxurious as you imagined?" He felt tongue-tied. Sri Sathya Sai Baba took him around the entire area, the small old-fashioned bathroom which did not even have running hot water, a small corridor and the unpretentious dining room – that was all. Why, he wondered, such stoic simplicity for himself when, for others, he had carpets and sofas in the visitor's rooms in Whitefield?

Sri Sathya Sai Baba explained, "Swami is like that. Simple living. My life is my message, *Bangaru*. I do all my work myself and look after my own needs. What would I do with luxuries?" It was an eye-opener to realize that someone who could command all the luxury and comfort the world had to offer would choose to live in such a simple, uncomplicated and down-to-earth way. How many, given the choice, would select this austerity?

Dr. Hanumanthappa enjoyed his breakfast in the divine company and, at the end of it, Sri Sathya Sai Baba held out the book he had admired the night before. "You wanted to buy this book, didn't you?"

Oh, the all-knowing Sai! For there was no way anyone could have reported his late night conversation with the young lecturer. Dr. Hanumanthappa was the first one to see Sri Sathya Sai Baba that day. Sri Sathya Sai Baba autographed the book for him and gave it to him along with the pen he had used to sign it, saying, "It is Swami's job to give *ananda* (joy) to his devotees."

"There are plenty of examples of his grace in our personal lives now, since we have surrendered everything to Swami's will," said Dr. Hanumanthappa, and then he related yet another incident.

One day, Dr. Hanumanthappa was driving recklessly fast on his scooter and it went out of control. The scooter hurtled madly, straight at an oncoming lorry. Suddenly, he felt a very powerful force pushing at the handle-bar and changing the direction of the careening scooter. The collision was avoided by a hair's breadth. There have been many other instances like this.

One day, at Whitefield, Sri Sathya Sai Baba said to Sharada Devi, "Ask him not to drive so recklessly. He goes much too fast at turnings and junctions."

Dr. Hanumanthappa recalled that though Sri Sathya Sai Baba had given him the book he wanted, he did not read it for several months. One day when he went to see him, he had a large technical tome with him. Sri Sathya Sai Baba, on seeing him, remarked to a student standing nearby, "You people will read all these useless books. Read also the useful books you have." It made Dr. Hanumanthappa think, and he understood that the remark was directed at his own lapse. Ultimately, when he did read the book, he learnt many things, including the nine ways of *sadhana*.

"Baba often avoids speaking to, or even looking at, someone who makes no conscious effort to improve," said Dr. Hanumanthappa. "Baba will make cryptic remarks, such as: what is the use of talking to people who are in daily contact with Swami, but do not genuinely improve even a little?"

Sri Sathya Sai Baba does not take this step unless a devotee commits a serious error, and then it invariably has the most effect. A genuine devotee cannot bear this kind of indifference and therefore does everything in his power to mend his ways. Genuine repentance and a real desire to atone make Sri Sathya Sai Baba forgive him and then, once again, he talks to him as before. This goes on frequently with close devotees, but normally, this is a silent issue between master and disciple. Others do not come to know of it and the devotee who is thus inwardly chastised returns to the fold with a more purified outlook.

"The greatness of Swami is that he takes an abiding interest in everything we do. It is this fullness, this whole hearted and complete giving that amazes me. Baba knows everything, even the most minute details of what we do. For, all his efforts are directed towards the spiritual upliftment of the individual. Any worry or problem that hinders the smooth spiritual progress of the devotee and distracts him from it, or shakes the usual calm of his mind, is immediately detected by Swami."

During the Summer Course, Dr. Hanumanthappa was rather frantically looking for a good car to buy. Salesmen and agents showed him the cars they had for sale and he often took them out on trial runs, in the process missing a few of the evening discourses of Sri Sathya Sai Baba.

Once, when he had missed the evening discourse, he had a dream in which Sri Sathya Sai Baba came and said, "Why are you so bothered about a car? What is a car, after all? Should you miss lectures because of it? You will get your car." And there in the dream was a car, a white one. He could not see all the digits on the registration plate, but the last two were quite clearly 27. The dream continued with Sri Sathya Sai Baba talking to him and an old lady appeared with a sick child. Sri Sathya Sai Baba went to her, materialised *vibhuti* and gave it to her. Then the dream ended.

Dr. Hanumanthappa took his cue from the dream and attended the remaining discourses faithfully, leaving all else to Sri Sathya Sai Baba's wish. Within a few days, he was approached by someone with a white Fiat who was going to America and so wanted to sell his car very quickly. The last two numbers on the registration plate were 27. It was, of course, the same white car he had seen in the dream. He bought it. That night again, Sri Sathya Sai Baba appeared in his dream and said, "I am very happy you got the car you liked the most."

Dr. Hanumanthappa took his new white car to Whitefield for Sri Sathya Sai Baba's blessings. When he came, Dr. Hanumanthappa put the car keys into his hands and prostrated himself. Sri Sathya Sai Baba said he was very happy. Just then, an old woman came forward from the *darshan* lines with a child in her arms. Sri Sathya Sai Baba walked across to her, comforted her and materialised some *vibhuti* which he gave her. Then she went back. Dr. Hanumanthappa stood stock still: it was the same sequence, the same old woman with the same sick child as in his dream about the white car. "That scene happened, sequence by sequence, as in the dream. So now do you see why I believe that my dreams are a hundred per cent true?" asked Dr. Hanumanthappa.

"Leelas are occurring in tens of millions of homes, Swami keeps his hands down so that publicity about the leelas will not spread."

. . . Sri Sathya Sai Baba

19

EXPERIENCES OF FOUR DEVOTEES

"How would you react to a diamond-studded ring with a Sai Baba portrait in the middle that rotates twenty-four hours a day everyday?" asked Mr. R. Ramanatha Chettiar, a successful diamond merchant of Madurai. For such was the ring he received on his sixtieth birthday from Sri Sathya Sai Baba. The diamonds were static, but the portrait within them slowly turned like the hands of a clock. However much one listened or looked, there were no ticking or whirring sounds, no mechanism to be seen. There was only a gold frame for the small picture surrounded by tiny diamonds, and yet, it turned . . .

Mr. Chettiar was intrigued and went to Sri Sathya Sai Baba to tell him that the picture never stopped turning. For almost ten years, the picture rotated with clock-like precision.

One day, during the Summer Course in 1978, Sri Sathya Sai Baba asked him, "Is the picture still turning?" He answered, "Yes, Swami." Sri Sathya Sai Baba smiled and went away.

A few days after that, in Puttaparthi, Sri Sathya Sai Baba asked for the ring. He took it and blew on it and, instantly, a new ring appeared, similar in every detail except that now the portrait was no longer mobile. It did not turn anymore. Sri Sathya Sai Baba said, "I had given you size 14 the last time, now it is size 13, a little smaller, so that it will fit you."

"The old ring was a size bigger than this present one; otherwise, it looked the same," said Mr. Chettiar, pointing to the new ring and adding, "I still don't know why Baba gave me a ring with a portrait that rotated for ten years."

Geraldine Brent, called Gerry, is a Sai devotee from the United States. She is a vivacious person, bubbling with life and laughter. She has brought out Sai *bhajan* books in English. During the Summer Course, she brought along and distributed a number of cassette tapes which she had produced herself. They were beautifully made and very professional. On one side was Sri Sathya Sai Baba singing *bhajans*, on the other, a commentary spoken by Gerry on *ashrama* life in Puttaparthi. I found the tape recording so very interesting that we got together one evening at my house.

Gerry is in show business. She first met Sri Sathya Sai Baba some years ago when she had travelled to India with some friends. And immediately, she had felt that he was the most perfect person she had ever seen. Somehow, the idea persisted in her mind that "there is a direct contact between him and heaven, like a rainbow."

One day, she was in the *darshan* lines at Dharmakshetra in Bombay. Sri Sathya Sai Baba appeared and Gerry experienced an ethereal sensation, like being wafted away from earth and being transported into the skies. The experience was so lovely, so out of this world, that it did many things to Gerry and she came to believe that Sri Sathya Sai Baba had divine powers. Gerry began to make frequent visits to India and to spend time in Puttaparthi and Whitefield. She was particularly drawn to Sri Sathya Sai Baba's *bhajan* singing which moved her very deeply. But, she had great difficulty in learning them, for there were no English transcripts of them; they were written, if at all, in various Indian scripts. So, she wrote down the words phonetically in the English alphabet and diligently learnt them. In a spirit of dedication, she resolved to ease the lot of the devout foreigner by collecting and then publishing the Sai *bhajans* in the English script. Gradually, her efforts bore fruit and she succeeded in bringing out a book of selected Sai *bhajans* in English.

Asked about extraordinary experiences, Gerry described one. At her flat in California, she had been putting some clothes into a suitcase. She heard a rap on the door, so she went and opened it. There was no one there. She came back and found that the clothes she had packed were all very untidily scattered about. She looked around puzzled. She decided that it must have been a stray cat. It had scratched at the door, she surmised, then come in through a window, disarranged the clothes in the suitcase and scampered off as it heard her returning footsteps. Then Gerry put the bizarre incident out of her mind.

Months later, she was in India with Sri Sathya Sai Baba and asked him when he would go to the United States. He answered, "I came to see you once. Only, you did not know." As she looked thoroughly bewildered, he laughed and added, "You thought I was a cat!" and proceeded to describe her room, her house, the street and the house next door, all completely accurately, in order to convince her that he had really paid her a call. Gerry was both aghast and amazed.

Gerry has no doubt at all about Sri Sathya Sai Baba's divinity. She is happy to be with him whenever she can. "Nothing else matters, except doing his work or thinking about him or meditating on him," said Gerry who is busy once again with another project to bring out a new set of Sai *bhajans* on cassette tapes.

Another devotee I met was Arlette Meyer. A translator and originally from Switzerland, she has settled in Venezuela and has translated a few Sai books into Spanish. She first came to India with a friend in 1972. She went to Puttaparthi. The first time she saw Sri Sathya Sai Baba, he was giving *darshan* from a balcony. She felt strong currents flowing from him to her.

Arlette had always been fond of travelling and so she set off on a tour of Southern India. But, having seen Sri Sathya Sai Baba, her heart was no longer in being a tourist and photographing all the sights, which used to be what she enjoyed the most. Her mind, she found, was full of thoughts of Sri Sathya Sai Baba. So, she cancelled her visits to Goa and Bombay and went instead to Whitefield to have the *darshan*, once more, of Sri Sathya Sai Baba.

She is, in fact, a very competent translator and so the idea of Sai books in Spanish soon took concrete shape in her mind. She wrote, "Can I translate?" on a piece of paper and gave it to Sri Sathya Sai Baba, – her way of seeking his permission.

The next time, Sri Sathya Sai Baba asked for her as "the translator" and she had an interview with him. He told her to go ahead with the translations and added, "It is your duty." When she said she would do it for him, he corrected her, saying "No, not for Baba, but for the good of the world, because of love for Baba."

Arlette had to study Indian mythology, Indian culture and Indian spirituality, and she had to learn some *Sanskrit* terms. She got hold of a good *Sanskrit* dictionary and began to translate.

Then a dampening thought occurred: who would print the Spanish book on Sri Sathya Sai Baba? Printing is very expensive in Venezuela. She completed the translation of *Man of Miracles* and returned to Puttaparthi. On her first day, at the bookstall, she was startled by voices speaking Spanish. She saw a gentleman who was saying, "All these books are in English. I want books in Spanish. I want to select some books for translation." He was the owner of a bookstall in Spain and a publisher. Arlette handed over her big folder to him and said, "Here, take this, your first Spanish manuscript, the *Man of Miracles*."

"Wasn't that a Baba miracle?" she asked. She was delighted to have a ready publisher. But then, Sri Sathya Sai Baba teased her for a few days. He would not see her or her manuscript which she carried to and fro. At last, he saw her but did not take much notice of the manuscript. He just leafed through it and murmured, "Lot of work." Well, thought Arlette, it was in Spanish so he could not have read it. "I told him I wanted to translate more books." He asked her to start a Sai Centre in Venezuela and gave her many packets of *vibhuti* to give to people, particularly the sick.

Sri Sathya Si Baba materialised a locket with an *Om* design and a double *rudraksha* pendant for her. She learnt that this kind of *rudraksha* symbolises *Shiva-Shakti*.

Arlette Meyer has started the Sai Centre in Venezuela and it has attracted many people who are interested in Indian religion and spirituality. The Centre conducts *bhajan* sessions and lectures, sells books and provides guidance for those who wish to visit India and Puttaparthi.

She is an ardent devotee and is learning *Telugu* so that she may understand the talks of Sri Sathya Sai Baba directly. This will also help her translation work as "Baba is so lyrical in *Telugu* . . . the translations somehow do not convey this musical quality; they are inadequate and do not convey cent per cent the same meaning." She even finds the books in "Indian English" very involved and not direct. Often, innaccurate words are used making correct translations more difficult. Fortunately, in her years of direct contact with India, she has become accustomed to Indian ways of expression and has learnt her subject thoroughly, too. So, she is able to pick up all the different shades of mood and meaning. She has translated *Prema Vahini* and *Sathya Sai Speaks* volume I and is continuing to translate other Sai books into Spanish.

When I met Arlette, she was with an arthritic and bed-ridden young girl. She had accompanied the girl and her father to Puttaparthi. The girl had been quite normal until, suddenly, she developed a very painful and virulent form of arthritis. Then one day, someone gave her some *vibhuti* which she rubbed on her painful joints and felt enormous relief. She began to apply *vibhuti* whenever the pain became unendurable. Soon, her longing to meet Sri Sathya Sai Baba became strong, but she knew it was useless to plan a trip to India while she could hardly sit up in bed. Then she heard of a doctor whose treatment she took and, gradually, she could sit up and begin to walk again, though very slowly. Now, the long journey to India seemed feasible – and here she was, at long last.

The young girl was thrilled with her first meeting with Sri Sathya Sai Baba. He materialised a locket for her and gave her two bottles of medicines. She returned home with happiness, a rare peace of mind and renewed faith.

Arlette has a friend who frequently goes into deep meditational trances and has spiritual experiences and mystic visions. For her, Sri Sathya Sai Baba materialised a three-faced *Shiva lingam* to fix at the focal point, between the eyebrows, to aid her in meditation.

Arlette spoke of a day when she went to the Elephanta Caves near Bombay with a group of people. Some of them touched a huge and damaged *Shiva lingam* there and, unexpectedly, felt a pull and vibrations, then jolting and churning sensations. It was without a doubt an "experience which was something out of this world" and which strengthened their belief and faith in *Shakti*, and the "power of the symbolic figures of yore."

Rajnandini Srivatsava has been living in Sri Sathya Sai Baba's *ashrama* for over three years. Seeing Raj today, it is difficult to imagine her as a modern outdoor sportswoman such as she used to be. She was the champion shot of the Kumaon Hills for many years, roving the forests with her gun on *shikar* (hunting) trips.

"I was trigger happy and loved the outdoors. At times, I would perch on steep slopes just to shoot scores of flying birds. The thrill and adventure of *shikar* used to be my life's blood. I loved it and lived it, killing game for glory!" Raj said this in a matter-of-fact tone.

"I was lonely and often afraid, I suppose, for I had a huge palatial mansion and not nearly enough people in it. I have only one son; he is married and I have a grandson, too. One day, I became fed up with it all. I felt that life could not just be parties and game hunting."

"I went in search of a *guru*. I found one and was initiated. I seemed to have found a little anchor, but it wasn't enough. Basically, everyone likes some fantasy, I think; from childhood even, the heart clamours for it. Every child likes to hear about miracles and incredible events. That is why children like mythological stories about gods: they can perform impossible feats and achieve superhuman things. A god can do so many wondrous things and the child grows up with a feeling of admiration and adulation for God who can do all the things that a mortal cannot."

"Baba fits admirably the image of God carved so strongly in every heart from earliest childhood. This is His uniqueness, His greatness and proof that everything happens according to His divine will. His is the last word in all things, though we may think that we do things, or that we are responsible for certain things," said Raj. She has surrendered herself to Sri Sathya Sai Baba after realizing his divinity.

How and why did she come to Sri Sathya Sai Baba?

Raj's brother was a Sai devotee and had a few photographs of Sri Sathya Sai Baba at his house in Delhi. But, Raj was neither drawn to them nor was she impressed by them. The pictures seemed to be of a huge person, like one of many affluent and well fed *sannyasis*. She was in Delhi when Sri Sathya Sai Baba came to her brother's house and Raj was surprised to see how very different he was from his photographs.

Sri Sathya Sai Baba gave *prasad* to everyone except Raj; he just looked at her. Why had he left her out? She asked him for *prasad* and he answered, "I will give you later."

The next time she saw Sri Sathya Sai Baba was in Puttaparthi. By then she knew that her place was at his feet and nowhere else. She asked Sri Sathya Sai Baba if she could stay with him and he agreed to let her stay in the *ashrama* in Puttaparthi. In Bangalore though, until the cottages were built, she had to stay in town and commute daily to Whitefield. She was overjoyed when one of the new cottages was allotted to her by Sri Sathya Sai Baba.

"This is real happiness. Nothing else really matters," she said. "Once upon a time, I used to have tiger cubs for pets at home. I was that wild! But, Baba has completely tamed me. He has opened my eyes and now I only hunt the God within."

"Come, I am the mender of broken hearts. I am like the smith who welds, mends and sets aright."

. . . Sri Sathya Sai Baba

20

THE SOUL HAS NO DEATH

Sri Sathya Sai Baba has often said, "The soul has no death. It is the body that dies. You should not worry about the physical body. It is the soul that matters."

Talking to two Italian devotees, Sylvie and Antonio Craxi, revealed how well they had assimilated this aspect of Sri Sathya Sai Baba's teaching.

Sylvie's son was spastic and suffered from severe paralysis. She roamed the world searching for a cure, even going to the psychic healers of the Philippines. At a time of desperation, an Italian parapsychologist told her about a man in India who, he said, was like Jesus Christ and renowned for his miracles. This sent Sylvie flying to India and to Whitefield where she waited in the *darshan* lines to see Sri Sathya Sai Baba.

He came to her where she sat with her small son and said, "Don't worry, I will make a straight future for your son." Then he gave her *vibhuti* for the boy. Sylvie was happy and returned home.

"I did not understand then that when Swami said he would give a straight future to my son that he meant it in another sense . . . that he would give me a new baby with a good and healthy body. I limited it to the body of this boy."

Andrea, the spastic son, took the *vibhuti* after which he did not have much pain. A few weeks passed. Then, Sylvie's little daughter had a dream. She came laughing to her mother and said, "Mamma! Sai Baba, Sai Baba! He came flying. He took away our Andrea . . . " Then she laughed again and said, "Mamma, Andrea is in your stomach."

Sylvie was perplexed. But soon, things fell into place. She was no longer tormented. She was at peace, prepared for any fate, fully surrendering to Sri Sathya Sai Baba's will with absolute faith in his assurance.

Very soon, she saw that Andrea was gradually sinking and, when he died, he died peacefully. The Craxi family by that time had the courage to bear the loss and to look forward to his rebirth in a sound body. They bade him farewell with serenity.

Sylvie would go to "Baba's room" and pray. She kept some milk in a covered glass and there were days when Sri Sathya Sai Baba would come and take a little from it. She realized this because the quantity of milk would lessen and there would be *vibhuti* on the milk and on the glass lid, and the room would be fragrant with the scent of *vibhuti*. And too, the milk would not curdle after that for days as it was Sri Sathya Sai Baba's *prasad* and blessed by him.

When Sylvie became pregnant again, she came to see Sri Sathya Sai Baba. Again, she was in a *darshan* line. He pointed to her stomach and smiled. Then he gestured, asking if she was happy about her new baby and if she had understood what he had meant about giving her child a straight future. Sylvie was rapturous. She returned to Italy then, with the intention that both she and her husband should return to India after the baby's birth to request Sri Sathya Sai Baba to give the child a name.

Sylvie's story is exemplary in showing how Sri Sathya Sai Baba gives people the courage to accept and face misfortune. It also demonstrates how he can pick out people from the *darshan* lines, especially those who have implicit faith in him. Newcomers in the *darshan* lines may wonder why Sri Sathya Sai Baba goes near only certain people, why he does not accept letters from all those who hold them out to him, or why he materialises *vibhuti* for just a few, and why he allows only some people to perform *namaskara*. He says he responds to genuine *bhakti* and to people's needs. It never matters where they sit and who they are; if the call from their hearts is sincere, he will always go to them. He knows and can spot such people.

People who wait in vain and do not get to speak to him may find it difficult to accept this explanation, but a few practical experiences of this would open their eyes to his seemingly incredible ability to pick out the most deserving or needy. Here is one touching instance.

Once, with a vast crowd milling about, Sri Sathya Sai Baba fixed his eyes on an old man. No one attached any special significance to this. Later, it was learnt that the old man had died happily and peacefully. According to the dead man's family, he had gone to see Sri Sathya Sai Baba that day with only one prayer in his heart: "Let me see you, Baba, and die in peace." His wish was granted. In that one moment, when Sri Sathya Sai Baba fixed his gaze on the old man, silent communion was established and it had thrilled the old man just before he died in the way he had prayed for.

"I do not take anything from anyone except their love and devotion."

. . . Sri Sathya Sai Baba

21

SAI BABA IS GOD

"Sai Baba is God! There is no doubt in my mind about it," says Terry Payne, a Hawaiian devotee, with deep conviction. "I believe in him. Oh, he is so great," he adds with undeniable devotion.

Terry heard of Shirdi Sai Baba some fifteen years ago and read a book about him which left a deep impression on his mind. But, he did not then become spiritual, since business tied him down to rather more worldly activities. Some years later, he came across an article entitled 'The Search for a Genuine *Guru*' and he pinned it up in his room. It was what Terry terms a "very heavy" article, but he felt that the author knew what he was talking about. (Editor's note: The author was Sri Sathya Sai Baba).

Once, at a sauna, Terry heard the word *Om*. It made him curious and he went on a quest which resulted in his joining *Kundalini Yoga* classes. There he met a man who spoke to him about Sri Sathya Sai Baba. He said that if he was looking for a *guru* in India, he should go to Sri Sathya Sai Baba, the reincarnation of Shirdi Sai Baba.

At that time, Terry was not thinking in terms of going to India or meeting Sri Sathya Sai Baba, but he continued taking an interest in things spiritual. At a spiritual gathering, he met someone from India who had a *rudraksha* bead. It fascinated him. The Indian, seeing his fascination, presented it to him.

Terry kept the *rudraksha* on him at all times, looking at it, turning it around, handling it playfully – so fond of it was he. The *rudraksha* bead cracked, but he still clung to it. He knew exactly which ridge was broken and the pattern the damage formed. He continued to carry it in his pocket, since it seemed to provide him with a spiritual base. It was something to cling to, a talisman.

Then it happened . . . the turning point of his life. Someone brought a record of Sri Sathya Sai Baba's discourses and *bhajans* and played it to Terry. "I heard his voice and, in that instant, I knew he was God. The voice was heavenly and transported me to great heights. It did all sorts of things to me that were indescribable. But I was definite he was God Almighty Himself and there was no doubt on that score in my mind. I was a different person from that moment. I also felt there was hope for the world. It made me feel real good!" said Terry, remembering the torrent of emotions and reactions the voice of Sri Sathya Sai Baba had released in him.

He was in tears and felt jubilant. He wanted to announce to the world that there is God, now, on earth. Everything in life changed for him and his general outlook underwent a sea change. He felt an inner peace that had a tremendous impact on the things he did. He no longer felt angry or impatient as he used to do, and he became more understanding.

Then, he had to go to California on business. He met some Sai devotees there at Sai Centres and felt he was becoming more and more inwardly involved with Sri Sathya Sai Baba. At a Sai gathering, he realised that he had lost his cherished *rudraksha* bead. He had no idea how he had lost it. The loss was a constant and painful wrench. He tried everything he could think of to trace the lost bead, but all in vain. All he could do was brood over its disappearance.

In 1974, Terry and his wife, Diana, travelled to India and had their first *darshan* of Sri Sathya Sai Baba on Christmas Day. "I saw him walking from the house to the *bhajan mantap*. He was so beautiful . . . and that was all I could think. There was no other thought. My mind kept saying 'so beautiful, so beautiful, so beautiful' and there was no other thought. Like a broken record, I kept mentally repeating 'so beautiful' and felt that Baba was something out of this world. Everything about him was so beautiful."

It was fascinating to see Terry relive the moments of his first *darshan*.

Sri Sathya Sai Baba saw him, said "Very happy," and moved on to others in the waiting throng.

The next day, Sri Sathya Sai Baba went up to Ooty and the Paynes followed. However, he never looked their way and they felt wretched. Then, Sri Sathya Sai Baba came near Terry and said "Tomorrow" and he was in seventh heaven.

They had their interview and when it was over, Sri Sathya Sai Baba rotated his hand and materialised a *rudraksha* bead for Terry. Stunned, he kept turning it around in his hands, inspecting it with awe – it was the very one he had lost. What had once been broken was repaired now, but there could be no doubt about it, it was his lost *rudraksha* bead, how could he not recognise it? All the little things were the same, the ups and downs, the ridges, scratches and smooth surfaces, they were all there.

He wondered how Sri Sathya Sai Baba had brought to the Nilgiri Hills what had been lost in California . . . As this thought raced across Terry's mind, Sri Sathya Sai Baba smiled and said, "Yes, it is the same one you lost in California."

"Baba actually stressed that it was the one I lost in California . . . how did he know? I had never mentioned it to him. Oh, he is omnipresent," said Terry for his spiritual protection. Terry always wears this *mala* with the bead, "If you say *Om* three times and place the *rudraksha* on your forehead whenever you are in trouble, I will rush to your help." Terry was ecstatic. He has not yet tried out the *Om*-and-*rudraksha*-on-forehead cry for help, but he feels that he has the greatest ally in his *rudraksha* bead.

On another occasion, Sri Sathya Sai Baba materialised a *japa mala* for Terry for his spiritual protection. Terry always wears this *mala* with the *rudraksha* as a pendant on it. He feels the close communion it gives him with Sri Sathya Sai Baba, physically and spiritually.

The Paynes have had several interviews with Sri Sathya Sai Baba. His words and counsel have had a supreme effect on Terry. They have experienced instances of Sri Sathya Sai Baba's omnipresence, for he subsequently repeated to them some conversations they had had in Hawaii, and even a quarrel or two! How could he know these things, living as he does in faraway India?

The Payne son attends the Satya Sai College at Whitefield. Sri Sathya Sai Baba is an integral part of their lives and they make numerous visits to India. Diana has learnt many *bhajans* and was given the opportunity to sing them in the presence of Sri Sathya Sai Baba during the 1978 Summer Course when a group of women Sai devotees from different parts of the world sang *bhajans*.

"To us, Baba means everything. Other things are all subsidiary, though we are in Hawaii and have to attend to our worldly life. Baba is God and we are indeed fortunate to have Him amidst us. What fantastic luck! We are all blessed indeed," says Terry Payne, devotion and adoration radiating from his eyes and giving his whole aspect the glow of infinite bliss.

PART III

Conclusion . . .

"The mind of man is as a blank sheet of white paper when he is born. As soon as thinking, feeling and acting start, then the process of tarnishing the mind also starts."

. . . Sri Sathya Sai Baba

ANSWERS FROM THE DIVINE *GURU*

(compiled from various meetings with Sri Sathya Sai Baba)

Question 1:
Why are some people born more beautiful, or more intelligent, than others? Why does not God give everyone equal beauty, abilities and talents?

Sri Sathya Sai Baba:
It is not God's partiality or fault. It is the human being who is responsible. His actions, thoughts and words are responsible for all good and bad. It is the mind that creates the differences. Pleasure is an interval between two pains. It is the way you look at things that matters.

There is a vast ocean of talents and qualities. All human beings have vessels to fill. Some people, through their actions, are able to fill the vessels to the brim; some fill only half; others can fill only a quarter, or less. They possess intelligence, beauty, talents, etcetera, according to how much they can fill their vessels.

You even judge beauty these days, as in Miss India, Miss World. But, that is all physical beauty, which is transient. What is important is the beauty of the *atma* (Self).

Question 2:
How are good or bad actions carried into the next birth?

Sri Sathya Sai Baba:
Swaasha (breath) carries the actions, for the breath stops when a person dies. The body is still there after death and we call it a corpse and burn it as useless. So, the body cannot carry anything with it, just as a flower cannot carry its fragrance. It is a breeze that wafts the scent of the flower and makes its fragrance reach you. Similarly, imagine a municipal lorry – the bad odour is carried to you by the breeze again! In the same manner, good and bad actions are carried by the breath and surround you in the next birth like an invisible garland. The pattern of your life is then governed by what the garland has – good or bad scent.

That is why man must understand that everything he does has a reaction, a reverberation and a reflection. It is he who writes his own destiny by his actions. It is essential for man to live a good life with good thoughts and good actions. Only through such a life can he realize the divinity in him. The concept *Aham Brahmasmi* (I am *Brahma* = God) is also incorrect, since it indicates duality. *Aham* (I) and *Brahma* (God) become separate. The statement ought to be *Aham Aham* (I am I).

Question 3:
Many people feel that *Hindus* worship countless gods. How did this happen?

Sri Sathya Sai Baba:
India has a wonderful religious tradition. It has something for everyone, to suit everyone's needs. Many people do not understand this excellent idea and make derisory comments on our having too many gods. This tradition has evolved to suit the needs of different people, just as we have shirts of varying types and sizes to fit different people. With the ideal of One God, there is only one shirt and, if it does not fit or if it is unsuitable, people turn away from God. But, here, if someone likes *Krishna*, they can worship *Krishna;* others can worship *Rama,* or *Narayana,* or *Shiva,* or even snakes and lions! What more do you need to propogate the idea that God is in everything everywhere? That is why I often say don't worship God as a picture, but worship the picture as God. This will slowly lead to the realization of God in you. That is where the *Hindu* spiritual path is practical and good.

Question 4:
Why does not God prevent cruelties in the world?

Sri Sathya Sai Baba:
God is only a witness *(saakshibhoota)*. He does not act. Man acts according to the dictates of his intellect *(buddhi)* and himself suffers the consequences of his actions *(karma)*. There is neither good nor bad for God. Take the knife as an example. A murderer uses a knife to kill another man, a slaughterer uses a knife to slay animals, a surgeon uses a knife to amputate, and a cook uses a knife to chop vegetables. If a magnet is placed

among all these knives, it will attract them all equally and not according to the kind of tasks they perform. God is like this magnet. All knives are the same to Him. However, the hands that wield the knives have to bear the consequences of their actions, dependent on right and wrong.

Question 5:
When we have troubles and are in difficulties and we pray to God, why does He not take them away?

Sri Sathya Sai Baba:
Troubles and difficulties are part and parcel of human life. They are the results of your *karmas*. There is no point in praying to God to wipe away all such troubles and difficulties. The right type of prayer would be to ask God for courage and strength to bear all the difficulties, problems and tragedy with equanimity.

Question 6:
What is the difference between the politics of yesterday and those of today?

Sri Sathya Sai Baba:
The present state of affairs can be described as the state of jumps and bumps. Now, take the example of your body and limbs. Each limb is important in forming the composite whole. All the limbs joined together make up the body, which is the *deha* (body, person). Similarly, in the *desha* (country, nation), every aspect should be tended to, just as one takes care of every part of the body – as your own *deha*, so your *desha* – that was the *Bharatiya Sanskriti* (Indian culture) and people have forgotten it. The ancient *rajakiya* (politician) never forgot this.

Question 7:
Some still hold the view that women should not take up *Brahma vidya* (spiritual knowledge), nor chant the *Omkara*. Is this correct? Also, in ancient times, were spiritual *sadhanas* (endeavours) forbidden to women?

Sri Sathya Sai Baba:
Brahma vidya and *chitta shuddhi* (spiritual knowledge and purity of consciousness) do not depend on whether a person is a man or a woman. All have an equal right to benefit from *Brahma vidya* provided only they are able to take it up with discipline and dedication.

At no time have there been any taboos against women. Lord *Vishnu* (the Preserver) taught *Bhu Devi* (the Goddess Earth) the glory of the *Bhagavad-Gita*. *Parameshwara (Shiva)* taught *Parvati* the *Brahma tatva* (divine essence) through the *Guru Gita*. *Ishwara (Shiva)* initiated *Parvati* into *yoga shastra* and *mantra shastra* (science of *yoga* and science of *mantra*). The *Brihadaranyaka Upanishad* mentions *Yajnavalkya* teaching *Maitreyi* the *Brahma vidya*. So, women in ancient times were not denied the pursuit of spirituality.

The *Brihadaranyaka Upanishad* mentions *Gargi* and *Maitreyi* basking in the splendour of *sannyasa* (renunciation) and *brahmacharya* (celibacy, chastity). *Madaalasa Chudaala* and others were able to receive *Brahma jnana* (divine wisdom) while in the *grahastha* (householder, i.e. married) stage of life. Even today, there are many who belong to this vast category.

It is sheer absurdity to deny women the right to earn *Brahma jnana*. But, in worldly matters, it is necessary for them to maintain certain limitations in the interests of *dharma* (righteousness) and *loka kalyana* (the good of the people/world). For the sake of safeguarding morality and for the social health of the world, women have to accept some restrictions. This is not to say that there is any fundamental inferiority in them.

Even *pandits* acquire their *jnana* through the reverential homage they pay to the feminine deity *Saraswati*. The divine patrons of learning, prosperity and wisdom are all feminine: *Saraswati, Lakshmi* and *Parvati*. This should show the reverence paid to women.

Question 8:
Why does Swami give gifts?

Sri Sathya Sai Baba:
Gifts of rings and pendants are an expression of Swami's love . . . It is not that Swami wants to draw people to him with gifts. When you wish to show affection to your son, or if you want to make someone happy, you make him a sports shirt or buy him a present, do you not? Swami also wants to bring happiness in this manner.

Question 9:
Does a gift also act as a protective talisman?

Sri Sathya Sai Baba:
Yes! They are also like my visiting cards and send me instant flashes when the person is in danger or in need of my help. Sometimes, these gifts are made for specific reasons: for the sake of a devotee's health, or I may give someone a gem stone so that rays from it may constantly influence him or her to follow the right path. I want to tell you that whatever Swami does has a purpose. He never does anything without reason.

Question 10:
Why does Swami give *vibhuti?*

Sri Sathya Sai Baba:
Flowers, leaves, fruit and other edibles have a temporary life. Even water breeds germs if kept in a vessel for days. Only *vibhuti* remains unchanged as it is the final result of the five elements of creation. Our desires have to be reduced to ashes and *vibhuti* is symbolic of this detachment and renunciation. One's mind has to become desireless and detached like the ashes in which everything is burnt out. It is that kind of pure mind that has to be offered to God.

Question 11:
Is it necessary to perform *pujas* (ritual worship) and ceremonies?

Sri Sathya Sai Baba:
Everything depends on the individual concerned. Whatever he or she does has to be done with faith and sincere devotion. God cannot be fooled with mere ritual.

Question 12:
What about ceremonies and rites for the dead? Is it wrong not to perform them?

Sri Sathya Sai Baba:
This again depends on one's mental attitude. After a person leaves the body, the soul takes birth and takes on a new body somewhere else. You must know this. Upto now you must have had so many lives, you must have been a mother and a daughter so very many times.

What is required really is gratitude to one's parents, by remembering them on the day of their death. Though they may shed these bodies in which they are your parents, you still owe them the debts of having given birth to you and of having given you their blood to give you your present form.

You can express this gratitude through the ceremonial *shraadha* rite, or by any other method, even by thinking of them with sincere and loving gratitude on the death anniversary. It is heartfelt feeling that is important.

Question 13:
Why doesn't God make people suffer for their sins in the same lifetime? Why in other lives when they cannot know why they suffer?

Sri Sathya Sai Baba:
Then how would you account for the *punya* (good deeds) they do? They have to enjoy the benefits of their *punya*, too! All that may not always be possible in one lifetime . . . .

Question 14:
Why does Swami have more restrictions for women? They do not have easy access to Swami!

Sri Sathya Sai Baba:
Everyone has the same kind of access to Swami. This does not depend on their being men or women. Everyone receives the same grace, depending on their devotion, their need, or their work.

Question 14 (continued):
Swami may say so, nevertheless women have more hurdles to overcome when they want to convey something to Swami.

Sri Sathya Sai Baba:
That is what they think! There are times when the man who stands next to me never catches my attention, as hard as he may try; while a devotee sitting far away in a corner amid a crowd easily catches it. It all depends on who has to receive what and when. Everything happens according to that will, not because of the physical form of man or woman.

Also – these differences are visible to you at your level of consciousness. For Swami, these are not differences that count. The *atma* is not different in man or woman. The *atma* is eternally conscious, pure and self-effulgent. The *atma* is neither masculine nor feminine, nor yet neutral. It is only the body that limits, deludes and wears names.

Question 15:
What is the principal cause of all troubles and sorrow?

Sri Sathya Sai Baba:
Attachment and ego are the main causes. Jealousy is another factor.

Question 16:
How can jealousy be conquered?

Sri Sathya Sai Baba:
By having love for everyone, by thinking of others with love and wishing them well. More than all, by realizing that jealousy is physically most harmful. It does damage your internal system and, later on, you will have to suffer the *karma* of the bad things caused by your jealousy.

Question 17:
Why has God created bad traits and negative tendencies in humans?

Sri Sathya Sai Baba:
These are results of man's own actions. God is only a witness to events. Human beings are themselves responsible for the good and the bad in them. Remember that you can never be hurt by the things you do not do.

Question 18:
But Swami says that there is nothing good or bad!

Sri Sathya Sai Baba:
Yes! this is from God's point of view. For humans, this is a relative matter, since what is good for one may be bad for another. What is good at one time may be bad in another season. Good and bad are thus two states – take two fruits, *phalam*, which are good. Once they are eaten and digested, they become excreta, *malam*, and that is bad.

Question 19:
Scientists say that something cannot be created out of nothing.

Sri Sathya Sai Baba:
Yes, but what they think of as nothing is not really nothing. There is no nothingness in the Universe. The scientist makes such statements because, with his limited vision, he cannot see all things or know them.

Both science and spirituality begin as inquiry, a quest. Spirituality comes full circle, like the letter O, while science reaches the half circle stage, resembling a C. Science has a lot of catching up to do, for it has only discovered a fraction of the truth. It is like a small piece of cloth you can see protruding from a fist: you can only conjecture about the whole, its looks and size, for it is hidden and you cannot see it.

Question 20:
But, science has made many advances – flights to the moon and other planets, for instance.

Sri Sathya Sai Baba:
Yes. Whatever science has done for humanity is to be welcomed, but it is still a growing and advancing field. Scientists used to say that you cannot split the atom, and today that is no longer true. The scientist learns as he progresses.

Today's investigations become old tomorrow and lead to new investigations which will become old the day after tomorrow. There is no end to this, and so the truth lies in something that contains within it both the old and the new. God alone envelops the old and the new and so the best way to advance is Godward.

SOME EXCERPTS FROM DISCOURSES GIVEN BY SRI SATHYA SAI BABA

On Meditation

In meditation, we close our eyes and try to focus on the inner vision. If our eyes are open, we see creation, but if they are closed, we cannot see any part of creation. The whole of creation has come to us from our own vision. If there is vision, there is creation; if there is no vision, there is no creation.

Just as external vision enables us to see exterior creation, internal vision enables us to see the interior self. Just as what does not flow is not water and what does not burn is not fire, so also a person who does not have inner vision cannot be called a human being. It is within the natural capacity of human beings to attain inner vision in relation to animals who possess only outer vision.

Everyone should spend at least one hour everyday in meditation on God. Even as a bale of cotton can be burnt by a tiny spark, the least grain of God's grace can burn away sins as great as mountains.

On the Quest for the Divine

Questions such as is there God, can we see God, can we reach God, are not new and have been asked ever since God created the Universe.

With *sadhana*, great *rishis* realized God and proclaimed that the quest for God should begin inside man since God, though omnipresent, reveals Himself to man through inner vision.

The quest for God can begin only when the individual is free from anger, jealousy and ego and does all his work, performs all his tasks, as offerings to God.

The women of the olden time, like the *Gopikas*, were *karma jivis*. They performed all their domestic chores but were surrendered to *Krishna*. When they fed their husbands and children, they felt they were offering *prasad* to God Himself. When they bathed their children, they thought they were performing *abhisheka* to their Lord. While chopping vegetables, they resolved to cut out anger and ego from their characters. Thus, in all their thoughts, words and deeds, they exemplified *dharma balam* (the might of righteousness) and *daiva balam* (divine might).

On Women

To save at least the next generation, women must be educated in a well planned manner and endowed with the wisdom, fortitude and faith to equip them for the great responsibility that rests upon them.

Women are the bulwark of spiritual culture. But, as is evident from the attitude and behaviour of educated women today, they are rapidly succumbing to the tinsel attractions of froth and frippery, cheap and tawdry literature and sensual films.

On the Law of *Karma*

The easiest path to self-realization is *sharanagati* (surrendering the ego). You might respond that the *karma* of the previous birth has to be consumed in this birth and that no amount of grace can save man from that. Evidently, someone has taught you to believe so. But, I assure you that you need not suffer from *karma* in that way.

When a severe pain torments you, the doctor gives you a morphine injection and you do not feel the pain though it is still present in the body. Grace is like morphine: the pain is not felt though you go through it. Grace takes away the malignance of the *karma* that you have to undergo. You know there are dated drugs which are ineffective after a certain time; well, the effects of *karma* are made null and void though the account is still there and must be rendered. Or, the Lord can save a man completely from the consequences as was done by me for the *bhakta* (devotee) whose paralytic stroke and heart attacks I took over some months ago during *Guru Purnima* week.

It is wrong to believe that *lalaata likhitam* cannot be wiped out, that what one has earned in previous births must be consumed in this birth. Grace can countermand all that, nothing can stand in its way. It is the grace of the Almighty, remember . . .

So, do not attach yourself too much to this body or to the things that bring comfort to it. You earn three friends in this life: first, the riches you accumulate and they do not go with you when you move out of this life; second, kith and kin and they accompany your body up to the burial ground or cremation *ghat*; third, the merit and demerit you have earned and they are with you to the last.

On Numbers

Man breathes at the rate of 900 times per hour: 21,600 times per day, of which he draws 10,800 breaths in the daytime. With every breath man repeats *SOHAM* (I am He). So, the figure 216 and its half, 108, has a deep significance. It is also 9 times 12, 9 being the number indicative of *Brahmam* since 9 is always 9, however many times you multiply it ($9 \times 12 = 108$ therefore $1 + 0 + 8 = 9$; $9 \times 9 = 81$ therefore $8 + 1 = 9$); and 12 is the number of suns; also the sun moves through 12 *rashis* (planetary houses, signs of the Zodiac), each *rashi* representing one month. Just as 9 is the symbol of *Brahmam*, 8 is the symbol of *Maya*.

On *Namasmarana*

The name of the Lord is the rifle that guards you against beasts of prey in the jungle of life. The rifle makes a loud noise when the bullet is ejected. So too, along with the sound of the name, eject the feeling so that the target may be hit.

You must cultivate love towards everyone, however distinct the character and capacity of each. Though the same blood flows through the whole body, the eye cannot smell, the ear cannot taste, the nose cannot see; do not emphasize the distinctions or the quarrel. Stress rather the basic brotherhood and love . . . Just as sugar that is dissolved in a glass of water is invisible but patent to the tongue in every drop, so too the Divine is invisible but immanent; it is capable of being experienced in every individual whether he is from the bottom rung or the very top.

Do *namasmarana:* taste the sweetness that is in the heart of everyone; dwell on the glory of God, His compassion summarised in His names. Then it will be easier for you to visualise Him in all and to love Him in all, to adore Him in all.

On Divinity Latent and Patent

If you want to make coal white, it would be foolish to wash it in milk; all that would happen is that the milk would become black. You have to heat the coal, make it red hot, and continue heating it until it is transformed into white ash. The ash remains forever.

Similarly, the *tamasic* mind (black or ignorant mind) has to be transmuted into the *rajasic* (red or active) and then into the *satvic* (white or pure) by the process of *sadhana* (heating, spiritual endeavour). The blackness and the redness are produced by the qualities of greed and lust. Regular treatment with the medicine of self-control *(nigraha)* will cure you of these.

These holy days are prescribed for inaugurating the treatment. The *Shastras* extol the medicine and have laid down the method of its administration. The lives of saints encourage you to seek it and save yourself with it. By these means, man can ascend from the animal to the human level and from the human to the divine. Yes, you too can become divine. I have nothing that you do not possess. It is latent in you, it is patent and potent here; that is the only difference.

On Activity

There is none to question me if I do not act. There is nothing I would lose if I did not engage in activity. Nor have I any great urge to be acting. Yet you see me ever active. The reason is that I must be doing something all the time for your sakes and as an example, as inspiritation and as a piece of training. Those who lead must themselves follow, those in command must themselves carry out what they expect others to do. I am engaged in activity so that you may learn to transmute every minute into a golden chance to ennoble yourselves into Godhood.

On Fullness (or Full minus Full)

This is full, That is full. When Full is taken from Full, Full remains. That is the *Upanishadic* axiom. The Divine is full, Creation is full; even when Creation occurred and the Cosmos appeared, produced by the Divine, there was no diminuation in the fullness of the Full.

Fullness is the attribute, the nature of the Supreme. It cannot be diminished by the process of creation of the Cosmos. Why is Creation also called the Full? Because it comes from the Full.

You go to the bazaar to buy a kilo of *jaggery*. The shopkeeper brings a big lump of it from his supply, he slices off a portion, weighs it and gives you, in return for the price in money, a kilo of *jaggery*. You go home and use a little of it to prepare the sweet refreshment called *panaka*. The *panaka* is sweet, the kilo of *jaggery* and the lump it came from, all are equally sweet.

Fullness is the quality of the Divine; it is found in part or portion or half or whole. Quantity is not the criterion, quality is. In the visible world that has been taken from the substance of the Divine, this quality is found equally full. We shall not consider the world as anything less than God.

On Miracles

The divine manifestations of Sai are called *chamatkaras* (miracles). Every devotee should try to understand the significance and the reason for these *chamatkaras*.

This particular phenomenon implies attraction and is a divine quality based on the power of the *atma*. How is this quality to be used? It is to be used for *samskara*, that is to say, for the transformation of human nature into divine nature. Intrinsically worthless human nature is subjected to *samskara*, so that it may change into invaluable divine nature, and the divine attraction of *chamatkara* is used for that purpose. This *samskara* forms the basis of *paropakara*. The path of *paropakara* (selfless service to and sacrifice for others) will ultimately bring you to *sakshatkara* (self-realization). The purpose of the *chamatkaras* is to lead you to the ultimate reality. The four steps are: *chamatkara* (miracles), *samskara* (development and evolution of character/nature), *paropakara* (selfless service) and *sakshatkara* (self-realization). Therefore, these *chamatkaras* are not an exhibition, but a divine manifestation with a divine purpose and they cause no harm to the world.

On *Lokas* in the Human Body

The *lokas* are all in the body of man. They are *Bhu-loka* in the feet, *Bhuvar-loka* in the genitals, *Suvar-loka* in the navel, *Mahar-loka* in the heart, *Jana-loka* in the throat, *Tapo-loka* in the centre of the brow, and *Sathya-loka* on the crown of the head. These are called the Upper *Lokas* and they are all situated in the human body.

There are Lower *Lokas*, too: *Athalam* in the soles of the feet, *Vithalam* on the nails, *Suthalam* in the heels, *Thalathalam* in the hips, *Rasathalam* in the knees, *Mahathalam* in the thighs, and *Pathalam* in the anus.

On True Peace

True peace is within your heart. To go out in search of true peace of mind is a waste of time. All that you wish to acquire is within you. You are God. That is why I often tell you that you are not one person, but three: the one you think you are, the one others think you are, and the one you really are. There are three different facets to your personality: the aspects of body, mind and *atma*. In these three aspects, promote good work, good ideas and good thoughts.

On Work

Work is like a flower bud. If we protect the bud, it will transform itself and become a flower. The same flower will slowly ripen and become a fruit.

On the Journey through Life

Life is a pilgrimage towards God when man drags his feet along the rough and thorny road of his years. But, with the name of God on his lips, he will have no thirst; with the form of God in his heart, he will feel no weariness; the company of the holy will inspire him to go on his way with faith and hope.

On Taking on the Illness of a Devotee

Take as an example the illness of the inflamed appendix that came into this body. It is the nature of the human body to generate disease as a result of wrong food or foolish habits. This explains the illnesses of ordinary men, but not the illness that you have witnessed during the past two days. That was an illness assumed, willed, in order to relieve a person who could not have survived or borne it without serious damage. This is one of the functions of the Divine, for which It has incarnated – the pouring forth of grace upon the devout.

The appendix was inflamed and became an abcess which the doctors said could only be cured if an operation was performed immediately. The devotee could not have borne that agonising pain. I have come with this body in order to save those other bodies from pain and suffering. This body will always remain free of illness and pain, disease can never affect it. That is the truth.

One day, Lord *Krishna* developed a headache. Everyone was upset. Sage *Narada* prayed that *Krishna* would reveal to him the means of removing the headache, and *Krishna* replied, "Bring me the dust from the feet of a true devotee." *Narada* thought, "I am the best devotee." He suggested to *Krishna* that he use the dust from his feet, but *Krishna* said, "No, egoism has tainted and contaminated that medicine." So *Narada* set off in search of the required dust, but all he met was reluctance. Everyone said that it might be sacrilege since they were all aspirants of the divine grace.

Then *Narada* went to Vrindavanam. As soon as the kind and simple *gopikas* heard of *Krishna's* plight and his pain, they collected the dust from their feet and made a packet which they gave to *Narada*. "Rush with this," they begged, "do not let *Krishna* suffer anymore. Please hurry." Not a single thought of pride, humility, fear, shame or any other emotion came to them. Their only thought was, 'The Lord is in pain, it must be cured.' They heard, they gave, they prayed, they were happy. They felt the pain of *Krishna* and they responded.

One should surrender to the Lord in this manner. It is such a devotee, a person who has surrendered all, even his judgement to me, that I had to save by taking on this illness and going through it. The signs of that illness have disappeared today and they will not occur again.

There is another reason that lies behind this episode. The Divine is realized by gifted people in the vast, the magnificent, the beautiful, the mighty, the majestic, the awesome. But, for the generality of mankind, the consciousness that each one is a miracle sustained by God, that each breath is a witness to God's providence, that each event is proof of His presence, comes but rarely in life. When this body that is apparently human behaves as if it is filled with supra-human potentialities, then amazement draws the attention of all towards the Divine, the Divine that is inherent in the nature of all humans. Off and on, it becomes necessary to give this lesson to mankind so that faith in God and the power to recognize Divinity are added to human faculties. Then only can the mind of man be turned from the world to the Master of all the Worlds.

On Religion

A word used frequently for religion is *matha*. A word used for mind is *mathi*. Putting both together one can say that *matha* is primarily for strengthening *mathi*.

The goal, the purpose and essence of all creeds, faiths and religions are the sublimation of the mind so that it can ensure liberation for the individual and happiness in society.

On Love

Only the cultivation of love can convince man of the truth that there is only one caste, the caste of humanity, and only one religion, the religion of Love.

EPILOGUE: THE ESSENTIAL SAI

I have tried in the preceding pages to portray the world of Sathya Sai and to present a glimpse of his multi-dimensional personality. The book is, at best, just a glimpse, for the Sai charisma is inscrutable. Words are totally inadequate to explain or attempt to answer the Why Sai Baba question.

People continue to come to Sri Sathya Sai Baba in their millions. The number of Sai devotees multiplies by the hour. It cannot be said that all are attracted by his miracles alone; although they certainly should not be brushed aside since they occur all the time and in different places. His miraculous manifestations are happening in hundreds of homes all over India and in countless other countries through his *sankalpa* (will, resolve) even as I write.

During a Summer Course at Whitefield, which lasts a month, Sri Sathya Sai Baba created more than a hundred gifts of gold, silver and precious stones, as well as sugar candy, sweets and *vibhuti*. He has been creating things in this way for the past forty years. If all the *vibhuti* he has created were to be collected, it would form a most enormous mountain. Can all this have been done by mere *yogic siddhis?*

Spiritual masters and religious leaders say that the power of *siddhis* wanes with the passage of time. So, divine *shakti* (power) is the only possible answer to such a vast and varied production of objects. Sri B. V.

Narasimha Swami, while talking about Shirdi Sai Baba, said that miracles are a concession made by Divinity to human blindness. He added that a feature common to both Sai Baba and to Jesus Christ is that people were to be convinced of their divine nature only through the miracles they performed.

Whatever the pros and cons in the argument about miracles, one fact is indisputable. The materialised objects produce immense joy in the recipients. I have seen ultra rich people joyfully clasping very simple silver rings materialised for them by Sri Sathya Sai Baba; more than the object, it is the giver and the way in which he gives that makes all the difference in the world. Sri Sathya Sai Baba also presents ordinary gifts bought in shops to his devotees, such as *saris* and *dhotis*. Though the recipients are pleased by such gifts, they cherish the materialised gifts far more.

Many people, devotees and others, love Sri Sathya Sai Baba's miracles as much as they love him. Therefore they ask: why should this aspect be questioned? It harms neither the giver nor the taker, quite the contrary, it produces joy in both. It is not as though people would stop coming to Sri Sathya Sai Baba if he were to stop materialising gifts. For, there are millions of Sai devotees who have never received a miraculous present from their Divine Master. One such devotee explained that he required nothing more since Sri Sathya Sai Baba had showered upon him the best gift of all: his grace, which had transformed his nature, turning him Godward.

The essential Sai is a melodious singer of *bhajans*, an eloquent orator and a prolific writer. His lucid and arresting interpretations of Indian philosophy and culture draw many people to him. The essential Sai is one who not only teaches the essence of spirituality in simple terms, but who then helps people to follow these teachings as a way of living and loving.

The essential Sai is a simple and straightforward person who practises what he preaches. He is a loving teacher, a firm father and a compassionate mother, all in one. Intensely concerned with the upliftment of mortal beings, he is the embodiment of humanity, love, goodness, self-abnegation and soul power.

The essential Sai is full of humility and says, "Don't think of me as Master or *Guru* . . . I am the servant of all." In the light of all that is happening around Sri Sathya Sai Baba, one cannot but wonder at this statement. Millions all over the world worship him as a living god; authors fill page after page of books and articles glorifying him; poets compose soul-stirring poetry about him in *Sanskrit, Hindi*, English and other languages; world famous artists and photographers are constantly using their creative talents in attempts to capture his physical form in all its moods; film and stage producers use his life story, message and *bhajans* on screen and stage to inspire vast audiences; musicians of varying traditions (North Indian, *Karnatic*, jazz and even pop) sing his praises at prestige performances; records and tapes of Sri Sathya Sai Baba are produced in a constant stream by well known artistes; dancers choreograph dances to explain the story of the Sathya Sai *Avatara*; researchers and scholars are at work analysing the various facets of his personality and his philosophy; and scientists are startled into taking note of and trying to understand the ceaseless flow of Sai miracles.

Regardless of all this, the essential Sai is simple, humble and full of sweetness and an unexpected and childlike innocence which is exquisitely touching. No ordinary being could remain so calm, so composed and unimpressed with so much glory.

Sri Sathya Sai Baba is not only himself fully divine, but asserts all the time that divinity is within each one of us. The essential Sai, therefore, is a divine humanist full of sweetness and light. He is also a perfectionist who expects high standards of conduct and moral values and absolute discipline, dedication and devotion to duty from students at his schools and colleges and from those living in his *ashramas*. The *ashrama* dwellers are not recluses. Since Sri Sathya Sai Baba is a dynamic leader with many organizational and educational activities, they share in the work and themselves remain active and agile.

Sri Sathya Sai Baba's love of the motherland, its languages, culture and traditions make him a patriot par excellence and he sets an example for all to follow. His love of beauty is reflected in the lovely buildings designed by him. His love of animals can be seen in his attitude towards his elephant called Sai Geetha, and the other animals kept on the grounds.

Sri Sathya Sai Baba is a born *guru*; this is so even when he is not performing miracles or manifesting superhuman powers. Every action of his proclaims his dictum: "My life is my message." He shows, completely successfully, how spirituality can be a reality in everyday life and the need for all of us to have our "heads in the forest" (quest for Truth) and our "hands in society" (goodness towards man).

Everyone may not be able to experience Sri Sathya Sai Baba's divinity. Nevertheless, I feel that they should at least study him as an example of perfection in humanity. Through such an attempt, they may come to understand the essential Sai who demonstrates in himself that the fully human man is fully divine.

GLOSSARY

(of Indian Words and Names)

A

aadi (adi) beginning; early, initial, primordial.

Aadi (Adi) Deva the first, primordial, original God.

Aadi (Adi) Sesha name of the mythological thousand-headed serpent who forms Vishnu's (q.v.) bed, regarded by some as an emblem of eternity.

aakarsh attraction, draw, pull.

aarati ceremony performed in adoration of a deity, or any outstanding personage or guest, by circular movements of a lighted lamp before his or her person or image.

abhaya an assurance of safety or protection; fearlessness.

abhaya hasta hand raised in protective gesture, blessing.

abhisheka (m) inauguration or consecration (by sprinkling water or other auspicious substance); inauguration at royal or sacred occasion.

achaara conduct; ethos; behaviour.

achaara sheela modest, pious, virtuous, moral, chaste of conduct.

acharya teacher, preceptor; professor; founder or leader (of a school of thought); an initiator.

adharma unrighteousness, breach of duty; injustice; not based on moral law.

adhyatma spiritual contemplation; spiritual knowledge.

adhyatmic spiritually contemplative; spiritually knowledgeable.

Advaita non-dualism or absolute monism; belief in and philosophy of the oneness of all.

Agastya (Agasthya) renowned rishi (q.v.) and enemy of the rakshasas (q.v.).

aikya oneness, unity; identity.

aikya stambha pillar of unity.

akarshana attraction; charm, allurement.

akhanda indivisible, entire; in this context it is used to mean unbroken and therefore uninterrupted.

akshaya imperishable, undecaying; perennial.

Alaknanda range and valley in the Himalayas in the State of Uttar Pradesh (q.v.).

Amma/ji mother; women are addressed thus in Southern India as a mark of respect; often it is appended to the first name, i.e. Sitamma (Sita), Sarojamma (Saroj), etc.

amrut (a) nectar; life-giving celestial liquid.

amrutatva essence of nectar; therefore truth, reality, very essence of eternity; immortality.

amsha part, share.

ananda joy, bliss.

anandaswarupa nature of joy, bliss itself; in this context used to denote pure bliss.

Anantapur town in the State of Andhra Pradesh (q.v.); nearest sizable town to Sri Sathya Sai Baba's ashrama (q.v.) in Puttaparthi.

anatma not soul, un-self; unbeing, state of unbeing.

Andhra Pradesh one of the states of the Republic of India, situated in the South East. Capital: Hyderabad. Languages: Telugu, Urdu, Hindustani.

anna food, especially rice or grain.

anubhuti perception, apprehension; by extension and in this context experience, experienced.

Apasthambha Sutra manual containing prayers and hymns devoted to the release of mental/physical hinderances and the reactivation of the Self, attached to the Yajur Veda (q.v.).

aradhana (araadhana) conciliating, winning; prospering, success; accomplishment; propitiation, gratification; adoration.

archana honouring; adoration.

Arjuna the third of the Pandavas, youngest son of Kunti called Pritha and of Indra. It is to him that Krishna addresses the immortal words of the Bhagavad-Gita (q.v.).

artharthi interested, selfish.

arthi desirous, avid; materialistic.

ashanti lack of tranquillity; passionateness, restlessness.

Ashoka Emperor of large parts of (present day) India, Pakistan and Bangladesh from 273 B.C. to his death in 232 B.C., he was a great lawgiver and codifier; he believed in the teachings of the Buddha and spread his philosophy to those parts of the world which are Buddhist today.

Ashokan of the age or law of the Emperor Ashoka.

ashrama shelter; hermitage.

ashtotara literally plus eight; eight utterings; certain prayers.

ashtotara archana a form of prayer and worship.

Assam one of the states of the Republic of India, situated in the East. Capital: Gauhati. Languages: Assamese, Bengali.

Assamese people and language of Assam (q.v.).

asura demon; demoniac being, person.

Atharva Veda the fourth and the last of the Vedas (q.v.).

atma self; breath; soul; life; Self; essence, nature; peculiarity; universal soul.

atma chintana thinking, reflecting upon the atma (q.v.); spiritual introspection.

atma tatva own nature; true nature of the universal soul.

Aum (Om) mystic monosyllable representing the deity, said to be the sound of the universe, cosmos; the sound of the Divine; the sound of creation.

avatara descent, especially of God or gods to earth; incarnation; manifestation.

ayusha life; age (of person, animal, thing).

B

badha repel, dispel; oppress, beset; check, thwart; influence, effect; remove, annul, set aside. Also tormentor; resistance; hurt, prejudice; exclusion from; contradiction.

Badrinath place of pilgrimage in the Himalayas in the State of Uttar Pradesh; one of the names of Shiva.

bahu-chakra-vahana composite word meaning literally many-wheeled-vehicle; denotes a train or engine.

bala young, not full grown; child. Also might, power, strength, vigour; force.

bali sacrifice, oblation. Also strong, powerful.

Bali name of an asura (q.v.) king from whom Vishnu, as the Vamana Avatara, reclaimed the worlds.

bangaaru golden (one). A term Sri Sathya Sai Baba sometimes affectionately uses when addressing a fortunate devotee!

Bangalore city in the State of Karnataka and its capital.

Benares correct appellation Varanasi. City which is a great pilgrimage centre on the River Ganges in the State of Uttar Pradesh. Sometimes also called Kashi.

Bhagavad-Gita literally the Song of God; name given to a chapter of the Mahabharata (q.v.), it contains the eternal message of Krishna to mankind as given to Arjuna on the battlefield of Kurukshetra.

Bhagavan God, the Lord Almighty.

Bhagavanta God, the Lord Almighty.

Bhagavatha(m) a Purana (q.v.) of Vishnu exalting Krishna. Also Bhagavata.

bhajan a devotional song; repetition of the name of God.

bhajji a savoury vegetable fritter.

bhakta devoted; devotee, worshipper.

bhakti devotion, worship; faith; faithful attachment.

Bhakti Marg the way (to realise God) through loving devotion; loving worship.

Bharadwaja a great rishi (q.v.) of the Vedic Age.

Bharat the Indian (Sanskrit) and correct name of the country called India.

Bharata Rama's half-brother, the son of Dasaratha and Kaikeyi, he ruled in Ayodhya during Rama's exile.

Bharatiya Sanskriti Indian culture.

bhoga eating, enjoying; consumption.

bhoomi ground, soil; territory, country, land; earth.

Bhopal town in the State of Madhya Pradesh and its capital.

Bhrugu name of a sage of the Bhrugu tribe said to be the son of Varuna; the planet Venus. Also Bhrigu.

bhu become; arise, happen, occur. Also place of being, space; earth; worlds. In this context ("bhur bhuvah suvaha"), our world, our place of being.

bhuvah the second world, as in "bhur bhuvah suvaha." One of the three vyahritis (q.v.) in that formula where it is taken to mean earth (when 14 worlds are assumed it is the first of an ascending series of seven.)

bilva a tree, the wood-apple (Aegle Marmelos).

Bodhi Tree tree of enlightenment; the holy tree in Gaya under which Prince Gautama Siddhartha attained enlightenment and thus became the Buddha.

Bombay city in the State of Maharashtra and its capital.

Brahma the Creator God of the Hindu Trinity comprising Brahma, Vishnu and Shiva (Maheshwara); God the Creator.

Brahmachari a celibate man.

Brahmacharini a celibate woman.

Brahmacharya celibacy; the first stage of life.

Brahmajnana knowledge of the Brahman (q.v.) or the Vedas (q.v.).

Brahma muhurtam the hour of Brahma; the first division of the day, i.e. the first one hour and 18 minutes from sunrise.

Brahman holy scripture, the Vedas; sacred learning. The Supreme Impersonal Spirit; the Absolute; Supreme Universal Soul.

Brahma tatva the essence of creation, i.e. divinity.

Brahmin the first caste, that of scholars and priests, the learned in Brahmajnana in tradition.

Brindavan name given to the grounds of Sri Sathya Sai Baba's residence and college at Whitefield, named after the forest in the State of Uttar Pradesh where Krishna spent his childhood and youth. Correctly written Vrindavan.

Buddha the enlightened one; name given to Gautama Siddhartha, prince of Magadha in the 5th century B.C. who was the 9th incarnation of Vishnu.

buddhi intelligence, understanding, reason, intellect, mind.

Buddhism name given to the spiritual teaching and philosophy of Gautama called the Buddha.

C

chaitanya consciousness, intellect, mind, soul; the quality of awareness.

chaitanya grantha a book, volume of deep and living perception.

chakra circle, wheel; in Yoga the chakras are centres of potential energy in the human anatomy.

chandan sandal wood, sandal wood paste.

Chandra the moon.

chapatti a flat round wheatflour bread.

charachara moving, running; the quality of mobility; quick, i.e. animals and plants, the whole of the living world.

charan foot; feet.

charan seva service of the feet; by extension devotion and worship at the feet of God or a venerated personage.

chintana thought, reflection.

Christianity name given to the spiritual teaching and philosophy of Jesus of Nazareth called the Christ.

chitta intellect, mind; perception.

chitta shuddhi purification of the intellect, mind; clarity of perception.

D

daiva peculiar to, coming from or having to do with the gods; divine.

daivamsham innate godliness, literally a share or part of divinity.

daiva prarthana prayer or praying to God.

daiva preeti love of God.

darshan view; seeing, looking at, beholding; sight of. Also doctrine or philosophical system.

Dasaratha king of Ayodhya, father of Rama.

Dasavatara (das = 10, avatara = incarnation). The ten incarnations (of Vishnu): 1. Matsya (fish), 2. Kurma (tortoise), 3. Varaha (boar), 4. Narasimha (man-lion), 5. Vamana (dwarf), 6. Parasurama, 7. Rama, 8. Krishna, 9. Buddha, 10. Kalki.

Dassera the 10th and culminating day of the nine days of celebration in honour of the Goddess Durga, usually in October.

daya sympathy, pity, compassion.

deha body; person.

desha country; point, spot; place, region.

deva heavenly, divine, celestial; deity, god, divinity.

devata divinity, divine power; deity.

dhairya (m) firmness, steadfastness, constancy, fortitude; gravity, resolute bearing; obstinacy.

dharma established order, usage, custom; rule; duty; virtue, moral merit; right; justice; in this context it is used to mean righteousness, the ideal of righteousness.

Dharmakshetra literally field of righteousness; name given to Kurukshetra, the great field of the final battle in the Mahabharata (q.v.); the name of Sri Sathya Sai Baba's institution in Greater Bombay.

dharma samsthapana establishment or re-establishment of righteousness in the right balance, proportion; hence establishment of righeousness in the world.

Dharwar town in the State of Karnataka.

dhee thought, conception; intelligence, insight; religious meditation, devotion, prayer, hymn. Also splendour.

dhoti a loose outer garment tied at the waist worn by Hindu men.

dhvani sound, noise; cry; thunder.

dhwaja banner, flag, ensign; token, symbol.

dhyana meditation; religious and spiritual contemplation (Note: Zen is a derivative of this word and concept).

dipa (deepa) flame; blaze; beam, burn; lamp, lantern.

divyaswarupalara one of Sri Sathya Sai Baba's terms of address for individuals in a multitude; it means aspects of the Universal Divine.

drishti sight, seeing; that which is visible.

dukkha (m) fraught with hardship, wretched; adversity, misfortune, sorrow.

Durga name given to Parvati for slaying the asura (q.v.) Durg; a widely worshipped deity in India.

Dvaita dualism; belief in and philosophy of the duality, separateness of God and man.

Dwapara Yuga — the third yuga (q.v.) in the Hindu method of dividing time into cycles.

Dwarka — town and island of the State of Gujerat; great pilgrimage centre dedicated to Krishna.

Dwarkadish — literally Lord of Dwarka, i.e. Krishna.

E

Elephanta Island and Caves — a name given by the Portuguese to a small island between mainland India and the 7 islands of Bombay. The caves are 8th to 10th century Hindu temples and monastic grottoes.

G.

gadaa — club, mace.

Ganapati — another name for the elephant-headed god, Ganesha (q.v.).

Ganesha — god of wisdom, remover of obstacles, elephant-headed son of Shiva and Parvati.

Ganga — the River Ganges; also personified as a goddess.

Gangotri — name given to the source of the River Ganges in the Himalayas, a place of pilgrimage 17,800 ft above sea level.

Garuda — name of the fabulous bird, son of Vinata and elder brother of Aruna, king of the feathered race; vehicle of Vishnu.

Gautama the Buddha — see Buddha.

Gayatri — Goddess; name of a powerful incantation, mantra (q.v.).

ghee — clarified butter.

ghunghuru — anklets with bells worn by dancers.

Gita — song. Also the popular abbreviation for the Bhagavad-Gita (q.v.).

Gitopadesha — the instruction, direction of the Bhagavad-Gita; its teaching, message.

Goa — former Portuguese colony on the West Coast of India, South of Bombay, now incorporated into the State of Maharashtra.

gopa — a male cowherd.

gopi (ka) — a female cowherd, or dairymaid.

gopuram — tall pagoda-like structure associated with temples in Southern India, usually but not always gateways.

gotra (gothra) — literally cowshed; hence house, race or family; surname; name; by extension descendant.

Govinda — one of the many names of Krishna.

graha — house; planetary house.

grahapravesha (m) — literally entering a house; therefore name given to the rite performed before settling into a new house, dwelling place.

grahastha — householder, a married man.

grahasthashrama — the second stage of life, that of family duties and worldly commitments.

grantha book, volume, tome.

guna property, quality; elemental quality (sound, feeling, colour, taste, smell); fundamental quality (satva, rajas, tamas which see individually); good quality, virtue.

guru venerable or highly respected person: father, mother or elder relative, especially teacher. Most frequently used for spiritual initiator and teacher.

gurukula teacher's house, teacher's family.

Guru Maharaj respectful appellation given to a personal or family spiritual preceptor.

Guru Purnima a particular full moon day set aside for the honouring of the guru.

H

halva an Indian dessert, sweetmeat. (Note: not like the Turkish or Middle Eastern sweet of the same name).

Hampi town in the State of Karnataka, the former Vijayanagar.

hamsa (hansa) swan; symbol of purity and freedom.

Hanumana god; half-monkey son of Vayu (q.v.); great devotee of Rama, ideal of strength and faithfulness.

Haridwar town in the State of Uttar Pradesh near where the River Ganges flows out of the Himalayas and into the plains; pilgrimage centre devoted to Hari (Vishnu).

Hindi an Aryan language chiefly of the Gangetic Plain, but understood by most of the peoples of Nothern and North-Western India.

Hinduism (Hindu) name given to all the religious and philosophical concepts, doctrines, philosophies and faiths of pre-Muslim India, ancient India and their modern derivations and forms. The only religion without an individual founder or defined dogma, it comprises all beliefs from atheism through animism and polytheism to absolute monism.

homa pouring into the fire, oblation; sacrifice.

homa kunda fire pit, cavity in the ground, where the homa (q.v.) is performed.

hookah (hukkah) a water pipe, "hubble bubble." (Note: this is not used exclusively for opium smoking).

hridaya heart; also as seat of mental operations; centre, core.

hridayasthayi He/she/it/they who stay, live in the heart; cherished in the heart.

I

ishta sought, wished for; desirable, agreeable; dear; favourable; approved; favoured.

Ishta Devata the chosen God, personal God.

Ishwar (Ishvara) lord, ruler; name usually given to Shiva.

Islam surrender (Arabic); name given to the religion founded by Mohammed called the Prophet in the 7th century A.D. in what is Saudi Arabia today.

J

jagata all that moves; animals; men; world, earth.

jagriti watchfulness, wakefulness.

jambu rose-apple; rose-apple tree.

Jamnagar town in the State of Gujerat.

Jam Saheb additional title of the maharajas of Kutch and Nawanagar, dropped by the rulers of Kutch in the 18th century A.D., but worn by the rulers of Nawanagar upto the Independence of India in 1947.

japa repeat in an undertone, mutter or murmur (prayers); pray silently.

japam muttering of prayers; repetition of prayers.

japamala rosary, prayer beads.

jhubba a tunic; a loose fitting garment hanging down from the shoulders to the waist or knees with or without fastenings.

jhula a swing.

jignaasu a learner; wishing to know or test.

jivatma the individual soul.

jnana knowledge; true or superior knowledge; wisdom.

jnanaswarupa nature of knowledge; wisdom itself; in this context used to denote aspect of highest and truest wisdom.

jnana vidya learning or science of wisdom (of Truth).

jnani knowing, understanding, wise; having the higher knowledge.

jyoti light, radiance; fire.

jyoti upasana attending, honouring the light or flame; devotion, worship of the light or flame.

jyotisha astronomical science; mostly used to signify astrology.

K

Kabir Das a great Indian saint of the 15th - 16th century A.D. who offended the rigid views of doctrinaire Hindus and Muslims alike and was persecuted by them. He saw God in everything and preached the way of bhakti (q.v.). A prolific composer of deeply moving bhajans (q.v.).

Kailasa mountain in the Himalayas of Tibet; the abode of Shiva.

kaala time; age, epoch; due season, appointed or right time.

kalaa artistic skill, art (of which there are 64).

kali bud.

Kali Goddess; name given to Parvati when she slayed Raktabija by sucking away all his blood. Also known as Mahakali. Widely worshipped in India.

kali dissension and strife, sometimes personified (Kali).

Kali Yuga the 4th yuga (q.v.) in the Hindu method of dividing time into cycles.

Kalinga name of a people and their country, the present day State of Orissa.

kalpa cosmic period (a day of Brahma = 1000 yugas, etc.); also wish, wishful imagination.

kalpataru fabulous wishing tree.

kalpa vruksha same as kalpataru (q.v.)

kalyana (m) good, excellent, noble; blessed, auspicious, prosperous; goodness, excellence, elevation; beneficence, prosperity.

kama wish, desire; sexual love; also personified as Kama, the god of (erotic and romantic) love.

kamandala ascetic's water-pot, sometimes made from a dried gourd.

Kamsa (Kansa) false king of Mathura, a usurper, uncle of Krishna who slayed him.

Kannada language spoken in parts of Karnataka and Southern Andhra Pradesh.

Kanya Kumari the southernmost tip of the Indian peninsula; the anglicised version is Cape Comorin.

karma action, deed, work; hence fate, i.e. result of an act done in a former birth or life.

Karnataka one of the states of the Republic of India, situated in the Southern or peninsular part of the country. Capital: Bangalore. Languages: Kannada, Malayalam, Telugu.

Kartika (Karthika) the first month of the Hindu calendar, usually November.

karuna doleful, pitiable; pity, compassion.

Kashi another name for Benares (q.v.).

Kashivishvanath literally the Universal Lord at Kashi; Shiva; name of the temple of Shiva in Benares popularly referred to as the Golden Temple.

Kaushalya queen of Ayodhya, wife of Dasaratha, mother of Rama.

kavacha armour, mail; here used to mean sheath or scales.

kavi poet.

Kerala one of the states of the Republic of India, situated in the South East. Capital: Trivandrum. Languages: Malayalam, Tamil.

khichri (khichadi) steamed rice and lentil preparation.

kiran ray of light. Also dust, mote.

kirtan mention, narration; by extension a hymn of praise or devotional song with a narrative element.

Koran the Divine Revelation as given to Mohammed the Prophet; the Holy Book of Islam.

Kosala (Koshala) name of a king of Kosala, the father of Kaushalya.

krishi husbandman; ploughman.

krishna dark; black.

Krishna name given to the 8th incarnation of Vishnu.

Krishnamurti, J. a contemporary Indian philosopher; he preaches the immanence of God. Author of many books, founder of several institutions in India and in some Occidental countries.

krodha	anger.
kshanika (m)	momentary; therefore often used for transient.
kshema	comfortable, agreeable; quiet; safe; rest; security; in this context it means tranquillity.
kshetra	field; sphere of activity; seat.
Kumaon Hills	range of foothills of the Himalayas in the State of Uttar Pradesh (Note: of Jim Corbett fame.).
kumar	a youth, an unmarried man; master.
kumari	a maiden, an unmarried woman; miss.
kumbha	pot, jar, urn.
kumkum	blood red powder used in puja (q.v.) and for ornamentation.
kunda	round cavity in the ground, round fire-pit.
kundalini	spiritual energy lying dormant in human beings.
Kundalini Yoga	the non-doctrinaire system of arousing the kundalini (q.v.) with the aim of union with the Absolute (in identity).
Kurma	tortoise; name given to the 2nd incarnation of Vishnu.
kurta	a loose fitting garment for the upper part of the body worn by some Indian men.
kusha	grass, especially sacrificial grass.
Kutch (Cutch)	a desertic region of Gujerat in Western India, on the Arabian Sea.

L

laddoo	a ball-shaped sweetmeat made of varying substances.
Lakshmana	Rama's half-brother who voluntarily shared his exile, son of Dasaratha and Sumitra.
Lakshmi	good fortune; royal dignity, glory; wealth; beauty, splendour. Goddess of all the above qualities, also known as Mahalakshmi.
leela	play, sport, pastime, diversion, amusement; mere appearance, semblance; charm, grace.
linga (m)	mark, token, sign, emblem, characteristic; in this context it is used in its Vedantic sense, that is, typical or subtle body, the indestructible original of the gross visible body. (N.B. not phallus or phallic).
lingodbhava	origin, birth, appearance, emergence of a linga; here it denotes the manifestation of a linga or several lingas by Sri Sathya Sai Baba on Shivaratri.
loka	world, division of the Universe; heaven; earth; mankind, folks, people.
loka kalyana (m)	beneficence, prosperity of the people, world.
loka upakara	service, benefit, help of the people, world.

M

maddala	a kind of drum.
Madhava	one of Krishna's names; often used as God in contrast to 'manava' which means man, mortal being.
Madras	a city in the State of Tamil Nadu; its capital.
Madurai	a city in the State of Tamil Nadu.

maha great; a prefix attached to proper and common nouns signifying an emphasis or the greater aspect of the same. Examples: Lakshmi and Mahalakshmi, atma and mahatma, raja and maharaja, Shivaratri and Mahashivaratri.

Mahabharata a great Sanskrit epic of about 100,000 stanzas relating incidents from the Dwapara Yuga (q.v.) The main story treats of the war of accession between the Pandavas and the Kauravas; it contains many digressions of religious, historical and cultural significance. The Bhagavad-Gita is contained in it. Vyasa (q.v.), the compiler of the Vedas, is believed to be its author and many devout Hindus therefore regard this epic as the fifth Veda.

Mahakali great Kali (q.v.).

Mahapurusha the Supreme Spirit. Also a great and eminent man.

Maha Purushottama the Highest Person, Supreme Soul, said especially of Vishnu or Krishna.

maharaj king; a term of respect, popularly used for persons of religious stature, especially Brahmins.

maharaja great king.

maharani great queen.

Mahashakti Great Shakti (q.v.).

Mahashivaratri literally Great Shiva's night. A sacred festival for all Hindus, observed with pomp and significance by Sri Sathya Sai Baba.

mahatma great soul; a term of veneration prefixed to great and beneficent personages, as with M.K. Gandhi.

mahavakya literally great utterance, speech, words; a profound and everlasting truth expressed in a phrase or sentence.

Maheshwara (Maheshvar) great lord, great ruler; Shiva.

mahila woman.

mahima greatness, majesty; might, power; glory; exaltation, dignity. A prayer that is called a mahima is praise, or singing the glory of a particular deity.

Mahishasura Mardini name given to Parvati for slaying the unconquerable asura (q.v.) Mahisha.

makki roti flat pancake-like bread made of cornflour.

mala garland, wreath; rosary, prayer beads; necklace; line, row, streak, series.

mala (m) dirt, filth, impurity; bodily secretion; excreta.

manana thinking, cogitation, reflexion; homage.

manas mind (in its widest sense as the seat of intellectual operations and of emotions), internal organ; understanding, intellect; thought, conception; imagination; desire, will, inclination. In the philosophical systems, manas is regarded as distinct from atman, of which it is only the instrument and is (except in the Nyaya) considered perishable.

mandala	circular, round; charmed circle; a division or book of the Rig Veda.
mandali	a circle (of people), group, company, assemblage.
mandir	temple.
mangalya	auspicious, fortunate, lucky; an auspicious object. In this context it is an object associated with marital or conjugal felicity.
mantra	pious thought, prayer, hymn; Vedic hymn, sacred text; mystical verse, incantation, spell.
Manu	name of celestial being, progenitor of mankind.
manushya	human; human being; man (as opposed to woman), husband.
Mareecha	son of Marichi, a rakshasa (q.v.).
marg	path, road, way, course.
Maruti	son of the god of wind and storms, Maruta; a name for Hanumana (q.v.).
Matsya	fish; name given to the first incarnation of Vishnu.
maya	art, marvellous power; illusory image; illusion. In Vedanta (q.v.), it is the power which causes the world to appear as really existent and distinct from the Universal Soul.
Mira Bai	a 16th century A.D. princess from the present State of Rajasthan who renounced worldly life to devote herself to worshipping Krishna. She was persecuted by her husband and his family. A composer of wondrously tender bhajans (q.v.) of longing for her lord, Krishna.
mithya	wrongly, incorrectly; falsely, untruly; not in reality, only in appearance; to no purpose, fruitlessly, in vain.
moksha	release, liberation; deliverance from further transmigration, final emancipation.
Mount Kailasa	see Kailasa.
muhurta (m)	moment, instant; an hour of 48 minutes (i.e. one 30th of a day).
mukti	release, deliverance from; emancipation from the bonds of existence, final beatitude; abandonment of; hurling, discharging.
muladhara	lower, main, basic stream; here it means the place which is believed to be the mainspring of energy.
Mysore	city in the State of Karnataka, its former capital.

N

naabhi	navel.
naada	sound; sound aloud.
naadi	vein; pulse, artery; by extension a single thread or narrative, object or aim.
naadopasana	devotion or worship with and through sound.
naga	serpent; especially Naga, as name of fabulous serpents with human faces inhabiting the city of Bhagarati in the infernal regions.

nagar	town, city; an urban area.
nagar sankirtana	group singing of songs of divine praise in the streets or in a public place.
Nagpur	city in the State of Maharashtra.
nama	name, title, appellation; good name.
nama sankirtana	group singing of the names of God.
nama smarana	remembering, recollecting the name of God; prayer.
namavali	a list of the names of God or of a god to be read or recited as prayer.
Narasimha	man-lion; name given to the 4th incarnation of Vishnu.
Narayana	son of the primal man, the personified Purusha (q.v.), identified with Vishnu and Krishna.
Nataraja	king of the dancers and performers; a name for Shiva.
navaratna	literally nine precious stones; they are specific stones, each associated with a planetary house and its particular property, aspect and characteristic.
Nawanagar	name of a former princely state, no longer valid as a name of the area now contained within the larger State of Gujerat in Western India (the area around Jamnagar).
netra	eye.
nidarshana	showing, announcing, teaching; example, illustration; prognostic.
nirvana	extinction; extinction of the vital flame, dissolution, final emancipation, union with the Absolute; absorption in; individual extinction; complete satisfaction, bliss.
nirvikalpa	admitting of no alternative, changeless, free from distinctions, undifferentiated.
nirvikalpa samadhi	immutable union.
nityananda	innate and infinite bliss.
niyama	restraint, limitation, fixed rule, certainty; observance, duty. Also self-imposed religious observance of certain restrictions and practices.

O

Om (Aum)	correctly should be A-U-M as it is a composite sound. Mystic monosyllable representing the deity, said to be the sound of the Universe, cosmos; the sound of Divinity; the sound of creation.
Omkar (a)	letter of the Sanskrit alphabet representing the Om; God.
Ootacamund	town in the Nilgiri Hills in the State of Tamil Nadu; a famous resort due to its scenic beauty and temperate climate.
Ooty	a colloquial and popular abbreviation of Ootacamund.

P

paada	foot, feet (of humans and animals); leg.
paada puja	worship of the feet (of God, respected elder or a venerable person).
paaduka	shoe, slipper, sandal; footwear in general.

padma lotus flower (which closes at night; nelumbium speciosum).

paisa/e money; the hundredth part of the decimal rupee (q.v.).

pan (paan) leaf; also specific edible leaves used to enclose the betel nut and spices.

panchamukhi literally five-faced; pentagonal; with five aspects or qualities.

pandit (pundit) learned; wise; scholar, learned or wise man.

papa (paapa) evil, bad, wicked, criminal, sinful; evil, trouble, misfortune; harsh, cruel, immoral; wickedness, offence, crime, villainy, guilt, sin.

papa bheeti fear, dread of evil and wickedness; disinclination towards offence, crime or sin.

Parabrahma Supreme Brahma.

Paramatma Supreme or Universal Soul.

Paramhamsa literally supreme swan (the swan being a symbol of other-worldliness, freedom and purity). It is an honorific for certain spiritual masters, as for Ramakrishna Paramhamsa and Paramhansa Yogananda.

paranjyoti the original, absolute, eternal light, flame.

paratpara of here and of beyond the remotest; everlasting.

parikshit dwelling around (Agni), extending around (heaven and earth). Also Parikshit, name of various princes.

paripalana protection; maintenance; nurture.

Parvati literally she of the mountain; daughter of the Himalayas; name of the goddess who is the consort of Shiva, another way of designating his active principle. She has many names: Shakti, Durga, Kali, Amba, Devi, Uma, Maheshwari, Nanda, Ishwari and many many more.

pati owner, master, lord, ruler; husband.

pati seva service to and of the husband.

Patri town in the State of Gujerat.

pavitra pure; purifying; beneficent; sanctified.

pavitratmaswarupa one of Sri Sathya Sai Baba's ways of addressing those in his audience, it means aspects of the pure atma (q.v.).

peon though not current in England, this English word is used in India to denote an office-messenger, attendant or orderly.

phala (m) fruit; by extension result, effect, issue, consequence.

Poona city in the State of Maharashtra, its former capital.

praasana pleasing, soothing, delighting; in this context a prayer or activity seeking to please (God).

prachara (prachaara) propoganda; publicity; currency, prevalence.

pradarshana appearance; showing, exhibition, designation; teaching; example; teaching by example.

Prahlada name of a daitya or asura prince, son of King Bali.

Prajapati lord of creatures; the genius presiding over procreation, protector of life; Creator. Also name of a supreme being above the Vedic gods; this epithet is in the post-Vedic period applied to various holy men regarded as demiurgic beings; time presonified.

prajopakara service, benefit of all creatures; therefore the good of the world.

prakanti the foremost radiance (kanti), grace, brightness.

prakriti nature; temperament, disposition. Also nature as in creation manifest.

pralaya dissolution, destruction, death; annihilation or end of the world; setting (of stars); cause of dissolution.

pralaya kaala the time of the dissolution of one cycle of time, or of the destruction of one civilization; the end of the world.

pranaam (pranama) reverential salutation; bowing with respect; a term used and pronounced in greeting elders.

pranava the sacred syllable Aum (Om q.v.).

prapti advent, occurrence; power of obtaining anything one wants, one of the 8 supernatural powers or siddhis (q.v.); attainment, acquisition, gain; obtainment, validity (of a rule).

prarthana solicitation, entreaty, prayer, request; petition, suit; supplication of anyone; here almost always used to mean prayer.

prasadam (prasad) kindness, graciousness, favour; gracious gift; food offered to an idol or respected persons and eaten by them; remnants of a preceptor's food (which may be taken as a blessing and eaten without scruple).

prashanti tranquillization, appeasement, alleviation; tranquillity, calm; abatement, cessation; extinction (of fire); mental calm, composure, quietude. In this context used to mean unbreakable and other-worldly peace.

pravesha (m) entry, entrance.

prema love, affection; tenderness; kindness, favour.

premaswarupa nature of affection, love itself; in this context used to denote the aspect of pure and true love.

prithvi the earth; also Prithvi, personified as a goddess.

puja honour, respect; homage, worship, adoration. Commonly used to signify rites and ceremonies of worship performed to honour a deity.

puja room a room in a private house or flat or other abode set aside for ritual worship; treated as a personal temple.

punar janma literally prior birth; previous or anterior life.

pundit see pandit.

punya auspicious, propitious, lucky, favourable; good, virtuous, righteous, meritorious; good work; the good, virtue; pure, purifying, holy; moral or religious merit.

punya bhoomi holy ground, sacred land; place of virtue.

Puranas collective name of 18 legendary works treating chiefly of cosmogony and divine genealogy; also belonging to the olden time, primaeval, ancient, old.

purna (poorna) full. Whole, entire; undivided, not partial.

purna kumbha pitcher full of water or other auspicious liquid.

purnima night of the full moon.

purohit appointed priest; domestic chaplain of a prince.

Purusha	personal and animating principle, soul; highest personal principle, Universal Soul, supreme spirit; primaeval male from whom the Universe was evolved (± Narayana); also purusha = a man.
Puttaparthi	village in the State of Andhra Pradesh, site of Sri Sathya Sai Baba's first and main ashrama (q.v.).

R

raga	musical mode (according to the particular school of music, there are 6, 7, 12 or 26 ragas). Colloquially, scales.
raj	realm, kingdom; hence state, area of political union or subjugation and administrative sway or domination.
raja	king.
rajakiya	servant of a king, hence politician, administrator, minister.
rajas	aspect, quality, characteristic of passion and energy; forcefulness.
rajmata	title of a dowager queen; literally the mother of the realm or kingdom (not, as is commonly assumed, an Indian version of the English 'queen mother').
rajpramukh	literally chief among kings; a title given to a princely governor of a newly created state of the Republic of India by its first governments.
raksha	protection, deliverance, preservation; guard, sentinel; preservative, amulet, mystical object.
rakshasa	evil spirit, demoniac being; nocturnal being, fiend.
Rama	name given to the 7th incarnation of Vishnu.
Ramakrishna Paramhansa	18th - 19th century A.D. spiritual master and fully realized soul born in Bengal. The guru (q.v.) of Swami Vivekananda.
Ramayana	great Sanskrit epic of 24,000 couplets composed by the rishi (q.v.) Valmiki. The incidents narrated are believed to have happened in the Treta Yuga. It is the story of Rama, 7th incarnation of Vishnu and prince of Ayodhya; his youth, exile, the abduction of his wife, Sita, and Rama's war on the King of Lanka to regain her, his triumphal return and reign.
rangoli	floor and ground decoration made with flowers and/or coloured powders and dyes in the manner of mosaics.
rani	queen.
ratna	precious stone, jewel; wealth, treasure.
ratna dataa	the giver, donor of precious stones and of wealth or treasure; God.
Ravana	mythical asura (q.v.) King of Lanka who abducted Sita and was slain by Rama.
Republic Day	the 26th of January, the day India celebrates in honour of its formation as a republic in 1952, 5 years after it gained independence from Britain.

Rig Veda — the first of the four Vedas; verses and hymns.

rishi — bard or author of sacred hymns, poet; saint or sage of the olden time; a special class of revered beings whose number is often limited to 7; a person renowned for wisdom and piety.

Rishikesh — a pilgrimage area in the State of Uttar Pradesh near Haridwar, where the River Ganges descends into the plains from the Himalayan heights.

roga — infirmity, disease, sickness.

Rudra — literally roaring, terrific; god of storms. Also a name for Shiva.

Rupee — the monetary unit of India. It is divided into one hundred parts called paisa or paise.

S

sadhaka — assistant; worshipper; aspirant (to spiritual knowledge).

sadhana — directing to the goal, guiding. In this context it refers to one's own endeavour to direct oneself towards God, i.e. spiritual effort.

sadhu — straight, right, unerring; noble, virtuous, good; saint, seer; holy man.

sadviniyogam — replete with all the true disciplines; of good behaviour, polite manners, good breeding, modest conduct.

sahadharmini — wife sharing duties with her husband (as against sharing *his* duties).

sahasranama — a thousand names. Also an expression for a large number of names.

sahukar — a money-lender; private banker; rich man, man of means.

saakshibhoota — literally a witnessing being; witness.

sama — even, smooth, level, parallel; similar, like, equivalent; same, identical with; equal.

samadhi — putting together, joining; deep meditation on the supreme soul, profound devotion, during which one can reach union with the Supreme Spirit; also said of the physical death of venerable people.

samadhi darshan — sight after union with the Supreme. In this context it means the seeing of a great soul who has "died".

Sama Veda — the third of the four Vedas.

sambhashana — conversation with; speaking to.

samithi (samiti) — coming together, meeting; council, assembly.

samsara — the world; circuit or cycle of worldly existence; the life of personal or private attachments, life in the physical and emotional spheres.

samsthapana — universal establishing; balancing of establishment. By extension the establishment or re-establishment of a missing or lacking quality or element.

Sanathana Sarathi — name of the journal published under the direct guidance of Sri Sathya Sai Baba. It means the Eternal Charioteer, an allusion to Krishna and thence to the Bhagavad-Gita (q.v.).

sankalpa — resolve of the mind, will, purpose, definite intention, determination; by the mere wish; originating in the will, produced by the mere will.

sankirtan — collective singing of kirtans (q.v.).

sanmarg — the path of virtue, the moral way; way of goodness, truth.

sannyasa — renunciation; asceticism; abandonment of worldly ties and interests; the fourth stage of life according to the ideal Hindu system.

sannyasi (n) — a renunciate.

Sanskrit — the ancient language of the Aryans in which are written nearly all the great religious, philosophical, scientific and cultural works of Hindu India. Also sanskrit which means prepared; cultivated language (as opposed to the vernacular).

sanskriti — preparation; formation; consecration; culture, refinement.

Saraswati — goddess of learning, science and all the creative arts; also Mahasaraswati = Great Saraswati.

sarvajna — all-knowing, omniscient.

sarva (m) — entire, whole; all, every; every kind of, all manner of; everyone, everything.

Sathyanarayana — literally the True Supreme Spirit. Name of Vishnu, sometimes used for Krishna. The given name of Sri Sathya Sai Baba.

satsang — intercourse or society of the good and pious; elevating and sacred company.

satva (sattva) — being, existence, reality; essence, nature, innate disposition, character; the first of the 3 gunas (q.v.) inherent in prakriti (q.v.); spirit; vital breath.

satya (sathya) — actual, real, genuine; true.

Satyabhama — one of the wives of Krishna.

satyam — truth.

Saurashtra — region of the State of Gujerat, the Western peninsula.

Savitra — name of a Vedic god belonging both to the sky and to heaven; personification of the generative power of the sun; sun-god; sun.

Savitri — another name for the Goddess Gayatri; Suryaa.

seva — service.

shabash (shahbash) — well done, bravo.

shakti — ability, capacity, power, strength, skill; regal power which comprises 3 elements: prabhava (majesty), utsaha (energy), mantra (counsel); active power or female energy of a deity, especially of Shiva. Also Shakti = name of Parvati.

Shakuntala — name of an apsara (celestial female being); name of the daughter of Vishwamitra (q.v.) and Menaka, also an apsara; mother of Bharata, a great king for whom India (Bharat) is named. A play of the same name written in the 4th century A.D. by Kalidasa.

shaligram — a round or oblong black stone containing fossil ammonite, it is considered sacred by the Vaishnavas (worshippers of Vishnu) who believe that such stones are pervaded by the presence of their Lord.

shamiana — canopy.

Shankaracharya — a great realized soul and teacher of the 8th century A.D., he preached the Advaita (q.v.) philosophy of Vedanta (q.v.). Also known as Adi Shankara.

shankha — shell; conch shell.

shanti — mental tranquillity, peace of mind; peace.

sharanagati — seeking protection, refuge; supplication for protection; by extension surrender.

shastra — command, precept; instruction, advice, good counsel; rule, theory; compendium, institutes (of any branch of learning); code, scientific or canonical work; scripture.

shastri (shastry) — learned; scholar; taught in the shastras (q.v.); belonging to theory (rather than to practice), theoretical.

shatarupa — one hundred aspects; figuratively many-sided, one with many forms.

Shatrughna — half-brother of Rama, son of Dasaratha and Sumitra.

sheela — good conduct or habits; noble character, uprightness, morality. Also a stone, rock or boulder.

shikar — victim, prey; commonly used to mean hunting, killing.

Shirdi — a village in the State of Maharashtra associated with the previous Sai Baba, Sai Baba of Shirdi. Now a pilgrimage in honour of Sai Baba.

Shiva — name of one of the gods of the Hindu trinity of which Shiva (Maheshwara) is the god of destruction and regeneration. Also shiva = kind, friendly, gracious; the Auspicious One.

shivam — kindness, friendliness, graciousness; happy; by extension goodness.

Shivaratri — literally night of Shiva; a great festival all over India in honour of the great god.

shloka — song; sound, noise; couplet, stanza. In this context it is always used as religious verse.

shraadha — literally faithful, believing. Its more common use is to denote an oblation to ancestors and household deities, funeral rites and feast (at which gifts and food are presented to Brahmins).

shraddha — putting faith in, trusting; confidence; trust, faith, belief in.

shri (shree) — splendour, beauty; prosperity, fortune, wealth; high position, glory, majesty, royal dignity. Also Shree = personified as goddess of beauty and prosperity, Lakshmi. Also an honorific for names of gods, men, women, places.

shriman — an honorific prefixed to masculine names.

shrimati — an honorific prefixed to feminine names.

shuddha — pure.

Shuka naadi literally the vein of Sage Shuka; a volume of writings by the sage of the same name.

Shukra bright, resplendant; white; pure, spotless; the planet Venus. A rishi (q.v.) personified as son of Bhrugu and teacher of the asuras (q.v.).

siddhi accomplishment, performance, fulfillment, complete attainment, successful; personal perfection entailing the acquisition of supernatural powers; magical power.

siddhi kshetra field of success, of attainment; successfully accomplished object, aim.

Sita daughter of King Janaka of Videha (Mithila), wife of Rama.

sitar stringed musical instrument of 16th century A.D. Moghul India evolved from more ancient instruments.

Somnath town in the State of Gujerat on the Arabian Sea famous for the temple of the same name dedicated to Shiva. Also a name for Shiva.

somya (saumya) cool and moist; moonlike, placid as the moon; gentleness.

sparshana contact, touch; feeling, sense of touch.

sphatika crystal.

Sravanabelgola a place in the State of Karnataka, site of a well known Jaina monastery and monuments dating from approximately the 4th century B.C.

sri another spelling of shri (q.v.), prevalent in the southern parts of India.

Srisailam town in the State of Andhra Pradesh.

srishti creation; the world, the universe, the cosmos.

sruti (sruthi) hearing, listening; sound, noise; traditional religious precept regarding sound; learning by sound.

stree woman; female gender; wife; feminine form or gender.

stotra hymn of praise, panegyric; name of chants corresponding to the Shastras (q.v.).

Subrahmanyam another name for Kartikeya, prevalent in the southern parts of India; he is the son of Shiva and the god of war.

Sufi a follower of a pantheistic form of Islamic mysticism.

sumangali said of a virtuous married woman in a state of auspicious felicity.

Sumantra minister of King Dasaratha of Ayodhya.

sundaram beauty, splendour.

sunyam nothing, nothingness; zero.

supari betel nut, areca nut.

suprabhatam literally good dawn; prayers sung or chanted at dawn.

Surya the sun, personified as a god.

sushumna asleep; quiescent.

sushumna naadi carotid vein.

sushupti sleep, drowsiness; quiescence.

sutra thread, string, cord; sacred cord (worn over the left shoulder by men of the 3 upper castes); figuratively thread running through and holding together; concise rule or aphorism; manual consisting of aphoristic rules.

suvaha the 3rd world as in "bhur bhuvah suvaha." One of the 3 vyahritis (q.v.) in that formula where it is taken to mean space, air, sky.

svaartha (m) own affair or cause, personal matter or advantage, one's own aim or object; egoistical.

svapna originally sleep and sleeping; now used chiefly for dream and dreaming.

swaasha breath; breathe, breathing.

swabhava nature, inherent nature; naturalness, peculiarity; literally self-aspect.

T

tala literally clapping of hands; by extension rhythm.

tamas (thamas) dark; the third of the 3 gunas (q.v.), connected with error and/or ignorance.

tambura musical instrument with 4 strings used as a drone.

Tamil a Southern Indian, or Dravidian, language spoken in the State of Tamil Nadu (formerly Madras) and by Tamil people in Sri Lanka.

Tamil Nadu one of the states of the Republic of India situated in the South, the most South Eastern state; capital: Madras. Language: Tamil.

tandava frantic dance; the dance of destruction or dissolution performed by Shiva.

tanpura musical instrument with strings used for accompaniment.

tapa (s) heat; also torment, penance, self-castigation, mortification; religious austerity, devotion.

tatva very essence, true nature; truth, reality; principle, especially one of the 25 in the Sankhya philosophy.

teertha (m) bathing-place, especially one to which pilgrims are made for the expiation of sins; in this context it is used for blessed water brought back from a place of pilgrimage; sanctified water.

tejas sharpness; edge; heat, fire, bright flame, light, brilliance; splendour, beauty; energy, vigour, force, vitality, strength; mental or moral power; dignity, majesty, glory.

Telugu a Dravidian language much influenced by Aryan elements spoken in the State of Andhra Pradesh and parts of the State of Karnataka.

Threta (Treta) Yuga the second yuga (q.v.) in the Hindu method of dividing time into cycles.

thruna (truna) grass, herb; blade of grass; straw. Often figuratively a mere nothing.

thumbe long gourd (lagenaria vulgaris).

tilak freckle, mole; hence coloured mark on the forehead as an ornament or sectarian distinction; also a mark of worship.

Tirupathi name of a temple and surrounding township, a great pilgrimage on the Andhra Pradesh-Tamil Nadu border.

tonga light two-wheeled one-horse carriage used as taxis in Indian towns and cities.

torana arched portal, triumphal arch; festoon, as in this context.

triguna the 3 fundamental gunas (q.v.) or qualities; consisting of 3 threads or cords; threefold; containing the 3 fundamental qualities.

trikala (m) the 3 times: past, present and future; knowing the 3 times, ergo omniscient.

Trimurti having 3 forms; the Trinity, that is Brahma, Vishnu and Shiva (Maheshwara).

tulsi the holy basil plant (ocymum sanctum).

turya fourth; fourth state of Vedantist's soul, i.e. complete union with Brahmam.

turyavastha in the fourth state, one with God.

tyaga abandonment, desertion; quitting; giving up, sacrifice, renunciation.

U

udhi ash.

upadesha reference; direction, instruction; precept, rule, lesson; advice; therefore also used as message, teaching, spiritual content of a talk, book or experience.

upakara (upakaar) friendly service, kindness; benefit; favour.

upanayanam investiture; in this context the investiture of the sacred thread.

Upanishad literally sitting down beside; secret or esoteric doctrine; name of a class of works treating of the inner or hidden meaning of the Vedas.

upasana attendance; honour; devotion, worship; practice.

upaveeta (m) wearing of the sacred thread; the sacred thread.

V

vadai a doughnut-like fritter made of flour.

vaidya versed in science (vidya), knowing one's subject, learned; one versed in medical science; physician, as in this context.

vajra thunderbolt, especially Indra's; adamant; diamond, as in this context.

vajra kavacha literally diamond armour; in this context shining sheath or scales.

Valmiki great rishi (q.v.) and author of the original Ramayana (q.v.).

Vamana name given to the 5th incarnation of Vishnu; also vamana = small in stature, dwarfish.

vanaprastha the 3rd stage of life, that of renouncing comforts and wordly ties to seek God.

vang sweet words, speech; eloquence; connected with or based on words or speech; verbal.

Varaha name given to the 3rd incarnation of Vishnu; also varaha = boar, hog, wild boar.

Varanasi correct name of Benares, also known as Kashi.

Vasishtha	name of one of the leading Vedic rishis (q.v.), composer of the 7th mandala (q.v.) of the Rig Veda classical Sanskrit, he is regarded as one of the Seven Rishis and is mentioned as a lawgiver; also vasishtha = best, most excellent.
vata vruksha	a tree, the India fig-tree (ficus indica), sometimes called the banian or banyan tree.
vayu	the wind; air; also Vayu, personified as a god.
veda	knowledge; ritual lore.
Veda (the Vedas)	sacred knowledge handed down in the fourfold form of the Rig Veda, Yajur Veda, Sama Veda and Atharva Veda.
Vedanta	literally end of veda (q.v.); text forming the conclusion or the essence of the Vedas, i.e. an Upanishad or the Upanishads (q.v.) and the theologico-philosophical doctrine based thereon (Uttara-mimamsa or Vedanta system).
vegetarian	Indian vegetarians not only do not eat meat, they also do not eat fish or eggs. The very strict followers of Jainism do not eat any of these nor do they eat roots (such as garlic, onions, carrots, etc.).
Vellore	a town in the State of Tamil Nadu known for its hospital and missions of care, both Indian and foreign.
vibhuti	extensive, abundant; mighty, powerful; manifestations of might, power; outstanding personality; ash, as in this context.
vibhuti abhisheka (m)	inauguration or consecration by the sprinkling of vibhuti (ash).
vidya	knowledge, learning, science (especially of the fourfold knowledge of the Vedas).
Vijayanagar (am)	former name of Hampi, a town in the State of Karnataka.
vina (veena)	musical instrument, the Indian lute, with a gourd at each end; it is said to be the oldest string instrument and is certainly ancient.
vipra	inwardly stirred, inspired; sagacious, wise (often of the gods); learned.
Vishnu	name of one of the gods of the Hindu Trinity of which Vishnu is the god of preservation and continuation; as such it is he who incarnates in every age to return us, when we have strayed, to the way of dharma (q.v.).
Vishwamitra	a celebrated rishi (q.v.), chief author of Rig Vida III; engaged in a great contest with Vasishtha (q.v.).
vishwaswarupa	aspect of the cosmos; the cosmic form (of God).
Visishtadvaita	qualified monism; the philosophy and belief that though there is only one God, soul and matter are also real and that God can be reached by devotion and total surrender.
volunteer	this term is used for those who serve to guide and restrain the public at meetings, celebrations and other similar occasions associated with and arranged for Sri Sathya Sai Baba.

vrata fast, fasting.

Vrindavan name given to the grounds of Sri Sathya Sai Baba's residence and college at Whitefield, named after the forest in the State of Uttar Pradesh where Krishna spent his childhood and youth. Sometimes mistakenly spelt Brindavan.

vruksha tree.

vyahriti utterance, declaration, statement; mystical exclamation.

Vyasa name of a mythical sage, the reputed editor or compiler of various extensive works (the Vedas, the Mahabharata, the Puranas, etc.) and regarded as the son of Parasava and Satyavati.

W

Whitefield a township 14 miles South-East of Bangalore in the State of Karnataka where Sri Sathya Sai Baba resides from time to time in a house attached to the Satya Sai College (for boys).

Y

yagna worship in prayer or praise; sacrificial rite, sacrifice.

Yajur Veda the second of the four Vedas.

yantra means of holding, support, barrier; apparatus, appliance, mechanical contrivance, engine, machine; amulet, mystical diagram used as an amulet.

Yashoda foster mother of Krishna.

yoga literally yoking; means, expedient; union, contact with; combination; connexion; systematic abstraction, Yoga system of philosophy; unity of the soul and nature (Samkhya philosophy).

Yogeshwar lord of mystic power; a name for Shiva.

yogi adept of the Yoga philosophy and system.

yuga generation; cosmic age (of which there are 4: Krita or Satya, Treta, Dwapara and Kali.).

Yugadi beginning of (an age); beginning of the world; sometimes used for New Year's Day as here.

Yugavatara the Incarnation of God for an age or yuga (q.v.).

Z

Zoroastrianism at one time, one of the great world religions, now practised only by the Parsis of Western India. Its basic tenet is the age-long war between good and evil, Ahura-Mazda heading the good spirits and Ahriman the evil ones. Morality is of paramount importance being the only way open to mortals to support Ahura-Mazda. The sacred book is the Avesta. Its name derives from Zoroaster (sometimes called Zarathustra), its 6th century B.C. Persian founder.

Bhajan I – Prema mudhita manasé kaho . . .

Prema mudhita manasé kaho
Rāma Rāma Raam, Rāma Rāma Raam,
Shri Rāma Rāma Raam,
Rāma Rāma Raam.

Pāpa ghaté dukkha mité
Léké Rāma naam,
Bhava Samudra sukkha danāva
Eka Rāma naam.

Parama shānti sukkha nidhāna
Divya Rāma naam,
Nirādhāra ké ādhāra
Eka Rāma naam.

Parama gopya parama divya
Mantra Rāma naam,
Shānta hridaya sadā vasata
Eka Rāma naam.

Mātā pitā bandhu sakhā
Saba hí Rāma naam,
Bhakta janara jivanādhāra
Eka Rāma naam.

Bhajan II – Subrahmanyam

Subrahmanyam, Subrahmanyam,
Sanmukhanāthā Subrahmanyam;
Subrahmanyam, Subrahmanyam,
Sanmukhanāthā Subrahmanyam.

Shiva Shiva Shiva Shiva Subrahmanyam,
Hara Hara Hara Hara Subrahmanyam;
Shiva Shiva Hara Hara Subrahmanyam,
Hara Hara Shiva Shiva Subrahmanyam.

Shiva Sarvanābhava Subrahmanyam,
Guru Sarvanābhava Subrahmanyam;
Shiva Shiva Hara Hara Subrahmanyam,
Hara Hara Shiva Shiva Subrahmanyam.

The Aarati

Om jai Jagadisha Haré,
Swāmi Sathya Sai Haré,
Bhaktajanā samrakshaka,
Bhaktajanā samrakshaka,
Parthi Maheshwarā,
Om jai Jagadisha Haré.

Shashivadanā Shridharā Sarvāprānapaté,
Swāmi Sarvāprānapaté,
Āshrita kalpalatikā,
Āshrita kalpalatikā,
Āpad bāndhavā,
Om jai Jagadisha Haré.

Mātā pitā Gurudaivam mariantayunivé,
Swāmi mariantayunivé,
Nādabrahma Jagannāthā,
Nādabrahma Jagannāthā,
Nāgendrashayanā,
Om jai Jagadisha Haré.

Omkārarupa Om jai Shiva Sai Mahādevā,
Sathya Sai Mahādevā,
Mangala aarati anduko,
Mangala aarati anduko,
Mangala Giridhāri,
Om jai Jagadisha Haré.

Nārāyana, Nārāyana, Om Sathya
Nārāyana, Nārāyana, Nārāyana Om
Nārāyana, Nārāyana, Om Sathya
Nārāyana, Nārāyana, Om Sathya
Nārāyana, Nārāyana Om,
Om jai Sadgurudevā.

Om . . . shānti shānti shāntihí.

The Shuka Naadi
(See Chapter 8 Part 1).

Sage Shuka and his palm leaf manuscript.

Tulasamma's miraculous collection
(See Chapter 11 Part 2).

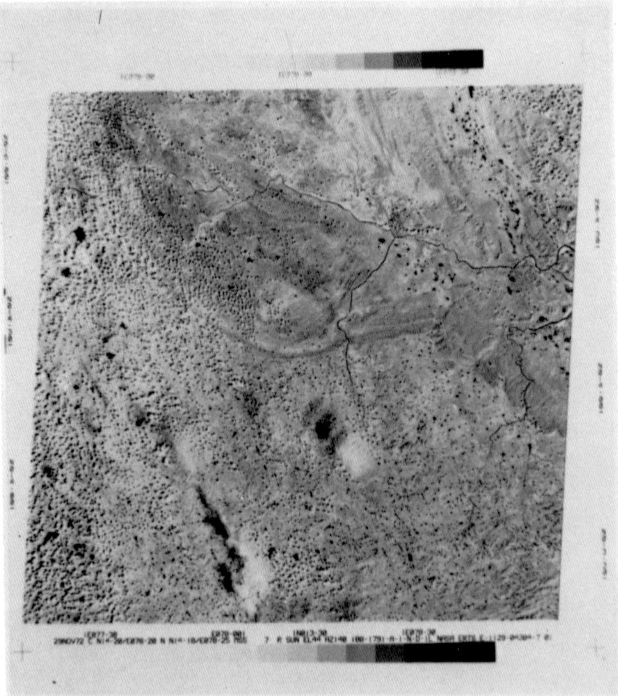

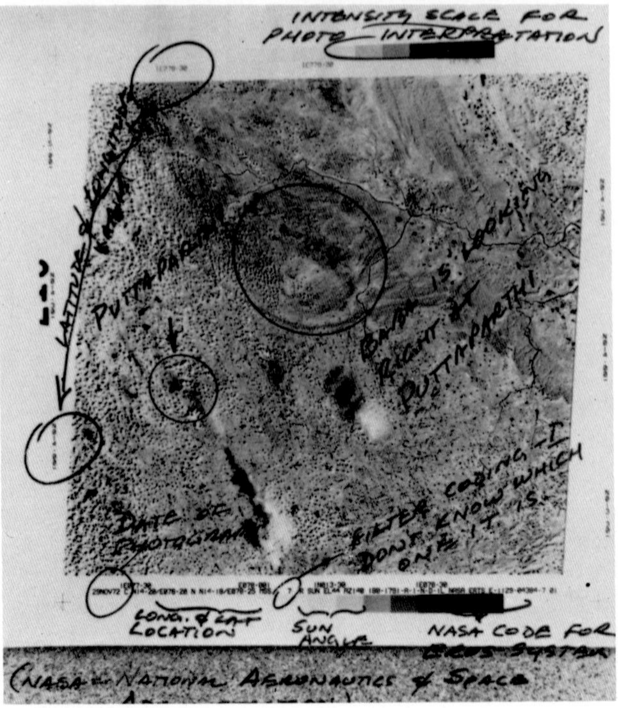

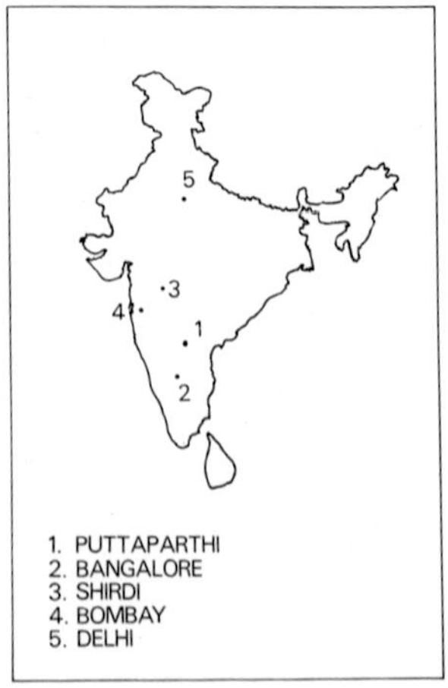

Map of India.

The Sai symbol of Concord or Unity has (clockwise). The AUM of HINDUISM, The CHAKRA of BUDDHISM, The Fire of ZOROASTRIANISM, The CRESCENT AND STAR of ISLAM and The CROSS OF CHRISTIANITY.

Top Left:
The satellite photograph that Homer Young had taken for his wife
(See Chapter 10 Part 1).

Bottom Left:
The satellite photograph explained
(See Chapter 10 Part 1).

Photograph sent to VEMU MUKUNDA in answer to his question (See Chapter 13 Part 2).

Bottom Left:
Vibhuti encrustations on a Sai photograph (See Chapter 9 Part 1).

Bottom Right:
Signor Bighi's divine portrait (See Chapter 11 Part 1).

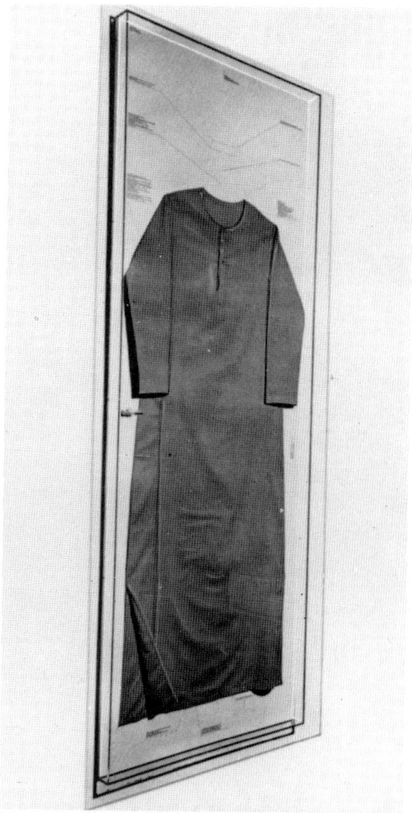

THE AVATARA, DIVINITY

Conversation at the darshan lines.

The LINGODBHAVA on SHIVARATRI DAY (See Chapter 20 Part 1).

The Divine Look.

Blessing.

PRASHANTI NILAYAM,
gate and temple
(See Chapters 19 & 20 Part 1).

PRASHANTI NILAYAM, PURNA CHANDRA AUDIT-ORIUM on left, Pillar of Concord right foreground, temple & abode (NILAYAM) right background (See Chapters 19 & 20 Part 1).

PRASHANTI NILAYAM temple with chalk RANGOLI in foreground (See Chapters 19 & 20 Part 1).

Sri Sathya Sai Baba with a rabbit . . .!

Sri Sathya Sai Baba with Sai Geetha. This photograph was autographed for the author.

In Bangalore.

The Divine GURU.

Batique painting by the author.

GOPALA AND SAI GOPALA.

The darshan lines at BRINDAVAN.

VIBHUTI ABHISHEKA
(See Chapter 20 Part 1).

VIBHUTI ABHISHEKA (See Chapter 20 Part 1).

Statue of SARASWATI in front of College building at Whitefield (See Chapter 16 Part 1).

College at Whitefield.

Assisting the future generation.

Sri Sathya Sai Baba with students of the College at Whitefield.

Sri Sathya Sai Baba on the jhula (See Chapter 20 Part 1).